Professing Literature

GERALD GRAFF

Professing Literature

An Institutional History

Twentieth Anniversary Edition

THE UNIVERSITY OF CHICAGO PRESS
Chicago and London

The University of Chicago Press, Chicago 60637
The University of Chicago Press, Ltd., London

Printed in the United States of America

16 15 14 13 12 11 10 09 08 07 1 2 3 4 5 6

ISBN-13: 978-0-226-30559-2 (paper)
ISBN-10: 0-226-30559-7 (paper)

Library of Congress Cataloging-in-Publication Data
Graff, Gerald.
Professing literature : an institutional history / Gerald Graff. — Twentieth anniversary ed.
p. cm.
ISBN-13: 978-0-226-30559-2 (pbk. : alk. paper)
ISBN-10: 0-226-30559-7 (pbk. : alk. paper) 1. Literature—Study and teaching (Higher)—United States—History. 2. Criticism—United States—History. I. Title.
PN70.G7 2007
801′.950973—dc22
2007010651

♾ The paper used in this publication meets the minimum requirements of the American National Standard for Information Sciences—Permanence of Paper for Printed Library Materials, ANSI Z39.48-1992.

Contents

Preface Twenty Years Later

One of the challenges for me in writing *Professing Literature: An Institutional History* was to keep the argument from overwhelming the history. I wanted my story of the emergence of professional academic literary study in America to be useful to readers who might disagree with my polemic on how the institution went wrong and how to set it right. And I wanted a book that would have a shelf-life after the controversies that shaped its writing had subsided.

Others will judge how well I succeeded, but *Professing Literature* is clearly history told from a point of view, an effort to change the institution it describes. Not surprisingly, many of the book's commentators have focused on my argument that the controversies that have roiled the waters of academic literary studies have possessed an overlooked and untapped pedagogical potential. As I frequently complain, the controversies that have divided literary academics have been largely hidden from undergraduates rather than made part of the object of study. The assumption has been that students should be exposed to the *results* of the disagreements between their instructors—results presumably representing settled knowledge—but not to the debates that produced these results, which are felt to be worthy of interest only to specialists. The curriculum, it is thought, should represent the enduring masterpieces and truths that are left standing after ephemeral turf wars and arcane controversies have fallen away. It is also thought that the heat and acrimony of controversy are threats to intellectual community and curricular coherence and a distraction from students' primary experience of literature. I challenge all these views, arguing that the effect of representing literary studies as if they were above controversy has been to diminish intellectual community and coherence and to leave many students clueless.

This diagnosis leads me to the conclusion that the best hope of achieving coherence in the literature curriculum is to make use of these controversies themselves (at least the most important ones) as a new kind of organizing principle—in short, in the motto that emerged in my subsequent work, "Teach the conflicts." Educators have always assumed that achieving coherence in the curriculum requires substantive agreement; I argue that sharply focused disagreement can serve as well or even better.

PATTERNED ISOLATION

The liberal arts colleges that dominated American higher education before the rise of the first departmentalized research universities enjoyed a high degree of consensus, made possible only because the vast majority of Americans were excluded from higher education. The coherence of the old college curriculum reflected a consensus that Greek, Latin, Christianity, and respectable upper-class social values were the foundations of good education. The new research universities that arose after the Civil War were more democratically open to the citizenry than the old liberal arts colleges had been, more receptive to the secular pursuit of truth, and therefore more diverse in the ideas and beliefs they represented. But this new diversity posed a new kind of problem: which of the now numerous contending groups would speak for the university itself? The new university dealt with this problem by evolving a structure of departments whose separation from each other—managed by a new cadre of academic administrators—guaranteed a level of peace and quiet.

Here was the emergence of what I call the "field-coverage" model of academic organization. Each department was composed of a set of subfields that were to be "covered," first by faculty members trained in the newly established system of graduate education, then by students taking courses. As I suggest, the advantage of the field-coverage model "was to make the [English] department and the college curriculum virtually self-regulating."

> By assigning each instructor a commonly understood role—to cover a predefined period or field—the principle created a system in which the job of instruction could proceed as if on automatic pilot, without the need for instructors to debate aims and methods. (7)

A related advantage of field-coverage was to give the department "enormous flexibility in assimilating new ideas, subjects, and methods" (7), especially those that might otherwise pose controversial challenges to entrenched thinking.

Thus whenever a threatening innovation arose—positivistic "scholars" who challenged the methods and assumptions of journalistic "generalists"; academic "critics" (the New Critics), who challenged both the scholars and the journalistic critics; eventually feminists, post-structuralists, new historicists, queer theorists, and other insurgents who challenged both the New Critics and the traditional scholars—the newcomers could be absorbed into the department by simply being added to the established array of fields. Though ugly flare-ups might occur in the pages of scholarly books and journals and at department meetings, the disconnection of the department and the curriculum screened warring factions from each other and kept their clashes largely out of the view of students. In a pluralistic spirit of live and let live, traditionalists and young Turks could pursue their incompatible projects in the privacy of their courses instead of confronting their differences out in the open.

But a result of this "patterned isolation," in Laurence Veysey's telling phrase (60), was to render the new university's curriculum notoriously incoherent. Specialization generally gets the blame for curricular incoherence, but the more serious culprit in my view is an entity we love to romanticize—the *course*. By configuring the curriculum as a set of courses taught by solo instructors not in communication with one another, the field-coverage model took a set of connected conversations and cut them into disconnected fragments. Thus a literary culture that insiders—literary journalists, literate readers, and professional academics—understood as a connected conversation was divided into courses whose implicit conversational relationship to each other was lost on most undergraduates. As those students went from course to course, the coherence of the conversation to which they were exposed tended to be intuited only by the high-achieving few—often if not always economically privileged—that had prior experience from family or church in entering intellectual discussions.

As the impenetrability of the intellectual culture of the university trickled down the school system, secondary and elementary schools were left unsure how to prepare their students to get into college or to succeed if they got there. The controversial recent report to Secretary of Education Margaret Spellings, *A Test of Leadership: Charting the Future of U.S. Higher Education,* is dead right in at least one claim: that higher education has done little to address the "poor alignment between high school and colleges" that often results in "substandard high school preparation" for college. Trickle-down obfuscation from the college curriculum has thus contributed to the much-discussed "achievement gap" in American schools between children of the rich and poor.

If making intellectual culture coherent and intelligible requires foregrounding points of controversy, as I believe it does, the college (and high school) curriculum needs to be restructured as a "learning community," in the fashion that has been successful in colleges and programs I have described in more recent writing. A learning community can be created by pairing courses and other forms of collaborative teaching in which students are exposed regularly enough to the interactions and the disagreements between the faculty that they become comfortable joining the club of literate intellectuals. The most practicable way to begin creating this club-like experience in the curriculum is to couple general education courses with first-year writing courses, whose freedom from a specific subject matter makes them easy to pair with virtually any discipline.

GUILLORY AND READINGS

Of course some might object that to speak as I just did of "the club of literate intellectuals" itself perpetuates the very snobbery that created the achievement gap in the first place. Yes and no. Historically, the idea of literacy as a "club" has indeed been tied to social exclusion, but the analogy can just as readily be used to further inclusion, as in the valuable book by educational theorist Frank Smith, *Joining the Literacy Club*. For Smith, seeing literacy as a club can help us understand why schools fail. Smith argues that from infancy certain kinds of learning—how to crawl, to walk, to eat, to communicate—occur without regular instruction, because children want to join the club represented by those around them who can do these things. Smith is struck by the paradox that learning flourishes almost everywhere but in schools. Schools fail, he suggests, because they replace the social, club-like experience that students can see the point of joining with decontextualized courses and programs. As Smith deploys it, then, the idea of literacy as membership in a club—as opposed to a mysterious and unexplainable spiritual bond—helps to demystify the intellectual culture of schooling and clarify the obstacles to democratic education.

The idea of literacy as a club, however, has certainly been intimately connected with class condescension and exclusion. This connection is the major concern of John Guillory, in his deservedly much-discussed 1993 book, *Cultural Capital: The Problem of Literary Canon Formation*. Guillory, who is influenced by the work of Pierre Bourdieu, covers some of the same history as does *Professing Literature* (which he generously cites). But Guillory goes further than *Professing Literature* in putting literary education in its external social and economic context, something he does by telling a story of the rise and decline of literature as a form of "cultural capital." Guillory also begins his history earlier than mine, with the rise of vernacular literary education in eighteenth-century England, allowing him to trace the fall of such education from its high point as an important form of cultural capital for the emerging bourgeois classes to its twentieth-century marginality, with the advent of a "technobureaucratic" economy that renders literary training irrelevant to today's social elites.

As Guillory puts it, technobureaucratic society has "rendered the literary curriculum socially marginal," in large part by transforming the university itself "into the institution designed to produce a new class of technical managerial specialists possessed of purely technical/managerial knowledge" (261). Guillory's point of departure is the canon debates of the 1980s and '90s, which, he convincingly argues, miss the point by focusing on the ideological values supposedly inherent in literary texts instead of on how texts are filtered through schooling and the social functions of schooling. To summarize one of his points reductively, why bicker over whether students should read canonical or noncanonical literature when the real problem is that literature as such has been devalued?

Guillory's argument raises some questions: is it really the case that literary education no longer serves as cultural capital? After all, corporate executives often express a preference for hiring humanities majors over MBAs because of their superior writing, critical-thinking, and interpretive skills. Anticipating this objection, Guillory suggests that it is rhetoric and composition, not literary study, that have arisen to meet "the task of providing the future technobureaucratic elite with precisely and only the linguistic competence necessary for the performance of its specialized functions" (264). But such a description underestimates the scope both of composition and literature programs and of the skills valued by "the future technobureaucratic elite." Robert Scholes, in his book *Textual Power,* is only one of many recent critics to argue that literary education is supremely useful training for reading and criticizing the wider "cultural text" of institutions, politics, and the popular media. Scholes is concerned with the training of citizens rather than workers, but it has become a familiar view that, with the emergence of an "information economy," the interpretive, critical thinking, and communication skills developed by literary studies and the humanities are highly sought after and rewarded. The demand for rhetorical mastery, the ability to make persuasive public arguments, may be as great as that for the mathematical competencies associated with the "technobureaucratic" sector, since such mathematical competence is of limited value if its possessors are unable to use language persuasively to intervene in policy arguments.

But even if we concede Guillory's point that literary education has lost some of its cultural capital, we would have to ask whether this has happened because "technobureaucracy" has no use for that kind of education, or because literary educators have failed to demonstrate to a wider public just how useful their work actually is. Might not some responsibility rest with the incoherence of literary education itself, which has arguably weakened its ability to persuade the wider culture of its usefulness? If this is the case, then patterned isolation as an organizing principle has not only made literary education nebulous to many students, but has compromised literary educators in the face of potential sources of economic support.

Some of Guillory's own points seem to suggest such an argument. Take for example his observation that the fragmented departmental organization of the modern university mirrors the "technobureaucratic organization of intellectual life." What Guillory calls the "technobureaucratic organization of intellectual life" sounds rather like what in *Professing Literature* I call the field-coverage model of academic organization, and its resulting patterned isolation. Similarly, just as I argue in *Professing Literature* for increased curricular connection as an antidote to the coverage of isolated fields, Guillory proposes an integrated humanities curriculum as a counterweight against the technobureaucratic ethos. Opposing both the traditionalists' monolithic core curriculum and the canon revisionists' dispersed pluralism, Guillory argues that the humanities need to become "an integrated program of study" (50). Borrowing a term from Antonio Gramsci, he claims that a democratic culture needs a "unitary school" in which all social classes study the same subjects and problems, in contrast to the "separate curricula for separate constituencies" and "different schools for different classes" characteristic of socially stratified societies (53).

It is striking that whereas Guillory sees the postmodern fragmentation of the university as a problem, the late Bill Readings, in his 1996 book, The *University in Ruins,* sees postmodern fragmentation as a welcome alternative to what for him is the danger of *too much* consensus. Readings, following Jean-Francois Lyotard's *Postmodern Condition,* goes so far as to equate consensus with "terror, " observing for example that "the assumption that we speak a common language lights the way to terror . . ." (184). In fairness to Readings, whose book is brilliant and well-argued, he does not reject or rule out local and pragmatic forms of agreement or shared language. What troubles Readings is the Enlightenment and modernist tradition from Kant to Habermas of universalizing metanarratives of "communicative transparency" (183). Nevertheless, for Readings, even my own argument for organizing the curriculum around controversy smacks too much of a new consensus, and so presumably would Guillory's argument for an integrated humanities curriculum. Readings's fear that a consensus may break out—a prospect that seems highly unlikely—tends to make his view of the university more complacent and fatalistic than today's situation warrants.

Thus Readings dissociates himself from "energies directed exclusively toward University reform" (169) and seems content to make the best of a bureaucratic institution that reserves oases for "intellectual variety." Readings calls this new bureaucratic model "the University of Excellence," which is essentially Guillory's "technobureaucratic" university, and this label suggests the satiric attitude he takes toward it. Yet Readings finally rather likes the University of Excellence because it gives him and others lots of space to do their thing. In Readings's words, such an institution "can incorporate a very high degree of internal variety without requiring its multiplicity of diverse idioms to be unified into an ideological whole" (168). What Readings here celebrates for warding off consensus appears to be the same disconnected structure that I criticize for disarming conflict—a structure that blocks both consensus and conflict by keeping parties isolated from each other.

Readings calls his ideal vision "the University of Dissensus." But Readings's utopian dissensus would seem to be already realized in today's pluralistic university, which is less a place of contentious dissent than one where academics tend to their separate gardens and tacitly agree not to bother one another. Readings claims that "dissensus cannot be institutionalized," because "the precondition for such institutionalization would be a second-order consensus that dissensus is a good thing . . ."(167). In my view, however, Readings's ideal dissensus has already been institutionalized in the live-and-let-live ethos that has long been the "second-order consensus" governing university faculty members, at least those with tenure. As I see it, the problem is the way academic dissensus has been institutionalized, in isolated and self-protected spaces rather than as a public sphere of debate inside the curriculum.

Why Patterned Isolation?

Guillory's discussion of "technobureaucratic" society suggests a materialist answer to the question of why patterned isolation, rather than a more connected and dialogical structure, became the dominant model of curricular organization in the modern university. In this respect, Guillory improves on the intellectual explanation I suggest in

Professing Literature when I point to the positivist world view of the late nineteenth century, which pictured knowledge as a set of discrete bricks of information that presumably form a kind of pyramid as each "investigator" adds a small research brick to the aggregate. According to this positivist view, the compartmentalization of the university into its departments corresponds to objective divisions both in external reality and in the human brain, cutting reality at the joints, as it were. It was this positivist picture of knowledge that George Santayana ridiculed when he described the Harvard faculty of the 1890s, which he found brain-dead, as "an anonymous concourse of coral insects, each secreting one cell, and leaving that fossil legacy to enlarge the earth" (98). An essentially positivist form of organization remains dominant today, despite long-standing and widespread repudiation of positivism and stiff challenges by interdisciplinary education. Since interdisciplinary programs tend to be assimilated into the university as add-ons, instead of building bridges between the disciplines such programs tend to reproduce the fragmentation they were invented to counteract.

Another explanation for the persistence of patterned isolation, one not suggested in *Professing Literature*, can be found in the habit of evading conflict that has often been seen as a distinctive feature of American culture itself. In many ways, the history of the American curriculum resembles the history of the American city: just as clashes between socioeconomic classes and races have been avoided, or at least made less visible, by emigration to the frontier and later to the suburbs, turf battles in the university have been avoided by adding new curricular outposts in the form of new fields, new courses, and new buildings. In both the urban and the academic arena, conflicts are avoided by expanding the playing field—a luxury that is less of an option in today's contracting higher education economy. As I note in *Professing Literature*, the academic curriculum becomes a geological overlay of wildly disparate ideas, texts, and methods that eventually do not even conflict so much as pass one another in the night, leaving it to students to connect what their teachers do not.

This is another way of putting my earlier point that keeping controversy out of sight contributes to leaving students clueless. Consider this passage from the introduction of my 2003 book, *Clueless in Academe: How Schooling Obscures the Life of the Mind:*

> For American students to do better—all of them, not just twenty percent—they need to know that summarizing and making arguments is the name of the game in academia. But it's precisely this game that academia obscures,

generally by hiding it in plain view amidst a vast disconnected clutter of subjects, disciplines, and courses. The sheer cognitive overload represented by the American curriculum prevents most students from detecting and then learning the moves of the underlying argument game that gives coherence to it all.

Professing Literature traces how this "vast disconnected clutter of subjects, disciplines, and courses" emerged—or why it emerged as a disconnected clutter rather than as a set of conversations that might have made more sense to students.

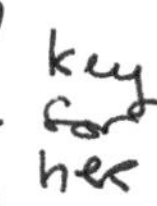

The Clarifying Power of Controversy

Which brings me back to my claim that clarification would result from exposing students to controversy. My assumption here, which is first formulated in *Clueless in Academe,* is that intellectual issues clarify themselves peculiarly at moments of controversy, or, as I put it in the later book, that "there exists a deep cognitive connection between controversy and intelligibility" (12). To put it another way, controversial issues are not tangential to academic knowledge, but part of that knowledge. That is, controversy is internal to the subject matter of subjects or disciplines—it *is* the object of knowledge or is inseparable from it. Debates about what a literary work means, or whether it deserves classic status or not, are internal to the study of that work, if only because such debates are part of the awareness of literate readers. Indeed, an awareness of what is regarded as controversial in any discipline at a given moment is generally a touchstone of whether someone is an insider to that discipline or not.

Another way to put it is to cite John Stuart Mill's famous maxim that we do not understand our own ideas until we know what can be said against them, that is, understand why and how they may be controversial. In Mill's words, which I quote in *Clueless in Academe,* those "who have never thrown themselves into the mental position of those who think differently from them . . . do not, in any proper sense of the word, know the doctrine which they themselves profess" (13). As I go on to say,

> our very ability to think depends on contrast—on asking 'as opposed to what?' This 'dialogical' or contrastive character of human cognition has long been a given of modern thought, but the academic curriculum with its self-isolated courses has yet to reflect it. When schooling is bad or dull, it is often because the curriculum effaces this element of contrast or as-opposed-to-whatness from students' view. Thus the academic habit of evading conflict helps obscure the life of the mind. (13)

Though I was not yet able to articulate them, these are the premises that underlie the argument in *Professing Literature* that hiding controversy from students robs literary studies of intelligibility.

Clueless in Academe argues that, in an academic environment increasingly characterized by intellectual and cultural difference rather than consensus, controversy—or what I call "the culture of ideas and arguments"—paradoxically becomes the only possible basis for consensus. It is an often-overlooked irony, especially in the heat of today's culture wars, that intellectuals with the most vehemently antagonistic ideologies are soulmates despite themselves—for their very antagonism brings them closer to each other than to nonintellectuals, who see their ideological passion as nebulous, boring, and alien. This point has been overlooked in recent battles over the humanities canon, where—to give a twist to one of Guillory's points—hostilities over *which* books to assign obscure the fact that the perennial problem for American students has been the culture of books and book discussion as such, regardless of who gets to draw up the reading list. These debates have become so fixated on *which form* of intellectual culture—traditional or trendy—should dominate the curriculum that they ignore the deeper problem, which is the alienation of most American students from any form of intellectual culture.

If this is indeed the deeper problem, then we are looking for curricular coherence in the wrong place when we seek it in the primary texts to be assigned rather than in the culture of ideas and arguments, the intellectual forms of talk and writing students need in order to make a literate response to a text or anything else. A curriculum that focused effectively on helping students talk the talk of the intellectual world could be admirably coherent even if it included clashing texts, ideas, and values.

Here, however, I come to some things I would do differently if I could write *Professing Literature* today. First, I would make clearer than I did that "conflict" and "consensus" are not antithetical concepts, but logically interdependent. To fruitfully disagree about *Macbeth,* say, we need to agree on a vast number of things: that *Macbeth* is a play, that it was written and performed in a particular historical period, that it contains characters intended to represent kinds of human beings. In order to teach the debate about the play, we would also need to agree on some educational axioms: that the play is worth assigning and arguing about, that reading it is valuable, that arguing about interpretations helps reading, and so forth. In short, in *Professing Literature* I was really arguing not against consensus, as I sometimes made it seem, but against looking for consensus in the wrong place, in the texts and subjects we assign rather than the literate discourse in which we talk about texts and subjects. The real point we need to agree on is that good education is about helping students enter the culture of ideas and arguments. If this point is granted—and a fair degree of consensus already exists on it—then teaching students to engage in intellectual debate at a high level is the most important thing we can do.

Here I can only plead guilty to Readings's charge in *The University in Ruins,* that my call to teach the conflicts requires "a consensus that would permit the determination and transmission of 'the conflict' as a unified object of professional discourse." This is not to concede Readings's rather different claim that behind my proposal to teach the conflicts "lies a desire for *final* consensus" (127, my italics). After all, there need be nothing "final" about a consensus that enables us to argue with one another. On the contrary, in good debates the parties often end up questioning the shared premises that enabled them to start talking. It is true that to make a particular controversy the "unified object of professional discourse," in Readings's words, would privilege some debates over others, but it would also allow the privileging of those debates to be questioned. Again, in good debates the terms of the debate itself are often challenged.

It follows from what I have just said that another thing I would do differently were I to write *Professing Literature* today is to give greater attention to the composition and rhetoric domain of English studies. I now see that in excluding composition from the scope of my study, I failed to recognize an important implication of my own argument. Since first-year composition is preeminently the part of the curriculum that has been charged with training students to "engage in intellectual debate at a high level," the logic of my own position should have led me to give composition greater prominence, as I might have done without losing sight of literary study or doubling the length of my book. Perhaps I now better appreciate the role composition should have played in my argument, because the focus of my teaching since the 1990s has shifted from literature to composition. Most recently, co-teaching first-year writing courses with my wife, Cathy Birkenstein, has led to a cowritten textbook, *"They Say/I Say": The Moves That Matter in Academic Writing,* a book that makes the "moves" of persuasive argument as explicit and accessible as possible.

Even while writing *Professing Literature* I had begun to think that the long-standing split between literature and composition programs in the English department (or between literary and language teaching in foreign-language departments) has been disastrous for *literary study itself.* After all, literary education flourishes only if students can write and speak proficiently about literature. Students may have a deep appreciation of literature, but their reading experience will be impoverished if they can't give an articulate account of it.

TEXTS DON'T TELL US WHAT TO SAY ABOUT THEM

To make this last point is to suggest that since no text tells us what to say about it, students need a critical conversation and a language of critical argument in order to effectively read and write about literature. For this reason, the very phrase *teaching literature* is misleading, since what teachers and students produce in literature courses is not literature, but *criticism*—that is, discourse about literature. Chris Baldick puts the point well:

> It is a fact too often forgotten that the real content of the school and college subject which goes under the name "English literature" is not literature in the primary sense, but *criticism.* Every school student in British education is required to compose not tragic dramas, but essays in criticism.

As I argued in *Clueless in Academe,* even in creative-writing courses, where students might conceivably compose tragic dramas, discussion is conducted in critical discourse. Like Molière's gentleman who realized he had been speaking prose all his life, literature teachers need to recognize that criticism is inevitably what we do when we talk about a work of art.

But if literature students are necessarily expected to produce criticism—and graded down when they do it badly—then they need to *read* some models of what they are asked to produce. To withhold examples from students of the kind of critical discourse they are expected to produce is in effect to tie one hand behind their backs. Yet college (and high school) literary study still overwhelmingly consists of reading primary literary texts with little or no literary criticism, much less critical debate or literary theory. To incorporate more criticism into literature courses, then, would be a way to give students some models of the critical discourse they need in order to talk and write articulately about primary texts. And to present these critical models in debate—rather than as isolated pieces—would help students see that criticism involves entering a larger conversation of readers who care enough to argue passionately about literature.

Perhaps the above comments will disabuse those who have gotten the idea that "teaching the conflicts" means essentially replacing literature with criticism or theory. The philosopher John Searle, for example, in a 1991 exchange in the *New York Review of Books,* summarizes me as follows: "instead of teaching Plato and Shakespeare Graff thinks we should teach the debate about whether Plato and Shakespeare should be taught." For me, however, the point has never been to replace Plato and Shakespeare, but to make it possible for students to enter a critical discussion of either writer.

The reluctance to acknowledge that "secondary" critical discourse necessarily comes between a text and what we are able to say about it often reflects long-standing resentment at literature's having become a professional subject at all. In *Professing Literature* I tried to avoid this pessimistic view, which sees professionalism and institutionalization as inherently corrupting to the spirit. This anti-professionalism, which has been acutely dissected by Stanley Fish and Bruce Robbins, can be felt hovering over recent culture war skirmishes. It gets passed on to students in the form of the belief that to analyze a literary work or otherwise "intellectualize" about it is to spoil the pleasure of reading. The conflict felt by many students and lay people between analyzing literature and enjoying it is one of the many that falls into the cracks between courses and fails to be addressed.

In concluding, I want to touch on a controversy that erupted after the publication of *Professing Literature*, the battle over "political correctness" and the prominence of the liberal-left in the academic humanities. The same inability to think productively about controversy—even to imagine productive controversy as an alternative—has impoverished recent debates about political correctness the same way it has impoverished debates about the curriculum. Such debates tend to be framed by two unsatisfactory options: either the classroom is a site of radical political advocacy, or else such advocacy has no place in the classroom at all. And as long as the debate is limited by "the classroom" understood as an isolated space, an alternative way of thinking about classroom advocacy is indeed hard to imagine. The possibility hardly arises that the antidote for irresponsible classroom advocacy might be *counter-advocacy* rather than the avoidance of advocacy. Let instructors take strong stands, but let these stands answer to the strongest available counter-voices, so that students gain models of true intellectual exchange.

In his recent book, *What's Liberal About the Liberal Arts?: Classroom Politics and "Bias" in Higher Education,* for my money the most nuanced discussion of the political-correctness controversy so far, Michael Bérubé challenges many of the standard conservative complaints of liberal bias in the humanities. But Bérubé does single out one conservative argument, made by Mark Bauerlein, which he calls "interesting" and "insightful." This is the argument, as Bérubé summarizes it, that the domination of the humanities by "liberal-left thought" is bad not only for the humanities, "but also for liberal-left thought." As Bérubé puts it, the liberal-left tilt of much campus culture "can envelop young progressives in a moral mist that leaves them complacent and thoroughly unprepared" for the opposition they will encounter from "the rest of American culture."

The insular mentality that Bérubé finds in leftist campus culture is greatly magnified for all academics by teaching in closed classrooms, the doors of which shut out the very colleagues who would be most disposed—and often best qualified—to question our pet beliefs. To be sure, students may challenge those pet beliefs. But being answerable to a captive audience of students is simply not the same as being answerable to an audience of peers. Since academics consider it normal to be accountable to our peers when our books and articles are reviewed or we give papers at academic conferences, why are we exempted from such accountability when we teach?

But perhaps the most damaging effect of this insularity appears when academics need to justify their existence to their society. If you tried to devise the poorest form of rhetorical training you could think of for justifying what you do to the wider world, it would be hard to improve on teaching in isolated classrooms, screened from the criticism of your peers. It is hard to imagine a worse form of training for changing people's minds about the legitimacy of feminist readings of Shakespeare, the merits of affirmative action, or the need for society to fund humanities research. We humanists spend a great deal of our time these days lamenting the lack of financial support for our enterprise, a disturbing result of which is the disappearance of full-time teaching jobs, as part-time instructors have come to make up more than half of American college faculties. Though this downsizing is indeed shameful, the failure of academics to mount effective resistance to it has exposed the disabling effects of patterned isolation. If the story told in *Professing Literature* is accurate, we have acquiesced in ways of organizing our work that undermine our effort to speak with a strong collective voice.

NOTES

Page

1 **the book's commentators**—The most substantial of these include Robert Scholes, "Three Views of Education: Nostalgia, History, and Voodoo," *College English* 50 (1988): 323–32; George Levine, "Graff Revisited," *Raritan* 8, no. 4 (Spring 1989): 121–133; Francis Oakley, *Community of Learning: The American College and the Liberal Arts Tradition* (New York: Oxford University Press, 1992), pp. 68–70,

159–61; Jeffrey Williams, "Gerald Graff," editor's headnote, *The Norton Anthology of Theory and Criticism* (New York: W. W. Norton, 2001), p. 2056–59. See also "Only Connect: An Interview with Gerald Graff," in Williams, ed., *Critics at Work: Interviews, 1993–2003* (New York: New York University Press, 2004), pp. 55–71.

2 **"teach the conflicts"**—The most comprehensive version of this argument appears in my *Beyond the Culture Wars: How Teaching the Conflicts Can Revitalize American Education* (New York: W. W. Norton, 1992); for other discussions, see William Cain, ed., *Teaching the Conflicts: Gerald Graff, Curricular Reform, and the Culture Wars* (New York: Garland Press, 1993), and the "Symposium: Teaching the Conflicts at Twenty Years," *Pedagogy* 3, no. 2 (Spring, 2003): 245–75.

3 **the "field-coverage" model**—My point was never to disparage the coverage of fields in itself, a fact I emphasize because some readers may have associated me with a certain critique of the university that attacks professionalism, specialization, departments, and the very division of labor into fields. My own view is that professionalization, specialization, and division of labor are necessary features of any complex modern organization. What I meant to object to in the field-coverage model was not the formation of specialized fields as such, but the separation and disconnection of these fields.

4 **"substandard high school preparation" for college**—*A Test of Leadership: Charting the Future of U.S. Higher Education,* A Report of the Commission Appointed by Secretary of Education Margaret Spellings, pre-publication copy (September 2006), p. 1.

5 **programs I have described in more recent writing.** See *Beyond the Culture Wars,* pp. 171–96; *Clueless in Academe: How Schooling Obscures the Life of the Mind* (New Haven: Yale University Press, 2003), pp. 62–80; and Graff and Jane Tompkins, "Can We Talk?" in Donald E. Hall, ed., *Professions: Conversations on the Future of Literary and Cultural Studies* (Urbana, IL: University of Illinois Press, 2001), pp. 21–36.

clarify the obstacles to democratic education.—Frank Smith, *Joining the Literacy Club: Further Essays into Education* (Portsmouth, NH: Heinemann, 1988).

literary training irrelevant to today's social elites.—John Guillory, *Cultural Capital: The Problem of Literary Canon Formation* (Chicago: University of Chicago Press, 1993). Page numbers henceforth given in the text.

7 **of institutions, politics, and the popular media.**—Robert Scholes, *Textual Power: Literary Theory and the Teaching of English* (New Haven: Yale University Press, 1985), p. 33.

9 **the danger of *too much* consensus.**—Bill Readings, *The University in Ruins* (Cambridge, MA.: Harvard University Press, 1996). Page numbers henceforth given in the text.

12 **argument game that gives coherence to it all.**—Graff, *Clueless in Academe,* p. 3. Page numbers henceforth given in the text.

13 **the doctrine which they themselves profess."**—John Stuart Mill, "On Liberty," in *Utilitarianism, Liberty, Representative Government* (London: Dent & Sons, 1951), p. 129.

16 **argument as explicit and accessible as possible.**—Gerald Graff and Cathy Birkenstein, *"They Say/I Say": The Moves That Matter in Academic Writing* (New York: W. W. Norton, 2006).

17 **not tragic dramas, but essays in criticism.**—Chris Baldick, *The Social Mission of English Criticism, 1848–1932* (New York: Oxford University Press, 1983), pp. 4–5; quoted by Graff, *Clueless in Academe,* p. 175.

18 **whether Plato and Shakespeare should be taught."**—John Searle, letter to the editor, *New York Review of Books* 38, no. 4 (February 14, 1991): p. 49. Searle was replying to my letter to the editor in response to his article, "The Storm Over the University," *New York Review of Books* 37, no.19 (December 6, 1990): pp. 34–42.

19 **This anti-professionalism, which has been acutely dissected**—Stanley Fish, "Anti-Professionalism," in *Doing What Comes Naturally: Change, Rhetoric, and the Practice of Theory in Literary and Legal Studies* (Durham, NC: Duke University Press, 1989), pp. 215–46; Bruce Robbins, *Secular Vocations: Intellectualism, Professionalism, Culture* (London: Verso, 1993).

19 **"but for liberal-left thought."**—Michael Bérubé, *What's Liberal About the Liberal Arts?: Classroom Politics* and "Bias" in *Higher Education* (New York: W. W. Norton), p. 87.

20 **from "the rest of American culture"**—Bérubé, p. 125.

Acknowledgments

My thanks to numerous colleagues and friends who read my manuscript at various stages and gave valuable advice and criticism. None should be held responsible for the shortcomings of the results. To Wally Douglas and Michael Warner, two colleagues at Northwestern University whose important work on the early history of English is acknowledged in the text, for comments on more than one draft. To Larry Lipking and Saul Morson for close and critical readings. To Michael Fischer, William Cain, and Jonathan Arac for challenging criticisms of the argument and the rhetoric. To Tim Bahti for help on the history of German universities and early professionalism.

For useful comments and productive disagreements on various sections of the manuscript, thanks to David Shumway, Steve Mailloux, Mac Davis, Melita Schaum, Fred Crews, Greg Jay, David Myers, and Claudia Springer. Two press readers, Jonathan Culler and John Ellis, made helpful critiques of an early draft.

My particular thanks to Mark Walhout and Carla Kaplan for invaluable research assistance and to Elizabeth Shaw for painstaking editing and patience.

My thanks to the John Simon Guggenheim Foundation for a grant that made it possible for me to undertake this project.

I am grateful to Alan Thomas, humanities editor of the University of Chicago Press, for suggesting this reissue and for his help with the new Preface. Ben Underwood of UIC also helped with acute suggestions on several drafts of the Preface.

CHAPTER ONE

Introduction: The Humanist Myth

When a sufficient number of specialists are assembled on a college faculty, the subject of which each knows only a small part is said to be covered, and the academic department to which they all belong is regarded as fully manned. In ancient Ireland, if legend is to be trusted, there was a tower so high that it took two persons to see to the top of it. One would begin at the bottom and look up as far as sight could reach, the other would begin where the first left off, and see the rest of the way.

JOHN ERSKINE

It's hard to organize literature.

IRVING HOWE

Professing Literature is a history of academic literary studies in the United States, roughly from the Yale Report of 1828, which assured the primacy of the classical over the vernacular languages in American colleges for another half-century, to the waning of the New Criticism in the 1960s and subsequent controversies over literary theory. Strictly speaking, there were no "academic literary studies" in America or anywhere else until the formation of language and literature departments in the last quarter of the nineteenth century. But the use of literature as a vehicle of education goes back to ancient times, and in America since the Colonial era literary texts had been studied in college classes in Greek and Latin, English grammar, and rhetoric and elocution. These early practices assumed a theory of the social function of literature that affected the shape of literature departments when they finally emerged.

But the idea that literature could or should be taught—rather than simply enjoyed or absorbed as part of the normal upbringing of gentlefolk—was a novel one, and no precedents existed for organizing such an enterprise. To "organize literature" is difficult under any circumstances, but particularly when it means reconstituting as a curriculum under more or less democratic conditions something that had previously been part of the socialization of a particular class. My account suggests that this project was never thought through in all its ramifications, but, if anything, early educators were more alert to its difficulties than we are today, since they had the advantage of a historical perspective that was lost once academic literary studies became established and complacent and once it no longer could remember a preacademic literary culture for comparison.

Any single-volume treatment of so vast a subject must omit some matters and reduce others to schematic proportions. Though I refer generically to "academic literary studies" and "the literature department," most of my evidence is drawn from research-oriented departments of English at major universites, and I make only occasional attempts to distinguish patterns in English from those in other modern language departments or departments of comparative literature. Perhaps I ought to have subtitled the book "A History of English Studies," but I decided that essential traits have been similar enough to warrant the broader label.

My account does not do justice to the small-college experience, however. And I suspect that some of the conditions I treat as chronic dilemmas will be seen as grounds for envy in institutions where literature, as distinct from composition, has become a luxury. I deal only in passing with the teaching of composition, though the pioneer work of William Riley Parker, Wallace Douglas, and Richard Ohmann has shown that without that enterprise the teaching of literature could never have achieved its central status, and none of the issues I discuss would matter very much. I have made only occasional mention of British universities, despite the influence they exerted on native developments.

The aim of my concluding chapter is not to examine recent controversies over literary theory in detail—something outside the scope of this kind of book— but to point out how these controversies echo old ones as far back as the beginnings of the profession. My aim here is also to suggest that literary theory can help illuminate old and new conflicts in ways that might infuse some welcome self-consciousness into literary studies. As I use the term, there is a sense in which all teachers of literature are "theorists" and have a stake in theoretical disputes. For that matter, there is a sense in which a literature department (and curriculum) is itself a theory, though it has been largely an incoherent theory, and this incoherence strengthens the impression that the department has no theory.

It is possible to defend the infusion of theory into the curriculum on traditional grounds, namely, that students need theoretical concepts in order to be able to make sense of literature and talk about it intelligently. We shall see that until recently, in fact, the word "theory" was embraced by educational traditionalists, in reaction against the atomized empiricism of research and explication, which trusted that the accumulation of facts and interpretations about literature would somehow of itself add up to a coherent picture. This is not to deny that much current theory amounts to a radical attack on the premises and values of traditional literary humanism. But such attacks on traditional literary humanism raise the kinds of questions about the nature and cultural functions of literature that used to be the concern of traditional humanists, even as they reject the traditional humanistic answers to those questions as no longer sufficient. The real enemy of tradition is the kind of orthodox literary study that neglects theoretical questions about ends, values, and definitions in the hope that they will take care of themselves. It was the breakdown of agreement (or ostensible agreement) on these questions that inspired the current theory explosion and ensures, I think, that it will not be a passing fad.

When I first began this inquiry I vaguely assumed that the founders of academic literary studies must originally have had a shared idea of their rationale that had somehow got lost along the way. I imagined that this shared rationale had something to do with concepts like "humanism" and "cultural tradition," more or less in the sense associated with the name of Matthew Arnold. What I discovered, however, was that although the transmission of humanism and cultural tradition in the Matthew Arnold sense was indeed the official goal of the literature department, there were from the outset fundamental disagreements about how that goal should be pursued. Early educators who identified themselves with the Matthew Arnold view of literature and culture strenuously objected to the philological and historical literary scholarship that had qualified literary studies for departmental status in the new research university.

The union of Arnoldian humanism and scientific research which gave birth to academic literary studies was never free from strain. Traditional humanists argued that the compartmentalization of literature in narrowly specialized and disconnected "fields" and the glorification of quantitative "production" in research tended to undermine Arnold's ideal of broad general culture and his view of literature as a coherent criticism of life. The research fetish seemed only another example of that triumph of practical and technical "machinery" over ethical and cultural ends that Arnold had deplored in so many features of the modern world—and that seemed peculiarly unrestrained in the United States.

It is worth pondering that the kind of scholarship we now think of as traditionally humanistic was regarded as a subversive innovation by the traditionalists of an earlier era, whatever its roots may have been in the classical humanism of the Renaissance. It is also worth pondering that traditional humanists of the same era indicted research scholarship for many of the very same sins for which later traditionalists indicted the New Criticism and present day traditionalists indict literary theory: elevating esoteric, technocratic jargon over humanistic values, coming between literature itself and the student, turning literature into an elitist pastime for specialists. Whatever the sins of recent theory, those who blame the problems of the humanities on them—and on other post-1960 developments—only illustrate their own pet maxim that those who forget the past are condemned to repeat it. The solutions they propose—a return to a great tradition with no investigation of why that tradition has come to be questioned—figures only to send us yet one more time around what we will see has been an oft-repeated cycle.

Of course the research scholars who were the targets of the earliest criticism did not see matters the way their critics did. They too saw themselves as legitimate heirs of Matthew Arnold, and they dismissed their detractors as dilettantes and victims of mere nostalgia, as many of them were. Even so, a surprising number of these early research scholars could not help agreeing with their critics that there was a disturbing disparity between their traditional humanistic ideals and their professional practices. They spent much of their time at the early meetings of the Modern Language Association exhorting one another to do something about the disparity, though few of them went beyond ineffectual assertions, reiterated countless times by now, that teaching should be restored to equal importance with research, that the "general culture" of the undergraduate college should be reasserted against the specialization of the graduate school, and (above all) that literature itself should somehow be restored to primacy over scholarship and methodology. The very nature of this diagnosis led the critics of the profession to lapse into fatalism, blaming their problems on the inherent philistinism of American democracy, the inherent vulgarity of the modern age, or the incurable inferiority of their students.

The complaint that research and publication have displaced teaching has always resembled the parallel complaint that technology or bureaucracy has displaced more human or communal relations. Whatever its justifications, such a complaint leads nowhere, for it envisages no role for the professional interests of the scholar except to extinguish themselves. The diagnosis on which the complaint rests blames the problems of the institution on the process of professionalization itself, not distinguishing between professionalism as such and the specific forms professionalism has taken under the peculiar circumstances of the new university, forms which—it must be stressed—need not be the only forms possible. But however limited their value as present guides, these early critics can at least cure us of the delusion that academic literary studies at some point underwent a falling-away from genuine Arnoldian humanism.

Helping prop up this humanist myth, however, is the habit of thinking of institutions as if they were unmediated projections of the values, methods, and ideologies of major individuals and movements. This procedure is convenient and seems to accord with common sense, but it ignores, for one thing, the substantial changes that even the dominant critical values, methods, and ideologies may undergo when they become institutionalized in the form of scholarly fields, curricula, and pedagogy. "Professionalization" and "academicization" are not neutral principles of organization, but agents that transform the cultural and literary-critical "isms" fed into them, often to the point of subverting their original purpose, or so deflecting them that they become unrecognizable to outsiders. What goes in is not necessarily what comes out, and this is one reason why the things the institution seems self-evidently to stand for to insiders may scarcely register on outsiders.

In calling this book an institutional history, I mean to underscore that its concern is not only with particular scholarly and critical practices, but also with what has happened to those practices once they have become institutionalized in modern universities—in ways that are not the only possible ones. My emphasis, in other words, is not only on what "goes in" in the shape of individual scholarly accomplishments and trends, but on what "comes out" as an operational totality and how that totality is perceived, misperceived, or not perceived at all by outsiders. Most histories of criticism properly ignore such matters and concentrate on major figures and movements, but for this reason their results may not yield a safe basis for an institutional analysis. For even major figures and movements can fail to stamp their values on the institution as a whole. In large degree

Arnoldian humanism has been the outlook of singular individuals, individuals who have exerted a powerful and still-present influence on students and followers, but who have repeatedly failed to make their values visibly characteristic of the totality. Without going into the complex history of the term, we can note that already by the turn of the century, "Humanist"—in its association with Irving Babbitt and his group—was the name of one particular professional faction, one "field" among many, more or less estranged from the established ones. It is no accident that many of the exemplary Arnoldian humanists from Babbitt to Walter Jackson Bate have ended up as bitter critics of the profession.

Their failure does not seem to me a state of affairs to be lamented, since it is after all the inability of their Arnoldian humanism to become an effective umbrella concept that has gradually opened academic literary studies to a variety of competing views of literature, scholarship, and culture. The discouraging thing is not that such institutional conflicts have gone unresolved—unresolved conflict being just the sort of thing a democratic educational system should thrive on—but how little of the potential educational value of such conflicts the professional system has been able to turn into part of what it studies and teaches, instead of a source of paralysis. Not all the conflicts of literary studies have been so esoteric as to lack potential interest to outsiders, and even those that have a large esoteric dimension (like the current cold war between theorists and humanists) have a surprising way of exemplifying cultural conflicts of potentially general interest. But educational-cultural battles tend at present to be fought out only behind the scenes, as it were, in specialized journals, technical vocabularies, and private faculty meetings. They are exemplified rather than foregrounded by the department and the curriculum and thus do not become part of the context of the average student's education or the average professor's professional life.

The pretense that humanism and the cultural tradition preside over the various dispersed activities of literary studies is one of the things which has permitted ideological conflicts to be kept out of public view. But another powerful cause lies in the field-coverage model of departmental organization, which has conceived literature departments as aggregates arranged to cover an array of historical and generic literary fields. The field-coverage principle accompanied the modernization and professionalization of education of the 1870s and 1880s, when schools and colleges organized themselves into departments corresponding to what were deemed to be the major subjects and research fields. For reasons having to do equally with ensuring humanistic breadth and facilitating specialized research, the literature department adopted the assumption that it would consider itself respectably staffed once it had amassed instructors competent to "cover" a more or less balanced spread of literary periods and genres, with a scattering of themes and special topics.

The field-coverage principle seems so innocuous as to be hardly worth looking at, and we have lived with it so long that we hardly even see it, but its consequences have been far reaching. Its great advantage was to make the department and the curriculum virtually self-regulating. By assigning each instructor a commonly understood role—to cover a predefined period or field—the principle created a system in which the job of instruction could proceed as if on automatic pilot, without the need for instructors to debate aims and methods. Assuming individual instructors were competently trained—and the system of graduate work which developed rapidly in America after the 1890's took care of that—instructors could be left on their own to get on with teaching and research, with little need for elaborate supervision and management.

The second advantage of the field-coverage principle was to give the institution enormous flexibility in assimilating new ideas, subjects, and methods. In the model of education that had preceded the modern school or university, where a primary goal was to enforce a Christian religious and social ideology, any innovation that challenged the prevailing way of doing things was disruptive and had to be excluded or expelled. In the coverage model, by contrast, innovation even of a threatening kind could be welcomed by simply *adding* another unit to the aggregate of fields to be covered. Fierce resistance to innovation arose frequently, of course, but since all instructors were on their own, the absorption of innovation did not oblige pre-established habits to change, so that in the long run—and increasingly it was not a very long run—resistance tended to give way. It is only the field-coverage principle that explains how the literature department has managed to avoid incurring paralyzing clashes of ideology during a period when it has preserved much of its earlier traditional orientation while incorporating disruptive novelties such as contemporary literature, black studies, feminism, Marxism, and deconstruction.

The field-coverage principle made the modern educational machine friction free, for by making individuals functionally independent in the carrying out of their tasks it prevented conflicts from erupting which would otherwise have had to be confronted, debated, and worked through. An invisible hand—fortified by the faith that humanism in the Matthew Arnold sense pervaded all the branches of the department's and the profession's activities—saw to it that the sum of the parts added up to a coherent whole. Yet these very strengths of the field-coverage principle were also liabilities. By making the teaching staff and the curriculum self-regulating, the principle let instructors get on with the job of teaching and research in an efficient and untroubled way, but it also relieved them of the need to discuss the reasons they were doing what they were doing. Organizational structure left the faculty without the need to confer about matters of fundamental concern with colleagues in their own and other departments. Not that there was any lack of controversy, of course—this has always been plentiful enough—but controversy was curiously screened from students and outsiders. The tacit assumption has been that students should be exposed only to the *results* of professional controversies, not to the controversies themselves, which would presumably confuse or demoralize them. The curriculum has been determined by political trade-offs, while the clashing principles that might at least have made the process edifying have been removed from view.

The division of fields according to the least controversial principles made the department easy to administer but masked its most interesting conflicts and connections. To put it another way, the field-coverage principle enabled administrative organization to take the place of principled thought and discussion. The presence of an array of fully staffed fields made it unnecessary for anybody to have a theoretical idea of the department's goals in order for it to get on with its work. The grid of literary periods, genres, and themes in the catalog was a sufficiently clear expression of what the department was about. Critics objected to the department's compartmentalization as if that in itself was the problem, but division of labor is necessary in any bureaucratized system. It was not the compartmentalizations which created the problem but their disconnection, which rendered invisible the relations and contrasts that could have forced the meanings of the department's divisions into relief. Since the courses in periods and genres did not address one another, teachers tended not to raise the question of what connections or contrasts the different periods and genres might bear to one another, what was meant by a particular periodization or by "period" in general, or what it might mean to approach literature in a historical or generic (and later a "New Critical") way. It was as if categories existed in order to make it unnecessary to think about them and to recognize that they were the product of theoretical choices.

By organizing itself on a principle of systematic non-relationship in which all parties tacitly agreed not to ask how they might be connected or opposed, the department prevented potentially edifying conflicts from becoming part of what literary studies was about. Students (and instructors) were thus deprived of a means of situating themselves in relation to the cultural issues of their time. For students learn not just by exposure to individual instructors, but by sensing how the teaching aggregate hangs together or divides, so that to obscure these relations robs students of one of the central means of making sense of education and the cultural world. Latent conflicts of method and ideology that had divided the faculty from the first did not have to be confronted; it was up to each instructor (within increasingly flexible limits) to determine method and ideology without correlation with one another. Thus, even though conflicts over method and ideology were becoming more frequent and intense as the profession developed, the myth of shared humanistic values and purposes could always be maintained. Not only was there no need to ask what theoretical assumptions underlay these values, the illusion could be kept up that nobody had a theory.

This effect operated vertically as well as horizontally, as the methodologies of literary study became detached from the cultural rationales that originally had given point to them. This pattern of detachment, whereby methods become separated from their goals, first arose in the pre-professional era, but professionalization, with its multiplication of technical methodologies, greatly intensified it. Usually the blame falls on the inherent tendency of methodology itself to become a monster grinding out research and criticism without their producers knowing why they are producing it. Again, however, it is arguably not methodology that necessarily invites such routinization, but a system which, by isolating functions, separates methodology from the contexts and theories which would keep its justifications visible.

The field-coverage principle effected at the administrative level what the humanist myth perpetuated at the level of ideology. In combination, the two provided a solution to the problem of how to "organize literature" that removed the need for continued collective discussion. Just as the literature faculty was self-regulating as long as periodization predefined the functions of individuals, literature was self-interpreting as long as it remained an expression of humanism. Hence there arose a curriculum that expressed the faith that exposure to a more or less balanced array of periods, genres, and themes would add up in the mind of the student to an appreciation of humanism and the cultural tradition. More succinctly, the assumption implicit in the humanist myth and the field-coverage principle has been that *literature*

teaches itself. Since the literary tradition is presumably coherent in and of itself, it should naturally dictate the way teachers collectively organize themselves. That literature teaches itself is not necessarily the conscious assumption of individual teachers (though many have embraced it, as we will see), but something presupposed by the overall structure.

Unfortunately the assumption has never proved true—but the dream still persists that it might, if the encumbrances of scholarship, criticism, or theory could somehow be prevented from getting in the way. One of the recurrent motifs in the present history is the appeal to "literature itself" against various forms of commentary *about* literature as a cure for institutional dilemmas. The hope is that salvation can be achieved if only the great literary works can be freed from the institutional and professional encumbrances that come between students or laymen and the potency of the work itself. For a long time it was positivistic scholarship that was the target of this view, then it became analytic criticism, and today it has become literary theory and various attempts to historicize literature. But the basic form of the "literature itself" argument remains the same, bespeaking the perennial wish to believe that if the quality of individual instruction is good and the right works are taught, the effect of the whole will take care of itself.

Literary studies have not yet found a way to institutionalize the lesson of recent criticism that no text is an island, that every work of literature is a rejoinder in a conversation or dialogue that it presupposes but may or may not mention explicitly. It is in this spirit that Robert Scholes argues, in his recent book, *Textual Power,* that to teach the literary text one must teach the "cultural text" as well. Many instructors already do so, but individual pedagogy alone can have only limited effects when it conflicts with institutional structure. The disconnection between the divisions that organize the literature department and the university tends to efface the larger cultural conversation to which works of literature refer. The cultural text tends to fall into the cracks separating periods, genres, and fields, criticism, creative writing, and composition. Nobody is responsible for it since it is nobody's field—or else someone is responsible for it only as one field among others.

One might expect traditionalists to show some sympathy with such a conservatively historical argument as this, yet the idea still remains powerful that students are best introduced to literature by being put in "direct" contact with texts themselves, with a minimum of contextualizing interference. Those who hold this view cling to it tenaciously, believing it has been validated by the historical experience they have lived through for the past thirty or forty years. They recall so vividly the disastrously mechanical kinds of contextualizing they were subjected to under the old positivistic literary history that when they hear words like "contextualize," "historicize," and "theorize," they envision students even more bored and disaffected than they were before the New Criticism put the old historicism out of its misery. But the remedy for a poor contextualizing of literature is not no contextualizing but better contextualizing. That did not arise out of the compromise between New Criticism and background study that resolved disciplinary controversies after World War II. Nobody can doubt that the turn to "close reading" at that time constituted an immense improvement over what came before, but it has proved to be a short-term solution whose costs are now increasingly apparent. By treating the contexts of literature as an extrinsic matter, however important, the compromise between New Critical and historical pedagogy that stabilized literature departments over the past three or four decades has only reinforced the inveterate assumption that these contexts will take care of themselves if a balanced spread of fields is represented, and thus that they do not need to be collectively worked out or organized. By treating the contexts of literature as an extrinsic affair, the New Criticism made it all the more unnecessary to worry about how those contexts might be organized institutionally. But without a context, the student's "direct" experience of literature itself tends to result either in uncertainty or facile acquiescence in an interpretive routine.

Current radical critiques of academic literary studies have effectively exposed the pretensions of "unproblematic" appeals to literature itself, and my analysis often echoes them. I agree with Terry Eagleton's argument, in *Literary Theory,* that literary studies have arbitrarily narrowed the concept of "literature,"and that the goal should be to repair the disabling dislocation of literature "from other cultural and social practices." I echo Foucault in looking at the way seemingly neutral, disciplinary classifications and boundaries actually constitute the fields they organize. Like certain deconstructionists, I am concerned with the way idealizations such as "humanism" have functioned rhetorically to mask the conflicts that constituted them.

At the same time, I see nothing inherently self-undoing or illegitimate about all idealizations, as the deconstructionists do, and I doubt that all institutional patterns can be explained as effects of ideology, power, "logocentrism," or subjugation. Valuable as they are, these forms of critique seem to lack a criterion that would enable them to distinguish between legitimate and illegitimate forms of institutional or rhetorical power. Furthermore, they tend to accept the same working model of institutional history as the traditionalists, merely "reinscribing" it in an accusatory vocabulary. Like the Right, the Left mistakes pious wishes and pronouncements for institutional fact. A case in point is Eagleton's account of the rise and development of "English" as a project of "controlling and incorporating the working class" through the consolidation of the national literature.

There is some truth in this "social control" theory of academic literary studies, for many members of the founding generation did conceive these studies explicitly and openly as a means of reinstating cultural uniformity and thus controlling those unruly democratic elements that were entering higher education for the first time after the Civil War. What Eagleton describes in England was true in the United States as well, that "in the work of 'English' pioneers like F. D. Maurice and Charles Kingsley, the emphasis was on solidarity between the social classes, the cultivation of 'larger sympathies,' the instillation of national pride and the transmission of 'moral' values." But the queston remains, how successfully was this nationalistic mission for literary studies carried out? Did the ideology of the founders remain "the distinctive hallmark of literary studies" down to the present, as Eagleton claims?

If their testimony can be taken seriously, those who most wanted the mission to succeed thought it had failed right from the start. The hope that the study of English would restore national leadership to the academic custodians of high culture disintegrated very early. On the one hand, high literary culture was increasingly marginal to the commercial and corporate interests dominating modern life, making laughable the pretensions of the literary elite to cultural leadership. On the other hand, even within the university the old elite was losing control—at least it complained bitterly that the new academic professionalism tended to place the interests of the research field above the interests of the nation. Underlying the animus of many early Arnoldian humanists against the profesional research industry was the view that research sacrificed literature's potential as an instrument of socialization to the narrow interests of a professional clique. Although the turn of the century saw the imposition of a uniform canon of English literature, traditionalists complained that the curriculum had all but dissipated the civic potential of the canon by breaking it up into such disconnected fragments that students could get no clear sense of its unity. Far from being organized on a centralized logocentric model, the American university is itself something of a deconstructionist, proliferating a variety of disciplinary vocabularies that nobody can reduce to the common measure of any metalanguage. This in fact is one of the reasons why such institutions are so hard to change.

My evidence, in any case, suggests that professionalization not only failed to turn academic literary studies into the effective instrument of nationalist ideology some of the founders hoped they would be, but in some ways it subverted that ideology. Again, the American situation may have to be distingushed from that of France and England, where the traditional social elites were more powerful and more able to resist professionalization than were their counterparts in the United States. In the American university, the frustration of cultural nationalism is particularly obvious in the late and grudging academic recognition accorded to America's national literature, which was at first excluded from departments because it did not suit the prevailing research methods and then, when at last incorporated, proceeded to be so assimilated to those methods that its coherence as an expression of the national spirit was rendered all but invisible. Professional literary studies would not have encountered so many problems of identity had they not come into being at the very moment when the principle of nationality, for most of the nineteenth century the major way of conceptualizing literature as a whole, was losing its effectiveness.

The point needs to be kept in mind when considering recent critiques of the canon. Unquestionably, the exclusion of blacks, women, and other heterodox traditions from the canon has had major ideological effects. What is prevented from "going in" to begin with can hardly have an effect on what comes out. But this is not to say that what comes out is ideologically of a piece. When critics like Jane Tompkins argue that the academic remaking of the American literature canon gave "the American people a conception of themselves and their history," they fail to ask whether the canon was ever taught homogeneously or effectively enough to convey a clear conception of the national spirit to students, much less to "the American people" as a whole. In order to specify the ideological effects of the canon, it should be necessary to do more than make inferences from the canonized texts and interpretations. Though recent reader-centered criticism has taught us that readers appropriate texts in heterogeneous ways, this lesson tends to be forgotten when the ideology of the canon is at stake.

Both the accusatory and the honorific view of literary studies—which turn out, curiously, to be the same view—rest on wishful thinking. They credit the institution with a more cohesive impact than it has ever achieved. Like other inventions of the Progressive Era, academic literary studies have combined class, ethnic, and gender prejudices with a genuinely democratic egalitarianism—that is what has made it possible for radical critics to find a home in them. Literary studies have been no beacon of political enlightenment, but they have not been an instrument of dominant ideology and social control either—or, if so, they have been a singularly inefficient one.

As I have told it, then, the story of academic literary studies in America is a tale not of triumphant humanism, nationalism, or any single professional model, but of a series of conflicts that have tended to be masked by their very failure to find visible institutional expression. This emphasis on conflicts is seen in the successive oppositions that organize my narrative: classicists versus modern-language scholars; research investigators versus generalists; historical scholars versus critics; New Humanists versus New Critics; academic critics versus literary journalists and culture critics; critics and scholars versus theorists. These controversies have seemed to me to possess greater richness and vitality than any of the conclusions they led to about the nature of literary studies as a discipline or the nature of literature as an object. Among the matters in dispute have been not just the nature of literature and the discipline, but whether there is—or needs to be—such a thing as a "discipline" of literary studies at all, or such a thing as "literature" in some univocal sense, as opposed to a variety of different literary and critical activities made coherent, if at all, only by their conflicts. If one conflict subsumes the others in my story, however, it is the one which has pitted scholars against critics. We tend to forget that until recently the terms were considered antithetical: scholars did research and dealt with verifiable facts, whereas critics presided over interpretations and values, which supposedly had no objective basis and therefore did not qualify for serious academic study. This state of affairs changed so rapidly that the implications of the change hardly had time to be assessed. Whereas "academic criticism" had been a contradiction in terms, it suddenly became a redundancy, as criticism, once the province of nonacademic journalists and men of letters, became (with important exceptions) virtually the monopoly of university departments.

Yet the old antagonism of scholar and critic did not disappear as much as it became submerged, after World War II, in an atmosphere where methodological and conceptual progress seemed more desirable than ideological confrontation. Many of the old issues reappeared under a realignment of the parties that has now set scholars and critics on the same side in opposition to theorists. Among these issues are the nature of literature (or whether it has a nature), the nature of literary interpretation and evaluation, the relation between the "intrinsic" domain of literature and the "extrinsic" ones of history, society, philosophy, and psychology, and above all, the issue of whether or in what way literature should be historicized and assimilated to social and political contexts.

Those who argue that the humanities have become disablingly incoherent seem to me right, but many of them fail to see that coherence can no longer be grounded on some restored consensus, whether it be traditional "basics," revolutionary ideological critique, or something else. In the final analysis, what academic literary studies have had to work with is not a coherent cultural tradition, but a series of conflicts that have remained unresolved, unacknowledged, and assumed to be outside the proper sphere of literary education. To bring these conflicts inside that sphere will mean thinking of literary education as part of a larger cultural history that includes the other humanities as well as the sciences even while acknowledging that terms like "humanities," "science," "culture," and "history" are contested.

Literature in the Old College: 1828–1876

CHAPTER TWO

The Classical College

The classical men made us hate Latin and Greek

EDWARD E. HALE

Until the later decades of the nineteenth century, the study of literature in American colleges, as elsewhere, was ancillary to the study of something else—chiefly to the Greek and Latin languages and to rhetoric, oratory, and forensics. The idea that works of literature could be profitably treated "as literature" was familiar enough in America by the 1840s, when Poe was attacking "the heresy of the didactic" and urging the aesthetic doctrines of Continental romanticism. But this idea had little effect on school or college teaching until the formation of the departmentalized modern university in the last decades of the century.

Throughout the preprofessional era, the college teaching of literature reflected the ancient view that, in William Charvat's words, "literature should be social in point of view, not egocentric." This meant there was nothing wrong with treating literature in an instrumental way—as an illustration of grammar, rhetoric, elocution, and civic and religious ideals. What teaching of English literature took place was informed by neoclassical theories, largely imported from Scottish rhetoricians, which viewed literature as an extension of public forms of speech and argument. This neglect or subordination of "literary" qualities drew complaints throughout the century, but certain conditions worked against making literature a special object of classroom study.

For one thing, the idea had hardly arisen that the literature of one's own language needed to be taught in formal classes instead of being enjoyed as part of the normal experience of the community. Literary  culture was already a flourishing part of the extracurricular life of the college and the general community. College and town literary and debating societies, college debating clubs, student literary magazines, undergraduate prize competitions, and frequent public lectures and readings constituted an informal literary education of impressive proportions. Educators therefore had reason to feel that the larger issues raised by literary works were amply attended to and did not need to be taken up in classes. This view was reinforced by the assumption that great literature was essentially self-interpreting and needed no elaborate interpretation. That is, its "spirit" naturally communicated itself at the mere contact with it. This may not justify the time college students were forced to waste on exercises on Latin and Greek texts where the question of what the text might mean never arose, but such practices seem less perverse when examined in context.

The subsequent rise of literature as a college subject with its own departments and programs coincided with the collapse of the communal literary culture and the corresponding estrangement of literature from its earlier function in polite society, where it had been an essential instrument of socialization. There was a paradox, then, in the literary education of the preprofessional era: literature was neglected or trivialized, taught—when taught at all—in an instrumental and mechanical way that seemed absurd or perverse to most thoughtful students. Yet this very trivialization and neglect reflected the fact that literature enjoyed a more secure social status than it would occupy when it came to achieve curricular autonomy.

THE OLD COLLEGE ATMOSPHERE

Nineteenth-century American colleges followed age-old patterns set by Oxford and Cambridge and the Continental universities. The typical American college was a quasimonastic institution where "the preparation of individuals for Christian leadership and the ministry," as one college president put it, was considered a more important goal than the advancement of knowledge. Since their beginnings in the seventeenth and eighteenth centuries, American colleges had been training schools for the professions—primarily medicine, the law, and the ministry. Yet their idea of professional education scorned vocational concerns in favor of "liberal" studies, studies designed to form gentlemanly character rather than to train directly for a vocation. College presidents spoke of "gentle breeding" as a primary concern, and saw the study of literature through the classics as a form of acculturation for "the cultivated gentleman."

The achievement of "culture" was theoretically open to everyone, but in practice it was considered "easier and more natural for young men who were well bred." As Carl Becker wrote, "the end desired . . .

was the disciplined and informed mind; but a mind disciplined to conformity and informed with nothing that a patriotic, Christian, and clubable gentleman had better not know." Colleges prided themselves on their democratic spirit and did admit a number of students from poor backgrounds, but their conception of democracy assumed the natural right of liberally educated men to national leadership. The college stood "on the side of God, the United States, and the governing class," locating "virtue and wisdom not in the people but in an educated few fit to be their leaders."

This idea of leadership was at once thoroughly hierarchical and hostile to capitalism, scorning the twin vulgarities of commercial enterprise and plebian labor-agitation. It assumed, as Edmund Wilson later wrote, that the country should be run by a "caste of trained 'college men' who were to preside over the arts and the professions." This assumed in turn that study of the classics was the best training for the professions, and that a cultured elite so trained would be able to control the twin excesses of grasping businessmen and unruly industrial proletarians.

But though the college spoke for the ruling class, it was a ruling class that felt curiously displaced from the rising sources of power and influence. Not only did higher education have "no organic relation to careers in civil service and diplomacy, as it had in England and in some continental countries," that education was not even a necessary prerequisite for the professions it trained men in. President Francis Wayland of Brown, the most penetrating critic of the college system before the Civil War, observed in 1842 that "the impression is gaining ground" that college preparation "is not essential to success in professional study. A large proportion of our medical students are not graduates. The proportion of law students of the same class is, I rather think, increasing." The industrial merchant and business class—in Wayland's words "the great agents of . . . production" and "the safest depositories of political power"—saw little reason to patronize an institution so antagonistic to its interests and values. Consequently, as industrialization proceeded, the gulf widened between the college and American life.

This situation caused Wayland to complain that "in no other country is the whole plan for the instruction of the business of the young so entirely dissevered from connexion with the business of subsequent life." Yet this estrangement was partly self-induced, expressing a desire to keep the college pure of the corrupting influence of practical life. College presidents like Noah Porter of Yale argued that "in such a country as ours, the peculiar influences of the common life of the college are of the greatest consequence, to deliver us from that gross vulgarity of taste and superficial conceit of knowledge to which it is especially exposed." By the 1870s, however, most educators had become resigned to the probability that the college could not survive unless it compromised with the "vulgarity" and "conceit" of the new business classes.

College literary culture was thus at once a "ruling class" culture and one that was increasingly "dissevered from connexion" with power and bitterly aware of its displacement from the center of things. It was this contradiction under which the old college eventually collapsed: the gap between its patrician conception of culture and the dynamics of an increasingly industrialized, democratic society grew too great to sustain. But the collapse did not come until the last quarter of the century.

The Curriculum and the Faculty

The standard college curriculum consisted in two to four years of Greek and Latin, plus mathematics, history, logic, theology, and a bit of natural science in the last two years. It culminated in the senior-year course in moral philosophy—sometimes called Evidences of Christianity—which more often than not was taught by the president of the college himself. English, foreign languages, and other subjects were frequently offered in the last two years, but usually only as electives for which most students, preoccupied as they were with classical requirements, had little time. The Yale Report of 1828, written in response to popular demands for a more flexible curriculum, had defiantly reasserted the primacy of the classics in instilling "mental discipline," and Yale's example was one few colleges could afford to challenge. A number of them tried, experimenting with new or alternate curricula, but these received so little support that they sooner or later had to give up the effort.

In 1842, Wayland judged "the system of collegiate instruction" to be "very much the same throughout the United States." Local variations existed, to be sure. Attending a small, private, denominational college in New England or Ohio was a different experience from attending Harvard or Yale and different still from attending one of the new state universities in the West or one of the women's colleges that sprang up after the 1860s. John W. Burgess, for example, who graduated from both Amherst and Columbia, found the two colleges as different as night and day: at Amherst "everything was as hard as it could be made. Study and recitation, investigation and discussion, from early morning till night and deep into the night, every day in the week, except Sunday," when students had "only" to hear two sermons and attend prayers. By contrast, a student in the School of Arts of Columbia attended class only from ten to one, regarded his "college attendance as a joke," and did not, "with a few rare and honorable exceptions," make "any preparation at all for his recitations, but chanced it every time, depending upon his wit for guessing and the help and indulgence of his teacher." Further variations appeared in the liberalizing reforms just after the Civil War at institutions such as Cornell, which was founded in 1867 on the principle of suiting college education to a wide diversity of interests; at Harvard, where Charles William Eliot installed the elective system in the early seventies; and at the land-grant colleges of the West, which initiated vocationally centered curricula.

Yet the extent of these forms of diversification and innovation was always limited, if not by the still-powerful conservative sentiment, then by lack of funds. Poverty was a powerful inducement to a small college to stick to a required classical course with few options, since such a course could be staffed by a small faculty largely recruited from the college's own graduates. For these reasons, "a little college of the period was likely to be a smaller version of Yale or Princeton." When the diversified research university finally began to emerge in the seventies and eighties, existing colleges conformed to its pattern at an uneven rate, some not abandoning the older pattern until after World War I, if then.

The old college derived its moral atmosphere from the patriarchal figure of the college president, who bore scant resemblance to the fund-raising, business-administering chief executives of today. The early college president personally supervised admissions procedures, corresponded with and greeted new students, negotiated and decided faculty appointments (though sometimes with faculty consultation), conducted compulsory daily morning chapel, and often taught every student in the senior class in the central course in moral philosophy, where he "ranged widely over the whole field of knowledge, pausing wherever he was interested." Faculties were unspecialized and largely recruited from the clergy, religious orthodoxy outweighing prowess in scholarship as a qualification for employment. Princeton's president, James McCosh, "took pains to quiz all prospective candidates for faculty positions upon their religious soundness."

Courses were assigned with little regard to special expertise, for there was not yet any system of advanced training for professorial work. Biology might be assigned to a returning missionary, and the professor of rhetoric might well double as the professor of history, logic, or metaphysics. Andrew D. White, whose reforms at Cornell were inspired by his dissatisfaction with his college experience at Yale in the 1850s, remembered that the lower classes there were "given mainly by tutors, who took up teaching for bread-winning, before going into the ministry. Naturally, most of the work done under them was perfunctory." College teachers "were likely to be well-connected failures in the law or the ministry content with a professor's pittance."

A pittance it was, most colleges being too poor to pay a salary sufficient for a teacher to survive without taking on private tutoring, and annual salary increases were unheard of. Wayland thought that "the instructors of Colleges in this country, are remunerated, at a lower rate than almost any other professional man," and this did not change after the Civil War. Wayland added that a professor's salary "is commonly unchanged during his whole continuance in office" and that in general "his calling presents him no reason for advancing. Were he ever so much distinguished, his compensation would be no greater nor his field of scientific labor more extensive." Wayland judged that the system as a whole offered "a bounty for indolence and incapacity, for it rewards them as well as industry and talent."

In William Riley Parker's words, the typical professor of English "was a doctor of divinity who spoke and wrote the mother tongue grammatically, had a general 'society knowledge' of the literature, and had not specialized in this or any other academic subject." "The professor who taught *only* English was still a great rarity." As late as the turn of the century at some colleges, there remained only a faint line separating professors of English from the clergy, and men continued to move freely between the two professions. One of Northwestern University's first professors of English was pressured to resign in 1902 and promptly became a Unitarian minister after his article suggesting that there might be myths and inaccuracies in the Bible had offended Evanston's predominantly Methodist community. Of the twelve professors of English appointed by the University of North Carolina between 1819 and 1885, nine were ministers.

The professor of Moral and Intellectual Philosophy and English Literature at Columbia in the 1860s and 1870s had earlier been a quasi-orthodox Presbyterian preacher in Edinburgh. According to John W. Burgess, a student at Columbia in the late sixties, this man's teaching "was a joke. He did not know one of his students from another, marked them all alike, and remonstrated only mildly when they played ball in his recitation room." This man's assistant "did most of his teaching for him. . . . He was an agreeable man personally, polite and deferential, almost shy, and in all practical matters as helpless as a child."

The student disorder Burgess described was a common problem for college professors, a part of whose regular duty was to police students by enforcing the usually severe college restrictions. College faculties acted as disciplinary tribunals, periodically reviewing violations of rules such as those requiring students to attend chapel services early every morning, to remain in their rooms for hours every day, and to avoid the snares of the town. Nor were these restrictions relaxed for the many students in their late twenties or older, who lived alongside freshmen as young as fourteen. The classes themselves, conducted by the system of daily recitations, were said to have "the fearsome atmosphere of a police-station. Teachers were not expected to inspire the student, but to cross-examine him on his prepared lessons."

Students took revenge on this oppressive system through practical jokes and, occasionally, more serious forms of violence. Ernest Earnest states that "the history of every college before the Civil War is filled with accounts of riot, violence and disorder," and not only in the frontier colleges but in Puritan New England as well. Andrew D. White said he never saw "so much carousing and wild dissipation" as he witnessed in 1849 as a student at a Protestant Episcopal "Church-college" whose "especial boast was that, owing to the small number of its students, it was 'able to exercise a direct Christian influence upon every young man committed to its care.' " The faculty minutes at North Carolina during the years before 1868 recorded "disciplinary action taken in cases of misconduct, intoxication from drinking 'ardent spirits,' fights, raising hell in the buildings, shooting off fire arms, riding horses around the grounds in the middle of the night, and so on. There are a few widely scattered cases arising from rows in bawdy houses outside the village, where apparently also, spirits could be drunk." Lyman Bagg of Yale '69, in one of the most revealing (and entertaining) memoirs of college life in the nineteenth century, described standard tricks that "prevail at other colleges," such as "locking an instructor in his recitation room or dormitory, throwing water upon him, stealing his clothes or other property, upsetting his chair in recitation or tripping him up outside, writing or printing derisive or scurrilous remarks in regard to him, and so on."

Bagg claimed that such crude tricks had become "obsolete at Yale," but he noted that cheating was winked at by students and faculty alike so long as the cheater was not trying to make a reputation as a scholar. According to what appears to have been the code at Yale, "skinning" (college parlance for cheating) was thought disgraceful only when practiced by one who aspired to become a "high stand man." In Bagg's typically candid way of putting it, "the general college sentiment in regard to all such matters is one of approval for all means calculated to circumvent and deceive those in authority—provided that these means are employed for the benefit of those who make no pretensions as scholars. For a high-stand man to skin, or for anyone to skin for a stand simply, is looked upon as mean and contemptible."

Bagg thought that "the boy who comes to college with the deliberate intention of shirking every possible study" was hardly admirable, but he was "less to be pitied than the one who goes through the four years, digging and grinding for a stand" and thus remaining "unconscious of the peculiar and delightful life about him." In Bagg's view the college student at his best was "a careless boy-man, who is chiefly anxious to 'have a good time,' and who shirks his work and deceives his instructors in every possible way." This way of thinking had certain class ramifications, for obviously the wealthier student must have had more luxury to act like a "careless boy-man" than the student from a poor background, who was more likely to have to "dig and grind for a stand" and be scorned and pitied accordingly. Some such code as this prevailed in many colleges as late as World War I or after, and traces of it can still be seen.

For nineteenth-century college professors, the intellectual incentives were as paltry as the financial ones. In an atmosphere hostile to specialization, the idea of a "major" in a particular subject was unknown, and graduate study was virtually nonexistent. By one estimate, in 1850 there were 8 graduate students in the United States in all subjects. By 1875, a year before Daniel Coit Gilman established Johns Hopkins as the first American research university, there were only 399, whereas by 1908 there would be almost 8,000. American college libraries, recalled a professor of modern languages in 1908, "were largely haphazard collections" and "the books of fundamental importance were often lamentably lacking. This was especially true of modern language collections." Only after 1875 was "the buying of books . . . put on a methodical basis, by men who have known exactly what was best in their particular fields." "A college library was likely to be a sorry accumulation, open an hour or two a week," and some librarians became legendary for their resistance either to purchasing books or to letting anyone borrow them. According to Morris Bishop, "the first President of the University of North Carolina kept the University Library in an upstairs bedroom of his house for twenty years. The librarian of Columbia resolutely fought every effort of the faculty to add a book, in order to turn back half his appropriation unused." The more forward-looking among the faculty viewed the college librarian as an enemy to be circumvented.

The poor state of the libraries did not overly trouble college authorities, who feared that reading too many books could only encourage student unorthodoxy. The Yale Report of 1828 defended the standard practice of teaching from a single textbook, whose lessons could be easily keyed to daily recitations, and it warned that reading a half-dozen different books tended to create confusion in the student's mind. Between 1855 and 1875 Northwestern University printed the titles of textbooks in its catalog, and there and elsewhere courses were formally and informally called by the name of the textbook—for example, "Paley," for William Paley's *Evidences of Christianity*. Such facts further testify to the highly static nature of the curriculum.

Educators felt that the social bonds of college life were more important than anything a student might actually learn. Noah Porter spoke eloquently of "the *common social life*" that "silently shapes and energizes [the student's] inner being," of "the intense and pervasive common life" and the common "social bonds" that inspired scholars in England and that "in this country . . . are needed more." The key to this common social life was the sentiment uniting the graduating class. Porter spoke of "the sacred import of the words 'class' and 'class-mate.' " He called the class "the charmed circle within which the individual student contracts the most of his friendships, and finds his fondest and most cherished associations," and he wondered if "an American college without fixed classes can have an efficient common life."

A major reason why conservatives like Porter of Yale and McCosh of Princeton so desperately resisted Eliot's elective system was their recognition that once students were allowed to choose classes for themselves, the uniformity of experience within the graduating class would be broken. To educational reformers, on the other hand, one of the singular merits of the German universities was precisely that there were "no classes, the students are not arranged according to their standing by years." When Gilman took over as president of the new Johns Hopkins in 1876, one of his most radical steps was to get rid of the traditional four-year class, encouraging students to enroll in courses irrespective of class-standing and to graduate in as few as two years if they could complete the requirements.

How deep the feeling of graduating class unity went is suggested by Yale's President Timothy Dwight's recollections of student days there in the forties. Dwight wrote of the "community of thought and purpose" which was "connected with the educational ideals of the time." "We had," he recalled,

> a certain oneness or harmony of intellectual life that cannot be so easily realized amid the multitude of studies and of interests now [1903] appealing to the tastes of different minds. This oneness or harmony was a good thing in itself. It was helpful in developing that friendly sentiment, or class feeling, uniting the brotherhood, which has been so marked a characteristic of our Yale life throughout the century.

Such statements suggest that college literary education fit into a well-defined social unity that, at its best, made sense of what was otherwise a deadly routine. At the same time, the kind of sense it made had increasingly tenuous relations to the new realities of American life.

LITERARY EDUCATION AND THE CLASSICS

The bulk of formal college literary education came in the courses in Greek and Latin, which occupied as much as half of an average student's time. In theory, the study of Greek and Latin was supposed to inspire the student with the nobility of his cultural heritage. The central justification for the primacy of the classics was "the special culture which it imparts." But in practice, in and out of class, instructors rarely spoke of what this special culture consisted in, and perhaps they could not have done so had they wanted to. Classroom concerns hardly ever went beyond the endless memorization and recitation of grammatical and etymological particularities.

Though hermeneutical theorizing in the nineteenth century had been generated by disputes over the interpretation of biblical and legal texts, there seems to have been a tacit assumption in the colleges that the meanings of literature were self-explanatory and thus in need of no elaborate explication. English literature was felt to be too easy to qualify as a college study, not a fit subject for examinations. As a later observer said, the refusal of the English universities "to admit the esthetic consideration of literature into the academic curriculum was based almost wholly upon the fact that it did not seem to adapt itself to the examination requirements upon which the whole foundation of the English university system rested." It was felt that "an examination in English literature on the terms proposed would call forth from the student merely a regurgitation of the instructor's hobbies and prejudices and opinions upon the unchartable areas of esthetics."

Greek and Latin called for a "close reading" of a different kind. It was described by Francis A. March, who had been a student at

Amherst in the 1840s, as a "study of small portions of text, dwelling in class on minutiae of pronunciation, etymology, moods and tenses, and points of classical philology." "Attention was drawn to etymologies illustrative of English, and to forms of syntax characteristic of scholarly English; quotable expressions were committed to memory. A sermon or lawyer's plea then lacked professional style if it had no happy quotations of that sort."

Fred Lewis Pattee, who went through the classical course at the New Hampton Institute in the early 1880s, recalled that sweating over Homer, Virgil, and Xenophon, he "had no suspicion that they were great literature, works of supreme art and beauty. From first to last, even into college days, they were simply conglomerations of ablative absolutes, vocatives, gerunds and gerundives, caesural pauses, conjugations and inflections, maddening irregular verbs. . . . Thus we were taught the classics." William Lyon Phelps, an undergraduate at Yale in the same period, recalled a course in Homer in which the instructor "never changed the monotonous routine, never made a remark, but simply called on individuals to recite or to scan, said 'That will do,' put down a mark; so that in the last recitation in June, after a whole college year of this intolerable classroom drudgery, I was surprised to hear him say, and again without any emphasis, 'The poems of Homer are the greatest that have ever proceeded from the mind of man, class is dismissed,' and we went out into the sunshine."

The tacit justification of these procedures derived from a way of thinking about language that had deep roots in European philosophy and classical philology. Classical education presupposed the belief, as Hegel put it, that not only did "the works of the ancients contain the most noble nourishment" of the human spirit "in the most noble form," but that this spirit was inherently bound up with the grammar and etymology of the languages in which these works were written. This richness of the ancients, Hegel said, was "intimately connected with the *language*," for "only through and in language can we obtain it in all its special significance." Therefore even "the mechanical elements in the learning of a language" have a spiritual value.

Hegel thus asserted the prime value of "*grammatical study*," as part of an education in that quality of *Bildung* or self-development of mind and character for which the nineteenth-century American equivalent seems to have been the phrase "self-culture." Grammar for Hegel, as for later philologists like Friedrich Max Müller, was the alphabet of the Spirit itself, having "for its content the categories, special products and definitions of the understanding." Because the young did "not yet possess the power of comprehending the many-sidedness of spiritual richness," grammar had peculiar educational value, providing them with "the single letters or rather the vowels of the spiritual realm, with which we begin in order to spell it out and then learn to read it."

At the core of this romantic view of language was a kind of linguistic "essentialism," as Hans Aarsleff calls it, which held that the origins and essence of "race" were traceable in a language's grammatical structure and the roots of its words. From this it followed that grammar and etymology could unlock the special culture embodied in a literary work. This view of language as an expression of national character came to inform Germanic and romance philology, studies which were able eventually to make Greek and Latin seem of less central importance educationally by evidently demonstrating that the roots of the Anglo-Saxon race lay in an "Aryan" or Indo-European *Ursprache* that predated the Mediterranean ancient languages.

A larger vision, then, underlay methods of teaching the classics that otherwise seem entirely pointless and mechanical. But since this larger vision was taken for granted rather than made explicit, little of Hegel's grand vision of the spirit informed classroom drill work, which students experienced as a set of exercises undertaken for their own sake or for the mental discipline they presumably imparted. Hegel himself objected to the way the teaching of Greek and Latin in German schools had "perverted the relation between means and ends in the field of linguistic studies . . . so that the material knowledge of a language was more highly esteemed than its rational aspect." This discrepancy between theory and practice was relentlessly pointed out by American critics of the classical system. The most powerful of these critics was Charles Francis Adams, a graduate of Harvard whose 1883 Phi Beta Kappa address, "A College Fetich," was the final nail in the classicists' coffin. Adams ridiculed what he called "the great-impalpable-essence-and-precious-residuum theory" of the classics, the theory that "a knowledge of Greek grammar, and the having puzzled through the Anabasis and three books of the Iliad, infuses into the boy's nature the imperceptible spirit of Greek literature, which will appear in the results of his subsequent work, just as manure, spread upon a field, appears in the crop which that field bears."

The most frequently stated justification for the way the classics were taught was the theory of "mental discipline," which was rooted in the mechanistic faculty psychology of the nineteenth century. The theory presumed that, like the body, the mind and character are strengthened by strenuous, repetitive exercise on disagreeably difficult tasks. The Yale Report of 1828 had laid down the official doctrine that the study of the classics "forms the most effective discipline of the mental faculties. . . . Every faculty of the mind is employed." For many, the very quality of seemingly pointless drudgery that critics objected to was precisely what made the classical pedagogy valuable as discipline. Speaking with brutal candor, Lyman Bagg argued that "there is this to be said in favor of a classical course, that it can, better than any other, be choked down a man's throat, whether he wishes to receive it or not. Spite of all his exertions to the contrary, spite of all his ponyings and cheatings of every sort, he must in time, by dint of reciting and hearing others recite, get a good share of classic lore forced into him, and receive the benefits of mental discipline." As a less sympathetic observer looked back on it in 1891, "the idea was that it was good for a boy to do things that are hard for him, simply because they are hard; and the harder they are, the better for him."

Though vocational considerations were presumably irrelevant, the discipline of the classics could be defended as good preparation for the practical affairs of life. This argument helped classicists hold the line against the mounting cry for vocational education after the Civil War. Even Porter, the scourge of vocationalism, was not above claiming that "the student who has acquired the habit of never letting go a puzzling problem—say a rare Greek verb—until he has analyzed its every element, and understands every point in its etymology, has the habit of mind which will enable him to follow out a legal subtlety with the same accuracy."

In most cases, however, the chief result of the classical drill work was to imbue the student with a lifelong hatred of classical languages. "The classical men made us hate Latin and Greek" is an altogether typical comment. "A more horrible torture could scarcely be imagined for criminals" is another. "The absurdity and the cruelty of the process are almost equally unimaginable." Andrew D. White remarked that at Yale in the fifties "the majority of the average class" looked on the classical professor "as generally a bore and, as examinations approached, an enemy; they usually sneered at him as a pedant, and frequently made his peculiarities a subject for derision." Charles Francis Adams wrote in his memoirs that the "fancy for Greek" which he brought to Harvard in 1853 was quickly dampened by methods of instruction that "were simply beneath contempt. . . . We were not made grammarians, and we were not initiated into a charming literature."

Much of the resentment against the classical system was inspired by the regimen of daily formal recitations. Lyman Bagg's description of freshman recitations at Yale gives a vivid picture of the process. The students

> are seated alphabetically upon the three rows of rising benches . . . and are requested to retain the same relative positions in future recitations, both in that and other recitation rooms. . . . The division officer sits behind a sort of raised box or pulpit, overlooking the whole. . . . most of the officers call up their men, by lot,—drawing their names, hap-hazard, from a box which contains them,—and so making each individual liable to be examined on every day's lesson. . . . In a Latin or Greek recitation one may be asked to read or scan a short passage, another to translate it, a third to answer questions as to its construction, and so on; or all this and more may be required of the same individual. The reciter is expected simply to answer the questions which are put to him, but not to ask any of his instructor, or dispute his assertions. If he has any enquiries to make, or controversy to carry on, it must be done informally, after the division has been dismissed.

Like most other aspects of student conduct, recitations were graded on elaborate point systems like the "Scale of Merit" at Harvard, which "granted a daily eight points toward graduation honors to the student who had recited his lessons properly."

Recitations frequently consisted of giving back verbatim the words of textbooks. James B. Angell, later president of the University of Michigan, said that when he started teaching modern languages at Brown University in 1845, "there was a general belief among the students, though no formal statement to that effect was made by the Faculty, that they would gain higher credits by repeating the language of the book than by reporting the substance of the thought in their own language." Not surprisingly, students became passive and acquired the habit, as Wayland described it, "of going rapidly over the text book with less and less thought" and cultivating "the passive power of reception instead of the active power of originality."

Noah Porter defended the process, however, arguing that having "to commit to memory, and to master by thought, the words and principles which the text-books present for study" aided a young man in learning to concentrate. For Porter, "enforced recitation" was crucial to "the training of the man to the power and habit of successfully concentrating and controlling his powers." Porter thus attacked Eliot's Harvard and White's Cornell for introducing written examinations and replacing recitations with lectures and discussion classes. Lecture courses have in our time come to be regarded as the epitome of conservatism in pedagogy, but in the old college they were a threatening innovation. As Andrew D. White said of Yale, "there was never even a single lecture on any subject in literature, either ancient or modern: everything was done by means of 'recitations' from text-books; and while young men read portions of masterpieces in Greek and Latin, their attention was hardly ever directed to these as literature." There was "too much 'reciting' by rote, and too little real intercourse between teacher and taught."

Yet for conservatives like Porter, it was lectures—and written examinations—that were depersonalizing: they made dry and abstract what was supposed to be a personal and communal experience. Writing in 1886, Porter traced a direct connection between the weakening of the "intense and pervasive common life" of the college and "the tendency to abandon or disintegrate the old college class" by substituting formal lectures and written examinations for "the lively question and answer in which man meets man with open face and loosened tongue." Porter conveniently neglected to mention that the question and answer had not always been especially "lively," but his point would have been that, even at their most dreary, recitations solidified the social bond that was more important than anything students might learn from them.

Occasionally a brave instructor departed from the Gradgrindian recitations, but anyone who went too far risked an official reprimand. Frederick Rudolph cites the case of a professor at Princeton in 1846 who discovered "that if he interspersed commentary on Greek literature with the study of the Greek language he could elicit a gratifying improvement in student interest. For this heresy he was called before the president, and a few days later his resignation was accepted." Phelps mentions a young teacher of Latin named Ambrose Tighe whom "the older members of the faculty looked upon . . . with suspicion. He made Latin interesting; and they got rid of him."

Charles Francis Adams charged that the classical training taught "the boy to mistake means for ends, and to make a system of superficiality." Yet the ultimate proof for him of the system's bankruptcy was that it did not even succeed on its own superficial terms: few students came out of it actually able to read Greek or Latin. Adams conceded that "Greek really studied and lovingly learned" would have been of great value," but "not only was the knowledge of our theoretical fundamentals to the last degree superficial, but nothing better was expected." As for Latin, Adams wondered "how many students during the last thirty years have graduated from Harvard who could read Horace and Tacitus and Juvenal, as numbers now read Goethe and Mommsen and Heine? If there have been ten, I do not believe there have been a score. This it is to acquire a language!" Adams believed that "learning by heart the Greek grammar" did him positive harm, that it "systematically suppressed" his "reflective powers," and he depicted himself as a victim of "a fetich worship, in which the real and practical is systematically sacrificed to the ideal and theoretical."

The unity of graduating "class" feeling admired by Porter and Dwight was possible only within a kind of class society that had been crumbling since the first quarter of the century, and the assumptions of which, as the century progressed, were no longer tacitly shared. After the triumph of Jacksonian populism in the 1820s, and even more after the rapid industrialization following the Civil War, the college's patrician conception of leadership had ceased to reflect the realities of American power. Throughout most of the century, the college occupied an ambiguous social status reflecting the increasing displacement of the educated class.

Hofstadter describes this class as

> a gentlemanly class with considerable wealth, leisure, and culture, but with relatively little power or influence. This class was the public and patron of serious writing and of cultural institutions. . . . But if one thinks of this class as having inherited the austere traditions of the older Republican order, the traditions crystalized by the Founding Fathers, one sees immediately the relative weakness of a type that kept the manners and aspirations and prejudices of an aristocratic class without being able to retain its authority.

In this "mugwump culture," Hofstadter says, "the intellectual virtues of the eighteenth-century republican type dwindled and dried up, very largely because mugwump thinkers were too commonly deprived of the occasion to bring these virtues into any intimate or organic relation with experience. . . . It was characteristic of mugwump culture that its relation to experience and its association with power became increasingly remote."

The fate of the classical system illustrates a pattern that will be encountered again and again in this history: what originates in an ambitious cultural and educational theory becomes detached from the methodology devised to carry it out, leaving students to grapple with the methodology without any notion of why they are doing so. The tacit social ideal that originally informed the methodology continues to be taken for granted even after it is no longer shared or understood. As long as the college failed to make explicit "the special culture" the classics were supposed to impart, the rationale for the classics remained hypothetical, and learning became a technical and mechanical exercise. In assuming that "the imperceptible spirit of Greek literature" would somehow rub off on students through contact with linguistic technicalities, the classical instructors assumed that great literature ultimately teaches itself. They would not be the last teachers of literature to assume that.

Yet a more generous verdict is still possible; namely, that the classical teachers felt no need to raise questions of more general significance about literature because they could count on those questions being taken up elsewhere, if not in the senior course in moral philosophy or in the extracurricular literary societies and debating clubs, then in the literary culture of the larger community. So far, we have looked at the classical education in isolation from the other forms of college literary education that complemented it and lent it meaning—or at least provided an alternative to it. Of particular importance was the oratorical culture which pervaded the college and linked the classical courses with the courses in English rhetoric and elocution, with the literary and debating societies, and with the literary culture outside.

CHAPTER THREE

Oratorical Culture and the Teaching of English

I remember that men were divided as Carlyleists or anti-Carlyleists, Coleridgeians or anti-Coleridgeians, and so on, and that literary, historic, and philosophic theories were as hotly discussed as the current political questions of the day.

JAMES B. ANGELL

The college teaching of English literature in the preprofessional era suffered from the same limitation marking the teaching of the classics: the routine of study obscured the theory supposedly justifying it. This was not surprising, since the earliest methods of teaching English literature were copied from those used to teach the classics. Literature was subordinated to grammar, etymology, rhetoric, logic, elocution, theme writing, and textbook literary history and biography—everything, a later generation would complain, except a truly literary study. And whatever the emphasis, the recitation method remained in force.

Still, the classroom study of English literature connected more creatively than did the classical work with the literary culture of the college and the larger society. English composition writing, declamation, and debate had practical outlets in college literary magazines, oratorical and writing competitions, and literary and debating societies. English courses were usually as drab as classical ones, but the surrounding literary culture provided an enlivening context that the courses themselves lacked.

"English Should Be Studied as Greek Is"

The prescribed course of study left little room for the modern languages and literatures, which were believed to lack the disciplinary rigor of the classics. The Yale Report had dismissed the modern languages as frivolous subjects, "to be studied, as an accomplishment, rather than as a necessary acquisition." A modern language scholar recalled in 1895 that at Yale he had "passed through four years of a college course without once hearing from the lips of an instructor in the class-room the name of a single English author or the title of a single English classic." The only textbook he had studied under the professor of "English" was "the oration of Demosthenes on the Crown in the original Greek. There had been nothing exceptional in this."

Outside conservative Yale, courses dealing with English, American, and European literary works had arisen sporadically since the eighteenth century. But these courses were usually optional and therefore unable to compete with the time-consuming classical requirements. Attempts at "parallel" courses of study offering the option of a modern language or scientific program were abortive. Even in the pioneering program in English begun at Lafayette College in 1855 by the philological scholar Francis A. March, students could take "two terms of Anglo-Saxon and Modern English" only after they had "nearly finished their Latin, Greek, French and German." Where English was required, as one scholar recalled in 1894, its "ill repute was increased . . . by the makeshift way in which time was grudged out to it in the curriculum. Under the name of 'rhetoricals,' English declamations, orations, and essays used to be sandwiched in where some little crevice opened between other studies, once a week perhaps, or at some irregular hour supposedly unavailable for anything else."

One reason for this neglect was that since the modern languages and literatures were considered mere social accomplishments, they were looked upon as feminine preoccupations. This explains why these subjects made earlier headway in the female academies that proliferated in the middle decades of the century. There the young women, as Ann Douglas notes, "were seldom asked to tackle the masculine subjects of mathematics, theology, Greek, and the natural sciences." Similarly, because the new women's colleges founded after the Civil War challenged the assumption that women's minds were incapable of rigorous intellectual tasks, they tended to adopt the classical curriculum. As Earnest says, "the best answer" to the sort of "male paranoia" that claimed women could not do the same kind of strenuous mental work as men "seemed to be a demonstration that women could excel in the sanctified classical curriculum." The curricula of Vassar, Smith, and Wellesley "derived from the old prewar classical course of study as it had been perfected at such places as Yale, Princeton, Amherst, and Williams." The decision to give the women of these colleges the standard fare for males "was dictated by the necessity to prove that women could undertake a serious course of study." The more ornamental the conception of women a college entertained, the more likely that that college featured modern languages and literatures. This reputation for effeminacy would have to be effaced from the modern languages before they could become respectable in the university. One of the attractions of Germanic philology would be that as a hard science its manliness was not in question.

The transition from classics to English was probably less dramatic and more gradual than it has generally been taken to be. Following the maxim that "English should be studied as Greek is," early teachers of English copied the dismal methods long used to teach the classics. Francis A. March, describing how he first conceived the "experiment" of an English course at Leicester Academy in 1845, stated that he taught "English like Latin or Greek." Teachers then, he said elsewhere, "were fond of repeating after Dr. Arnold of Rugby, 'What a treat it would be to teach Shakespeare to a good class of young Greeks in regenerate Athens; to dwell upon him line by line and word by word, and so to get all his pictures and thoughts leisurely into one's mind.' " March was an Amherst graduate whose interest in language studies was said to have been inspired by hearing a series of lectures given by Noah Webster. He would become a pioneering figure in the modern languages' dethronement of the classics, but his methods show how strong a link remained between classical and modern philology. For March, dwelling "line by line and word by word" on a literary text merely meant adapting the old formal recitations to English texts. March's classes at Leicester consisted of "hearing a short Grammar lesson, the rest of the hour reading Milton as if it were Homer, calling for the meaning of words, their etymology when interesting, the relations of words, parsing when it would help, the connection of clauses, the mythology, the biography and other illustrative matter, suited to the class."

March's description makes no mention of the meaning of Milton's works. When he adapted his Leicester English courses to college work at Lafayette in 1855, March tried to put things "on a higher plane," assigning "work upon Anglo-Saxon and English texts to read and understand them." By "understand," though, March did not mean the grasp of a work's larger meanings, but a "linguistic study" that did not get beyond the analysis of isolated words and constructions. What this must have come down to in practice is grotesquely illustrated by the textbook March published in 1879, *Method of Philological Study of the English Language*. At the head of each page of March's text appear at most one or two lines from *Pilgrim's Progress*, *Julius Caesar*,

Paradise Lost, and other classics, festooned with an enormous battery of questions entirely on philological points: for example, "*On* is the sign of a combination between what words? *Lighted* + *on place* is what kind of combination? Does *on place* complete or extend the predicate?"

In principle, March's manual was only an extension of the kind of philological texbook of English that had come into popularity in the schools as early as 1867 with William Rolfe's American version of Craik's *Julius Caesar*. March went Craik one better, for to Craik's ratio of 82 pages of philological notes to 102 pages of Shakespeare's play, March managed a full page of notes for every one or two lines of Shakespeare or Bunyan. Except for its superior pedantry, March's text was typical in the stress it put on material that lends itself to memory work and its assumption that the English studies of undergraduates should consist of memorizing grammatical and literary-historical facts from a manual.

Brander Matthews described having at Columbia "to procure a certain manual of English literature, and to recite from its pages the names of writers, the titles of books, and the dates of publication—facts of little significance and of slight value unless we happened to be familiar with the several authors as a result of home influence, or of private taste." Matthews says his class was "not introduced to the actual writings of any of the authors, nor was any hint dropped that we might possibly be benefitted by reading them for ourselves."

How teachers must have used the manuals can be inferred from the suggested examination questions appearing in many of them, always closely keyed to the commentary. Here are some on Edmund Spenser from Cleveland's widely used *Compendium of English Literature* (1857):

> Date of birth and death? In whose reign did he flourish? Repeat Thomson's lines. What is said of his parentage? What does Gibbon say? How did he enter Cambridge? What is a "sizer," and why so called? What work did he first publish? What is it? In what capacity did he go to Ireland? What grant did he receive? Where did he go to reside? Who visited him there? What did he style him? What was he persuaded to do? What does Campbell say of Raleigh's visit to Spenser? What is Spenser's great work? Of how many books does it consist? How many is it said he intended to write? Did he probably finish his design? What happened to him in Ireland? Where did he die and when?

We can only speculate whether the students who memorized and recited the answers to these questions actually read any of Spenser's verse. The chances are they did not, if only because texts even of standard authors were either unavailable or too expensive. The publication of annotated classics in cheap editions was a condition of the growth of high school and college teaching of English literature in the 1880s.

Teachers who deviated from the usual textbook approach to literature tended toward the other extreme of impressionism. This word seems fairly to characterize the popular Harvard courses in Dante given by Henry Wadsworth Longfellow (1835–54) and James Russell Lowell (1855–86) as well as Lowell's senior course in Modern Literature, begun in 1858. According to Lowell's biographer, Horace E. Scudder, "the formalities of academic work were of little concern to Lowell." He found "examinations of his classes . . . wearisome functions," and he often neglected to attend faculty meetings and to read student papers. Lowell "turned the lecture and recitation hour into a *causerie*." In his Dante course, for example,

> The actual exercise in the class-room was simple enough and unconventional. The classes were not large, and the relation of the teacher to his students was that of an older friend who knew in a large way the author they were studying, and drew upon his own knowledge and familiarity with the text for comment and suggestion, rather than troubled himself much to find out how much his pupils knew. . . . Toward the close of the hour, question and answer, or free discussion yielded to the stream of personal reminiscence or abundant reflection upon which Lowell would by this time be launched. Especially would he recall scenes in Florence, sketch in words the effects of the Arno, Giotto's Tower, the church in which Dante was baptized, where he himself had seen children held at the same font. . . . Suddenly, glancing at his watch before him,—a time-piece which was as idly whimsical as its owner,—he would stop, bow and walk quickly out of the room, the men rising respectfully as he left.
>
> And the listeners? They went away, a few carelessly amused at the loose scholastic exercise and complacent over the evasion of work, but some stirred, quickened in their thought.

Lowell, with his reputation as a celebrated writer and editor—he edited the *Atlantic Monthly* while at Harvard—was one of the few who could gracefully ignore the standard pedagogical practices. It was only later that Lowell's relaxed style become the badge of a distinctive professorial type.

It is symptomatic, for example, that Lowell's friend, Francis James Child, who joined the Harvard faculty in 1851 and was recognized as a far greater scholar than Lowell, was not able to concentrate on teaching literature courses until 1876—and then only after an offer from the new Johns Hopkins University "led to his being wholly relieved at last from the burden of correcting undergraduate compositions." In what may be the first case of an "outside offer" improving an English professor's lot, this incident showed the way professionalization would shape the curriculum.

Literature as Rhetoric

Textbook learning and forced recitations on one side, misty impressionism on the other, and nothing in between: this pattern will emerge even more starkly when we move into the early professional period. Yet in the old college, the rhetorical and elocutionary study of literature provided a certain middle ground. Theme writing, declamations, and the study of rhetorical principles in passages from great literary works were part of a single, undifferentiated process. At Harvard, while Lowell and a few others were teaching European works in a belletristic fashion, "English" as late as the sixties still exclusively meant elocution and rhetoric. "In 1858–59 the Freshmen had Lessons in Orthoepy and lessons in Expression; the Sophomores, Lessons in Expression, Lessons in Action, Themes; the Juniors, Themes, Declamation, Rhetoric; the Seniors, Forensics: nothing more."

Rhetoric courses had their own textbooks, more or less modelled on eighteenth-century British or Scottish prototypes. One type was the anthology of excerpts, suitable for analysis and declamation, from Shakespeare, Milton, and the great orators and statesmen, along the lines of the widely used Lindley Murray's *English Reader* and William Enfield's *The Speaker* (fully entitled *Miscellaneous Pieces Selected from the Best English Writers and Disposed under Their Proper Heads, with a View to Facilitate the Improvement of Youth in Reading and Speaking*). It is possibly Enfield's text, published in England in 1782, that should be blamed or credited with first immortalizing Mark Antony's funeral oration for Caesar and Burke's "Essay on Conciliation" as standard anthology selections, of which at least the first continued to be in American grammar schools as late as World War II.

The other common type of text was the rhetorical handbook such as Hugh Blair's *Lectures on Rhetoric and Belles Lettres*, a popular book in America before the Civil War. Blair's work epitomized the rhetorical idea of literature governing the college, but it also reflected conflicts between new and old theories of literature that neither Blair nor the college confronted. Blair recognized that in the modern age poetry had become specialized and marked off sharply from other forms of discourse. He said that prose and verse "require to be separately considered, because subject to separate laws," and he observed that whereas "the historian, the orator, the philosopher address themselves, for the most part, primarily to the understanding" and aim directly "to inform, to persuade, or to instruct," by contrast "the primary aim of a poet is to please, and to move; and, therefore, it is to the imagination, and the passions, that he speaks." But these statements came late in Blair's treatise. Through most of it, Blair treated poetry as a subcategory of rhetorical eloquence, an exemplification of the qualities of "personal character and disposition" expressed by all great writing. Finally, for Blair, "poetry, eloquence, and history" were alike in that all conveyed "elevated sentiments and high examples" that "naturally tend to nourish in our minds public spirit, the love of glory, contempt of external fortune, and the admiration of what is truly illustrious and great."

Blair conceded that poetry's immediate function may be pleasure rather than instruction, but he argued that this pleasure was only a means to an ultimately didactic purpose: the poet "may, and he ought to have it in his view, to instruct, and to reform; but it is indirectly, and by pleasing and moving, that he accomplishes this end." Thus "it is hardly possible to determine the exact limit where eloquence ends, and poetry begins." This rhetorical conception of poetry (and of prose fiction, to which Blair devoted a brief section) was perhaps most revealingly conveyed in Blair's indiscriminate choice of paradigm-passages from poets and orators. Blair's assumption that all the kinds of expression form a unity testified once again to the reigning conception of literature as a public or civic discourse fit for socializing future citizens.

Translated into the classroom, this rhetorical approach to literature could degenerate into the same dreary grind as classical grammar and textbook literary history. The student reader of an 1829 American edition of Blair's *Lectures* was evidently expected to memorize not only the passages of oratory and poetry copiously quoted by Blair, but large portions of Blair's commentary itself. This can be inferred from the study questions appended to each chapter, described by the editors as "greatly facilitating the recitations of classes, and, at the same time, . . . *compelling each scholar to learn every word of the author*" (emphasis mine). Considering the length of the book and the number of questions—the editors boast 5,750—one has to wonder if any unlucky student actually fulfilled the editors' hopes.

Yet when English declamations supplemented the study of rules, the rhetorical approach amounted to something more appealing. According to Walter P. Rogers, the "declamations given by the student before the assembled student body" and closely criticized by the faculty were perhaps "the most characteristic feature of the old classical college. Here the student felt that he was engaging in an activity which would be of immediate practical value in later life. A large proportion of the students would one day enter law, politics, or the ministry, callings in which oratorical powers were essential." It was exercises in elocution that brought students into close contact with English and American classics for the first time and created a link between technical analysis and appreciation.

Hiram Corson recalled that in school in the 1820s the students "read aloud twice a day; the several classes standing while they read, and toeing a chalk line," from such texts as the New Testament and Murray's *English Reader*. Andrew D. White fondly remembered the preparatory course in English at Syracuse Academy in the forties where "great attention was given to reading aloud from a book made up of selections from the best authors, and to recitals from these. Thus I stored up not only some of the best things in the older English writers, but inspiring poems of Whittier, Longfellow, and other moderns. I only regret that more of the same sort was not done."

White wished that there had been as much literary stimulation when he went on to Yale. Yet Lyman Bagg's picture of oratorical studies there in the sixties puts White's complaints somewhat in perspective. According to Bagg, Yale freshmen were relieved of recitations once a week to read their compositions aloud, on subjects previously announced, to the professor of rhetoric. During the sophomore year, the oral reading of compositions "took the place of the noon recitation on Saturday,—each person furnishing four compositions a term," and "the entire class attended declamations in the Chapel,—each person 'speaking' twice a term." Junior year, "extempore speeches were sometimes called for by the professor of Rhetoric at the recitations in English literature," and also "forensic disputations" in which writers were allowed to choose their own subject. Juniors and seniors engaged in disputes every Monday and Tuesday evening, and "twice a week, five or six deliver a declamation memoriter from the oratorical rostrum. The president makes some observations upon the manner of delivery and sometimes upon the subject, and sometimes gives some small laurel to him who best acts the part of an orator." These exercises were preparation for the exciting public oratorical displays and competitions at which the whole college turned out. For commencement ceremonies, Yale nominated its twelve best speakers of the class, who competed for prizes. Writing competitions were closely tied to oratory, for, as Bagg says, the "best literary man" elected by each Yale class was designated as "the orator to represent it upon Presentation Day," and the class poet fulfilled a similar obligation. These literary " 'first-prize men' " became "famous through all college, and enjoy[ed] a celebrity far more general and lasting than that accorded to the 'scholars' and 'high-stand men' who are not also 'writers.' "

The establishment of the course called Harvard Composition shows how the study of English literature could evolve from oratory and elocution. Harvard had introduced a requirement in "reading English aloud" in 1865, which it transmuted into its composition requirement in 1873. Instead of orations this early course in English composition required the writing of themes on subjects "to be taken from such works of standard authors as shall be announced from time to time." In 1874, for instance, the subjects were to be chosen from among "Shakespeare's *Tempest*, *Julius Caesar*, and *Merchant of Venice*; Goldsmith's *Vicar of Wakefield*; Scott's *Ivanhoe*, and *Lay of the Last Minstrel*." Arthur Applebee says that "this requirement institutionalized the study of standard authors and set in motion a process which eventually forced English to consolidate its position within the schools," for in the nineties colleges began to require standard works of English literature on their entrance examinations.

LITERARY SOCIETIES

No institution better offset the aridity of the college classroom than the cluster of literary societies, debating clubs, student literary publications, and public lectures and lyceums that impinged on college life. Earnest says that the activities of the literary societies alone refute "the commonly held notion that American colleges were, until recently, ivy-covered retreats from the world." Literary education did not yet depend wholly on the classroom, as it would for most students after the turn of the century, when the literary societies lost their centrality to fraternities, sororities, and athletics.

College literary societies were the formative literary education for numerous nineteenth-century American writers, including Emerson, Hawthorne, Dana, Holmes, Lowell, and Henry Adams. The societies had their own libraries, which "almost everywhere were larger, more accessible, and broader in range of interest than the college libraries." Historians agree that "English literature and American fiction were first welcomed in the American college by the literary societies, their libraries, and the student magazines." Owing to such societies, "outside the classroom a student in the 1840s was doing an amount of reading comparable to that covered in a modern survey course in

literature." "The societies absorbed the free time of students who pursued such extracurricular modern subjects as science, English, history, music, art, literature, and contemporary fiction." At Cornell, the winner of one of the society-sponsored literary competitions "was regarded as a college hero, marked for future eminence."

The work of the societies merged with other forms of local and extracurricular literary activity. After 1810 student literary magazines sprang up on numerous American campuses in imitation of Harvard's *Lyceum* (founded 1810), *Register* (1827), *Collegian* (1830), and *Harvardiana* (1836), and the *Yale Literary Magazine*—or "*Yale Lit*" (1836). In addition, there were evening lectures on campus to which the whole community was invited, delivered by members of the college faculty or by visiting luminaries. In the 1840s, Amherst sponsored lectures on Chaucer, the ballads, and "Milton's obligation to Caedmon." Andrew D. White called the fifties and sixties "the culminating period of the popular-lecture system." During his tenure at the University of Michigan, White gave "university extension" lectures all over the state and heard lectures in Ann Arbor by such figures as Emerson, George William Curtis, E. P. Whipple, and Wendell Phillips, one of many who disseminated abolitionist sentiments on campuses. Matthew Arnold lectured at Williams on his 1883–84 American tour, though Bliss Perry found his delivery inaudible.

By bringing the local culture into contact with contemporary currents of taste, public readings and lectures and the activities of the literary societies and student magazines had an important influence in breaking down genteel moral opposition to secular literature. It was said that Oberlin students dropped their belief in the wickedness of novels after discussing *Uncle Tom's Cabin* on campus. Byron was a particular favorite at colleges like Oberlin, where the male students "hotly debated the propriety of the Ladies' Literary Society Library Association owning a copy of Byron." Emerson and Whitman were invited to campuses by students at a time when both writers were considered suspect by authorities.

The literary societies not only stimulated interest in literature and ideas, they dramatized the central conflicts and controversies of contemporary culture. Burton J. Bledstein points out that in the literary societies students "debated national public issues like slavery—issues which transcended the provincialism of the college and led a few committed students to form antislavery societies on campus." Such actions were significant in a period when "conservative interests suppressed or disciplined antislavery organizations and abolitionist teachers and faculty in the academies and colleges." Members of literary societies also "openly discussed religious doubts" and "wrote essays on current heresies like the foundation of divinity in 'nature.' "

In this way the literary societies did far more than formal classes to situate students in relation to the cultural issues of their time. Participating in the societies' debates made possible the experimental trying out of ideas so necessary for intellectual self-definition. Most colleges had rival societies exemplifying opposed cultural, intellectual, and political orientations. James B. Angell recalled the "profound interest in literary culture" at Brown in the 1840s. He noted that students "divided as Carlyleists or anti-Carlyleists, Coleridgeians or anti-Coleridgeians," and that "literary, historic, and philosophic theories were as hotly discussed as the current political questions of the day." Bliss Perry spoke similarly of the rivalry between the Philologian and Philotechnian literary societies at Williams. There should be no question of idealizing the societies, for their success depended on a social homogeneity that created a common framework of interests. Yet it is difficult to ignore the fact that the societies provided something that was not fully recreated by the later university—a context of cultural debate through which students could make sense of their studies.

THE WANING OF ORATORICAL CULTURE

College writing and declamation competitions and literary and debating societies constituted a link between classroom work and the world outside the college. Yet the heyday of American oratory had passed by the late 1860s, and "elocution was fast fading from respectability in the academic community." Lyman Bagg, whose account of oratorical activites at Yale I quoted at length above, observed in 1871 that " 'the gift of gab' is thought less of than formerly," so that a "declamation prize counts for but little; and even a successful speaker in prize debate cannot be sure of his reputation as a 'literary man,' until he has strengthened it by winning a prize competiton." In 1873 Harvard made elocution an optional subject, substituting as a requirement its new course in English Composition, and the School of Oratory at the University of Texas "included a disclaimer in their catalogs to the effect that their objective was *not* to train elocutionists." Charles Francis Adams, with his characteristic pungency, adverted in 1883 to "that display of cheap learning which made the American oration of thirty and fifty years ago a national humiliation. Even in its best form it was bedizened with classic tinsel which bespoke the vanity of the half-taught scholar."

Still, elocution hung on as a central college subject after it outlived its vogue in literature departments and before it was given new life in the 1920s by schools of speech. The final third of the century saw several notable attempts not just to revitalize elocution as a literary study but to advance it as a humane alternative to the scientific philology of the modern language scholars. One of the most famous and controversial teachers to identify himself with this cause was Hiram Corson, who taught English at Cornell from 1870 to 1903. Corson was born in Philadelphia in 1828 and went to Washington as a youth to work as a stenographic reporter in the United States Senate, where he came to admire the oratory of Daniel Webster. The young Corson became a librarian at the Smithsonian, a position that afforded him the leisure to make an extensive private study of English literature. This led to a career as a popular lecturer, which in turn led to teaching posts at Girard College, St. Johns College at Annapolis, and eventually in 1870 at Cornell, where he was offered a position in English by President White despite his never having enrolled in any college.

White at the time "was inclined to scorn pure literary scholarship," thinking that "what is needed is not more talk about literature, but the literature itself." He could not have found anyone better suited to carry out his views than Corson, who believed obsessively that the oral reading of literature was the sole and sufficient form of authentic literary experience, and that mere talk about literature can easily become an obstacle to literary appreciation. One can see, in the primacy Corson attributed to the spiritual realization of literature through oral reading, an echo of earlier Quaker and Protestant evangelical appeals to the authority of faith over the encumbering externals of formal churches, rituals, and doctrinal disputes. Looking ahead, one can also see in Corson the prototype of the disaffected professorial humanist who tries to rescue the spirit of literature by disencumbering it from pedantic analysis.

A trained philologist himself, Corson from his position as chairman of the Cornell English Department in the 1890s vehemently attacked the philologists who had spearheaded the formation of departments of English in the previous decade. His manifesto, *The Aims of Literary Study* (1895), denouncing "German literary and philological scholarship" as "a great obstacle to the truest and highest literary culture" and a "degeneracy" manifesting itself in "a piddling analysis which has no end but itself," was an American equivalent of the influential English polemic by John Churton Collins, *The Study of English Literature* (1891). But what distinguished Corson from other such opponents of the new philology (who will be discussed in a later chapter) was his passionate defense of "interpretive reading," which—to his credit—he did not merely assert but attempted to justify theoretically.

In *The Voice and Spiritual Education* (1896), Corson argued that the spiritual essence of a poem, which was part of "the non-intellectual, the non-discursive" aspect of man, expressed "*man's essential absolute being*." This spiritual essence was accordingly the true object of teaching, and in Corson's view the only means of capturing it was through proper oral reading. For Corson, "a slovenly articulation" was a presumptive index of "moral slovenliness," and the touchstone of one's understanding of any text was how well one could render the text in oral performance. He recalled his childhood experience reading aloud and being corrected by his father when his enunciation betrayed that he had not understood what he was reading, and he pointed out that Milton had applied this very test to one of his own young pupils. Reading Corson, one becomes convinced at least for the moment that the great writers are indeed on his side, bound together in a tradition in which the speaking voice is the test of spiritual community.

At Cornell, "encouraged by the president, Corson let himself go, thundering Shakespeare to his classes and giving public readings every Saturday morning," some of them in Sage Chapel to the accompaniment of organ music. Corson may have been the first of the spellbinding professors of English who would be credited in generations of reminiscences with inspiring conversion experiences in heretofore indifferent students. One such student in the nineties described how "one day in Corson's class he felt a kind of rapture, almost a mystical experience. He was no longer the sullen undutiful scholar, he was the poet and the poem, he was rapt in beauty, he was plunged in an emotion never suspected. This was the capital experience of his life. Ever after, poetry was his companion, his solace, his hidden joy."

The declamatory style that produced such effects did not seem extravagantly emotional to Corson, who in fact disparaged cheap melodramatic effects. Some of Corson's colleagues thought otherwise, however, and "regarded his popular performances with a jaundiced eye." One of them complained that Corson seemed "half crazy" and thought that Corson's habit of filling the classroom hour by reading was a pretext for neglecting the teaching of writing. Students, this detractor said, were complaining "that Corson's classes were out of control; the students were disrespectful, read newspapers in class, and so on." One student of the class of 1872 wrote in his diary: "Prof. Corson spouted today and as usual he was not appreciated, and a shoe was thrown over the banister from below and came up near the desk." Corson's later behavior became increasingly erratic. He "became a convinced spiritualist, and held seances with a chair set for Tennyson or Browning, solemnly recording their poetic messages from the other world." However, the division of opinion on Corson bespoke not just his personal idiosyncrasies but the uncertain status of the evangelical, antiscientific style of literary study he embodied.

A second promoter of literary elocution, less well known than Corson, was Robert McLean Cumnock of Northwestern University, who built a divinity school appointment at Northwestern into its Cumnock School of Oratory and Elocution. Cumnock was born in 1840 in Scotland of Presbyterian parents, who shortly emigrated to Lowell, Massachusetts. In 1864 he matriculated at Wesleyan, where the general course work "emphasized public speaking and debate." Cumnock practiced for hours to develop "force and animation" in declamation and won prizes as a junior and senior as outstanding speaker in his class. On graduation in 1868, Cumnock, who had by then embraced Methodism, accepted a teaching position in Northwestern's Garrett Theological Seminary, whose faculty was expected to conform its thinking to "the doctrines held and maintained by the Methodist Episcopal Church, as embraced in her Articles of Religion."

Like Corson, Cumnock immediately became celebrated for his public performances, "which were often readings in Scottish dialect or selections from the Bible and Shakespeare." His classes were soon among the most popular in the university, especially among young women, who had been admitted to Northwestern in 1869 and who were fashionably expected to acquire "at least a minimal exposure" to elocution. One exception to the predominantly female enrollment was the future evangelist Billy Sunday. Cumnock became active in the Chautauqua movement of the midseventies, as both a public reader and an adviser. In 1878 he published an anthology of his favorite pieces, classified by types such as "Solemn Selections" ("Thanatopsis"), "Humorous Selections" ("The One-Hoss Shay"), and "Selections of Bold Address, Anger, Hurry and Commotion, Etc." ("The Charge of the Light Brigade"). He taught courses in literature as well as elocution, mixing "vocal interpretation" of Shakespeare, "Bain's Rhetoric, Taine's [History of] English Literature," with "special study of Chaucer, the early dramatists and the modern poets."

Describing Cumnock, one former student nicely epitomized the old college literary and social ideal:

> He was not interested in and had no part in our present day political and social institutions. He knew little of the literature of his day. He was a heroic figure from an earlier age, an age which expressed itself in scrupulous devotion to duty (to one's work), and to maintaining inviolate the integrity of character inherited from high Scotch tradition, an age that expressed its emotional nature in a formal and noble literature, a literature which found its completeness in bold address and the grand, sublime, and reverential style.

Unlike other elocutionists at the time, Cumnock resisted the scientific spirit that was entering the universities and casting a certain "academic contempt for all that is emotional." Some elocutionists were trying to emulate this new scientific spirit by developing a technical vocabulary of terms like force, stress, pitch, ditones, tritones, and pectoral and nasal qualities. This only caused elocution to seem all the more ridiculous, and, as one observer put it, "the colleges became impatient with it, as did sensible people everywhere."

At Cumnock's retirement in 1913 the school of Oratory was still prospering, and in 1920 it was assimilated into the newly founded School of Speech, which continues today to harbor a Department of Interpretation that just recently was renamed the Department of Performance Studies. Thus a survival of the declamatory tradition coexists with the conventional literature departments of which it was once an implicit criticism. The formative controversy this division reflected, however, is long forgotten.

What finally should be the verdict on the literary education provided by the old-fashioned college? In many ways it was worse than a waste of time, a form of unredeemed drudgery carried on in the name of archaic social ideals. Yet the very class restrictions of the old college enabled it to create certain educational conditions that a more democratic modern university has had trouble recreating. The education it provided had the advantage of coherence, if only a coherence made possible by the fact that, in the heyday of American colleges, no more than 2 percent of eligible Americans attended them.

From the point of view of subsequent literary criticism, the old college's conception of literary study as an extension of grammar, rhetoric, and elocution was merely an evidence of hopeless provincialism. But this modern view was formed only after literature had largely ceded to journalism and other media whatever power it had had to shape public opinion. By contrast, the old college maintained a socially "committed" view of literature in its very conservatism. It bespoke a culture that still assigned a social function to a humanistically educated class.

But then, how effectively did the college make literary ideals into a socializing force? It is tempting, but finally misleading, to describe the story of the transition from the old college to the modern university as a falling away from organic traditional "community" into fragmented modern "association," from *Gemeinschaft* to *Gesellschaft*. Organic community hardly existed outside New England, and even there it weakened progressively throughout the century. The mounting criticism of the classical curriculum before and after the Civil War suggests that the college curriculum was failing to transmit the traditional culture. Without the student literary societies and magazines and the class-day orations and declamations, the old college literary education would make a very poor showing indeed.

The Early Professional Era: 1875–1915

CHAPTER FOUR

The Investigators (1): The New University

The German professor is not a teacher in the English sense of the term; he is a specialist. He is not responsible for the success of his hearers. He is responsible only for the quality of his instruction. His duty begins and ends with himself.

JAMES MORGAN HART

The appearance of departments of language and literature in the last quarter of the nineteenth century was part of the larger process of professionalization by which the old "college" became the new "university." In literary studies, as everyone knows, the advance guard of professionalization was a German-trained cadre of scholarly "investigators," who promoted the idea of scientific research and the philolological study of the modern languages. Yet the philologists' right to define the terms of professionalism in literary studies was contested from the beginning. A competing model was defended by a party of "generalists," as I shall call them, who were also committed to the idea of departments of English and modern languages, but who upheld the old college ideal of liberal or general culture against that of narrowly specialized research. In some ways they epitomize the viewpoint that Stanley Fish has recently called "anti-professionalism." Yet they insisted they were not opposed to professionalism itself, but only to the narrow forms it had taken—a distinction which tends to be lost in Fish's discussion.

This generalist group (to be fully discussed in a later chapter) formed a "dissenting tradition," in Applebee's term, which defended appreciation over investigation and values over facts. Applebee reminds us that "much that was not philological went on in the early departments of English, stemming from the earlier traditions of rhetorical analysis, from the long tradition of popular, nonacademic criticism, and from oratory (itself a child of rhetoric), which placed more emphasis on sensitive reading and 'interpretation.' " "The prestige of philology," Applebee says, "served to *justify* English studies without necessarily *limiting* them."

Nevertheless, the new research model dictated the organization of the department and, in the long run, the literary curriculum. In part, the success of the research model in shaping academic literary studies is explained by its appeal to science and modernity, but research succeeded also because it promised to serve certain traditional purposes never fulfilled by the classical regimen. Despite its secularism and distrust of tradition, the research ethos comported with the traditionalist orientation of literary culture in ways which need to be sorted out.

GILMAN'S NEW UNIVERSITY: 1876

Daniel Coit Gilman, born in 1831 and educated at Yale in the late forties, was not among the numerous nineteenth-century Americans who studied at one of the famous German or French graduate schools. But Gilman visited Europe in the 1850s and, visiting several of the universities there, noted their many points of superiority to American colleges. Gilman sensed that among the young men of America there might be "a strong demand . . . for opportunities to study beyond the ordinary courses of a college or scientific school," in other words, for a true "university," offering advanced instruction in all the modern branches of knowledge.

Gilman returned to New Haven to work as a fund-raiser for the Sheffield Scientific School, as yet a neglected appendage to the classics-dominated Yale College. Hoping "to win adherents to the teaching of science" against Yale's classicists, who "fought hard to maintain their monopoly," Gilman in 1856 published "a plan for the complete organization of a school of science." The plan called attention to "the woeful lack of opportunity in this country for those who wish 'to study science for its own sake' " or to fit themselves for practical occupations. Gilman was soon able to implement his ideas as a member of the governing board of Sheffield, and his accomplishments proved a stepping stone to the presidency of the University of California, which he assumed in 1872. This in turn led to an invitation to apply to the new Johns Hopkins, then in the planning stage and actually little more than an endowment looking for new ideas.

Chosen as the first president of Johns Hopkins, Gilman had the enviable opportunity of starting from scratch, unimpeded by inherited local tradition and armed with large, unrestricted funds bequeathed by the Baltimore grocery merchant from whom the institution took its name. Gilman proceeded to shape "the Hopkins" in the image of the great European universities, decreeing that the institution should "forever be free from the influences of ecclesiasticism or partisanship." Its power would "depend upon the character of its resident staff of permanent professors," and the quality of "their researches, their utterances . . . their example as students and investigators and champions of truth." In its faculty appointments, Johns Hopkins would consider above all "the devotion of the candidate to some particular line of study and the certainty of his eminence in that specialty; the power to pursue independent and original investigation, and to inspire the young with enthusiasm for study and research." The faculty's accomplishments would be reflected in "publications through journals and scientific treatises."

If these ends were to be accomplished, instructors could not become so "absorbed in routine" that they would be "forced to spend their strength in the discipline of tyros," as they were doing in the old college. Instead, they "should have ample time to carry on the higher work for which they had shown themselves qualified." Johns Hopkins students were to be shown "how to extend, even by minute accretions, the realm of knowledge; how to cooperate with other men in the prosecution of inquiry; and how to record in exact language, and on the printed page, the results attained." The embodiment of these ideals was the graduate school: had Gilman had his way, Johns Hopkins would have offered *only* graduate study and left "the kind of work now done by undergraduates to be done elsewhere." This was too impractical for the trustees, however, who persuaded Gilman to include an undergraduate college.

Even so, no institution in the United States had ventured on so bold and novel a program, and the Johns Hopkins model shortly began to be imitated by Harvard, Yale, and the new University of Chicago, opened in 1892. President Eliot, who had served on the committee recommending Gilman's appointment, later admitted that "the graduate school of Harvard University, started feebly in 1870 and 1871, did not thrive, until the example of Johns Hopkins forced our Faculty to put their strength into the development of our instruction for graduates. And what was true of Harvard was true of every other university in the land which aspired to create an advanced school of arts and sciences."

Lesser institutions followed suit. Sooner or later any ambitious college president had to ask the sort of questions put by the new president of Northwestern University in 1891:

> Are we keeping our University in the foremost ranks of modern discovery? Are we taking up the new branches of knowledge as they come successively into existence? Are we meeting the demands which the changed conditions of modern life make upon us? Are we continually harmonizing the knowledge which we have inherited from previous generations with the knowledge which this generation has acquired, or are we simply guarding ancient truth?

President Rogers's assumption that there need be no incompatibility between "ancient truth" and the demands of "the changed conditions of modern life" typified the optimism of the era's reform generation of university presidents. Few of these reformers foresaw that it might not be so easy to "harmonize" the old and the new, much less translate the harmony into curricular terms.

Gilman's vision called for specialized departments and courses of study after the German pattern. The word "department" had been in use in colleges through the nineteenth century, but only now did it take on connotations of disciplinary specialization and administrative autonomy. To stock his departments, Gilman proceeded to lure famous scholars from other institutions, engaging in the first large-scale "raiding" in American higher education. The new arrangement transferred to departments the responsibility of recommending their appointments, promotions, and salary increases and of judging the suitability of their courses and programs, a significant step that had the effect, among others, of turning departments for the first time into competitive entities with respect to other departments. As Parker writes, "departments soon became competitive and ambitious, looking anxiously at any unoccupied territory between themselves and neighboring departments." Departments remained small, however, until well after the turn of the century, most consisting of a single professor, two or three instructors, and a few graduate assistants.

To assure that his professors had outlets in which to publish their investigations, Gilman encouraged the formation of scholarly journals in various fields, including *The American Journal of Philology* and *Modern Language Notes*, founded at Johns Hopkins in 1880 and 1886 respectively. Gilman also founded the first American university press in 1878. (It was followed by the university presses of Chicago [1892], Columbia [1893], Yale [1908], and Harvard [1913]). As René Wellek has said, the practical necessity of "bulk in production" and "the convenient grading of teachers" implied "an industrial ideal" for scholarship, but bulk publication expectations in English were small in the early years. In accord with the austerely scientific ideal of truth, "study much, publish little" was then and for some time after the motto. Perishing for not publishing did not become a widespread phenomenon until later, perhaps not till after World War II, when postwar affluence made possible both departmental empire-building and the expansion of the university presses that created outlets for publication.

A commentator in 1925 said that "the professor must publish if he is to be promoted in rank and salary. The cry of deans and heads of departments is emphatic now: 'Produce! Show the stuff that is in you by publishing!' and the implication inevitably follows: 'Neglect this and you lose your job. If you cannot put your college on the map with your publications, we must get somebody else who can.'" But how serious such threats were and how widely they were carried out is unclear from this statement. For a long time the article or scholarly note, rather than the book, was the unit of production, as it still tends to be for scholars in the earliest periods of English literature. My guess is that, measured by current high-pressure standards, production demands in the early departments would seem mild. It would be interesting to know exactly when professors first began to be fired for insufficient publication.

Other standard features emerging in the late seventies and early eighties, more or less influenced by the example of Hopkins, were the undergraduate major, with greater or lesser allowance for electives; the numbered courses; the unit system of credits and requirements; the Ph.D. program with its research seminars taught by scholarly specialists; and the doctoral dissertation constituting "an original and important contribution to knowledge." In order to regulate this diversified complex there arose the bureaucratized, administrative "chain of command involving presidents, deans, and department chairmen." All these things, in Veysey's words, "emerged in an astonishingly short period of time and with relatively little variation from one institution to another." Bureaucratic standardization became necessary as American universities underwent a period of rapid growth, nearly doubling in enrollments every decade from 1890 to 1930.

The Secularized Professional

With these changes there arose between 1875 and 1915 a new type of secularized educational professional. The outlook of this type was tied not to maintaining the traditional ideal of liberal culture, but to facilitating the advancement of knowledge wherever it might lead—though, again, it was characteristic of the new professional not to worry about the possibility that these goals might conflict. Veysey points out that as the old college disintegrated, bureaucratic administration took the place of traditional ideology as the bond holding the institution together. "Neither the Christian religion in any of its varieties, nor positive science, nor humane culture proved self-evidently capable of making sense out of the entire range of knowledge and opinion." The university "was fast becoming an institution beholden to no metaphysic," and "talk about the higher purposes of the university" was becoming "increasingly ritualistic." "Bureaucratic modes served as a low but tolerable common denominator, linking individuals, cliques, and factions who did not think in the same terms." "Bureaucratic administration was the structural device which made possible the new epoch of institutional empire-building without recourse to specific shared values." This meant that "quarrelsome debate, including that based upon conflicts among academic ideals, must be minimized or suppressed whenever it became threateningly serious." Indeed the new structure of "patterned isolation" imposed a positive "need to fail to communicate," in which "each academic group normally refrained from too rude or brutal an unmasking of the rest." "The university throve, as it were, on ignorance."

Other historians corroborate Veysey's striking analysis. Rudolph says that the modern university characteristically dealt with conflicts by "walking away" from the choices that had troubled college authorities throughout the century: "practical or classical studies, old professions or new vocations, pure or applied science, training for culture and character or for jobs." Bledstein says that the new "universities quietly took divisive issues such as race, capitalism, labor, and deviant behavior out of the public domain and isolated these problems within the sphere of professionals—men who learned to know better than to air publicly their differences."

Bureaucracy entailed its own kind of ideology, tied to faith in science, expertise, and administration, but it was a dynamic ideology not bound by traditional fixities and compatible at least within limits with a wide variety of conflicting beliefs. New-style administrators like Nicholas Murray Butler, who became president of Columbia in 1902, had the power to get rid of offensively heterodox professors and students and did not hesitate to use it, and the patriotic hysteria of World War I and its aftermath led to frequent persecutions of suspected subversives. It was only through the agitation of the

American Association of University Professors—founded in 1915—that university presidents grudgingly began to concede the principle of faculty freedom from institutional censorship and to accept the concept of academic tenure. Still, by comparison with the old college's rigidity, the new professionalism was willing to give a wide berth to unorthodox opinion provided it did not tread too openly on accepted principles. The scholar's business was the search for impersonal truth, and the formulation of values and ideals was theoretically left to others.

Thorstein Veblen described this positivist ideology in *The Higher Learning in America* (1918). He noted that though much of the external "apparatus of the old order" had survived in the new university, including "the sentimentally reminiscent endeavors of certain spiritual 'hold-overs' . . . the power of aspiration had shifted to the concerted adulation of matter-of-fact." The president of the Modern Language Association in 1913 went so far as to say that "in academic circles, words like 'pious' and 'virtuous' have lost caste to the point of becoming terms of reproach among those who have cut their eye-teeth; even 'benevolent' and 'philanthropic' are not without a shade of suspicion, while puritanical restraint and Sunday-scool [*sic*] goodness have become if not anathemas then at least taboos." The modernized spelling in which this scholar's very words were printed in the *Publications of the Modern Language Association* was a small example of the secularism that was making him uneasy.

No doubt these statements underestimated the degree to which certain "spiritual hold-overs" remained compatible with newer ideas. Anti-Semitism, for instance, was all-pervasive in universities, and more pervasive in English departments than anywhere else. The Jewish Ludwig Lewisohn was denied a fellowship to the Ph.D. program at Columbia in 1905 and finally, when no English department would hire him, had to accept a teaching post in a German department. Lewisohn said that anti-Semitism had not, "to my knowledge, relented in a single instance in regard to the teaching of English. So that our guardianship of the native tongue is far fiercer than it is in an, after all, racially homogeneous state like Germany."

The secular tendency of the new academic type was most eloquently described (if somewhat exaggerated) by George Santayana, who taught philosophy at Harvard between 1889 and 1912. As Santayana wrote in *Character and Opinion in the United States*,

> many of the younger professors of philosophy are no longer the sort of persons that might as well have been clergymen or schoolmasters: they have

> rather the type of mind of a doctor, an engineer, or a social reformer; the wide-awake young man who can do most things better than old people and who knows it. He is less eloquent and apostolic than the older generation of philosophers, very professional in tone.

Though the new professionals gave lip service to the old dogmas of spiritual idealism and culture, there was a certain democratic relativism in their outlook. As Santayana paraphrased it, "we accept no claims; we ask for no credentials; we just give you a chance. Plato, the Pope, and Mrs. Eddy shall have one vote each." It was not that the new professionals opposed the older idealisms, they were simply indifferent to them. "It is evident," Santayana wrote, "that such minds will have but a loose hold on tradition, even on the genteel tradition in American philosophy. Not that in general they oppose or dislike it; their alienation from it is more radical; they forget it." One mainstay of the old guard, President James McCosh of Princeton, learned this lesson in the 1880s when he tried to pick a quarrel with Eliot's "new departure," the elective system: "The wise leaders of the new departure," McCosh sardonically observed, "do not propose to fight against religion. They do not fight with it, but they are quite willing to let it die out, to die in dignity."

The new academic professional thought of himself as an "investigator" devoted to advancing the frontiers of knowledge through research, and his loyalties went to his "field" rather than to the classroom dedication that had made the older type of college teacher seem a mere schoolmaster. The prototype of the new professional was the German university professor in his lecture room or seminar, a man who supposedly transcended morality and ideology in his disinterested search for truth. The German professor, it was admiringly said, is "not a teacher" at all "in the English sense of the term; he is a specialist. He is not responsible for the success of his hearers. He is responsible only for the quality of his instruction. His duty begins and ends with himself." "His time is not wasted in cudgeling the wits of refractory or listless reciters." Conservatives like Noah Porter protested in vain that the main business of the professor was still "to educate the young," and that "the American college is not designed primarily to promote the cause of science by endowing posts in which men of learning and science may prosecute their researches, but to secure successful instruction for our youth."

The new assertion of freedom with respect to the modes of instruction echoed the German academic ideal of *Lehrfreiheit*, which conceived the professor as "a law unto himself," a man who had "but one aim in life: scholarly renown." "Accountable only to himself for his opinions and mode of living," the German professor, it was said, "shakes off spiritual bondage and becomes an independent thinker." The laudatory descriptions were by James Morgan Hart, an American who studied law at several German universities in the 1860s and 1870s and later became a professor of English philology at the University of Cincinnati and at Cornell. Hart's book, *German Universities*, published in 1874, two years before the opening of Hopkins, depicted the German university as "a training-ground of intellectual giants" who dwarfed their encumbered American counterparts.

It is easy enough with hindsight to deride the naïveté of these claims to being above mere ideology. But at the time, they represented a radical challenge to social pieties, a declaration that truth was independent of whatever the traditional cultural authorities might dictate. At the same time, the form of the challenge entailed such an exaggerated disjunction between the impersonal facts of the investigator and the value-tainted experience of everyone else that it encouraged a new kind of irresponsibility and arrogance, as well as a pedantry whose narrowness was not lost on the Americans studying in German universities.

It is in some ways surprising that the emulation of literary studies in Germany caught on as easily as it did in the United States, in view of the dreary picture painted by many who sent back accounts of their student experiences. One scholar, for example, describing the historical seminar at Leipzig in the late eighties, said that "the work was scientific and thorough, but there was no debate, no lively interest in the questions discussed, and no one attempted to conceal the fact that the exercise was decidedly long and tiresome. Even [the professor] covered his face with his hand, now and then, to conceal—or attempt to conceal—the big yawn that he could not restrain. . . . I went in prepared to 'behold and wonder'; it took my entire stock of admiration to pull me through." Evidently the myth of Germanic superiority caused Americans to ignore the evidence before their eyes. As another observer put it in 1891, "there is a general and almost impregnable superstition in America, and even in Great Britain, about German universities and scholarship." By this time, however, respect for Germanic methods had actually begun to wane.

Aspirations toward national identity clearly had something to do with the superstitious emulation of German methods. In depicting the professor as a bold, heroically individualistic searcher for truth, James Morgan Hart suggested a connection between professorial independence and national prestige. The Germans, Hart said, "know that speculative thought alone has raised Germany from her former condition of literary and political dependence to the foremost rank among nations." The attractions of such a picture for a nation increasingly aware of its power in the world are not hard to imagine. The new professionalism could not have succeeded had it not accorded with a new national respect for the progressive claims of science, specialization, and expertise. It was later said of Gilman—by another pioneering university president, G. Stanley Hall—that he had "realized that as civilization advanced, all critical decisions and new steps must be made by experts who could command all the available knowledge in their field and perhaps add something new to the sum of the world's knowledge." This statement suggests how "the culture of professionalism," in Bledstein's words, incarnated "the radical idea of the independent democrat, a liberated person seeking to free the power of nature within every worldly sphere, a self-governing individual exercising his trained judgment in an open society."

Faith in professional expertise gave a measure of reassurance to Americans who had always lacked traditional authorities and now, after the Civil War, found themselves confronted by bewildering industrial and social changes. But in exchange for this reassurance, these Americans were obliged to surrender their independence of judgment to experts. Professional expertise defined itself precisely by its contrast with the ineptitude of "laymen," who were "neither prepared to comprehend the mystery of the tasks which professionals performed, nor—more ominously, were . . . equipped to pass judgment upon special skills and technical competence." The growth of a cult of expertise in the university mirrored the development of bureaucratic corporations and of scientific modes of management. As Richard Ohmann observes, the university in this period "was gearing itself up to be a supplier and certifier of the professionals and managers needed by . . . large integrated corporations and by the other institutions that came into being to monitor and service the corporate social order. . . . The new universities came into being along with the professional-managerial class they educated."

Of course what "professional expertise" meant and how it related to its lay clientele were reasonably obvious as long as one remained in the spheres of marketing, engineering, or management. But what did it mean for those who worked on Middle English poems and homilies? It was one thing to professionalize the health industry, another to professionalize the culture industry; and though many patterns can be assumed to have carried over from the one sphere to the other, we cannot assume a perfectly homologous relation between the two. Reconciling professional secularism with the traditionalism of liberal culture proved to be a problem.

CHAPTER FIVE

The Investigators (2): The Origins of Literature Departments

A scientific basis dignifies our profession. . . . By introducing scientific methods, we shall show before very long that every body cannot [teach English], that the teacher must be as specially and as scientifically trained for his work in our department as well as in any other.

H. C. G. BRANDT

President Gilman was nowhere more radical than in the scientific conception of knowledge that animated his thinking about the new university. Whereas the old college curriculum had left the sciences to be taught as if they were analogous to the classical learning, Gilman, whose formative experience had come in a scientific school, naturally gravitated to a scientific model of knowledge. At Johns Hopkins he dramatically reversed traditional priorities, taking the sciences as the central model of knowledge and letting humanistic subjects adapt themselves as best they could. Departments were themselves an expression of the scientific view of knowledge, being efficient instruments for facilitating research breakthroughs rather than custodial agencies for conserving tradition.

In literary studies, however, departmental identity from the start reflected conflicting conceptions of the department's mission, which resolved themselves in varying degrees of compromise, stalemate, and peaceful but distrustful coexistence.

Composition of Departments

Not surprisingly, the extreme type of the "advanced" English department was Johns Hopkins itself, which was so far ahead in one respect that it turned out to be retarded in another when the winds shifted from philology to literature in the nineties. Having begun from scratch, Johns Hopkins had had no tradition of generalist culture like that at Harvard and Yale. Its early work in the modern languages was so wholly monopolized by philologists that it was late in developing courses in literature proper. At Harvard, on the other hand, philologists like Francis James Child and George Lyman Kittredge uneasily coexisted with generalists like Barrett Wendell—the one type dominating the teaching of language and literature, the other the teaching of writing.

Harvard's "courses of instruction were not grouped by departments in the catalog until 1872," at which point English, German, French, Italian, and Spanish achieved departmental status. In 1876 Harvard appointed Child to its first professorship in English after his offer from Johns Hopkins. Child developed a course in Shakespeare consisting of "a close reading of eight or ten of Shakespeare's plays," and "a literature course emphasizing Chaucer, Bacon, Milton, and Dryden." At least one student remembered that Child's Shakespeare course involved "much thumbing of Schmidt's *Shakespeare Lexicon* for parallel references, useful on examination papers. There was no mention of the fact that Shakespeare had a personal history or that he wrote for the Elizabethan stage. . . . [Child's] method of conducting the class was to summon to the front row eight students to read and comment on the text, while the rest of the class listened or slept."

Kittredge, who joined the Harvard faculty in 1888, established himself as the quintessential philological scholar, even though he had no Ph.D. ("Who could have examined me?" he is said to have answered, when asked why not.) Kittredge introduced courses in Icelandic, Germanic mythology, and historical English grammar, and took over Child's Shakespeare course after Child's death in 1896. It was largely Child and Kittredge who set the pattern described by Wellek, whereby "Shakespeare on the graduate level" came to mean "the distinctions of quartos and folios, sources, stage conditions." In the seventies and eighties this description would often have suited Shakespeare on the undergraduate level as well.

While Child and Kittredge were teaching sources and parallel references, composition flourished under idiosyncratic, unscholarly men like Barrett Wendell, Le Baron Russell Briggs (later "Dean Briggs"), Lewis E. Gates, and Charles Townsend Copeland. Robert Morss Lovett, a student during the late eighties and later an instructor at Harvard, said that Harvard's composition courses had been established by President Eliot as an attempt "to maintain the traditional culture of Harvard, threatened by the loss of social exclusiveness and of the protection of the classics."

Composition at Harvard, when taught in classes as large as five hundred students, was later described as a "huge concern which (despite many experiments) has never been carried on to anyone's satisfaction." But it also meant advanced courses similar to what would later be called "creative writing," mixing essays and fiction, and pungently reflecting the personalities both of its instructors and that Harvard culture that Eliot wanted to preserve. Harvard thus became the first great university to dramatize the split between scholarship and composition that would become so typical of English departments down to the present day.

At other universities, the initial departmentalization of literary studies reflected more or less directly the influence of Germanic philology. At Indiana University in 1885, the professor of English, Orrin Clark, went on leave, travelling in Europe and taking an M. A. at Harvard, probably at the suggestion of Indiana's new president, David Starr Jordan, who "pressured his faculty to pursue advanced training and distinction in their fields." According to Richard Ohmann's account, early in Jordan's administration, the old "composite structure" of standard required courses was declared unsatisfactory and replaced "by a differentiation of previously existing departments and the introduction of new ones." Instead of three courses of study—classical, scientific, and modern languages—there were now eight, including English literature, history, political science, mathematics, and physics, biology, geology, and chemistry.

As Jordan described the new arrangement, "each junior or third-year student was required to choose a specialty or 'major,' and to work under the immediate advice of his 'major professor.' . . . The natural extension of this emergence of specialized undergraduate study was the introduction of graduate work." From this time on at Indiana, Ohmann comments, "English, though it still had a viable role in what we would call 'general education,' was a separate field of study. Jordan had invented the English major or gotten Clark to invent it. . . . In making his university serious, scholarly, and professional, Jordan had created there the field of English."

"Any Body Can Teach English"

The generalist professors might be popular teachers, but as Applebee points out, they "lacked an adequate methodology to offer in place of the new-found rigor of philology," and their lack of special expertise was a real liability in the fight for respectability being waged by the departments. As H. C. G. Brandt, a professor of German at Hamilton College, put it in 1883, at the first meeting of the Modern Language Association, as long as "teachers of modern languages . . . do not realize, that their department is a science," the feeling will continue to be that "*any body* can teach French or German or what is just as dangerous, any body can teach English." Brandt hastened to add that "our department *is* a science, and that its teaching must be carried on accordingly," for "a scientific basis dignifies our profession."

"By basing our instruction and text-books upon a scientific groundwork," Brandt continued, "our department and our profession gain dignity and weight. . . . By introducing scientific methods, we shall show before very long that every body cannot [teach English], that the teacher must be as specially and as scientifically trained for his work in our department as well as in any other." As another modern language professor declared at the first MLA meeting in 1883, "the student expects hard work in Greek, but modern languages he considers a 'soft snap.'" A third, also at the first meeting, deplored the fact "that English literature is a subject for the desultory reader in his leisure hours rather than an intellectual study for serious workers; that it ranks as an accomplishment only, and that the terms literary and philosophic, are mutually exclusive."

It now seems odd that the philologists could have confused literary and linguistic study so badly—though perhaps no more odd than the confusions of their classical predecessors. But the earliest academic philologists did not think of themselves as teachers of literature primarily, but as teachers of language. As Michael Warner points out, "the MLA . . . was not primarily, either in intent or in membership, a literary organization." Its members "had in most cases begun their academic careers with little or no interest in teaching literature," but "thought of literary texts as pedagogical tools." Purists like James Bright of Johns Hopkins thought that literary concerns could only corrupt philology: Bright, it was said, thought that "describing a philologist as a professor of literature would be as absurd as describing a biologist as a professor of vegetables." We have already seen that the idea that literary works could be taught "as literature"—as opposed simply to being read in one's leisure hours—was a novelty.

In other words, philological study proved a dismal failure only in relation to expectations that few of its early proponents were attempting to meet or would have thought they could meet. On the other hand, the traditions of philology, like those of classical study, implied a larger cultural vision. René Wellek has written of "the useless antiquarianism, the dreary factualism, the pseudo-science combined with anarchical skepticism and a lack of critical taste" characteristic of the scholarship of the early professional era. But Wellek reminds us that such abuses "represent the decadence of a worthy ideal, that of philology conceived as a total science of civilization, an ideal originally formulated for the study of classical antiquity and then transferred by the German romanticists to the modern languages." The nineteenth-century passion for philology "satisfied the nostalgia for the past, especially the European past and the Middle Ages, and at the same time it met the desire for facts, for accuracy, for the imitation of the 'scientific method' which had acquired such overwhelming prestige" in the United States.

The history of the word "philology" itself reflected a conflict between broad, humanistic generality and narrow, positive science. Originally dating back to Plato, the word was revived in 1777 by Friedrich Wolf of the University of Göttingen, who included in it "attention to the grammar, criticism, geography, political history, customs, mythology, literature, art, and ideas of a people." Modern language scholars liked to invoke the names of great nineteenth-century philologists like Boeckh, Max Müller, Bopp, and Jacob and Wilhelm Grimm, for whom philology had meant not only linguistics but "the whole study of the history of cultures." According to Richard Macksey, "at its best, this first vision of language and critical method could aspire to a total view of civilization and a command of its languages." Philology expressed "the Romantic welling up of a search for method that was to be the common concern binding together the humane disciplines." Boeckh insisted on the speculative unity of knowledge, objecting to those who conceive science as something expressed "through counting, piece by piece, what comprises it," and who thus view "philology merely as an aggregate."

British Victorian philologists had similarly large pretensions, arguing that there was an "affinity between Darwin's evolutionary hypotheses and the kind of patterns drawn by the philologists."Friedrich Max Müller, the Sanskrit scholar and the first German philologist to be appointed at Oxford, argued that the study of linguistic roots demonstrated the unity of "all Indo-European nations," proving their membership in a "great Aryan brotherhood." Anti-Semitic and imperialist as this "Aryan hypothesis" was, it was not pedantic. "In order to know what we are," Max Müller said, "we have to learn how we have come to be what we are. Our very languages form an unbroken chain between us and Cicero and Aristotle, and in order to use many of our words intelligently, we must know the soil from which they sprang, and the atmosphere in which they grew up and developed."

Philologists like Max Müller were central voices in the Victorian ethnological controversy over the origins of the English "racial" strain. This controversy, conducted not only in scholarly journals and societies but in popular organs such as the *Gentleman's Magazine*, pitted those who saw the national character as "Teutonic" and Anglo-Saxon against those who maintained the presence of a significant "Celtic" admixture. Among the latter party was Matthew Arnold, who took a keen interest in the researches of the philologists for their relevance to those questions of national cultural identity that so interested him. As Frederic E. Faverty pointed out in a now neglected book, that "best self" against which Arnold measured the Hebraic and Philistine character of the British confused the idea of universal human nature with the "scientific" theory of Celtic racial superiority which Arnold had borrowed from Ernest Renan, Amédée Thierry, and others. Arnold drew heavily on current ethnological researches in the lectures he delivered at Oxford in 1857 as Professor of Poetry, later published as *On the Study of Celtic Literature*. It was significant that Arnold concluded his lectures with a plea for the formation of a chair in Celtic philology.

The historical studies of Hippolyte Taine were also widely invoked as a model by the early modern language departments. Like Boeckh, Taine conceived the object of historical science to be not a mere accumulation of disconnected data, but a search for the underlying unity that draws together the disparate aspects of a culture. Taine wrote that "it is a mistake to study the document, as if it were isolated." The historian, "if his critical education is sufficient, . . . can lay bare, under every detail of architecture, every stroke in a picture, every phrase in a writing," the "master idea" defining the characteristic tendency of a national culture at a given moment. According to Taine, "everything is a symbol" to the historian, no cultural fact is without significance for the whole; therefore historical study can open "all the wealth that may be drawn from a literary work: when the work is rich, and people know how to interpret it, we find there the psychology of a soul, frequently of an age, now and then of a race."

One cannot minimize the importance of these theories of "race" in the formation of language and literature departments in the 1880s. As Hofstadter points out in *Social Darwinism in American Thought*, this was the decade in which the Anglo-Saxon mystique reached its high point in America. John W. Burgess, who would help found the discipline of American political science at Columbia, wrote in 1884 that "the creation of Teutonic political genius stamps the Teutonic nations as the political nations *par excellence*, and authorizes them, in the economy of the world, to assume the leadership in the establishment and administration of states." In *The Winning of the West* (1889), Burgess's student at Columbia, Theodore Roosevelt, described the world domination of "the English speaking peoples" as an irresistible impulse that acted in "obedience to the instincts working half blindly within their breasts," and in so doing "wrought out the destinies of a continental nation."

Such a nationalistic vision obviously encouraged a consciousness of the racial element in literature. The very decision to divide the new language and literature departments along national lines was an implicit assertion of pride in "the English speaking race." Brander Matthews wrote in an American literature textbook of 1896, "as literature is a reflection and a reproduction of the life of the peoples speaking the language in which it is written, this literature is likely to be strong and great in proportion as the peoples who speak the language are strong and great. English literature is therefore likely to grow, as it is the record of the life of the English speaking race and as this race is steadily spreading abroad over the globe."

Statements like these can be amassed in order to make a case for the argument that the professionalization of literary studies in the university was a means by which "the old elite and their allies" sought "to impose middle-class American 'likemindedness' on a heterogeneous, urban, working-class population." Calling it "professionalization," Paul Lauter says, the old elite "reorganized literary scholarship and teaching in ways that not only asserted a male-centered culture and values for the college-educated leadership, but also enhanced their own authority and status as well." In other words, the interests of professionalism and of cultural nationalism coincided—as indeed the official humanist view assumed.

While not wholly false, this view is misleading in several respects. It not only reduces a tangled and contradictory complex of ideologies to a single one, but ignores the ways in which an ideology can be deflected or subverted in the process of being institutionalized. Certainly many among "the old elite" did hope that academic literary studies would help impose a unified, "male-centered" American culture and values on an increasingly heterogeneous population. But this hope was at least to some degree frustrated by the dynamics of professionalization itself, which the old elite did not fully control.

Like the British John Churton Collins, whose polemic *The Study of English Literature: A Plea for Its Recognition and Reorganization at the Universities* (1891) was widely read and discussed in America and invoked at MLA conventions, American educators often conceived the study of English literature as a potential "instrument of political education . . . to warn, to admonish, to guide." But it was this very vision of national, cultural unity that seemed to be traduced by the research scholars, whose loyalties lay less with their national traditions than with their professional research fields. Collins attacked the "degrading vassalage to philology," and argued that the "national interests of culture and education" had been subordinated to "the local interests of specialism and Philology."

It was not the research scholars but their belletristic detractors—men like Brander Matthews, Henry Van Dyke, and Bliss Perry—who kept alive until World War I the nationalist idiom of Taine, Boeckh, and Arnold, and it was they who championed the teaching of American literature in college classrooms against the resistance of the scholars. Like the high-school teacher who cited Collins's polemic at the MLA meeting of 1886, they argued that "the progress of a nation's thought and literary style" could not advance until literature "has been divorced from philology," and that American literature was "highly serviceable to education precisely because it admits of a complete severance of literature from philology." Such statements suggest that the vision of national culture which animated the founding of English was becoming detached from and turned against the methodology it had spawned.

English as Mental Discipline

The new philologists paid lip service to the rhetoric of cultural nationalism and the broadly comprehensive view of their discipline. In actuality, however, they found it more effective to establish their credentials on practical grounds than to propound grandiose cultural visions. They put their subject forward not as a philosophy of culture, but as the replacement for Greek and Latin as the up-to-date form of mental discipline. Perhaps the polemical situation required such a strategy. Scornful as the philologists were of the educational philosophy of the old college, when it came to making a case for their enterprise in the university, they assiduously set out to prove that it met that philosophy's requirements. This will not be the last time we will see the reformers of literary studies opportunistically acceding to the standards of their opposition and losing sight of larger ideals in the process.

The theory of mental discipline had a flaw that proved fatal to the classicists' interests. In making the worth of the classics rest on their

disciplinary value, the classicists opened themselves to the objection that the same discipline could be provided by other subjects. Charles Francis Adams, Jr., argued that "there is no more mental training in learning the Greek grammar by heart than in learning by heart any other equally difficult and, to a boy, unintelligible book. As a mere work of memorizing, Kant's 'Critique of Pure Reason' would be at least as good." Following Adams's logic, the proponents of the modern languages had only to point out that if difficult problems of translation, etymology, and grammar were what was wanted, the modern languages provided as many of these as anyone could desire.

Even English could be made sufficiently taxing if its teachers concentrated on early texts and taught them philologically. As Brandt put it in his MLA paper of 1883, "When 'English' meant, and too often still means, a certain amount of orthoepy, elocution, style, and literature, when we teach French and German as if they were accomplishments like dancing, fencing, or final touches to be put on . . . young ladies in their seminaries, . . . our department is justly charged with affording no mental discipline." But "let 'English' mean as it should and as it is bound to mean more and more, the historical scientific study of the language, Beowulf and Chaucer," then the objection is overcome.

Perceiving that their disciplinary rhetoric was being co-opted by the opposition, the classicists tried belatedly to liberalize their position. In 1870 Noah Porter of Yale conceded that "mere grammatical analysis has . . . been pushed to a one-sided extreme so as to be over-refined, unnecessarily complicated, and unreasonably prolonged." Porter suggested that "the drill-work of classical study might be exchanged by degrees for those higher enjoyments to which the ancient writers invite when their works are read as literature, or are studied with logical or aesthetic analysis, or are recited with a distinct regard to rhetorical praxis and improvement."

But it was too late for such concessions. As it happened, the proponents of modern languages were less interested in reducing traditional drill work than in demonstrating that their own subject lent itself to it:

> Let "German" for students of the grade with which we have mainly to do mean an intelligent acquisition of its sounds, a drill in the various laws of its phonology, Ablaut, Umlaut, Grimm's Law, English and German corresponderes and cognates, syntactical analysis of Lessing's and Schiller's Prose, and of the difficult parts of Faust and of Nathan der Weise, the reading of the masterpieces of German literature, speaking and writing the language, and we claim without presumption, that the discipline acquired by going through such courses, while *different* from the discipline afforded by the study of Greek is not *inferior* to it.

Doubtless Brandt was right: philology did make the modern languages, even English, as difficult as the classics. The philologists had solved the problem that had perennially thwarted the claim of English literature to be a classroom subject: that you could not examine in it.

Francis A. March made the point with mild sarcasm in another MLA paper in 1892: whereas "the early professors had no recondite learning applicable to English, and did not know what to do with classes in it, they can now make English as hard as Greek." March's top-heavily philological manual of 1879 bore out his statement: pages and pages about pronominal elements and grammatical equivalents, and not a word about the Teutonic national character or the ultimate unity of civilization.

"Generalization Is No Longer as Easy as in the Days of Taine"

What was supposed to promote a unified vision of civilization, then, became an exercise in what Norman Foerster later described as an "atomistic view of learning," in which "it was apparently assumed that the facts, once in, would of themselves mean something. Synthesis, interpretation, and application were postponed to a steadily receding future." In Wellek's words, "the romantic concept of the evolution and the continuity of literature decayed so quickly that nothing was left of it save the superstition that works of literature could be reduced to compounds of parallels and sources." There is some evidence that this degeneration had in fact already occurred in Germany and was merely recapitulated in the United States some fifty years later.

Wellek says that "Teutonic racialism, the inspiration of the founders of Germanistics, was, for very obvious reasons, a very artificial growth in America; and so was romantic medievalism." But Teutonic racialism, as we have seen, did not seem such an "artificial growth" in the America of the seventies and eighties—it was not until World War I that it came to be regarded as wholly alien—and racialism of other kinds did not seem artificial at all. The narrowed scope of philological science and the deterioration of literary nationalism in the early modern university cannot be explained by the decline of Teutonic or other kinds of racialism because there was no such decline. The phenomenon is more plausibly explained by the positivist temper of early professionalism, which worked against broad cultural generalization.

What excited the new academic professionals about the historical program of Taine was not its Anglo-Saxon patriotism—which they took for granted—but its susceptibility to scientific observation and formulation. Taine thought that his famous triad of "race, milieu, and moment," the components of any national culture, was in principle as susceptible to analysis and even to prediction as were the quantifiable phenomena of matter. "If these forces could be measured and computed," Taine speculated, "we might deduce from them as from a formula the characteristics of future civilization."

Edmund Wilson later pointed out what was spurious in Taine's pretense that "he will merely present the evidence and allow us to make our own conclusions," for it never occurred to Taine "that we may ask ourselves who it is that is selecting the evidence and why is he making this particular choice. It never seems to occur to him that we may accuse him of having conceived the simplification first and then having collected the evidence to fit it." Overconfidence in generalizations tends to produce a distrust of generalizations, and Wilson notes that already, "by Taine's time, the amassment of facts for their own sake was coming to be regarded as one of the proper functions of history." By the 1880s philologists had come to regard it as almost the only function.

The great British philologist, W. W. Skeat, who was elected to the Chair in Anglo-Saxon at Oxford in 1878, became famous for puncturing the fanciful etymologies by which gentleman scholars gave words a colorful folk-significance. For example, Skeat ridiculed those scholarly amateurs who derived the word "foxglove" from "folk's glove," observing that though such derivation might be "poetical," "this does not alter the fact that it is entirely false." Skeat proceeded to state the essential creed of the modern philologist:

> The business of the student of language is to ascertain what were the actual forms of names in olden times, and not be wise above what is written by inventing names which our forefathers *ought* to have employed. The philologist is not concerned with what ought to have been said; his business is to pursue strictly historical methods. . . . If etymology is to be scientific, the appeal lies to the facts; and the facts, in this case, are accurate quotations, with exact references, from all available authors.

Skeat would not have regarded it as a pertinent objection that "facts" of this order did not deserve to be put at the center of English education.

Yet Skeat's corrosive scepticism could not be conjured away by well-intentioned pleas for breadth. For all Taine's pretensions to laboratory precision, his characterizations of national types were for the most part unintentionally comic sterotypes. Consider, for instance, Taine's description of the ancient Greeks as

> men who live half naked, in the gymnasia, or in the public squares . . . bent on making their bodies lithe and strong, on conversing, discussing, voting, carrying on patriotic piracies, nevertheless lazy and temperate, with three

urns for their furniture, two anchovies in a jar of olive oil for their food, waited on by slaves, so as to give them leisure to cultivate their understanding and exercise their limbs."

By professional standards, this "olive oil" picture of the ancient world would seem merely embarrassing by the 1880s, as would Taine's account of the history of English literature as a series of permutations in which crude Saxon vitality is tempered by subtle Norman intelligence. As a scholar would put it in 1915, "easy generalization is no longer as easy as in the days of Taine. To a conspicuous degree we would rather be right than interesting."

This comment neatly points up the problem facing any philologist who tried to go beyond the accumulation of facts. Consider the case of C. Alphonso Smith, a Ph. D. product of Johns Hopkins and the founder of *Studies in Philology* at the University of North Carolina, but also a possessor of unusually broad interests who gave courses in the novel and American literature and became a popular lecturer to lay audiences throughout the South. In an 1899 MLA paper, Smith urged the necessity of rescuing the study of syntax from the "barren array of statistics" into which it had fallen. "Counting has . . . taken the place of weighing," Smith said—he here echoed Boeckh's scorn for mere "counting, piece by piece"—and consequently the study of syntax had been "divorced from the vitalizing influence of literature."

Smith's response was to reassert the ideal of Taine. Why, he asked,

> should not syntax aid in the interpretation of history? History is one: a nation's art, science, architecture, laws, literature, and language are but parts of a larger whole. . . . Shall we study the evolution of a people's character in the way they build their bridges and highways and homes, and not in the way they build their sentences?

Smith's intentions were admirable, but his execution fell short. He argued, for example, that because syntactical peculiarities "testify to a fund of common intelligence and common interests," a purely syntactical study could yield conclusions about "a people's gradual nationalization, and indicate how far collectivism was replacing individualism." Such a desperate attempt to make syntax "interesting" could only induce scholars to stick to counting.

The example suggests why, increasingly, Aryan racial theory could be expressed in its old sweeping form only by the kind of generalist critic who felt under no obligation to provide scholarly evidence. And even that kind of critic was becoming cautious, as we will see.

From Philology to Literature

According to Michael Warner, in the 1880s, philologists "in increasing numbers . . . decided that they could do more than their philological work. Literary studies, some of them argued, could be *added* to the purview of the profession." This argument was in some ways only an extension of the logic of professional study: the same specialized rigor and impatience with amateurism that had produced the scientific study of the modern languages led to the conclusion that literature should be treated as a domain in its own right. But the move to include literature was also a response to the growing expectations placed on English as a potential cultural force and the consequent recognition that linguistic study alone could not meet them.

At the MLA convention of 1888, Morton W. Easton, a French philologist at the University of Pennsylvania, argued that

> the teacher of the undergraduate . . . is a member of the guild of literature, and it is only as such, and not as an imperfect imitator of the teachers of the exact sciences that he, or the teacher of any other tongue, dead as well as living, can attain to the true dignity of his post. . . . All this study of [philological] origins, in whatever field we find it, is work of a partly ephemeral and in one sense a lower order and should be regarded merely as the road to something else. We could make scholars in this way who should remain essentially barbarians.

Even more pointedly, former president E. H. Magill, another French philologist from Swarthmore, addressing the membership at the 1892 convention, tartly speculated that it was "as much as you can hope for" if 5 percent of the students under the professors' tutelage "pursue courses of study which would make the investigations which you are pursuing with great interest and value to science valuable to them directly. . . . Now what are you going to do with the other 95 percent? that is the point."

The interests of "the other 95 percent" clearly seemed to call for a more "literary" way of treating literature. In 1883, T. H. Hunt of Princeton had called for "philosophic and critical methods" to replace "the purely historical method of names and dates, incidents and events"—the staple of textbook literary history taught out of manuals like Shaw and Cleveland. Invoking the old, broad idea of philology, which had envisaged a unity between linguistic fact and the higher "thought" and "spirit" of literary expression, Hunt argued that "by safely gradationed stages" the study of the English language should "rise from a somewhat formal examination of phraseology and structure to a real philological study of the tongue in its content and its great linguistic changes . . . ," and that this should in turn lead to "the study of literature and style." Thus the student would move from such matters as "First English Philology in Caedmon, Beowulf and Alfred" to the "historical, linguistic, legendary, poetic, and rhetorical" topics gathered "about one such poem as the Faerie Queene or Comus." English would culminate in "the study of the great forms of poetry, of the principles of poetic art, of the leading canons of style as illustrated in English classics, of the life and times of an author as related to his literary productions, of the influence of other literatures upon the English." Here, at last, was a conception of "English" that was liberated from linguistic restrictions without sacrificing anything in mental discipline. As Hunt put it, describing his program in a book of 1891, "all this, we submit, is in the strictest sense disciplinary; tending directly to the education and enlargement of mental power; entering, at once, as a vital factor into what we call a man's intellectual life."

But what were the "philosophic and critical methods" that would inform the "gradationed stages" from the narrower to the broader kinds of literary study? How would "historical, linguistic, legendary, poetic, and rhetorical" considerations come together coherently in a study of *The Faerie Queene*? For all his talk of philosophic methods and disciplinary rigor, Hunt's suggestions about how such goals were to be accomplished were weak. Hunt's view of the "literary" as an expression of "great thoughts" hardly got beyond the commonplaces of the old oratorical tradition of the college, though even those commonplaces might have been more nourishing than philological analysis.

In any case, as long as the procedures of professional accreditation remained narrowly philological, they lagged behind the newly literary and cultural conception of the profession's goals and were curiously irrelevant to them. As Warner points out, the profession trained its teachers as philologists and trusted that somehow that training would fit them to teach literature. Warner cites the case of Harvard's F. N. Robinson, who "wrote a philologist's dissertation on Chaucer's syntax. But as the profession changed, and as its practices of research and interpretation brought about the conception of literature as a field of discourse and inquiry, his accreditation was in no wise diminished, and that dissertation on Chaucer's syntax qualified him to teach *The Canterbury Tales*." Robinson exemplified the anomaly that would become notorious in the later hortatory literature of the profession:

what the professor of literature is trained to do has little relation to what he or she teaches.

In retrospect, we can see that the anomaly resulted from a cultural transition the institution was not prepared for. Early philologists were suddenly being asked to shoulder general education responsibilities that to many of them, trained as professional research men, seemed no part of their proper business. But as the profession expanded and became the beneficiary of increasing institutional support, the excuse that one was after all a mere scholar, not an educator, or at least that it was not one's concern if one's teaching appealed only to a tiny fraction of the student body, seemed lame or irresponsible. There remained an ambiguity as to how far the profession could be blamed for failing at its larger responsibilities, and this ambiguity showed up in professional self-justifications.

On the one hand, as Albert S. Cook of Yale sadly noted in his MLA presidential address of 1906, it was said that the literature department had been caught up in changes it had not anticipated. "English has been thrust forward with a rapidity almost alarming," Cook said, "in view of the fact that most of us who represent it have been brought up with a lower conception of our responsibilities, and with a more restricted view of our opportunities, than is indicated by the present exigency." On the other hand, Cook had only a few years earlier refused to accept any "lower conception" of the profession's responsibilities. In 1897 he had admonished the association regarding the need to make the older, comprehensive meaning of "philology" "the prevalent one, by consistently adhering to it in our practice, and, so far as possible, inducing others to accept and adopt it."

This contradiction with respect to the breadth of the profession's aims was reflected in Cook's own career. Cook would later be described by a former student, Henry Seidel Canby, as "a finished product of the German philological mill, who had been brought to the university to introduce methodology—how he rolled the word on his tongue!—into our somewhat haphazard graduate school of language and literature," and who "brought the gospel of science in literary studies." Cook had taught at Johns Hopkins, where he had been the first professor of English and had organized the department in 1879. He was an indefatigable contributor to *Speculum*, *Modern Language Notes*, and *Philological Quarterly*, and eventually the editor of seventy-five volumes of the *Yale Studies in English*, in which he published many of his graduate students' papers.

Cook was capable of speaking grandiloquently, in a published graduation address, about "the artistic ordering of life," and of praising "the palmy days of the Renaissance" when "men were not so one-sided as they have become in the epoch which has since intervened." He evidently identified himself with the humanism of Sidney's *Defence of Poesie* and the other great poetic treatises that he edited. Yet Canby could discern little connection between Cook's humanistic ideals and his philological teaching and publication. Cook's scholarly discoveries were not steps leading to a broader study, Canby observed, "but rather chips of literary history, the date of a Northumbrian cross, the classic parallels to a line in Milton." Cook's scholarship and his larger cultural interests were apparently closely related in his mind, but he had no way of uniting them in his work.

So it was primarily a ritualistic event when philologists like Cook reminded their colleagues of the need to revive the older, comprehensive meaning of philology. By 1897, when he spoke these words, Cook conceded that philology had in fact become "a totally independent branch of learning," creating an "estrangement of the study of language from that of literature." Henceforth, invoking the old meaning of philology would be a ceremonial gesture, when it was not a useful way of warding off criticism by depicting literary studies as they were supposed to be, rather than as they were.

The estrangement Cook described was arguably not accidental but a result of the peculiar way in which professional literary studies had developed, their course having been determined not by any analysis of the larger educational, cultural, or literary situation, or by much collective debate over that situation, but by professional opportunism. An ideal of synthesis continued to be honored in theory, but in practice the department was merely the sum total of the research interests of individual faculty, without structural correlation or contrast between them. As Wellek says, "the gestures toward criticism,  synthesis, the history of the human mind, remained mostly gestures or the private virtues of an individual who was unable to make his ideas felt institutionally."

CHAPTER SIX

The Generalist Opposition

The great difficulty is that Kittredge and his band are in their own field strong men, whereas the so-called "literary" men are likely to be weak-willed dilettantes. . . . The great field of virile ideas is left deserted by the philologists on the one side and the semi-aesthetes on the other.

IRVING BABBITT

The "individual who was unable to make his ideas felt institutionally" was likely to be the generalist, an academic type that begins to take on distinct identity in the 1870's. The generalists defined themselves by contrast with the specialized investigators, but the gulf between the two was never absolute. An investigator might himself be a generalist in his views of literature, culture, and teaching, or he might vent his generalist side on public occasions (such as MLA presidential addresses) which called for opinions on matters beyond the scope of his research. In theory, professional research was only a vehicle of general humanistic culture, but in practice very few individuals and fewer departments managed to integrate the two.

The generalists were spokesmen for the missionary view of literature they inherited from Arnold, Ruskin, and other Victorian apostles of culture. Their idea of culture played an important role in legitimating the claims of literary studies in the university. We saw earlier that "the prestige of philology served to *justify* English studies without necessarily *limiting* them." In a similar fashion, the prestige of the generalists' humanism served to justify literary studies without determining their intellectual character.

The generalists thus embodied the clash between humanism and professionalism over what they referred to as cultural "leadership." It was because they believed that Arnoldian culture should exert national leadership that the generalists eagerly supported the profes-

sional ambitions of departments of English and urged the legitimation of American literature as a college subject. Yet this larger vision of cultural leadership was precisely what led the generalists to find fault with those departments for betraying this leadership responsibility to professional interests.

The Generalist Creed

Harvard virtually invented the generalist-professor before the Civil War when it engaged Henry Wadsworth Longfellow and later James Russell Lowell to teach Dante and other modern European writers, and Lowell became famous for the casual, impressionistic style of teaching described in an earlier chapter. After the war, the type reappeared at Harvard in the splendidly imperious figure of Charles Eliot Norton, another great teacher of Dante who was Professor of Fine Art from 1871 to 1898. It appeared again in the writing teachers of the nineties—Wendell, Briggs, Gates, and Copeland—who divided Harvard English with research men such as Kittredge. Other early figures who notably fit the pattern were Corson of Cornell (1870–1903); George Edward Woodberry of the University of Nebraska (1870–78), Amherst (1880–82), and Columbia (1891–1904); and college professor–presidents on the fringes of literary culture such as Woodrow Wilson of Princeton and Franklin Carter of Williams.

Second-generation generalists included such figures as Charles Mills Gayley of the University of California at Berkeley (1889–1923); Vida D. Scudder of Wellesley (1887–1927); William Lyon Phelps of Yale (1892–1933); Brander Mattews of Columbia (1891–1924); John Erskine of Amherst (1900–1903) and Columbia (1903–37); Bliss Perry of Williams (1881–93), Princeton (1893–1900), and Harvard (1907–30); Fred Lewis Pattee of Penn State (1894–1927); Robert Morss Lovett of the University of Chicago (1893–1921); Henry Van Dyke of Princeton (1899–1923); Irving Babbitt of Harvard (1892–1933); and Stuart P. Sherman of Illinois (1907–24). Like the research scholars, the generalists had their lineages of descent from teacher to pupil. Lionel Trilling, a student of Erskine at Columbia in the mid-twenties, was aware that "Erskine had the been the pupil at Columbia of Woodberry, who at Harvard had been the pupil of Charles Eliot Norton, who had been the friend of Carlyle, Ruskin, and Matthew Arnold." Norton taught Babbitt at Harvard; Babbitt taught Sherman (as well as T. S. Eliot) and met Paul Elmer More; Norton and Lowell taught Barrett Wendell, who taught William Lyon Phelps, and so on. On the other hand, not all of the figures I have listed saw themselves as part of a group at all. Irving Babbitt, in some ways the arch-generalist, whose *Literature and the American College* could be taken as the definitive statement of the generalist philosophy, felt little solidarity with men like Phelps, Van Dyke, and Erskine, whom he regarded as dilettantes and popularizers. Despite such differences, a certain common outlook can be discerned, based on a shared distrust of the research establishment and a common attitude toward the place of culture in America.

In social outlook, the generalists tended toward a "mugwump" view that saw national leadership as the virtual birthright of the cultured classes. Norton believed that "only the *Nation* [which Norton helped to found with his friend E. L. Godkin] & Harvard & Yale College" stood as "barriers against the invasion of modern barbarism and vulgarity." A friend of Ruskin and the executor of his estate, Norton gave lectures that were described as "fiery denunciations of the vulgarity and corruption of modern society, in Ruskin's best vein." These were parodied by undergraduates in statements like, "I purpose this afternoon to make a few remarks on the hor-ri-ble vul-gar-ity of EVERYTHING." Another Harvard wit observed that "Mr Norton is so fastidious that sometimes he can't even tolerate himself." Barrett Wendell at the turn of the century still regretted the freeing of the slaves, an event he blamed for having permanently "lowered the personal dignity of public life, by substituting for the traditional rule of the conservative gentry the obvious dominance of the less educated classes." Wendell thought "modern ethnology" had proved that "though native Africans are not literally neolithic, they certainly linger far beyond the social stage which has been reached by modern Europe or America."

Yet the same reactionary outlook that scorned the vulgarity of the masses scorned also the vulgarity of organized business and the assimilation of higher education by the values of the industrial marketplace. Lowell in 1889 had deplored the "barbarizing plutocracy which seems to be so rapidly supplanting the worship of what alone is lovely and enduring." Hiram Corson, who had been "a zealous opponent of slavery," was "strenuously apprehensive of the social effects of concentrated wealth." Henry Van Dyke attacked not only "the red peril of the rise of the demagogue," but also "the yellow peril of the dominance of wealth" and "the black peril of the rise of the boss." Norton promoted the cause of education for blacks, and his harsh attacks from the lecture podium on American imperialism during the Spanish-American War earned him a public rebuke from a United States senator. It was Norton above all who established the pattern of the professor as a kind of internal *emigré* from American culture. In Alan Trachtenberg's words, Norton was among "the first group of writers and thinkers. . . . to view themselves as alienated, and to describe and judge their times against the measure of their own alienation."

To be sure, this alienation did not necessarily prevent one from remaining on comfortable terms with American culture. Van Dyke, who continued to practice as a Presbyterian minister after coming to Princeton in 1899, wrote tracts glorifying patriotism and Christmas and preached "every Sunday, usually at university and college chapels," professing as his one aim "to lift the world up and make it a better, happier one than he found it." Even more conspicuously at one with his surroundings was "Billy" Phelps, described as "a sort of academic Rotarian" and a man of "abounding health and energy, . . . a complete extrovert [who] loved travelling about, and was a prodigious 'mixer.' " Santayana, though he could not help liking him, was uneasy at the way Phelps (and Yale generally) cultivated "enthusiasm . . . for its own sake, as flow of life, no matter in what direction" and "let the drift of the times dictate [his] purposes."

At the other political extreme, and virtually in a category by herself, was one of the most remarkable of the forgotten figures of early American literary studies, Vida Dutton Scudder of Wellesley. A relative of the publishers, E. P. Dutton and Horace E. Scudder, a follower of Ruskin, whose lectures she attended at Oxford in 1884, Vida Scudder revived the social radicalism latent in respectable New England idealism since the Puritans, preaching Christian socialism at a time when the mere expression of sympathy for labor unions was a dangerous act. Scudder's course in "Social Ideals in English Letters" must have been the first of its kind anywhere. Only Robert Morss Lovett of the University of Chicago, who dropped out of teaching after World War I, matched Scudder's combination of high literary culture with left-wing social radicalism. Scudder remained active, to the end of her life, in the trade union movement and in the settlement houses of Boston and the Lower East Side of New York. Her autobiography, *On Journey*, refutes the current tendency to assume that traditional humanistic idealism must always have embraced retrograde politics.

A few generalists like Corson and Woodberry had drifted into teaching from public lecturing or literary journalism, and several of them moved freely between the academic world and that of editing and publishing. Several mastered the philological rigors of German graduate training, but, with the exceptions of Norton and Gayley, none of them aspired to a reputation as a scholar in the conventional sense. It was symptomatic that Bliss Perry, who excelled in graduate work at Heidelberg and Strassburg, never found a way to draw on this background in his later writing and teaching.

The common bond of the generalists was their belief that, in Trilling's words, "great works of art and thought have a decisive part in shaping the life of a polity," and their consequent impatience with the narrow pedantry of research, which in their most pessimistic moods they regarded as a betrayal of everything Matthew Arnold had stood for. As John Henry Raleigh points out in his study of Arnold's American influence, Arnoldians like Stuart P. Sherman contrasted Arnold's views with those of prevailing literary studies. They argued "that Arnold, despite the fact that his standards were unsound according to the rules and regulations of modern scientific scholarship, was more truly a cultural leader than a medieval specialist could be."

The generalists' educational aim was essentially to adapt the old college ideal of liberal culture to the challenges of modern times. With Reverend Van Dyke they thought the university "exists for the disinterested pursuit of truth, for the development of the intellectual life, and for the rounded development of character. Its primary aim is not to fit men for any specific industry, but to give them those things which are everywhere essential to intelligent living." With Vida Scudder they believed that "teaching English literature means something other than investigating details of literary history, or studying technique," that it "means, in last analysis, establishing vital contacts between one's students and racial experience at its most intense." With Erskine they were "distrustful of colleagues who lecture on poems or novels or plays and put the authors in this or that pigeonhole, but cannot themselves write a page that anyone would print or that anyone would read."

The generalists channeled into literature emotions that, a half-century earlier, would have likely been expressed in evangelical Christianity, Unitarianism, or Transcendentalism, investing the experience of literature with the redemptive influence their ministerial ancestors had attributed to the conversion experience. Whether they were pessimists like Norton or healthy-minded enthusiasts like Van Dyke and Phelps, they saw themselves as the upholders of spiritual values against the crass materialism of American business life, of which the "production" ethos of the philologists was for them only another manifestation. Like Erskine, they held that the successful teacher of literature "must believe in a spiritual life, he must assume in every being a soul," and that "it is impossible to interpret the masterpieces of the last three thousand years by impoverished philosophies which define man as a biological or chemical accident, or as the byproduct of economic forces." Like Bliss Perry, the generalists defended "the amateur spirit," hoping it could somehow "penetrate, illuminate, idealize, the brute force, the irresistibly on-sweeping mass, of our vast industrial democracy."

GENERALIST PEDAGOGY

The generalists tended to dispense with elaborate pedagogical theories and methods in the effort, as they saw it, to let the great masterpieces of literature teach themselves. Erskine summed up their creed when he said that a book should "speak for itself," needing no elaborate "screen of historical and critical apparatus to make it available to students or general readers." Woodrow Wilson, who taught political science at Princeton before becoming its president in 1902, wrote in 1893 that literature "has a quality to move you, and you can never mistake it, if you have any blood in you. It has also a power to instruct you which is as effective as it is subtle, and which no research or systematic method can ever rival." Such a view led generalists to think of their writing and teaching not as an application of methodology, but as an attempt to disencumber literature from methodology and superfluous information—rather the way evangelical ministers had tried to free the holy spirit from the mediation of church and dogma.

This attitude produced an inspirational style of teaching that aimed to restore "an awakening touch" between teacher and student. This "spellbinding" manner, as practiced by Reverend Van Dyke, was described by a student, who recalled "a crowded lecture-room with the sun streaming into it, and perhaps a hundred young men or so, naturally inattentive, at the moment completely absorbed, and amongst them a goodly number, at least, who find themselves in the position of one young man who is suddenly lifted up and caught up and held by the thrilling beauty of words," by a lecturer who is able to "reincarnate the poetry and personality and thoughts of poets who are dead."

The same spellbinding style that drew hundreds, sometimes thousands, of undergraduates to the generalist's courses also tended to attract the scorn and derision of his scholarly colleagues. As if in deliberate contrast, scholars went out of their way to cultivate a dry, impersonal teaching style, a signal of their refusal to stoop to mere entertaining. Michael Warner nicely captures the contrasting stereotypes which grew up around the two styles. The generalist

> is pictured as setting afire the imaginations of undergraduates in his lectures, or as warming their hearts in private conversations in his quiet but

cozy study, or as pausing to speak to the elder ladies of the town while on a stroll. Above all, he is pictured as present, as personable. The professional's ideal type, on the other hand, is the researcher. As a teacher and mentor, he is a failure. His setting is a solitary office. He is conspicuously absent from the circles in which the teacher is thought of so warmly. Those with whom he associates communicate with him by writing—especially through published articles.

Again, one has to remember that these opposing styles might combine in one person. Babbitt pointed out that "the curious interplay of philology and impressionism" (of the "Baconian" and the "Rousseauist") were "sometimes united in the same person." He said that even "the more vigorous and pushing teachers of language," who "feel that they must assert their manhood by philological research," at bottom agree with the dilettante in seeing literature as a source "of more or less agreeable personal impressions." The occasional scholar might show surprising gifts as a spellbinder in the classroom, reading poetry aloud in an emotional manner. As Wellek says, scholars "taught graduate students bibliography and sources . . . , and meanwhile they read poetry to undergraduates in a trembling or unctuous voice." Even when present in one person, the two functions rarely meshed.

If the generalists were dismissed by scholars as superficial, they could strike back by depicting the scholars, in Warner's words, as "maimed men whose lives had been forgotten in the perverse development of mere intellect." In the professional setting, however, it was the generalists who were most likely to feel like "maimed men." When Erskine published a popular book, *The Private Life of Helen of Troy*, his department chairman at Columbia, the Shakespearean A. H. Thorndike, "remarked to a colleague that he had always feared I was at heart a journalist rather than a scholar." Even Barrett Wendell, seemingly the epitome of Harvard culture at its most self-confident, could be apologetic about his situation. When Phelps became a graduate student at Harvard in 1890, Wendell bleakly admitted to him, "I don't know anything. You have probably already taken my measure." Phelps saw that Wendell "felt out of place in a modern German-trained American college Faculty, surrounded as he was by research scholars and philologists. He had never studied Anglo-Saxon, he knew no German, he had never studied for the degree of Doctor of Philosophy, which had in general become the sole gateway to college teaching."

The system of accreditation that made a "gateway" of the philologically oriented Ph.D. put the generalists at a disadvantage. Again to quote Warner, "Non-professional critics such as Corson . . . had no means within the institution of producing successors and no particular interest in producing successors." Babbitt noted that "the philologists are better organized than the dilettantes, and command the approaches to the higher positions through their control of the machinery of the doctor's degree." Babbitt himself, according to More, "felt 'bitterly the way in which Kittredge and one or two others' had 'blocked his advancement' at Harvard." When Thorndike became chairman at Columbia in the twenties, he prevented Stuart Sherman's appointment there. Erskine had "wanted Stuart because he was a writer, a distinguished practitioner of the art he taught. That was the very reason Thorndike wouldn't have him."

THE GENERALIST CRITIQUE OF RESEARCH

The generalists produced a cogent critique of the research system, yet their own position was often either self-contradictory or devoid of substance. Generalist manifestos were frequently no more than vapid attacks on the analytical approach to literature as such, incanting words like "literature" in a talismanic fashion, as if the power of literature were in and of itself sufficient to overcome an institutional problem. For example, Woodrow Wilson, in "Mere Literature," seemed to question the need for any principled study of literature, maintaining that "there is no science of literature," that "literature in its essence is mere spirit," and that "you must experience it rather than analyze it too formally." Literature, Wilson said, is an instrument that "opens our hearts to receive the experiences of great men and great races." James Russell Lowell, urging the MLA in 1889 to shift the emphasis from philology to literature, spoke of literature as a "mysterious and pervasive essence always in itself beautiful, not always so in the shapes which it informs, but even then full of infinite suggestion."

Such vague phrases obviously assumed an audience that, by class and breeding, already took their meaning for granted. Since by the time Lowell and Wilson expressed these views, that kind of audience was on the defensive, if it still existed, such an approach was self-defeating. If Wilson was right that "if you have any blood in you," "you can never mistake" literature's power "to move you," then it was not clear why anyone needed to be *taught* literature at all. Presumably students would respond instinctively when in the presence of the real thing—but if they did not, what good would be done by talk of "literature's mysterious essence"? How was such talk more illuminating than biographical and linguistic facts?

We begin here to see a contradiction in the generalists' position that

helped make their criticisms of the research system ineffectual. The very fact that the common literary culture the generalists wanted to restore had broken down meant that merely to invoke the catchphrases of that culture—literature's mysterious essence and so forth—was an ineffective tactic. It was ineffective in the same way as the old classicists' rhetoric had been when they invoked "the great-impalpable-essence-and-precious-residuum theory" of the classics, to the derision of Charles Francis Adams.

To put it another way, as long as the generalists distrusted analysis and theory, they were necessarily inhibited from elaborating their case against the research professors. Even as they urged "literature" as a sufficient and self-interpreting end that presumably made theory and methodology superfluous, the generalists could not help seeing that the departments around them were deplorably lacking in theoretical vision, as their own persistent complaints about these same departments' paucity of "general ideas" implied. The generalists seemed dimly to perceive that they were themselves calling for a "theory" of some kind, in opposition to the mindless stockpiling of information. But instead of following through on that perception, they retreated to the social pose of an earlier era, when literary men could still act as if reflection was beneath the dignity of the gentleman, whose culture was tacitly presupposed.

Erskine, for instance, wrote a celebrated essay entitled "The Moral Obligation to Be Intelligent" (1913), in which he argued that Americans harbored a national prejudice "against mind." Yet did not Erskine exemplify some of that prejudice when he argued that literature should be taught with a minimum of "historical and critical apparatus"? Only Babbitt among the generalists readily acknowledged the need for a theory, complaining that "the modern languages have had so much practical success in supplanting Greek and Latin that they have hardly felt the need as yet of justifying themselves theoretically." But unlike Babbitt, other generalists tended to identify theoretical justifications with academic methodology and thus with the threat to "mere literature"—which is one reason why Babbitt tended to write them all off as dilettantes. As Babbitt saw, by surrendering matters of theory to the research scholars, the generalists were left with a position whose very efficacy depended on a literary culture that had disappeared.

The lack of content in the generalists' position was compounded by a certain reluctance to offend. Even when they attacked the new philology, they frequently hedged their remarks with conciliatory qualifications. Perhaps their gentlemanly conception of culture, or the social bonds they shared with their scholarly opponents, made them reluctant to polemicize. Perhaps they hesitated to dwell on difficulties in an enterprise that was otherwise enjoying a splendid boom. Or perhaps they felt they had to adopt a conciliatory tone in order to get a hearing. Whatever the reason, it is notable that even men like Lowell and Franklin Carter, who strongly regretted the trivialization of literature by pedantic scholarship, muted their criticisms when addressing their colleagues.

Lowell, in his 1889 address, while objecting that "the purely linguistic side in the teaching of [the modern languages] seems in the way to getting more than its fitting share," and urging the Association to "rescue ourselves from what Milton calls 'these grammatic flats and shallows,' " inconsistently rejoiced that "already a very great advance has been made. The modern languages have nothing more of which to complain. There are nearly as many professors and assistants employed in teaching them at Harvard now as there were students of them when I was in college."

Carter of Williams, at the meeting of 1885, objected that "etymologies and comparative grammars are luxuries in modern language study—necessary to the teacher, to his knowledge, his enjoyment, his self-respect, but rarely contributing much to the pupil's better knowledge of the author." Indeed, "the things that interest the teacher for the time being are not for that reason best for the pupil." Yet Carter still asked that "all honor be paid to that enlarging brotherhood of scholars, worthy teachers, who have changed this conception [of modern language study] and who are in this country pushing their scientific studies in modern philology in every direction." Carter praised the "attempt to teach the modern languages in the scientific spirit of modern philology," which he said had "elevated the conception of modern language study and banished the associations" that once linked "the title of professor of French" with "dancing, and chirography," or defined an Italian professor as "one who taught the language of Dante and the music of the banjo."

Carter even praised "the new, resistless spirit of inquiry, guided by natural systematic methods." If irony hedged Carter's enthusiasm it was diplomatically masked, as when he took note of "the minuteness with which studies are prosecuted, the readiness with which an earnest man limits his field, but seeks to know all that has been done in it, the rapidity with which investigations are made and old theories attacked and sometimes supplanted," and observed that all these things "make it imperative on a true scholar to keep up with the published results in his special line of research in all modern tongues." Carter may or may not have considered such "keeping up" as a pointless mania, but here he was careful to stop short of giving offense.

The Failure of the Generalists

Another way the generalists acquiesced in their own defeat was by accepting the sharp territorial division between the graduate school and the undergraduate college. Lowell said in his 1889 address that in objecting to the overemphasis on "the linguistic side" of literary study, he meant only to insist "that in our college courses [that side] should be a separate study, and that, good as it is in itself, it should, in the scheme of general instruction, be restrained to its own function as the guide to something better," that is, literature. It was as if a kind of unspoken partition treaty had assigned professional methodology to graduate study, leaving liberal or "general instruction" in command of the undergraduate major and other college courses. But Lowell did not ask how any "scheme of general instruction" could take shape when the curriculum was an uncorrelated assortment of philological and historical specialties. The problem was not merely that some departments put philological methods at the center of the undergraduate curriculum or employed teachers whose interests ill prepared them to think about what general instruction might mean. It was also that nothing in the department's organization caused the question to be raised of how the parts related to one another, leaving the conception of general instruction to take care of itself.

Once it had become clear that the graduate school conception of literary study was inevitably shaping the way literature was taught to undergraduates, the strategy of speaking as if the undergraduate college could be kept free of contamination by the graduate school became hypocritical. The very idea of "the college" became a form of sentimentality, acquiring emotional connotations in proportion as the thing itself ceased to exist. But as long as the college idea remained intact on the level of sentiment, and as long as a few conspicuous generalists remained on hand to personify it, departments did not feel obliged to confront the fact that neither it nor any other coherent idea integrated their activities.

The lack of connection between research and teaching could always be covered over by the chestnut—still dear to college deans—that research and teaching are inseparable. Had not President Gilman and Thomas Henry Huxley said so at the inauguration ceremony of Johns Hopkins, where Huxley repeated with approval Gilman's statement that "the best investigators are usually those who have also the responsibility of instruction"? There need be no incompatibility between the investigator and the teacher, for, as Felix Schelling later said, the "teacher interested in some investigation of his own" thereby keeps "his work in the classroom fresh and vitalized by a larger outlook than mere pedagogy can give him." The point was true enough as far as it went, but it conveniently passed over the fact that the "larger outlook" was rarely present in "investigation." So there was either a gap between research and teaching or else the kind of questionable concurrence in which the professor simply taught his research. An educator of a later era, Harry Gideonse, put it best: "solemnly the customary banalities about 'the teacher vs. the research man' are repronounced and reevaluated, and equally solemnly the conventional conclusions are rediscovered about the inevitable togetherness of good teaching and good research. . . . To me, however, all these questions are like an argument about the cabin decorations, while the steamer has a hole in her bottom."

How circumstances conspired to force the generalists to conform to the research model is seen in two anecdotes. The first involves Woodrow Wilson, who, on becoming president of Princeton in 1902, embarked on a strenuous campaign to restore the centrality of the college. By this time the whole social atmosphere of higher education was changing, so that for Wilson, the enemy was not merely the research interests, but the social snobbery of the fashionable "eating clubs" that functioned as a postgraduate sorting system for elite positions in business and management. Wilson called for "a period of synthesis" that would "put things together in a connected and thought-out scheme of endeavor" to counteract "dispersion and standardless analysis." He installed his preceptorial system, in which young doctors of philosophy would "live in the dormitories and direct the reading and studies of the students," thus restoring something of the primitive democracy of college life. He fought a plan for a new graduate school that would be separate from the college and in Wilson's view would threaten its unity. Appropriately, what finally defeated Wilson was the very success of Princeton's modern fund-raising machine. In 1910, an alumnus died leaving over ten million dollars earmarked for a separate graduate school. "This means defeat," Wilson said. "We can never overcome ten millions."

A second anecdote comes from Fred Lewis Pattee, who became professor of English at the land-grant university of Pennsylvania State in the 1890's. The Morrill Act of 1862 had specified that land-grant institutions should stress "agriculture and the mechanic arts . . . without excluding other scientific and classical studies," but land-grant institutions tended to measure all subjects by vocational yardsticks. Pattee recounts in his autobiography how, during the first years of his appointment, the administration at Penn State dropped a requirement in history in order to make room for a practicum in more technical subjects. "In vain," according to Pattee, "did the liberal arts minority on the faculty argue that the two subjects were in utterly different worlds." The decision posed an immediate problem: "All the students were required to take carpentry courses and other laboratory work, but what practicums could be found for liberal arts juniors and seniors?" Struggling with the problem, Pattee writes, I "at length thought of research as a solution. I could give the students the kind of work given those preparing for a graduate degree. I at once introduced what I called research courses in English."

The incident nicely illustrates the way even generalists like Pattee had no choice but to align themselves with the cause of research in order to make a place for their own interests. It also illustrates the usefully protean nature of the concept of research in the humanities. As Magali Sarfatti Larson observes, the fact that its early proponents valued research in the university as a "pure" inquiry with no ulterior purposes did not prevent them from touting it to outsiders for its usefulness.

"Life Is a Dirty Game"

At their most eloquent, the early generalists expressed a reaction against American materialism that would continue after them to be a powerful theme in American criticism. Yet their social criticism led for the most part to a defeatist feeling that the world had passed them by, that the spirit of vulgar materialism had taken over higher education itself and rendered their very lives a contradiction. This feeling induced some of them to drop out of teaching—most notably, George Edward Woodberry, who resigned his position at Columbia in 1904, and who, according to his colleague and former student Erskine, conveyed "a general sense of defeat" with regard to the college:

> He was living, he felt, in an age hostile to the finer things. Of President Butler and the Trustees he spoke always with respect, but with the implication that they shared the spirit of their time, and must therefore slight that side of man's nature which goes into the arts. It is no use trying to combat so strong a trend, he would say; life is a dirty game.

Woodberry told Erskine that "it was useless and perhaps harmful to make boys live a—for them—unnaturally ethical life which later they would be compelled to give up as soon as they got into that other life, which, as he insisted, is a dirty game."

The cheerful Erskine replied that he "had no sympathy with such ideas." But Erskine himself would leave teaching for public lecturing and a position at the Julliard School of Music. And to *his* former student, Randolph Bourne, Erskine's healthy minded optimism was not a much more helpful means of confronting the modern world than the pessimism of Norton and Woodberry had been. Bourne quoted Erskine's statement that his purpose as a teacher was "to give my boys the spirit of the authors, and let them judge between them for themselves," and he cited Erskine's belief that he could "trust my boys to feel the insufficiency of any purely materialistic interpretation of life." This was not enough for Bourne, who noticed that, impeccable as was Erskine's "critical taste where the classics are concerned," he was "reluctant about giving his opinion to those students who had come for some clue through the current literary maze." In a world of change, Bourne concluded, Erskine kept "the faith pure," but Bourne felt the need for a faith less pure.

Bourne wanted college education to become "a field for working out a background for the contemporary social world," but to do so it would have to overcome the polarities of hard investigation and soft appreciation, of specialized research and general ideas. The perception of a "division of sentiment . . . right in our own camp" became a commonplace in literature departments as early as the nineties. A neat statement of it was made by Calvin Thomas, a Germanist from Columbia, at the 1896 MLA meetings:

> On the one side are the men of letters and those whom they inspire, looking a little disdainfully upon the patient plodding, the extreme circumspection, of the philologists, and teaching by example that the important thing in dealing with literature is, as M. Tissot expresses it, "to talk well rather than to think well." Their ideal of the literary discourse tends toward the elegant *causerie*, which is apt to be interesting but not true.

On the other side were the philologists, who

> feel that what the literary men say consists pretty largely of cunningly-phrased guess-work, superficiality and personal bias. For their part they wish their work to rest on good foundations. It is the solidity of the fabric, not its beauty, that they care for. Thus they are tempted as a class (for every class has its besetting danger) to undervalue form and to confine themselves to somewhat mechanical investigations, such as promise definite, exact and unassailable results. They are suspicious of the larger

and more subtle questions of literature; and so their ideal gravitates in the direction of the amorphous *Abhandlung* which is apt to be true but not interesting.

Dilettantes versus investigators: the one all interesting but untrue generalizations, the other all true but sterile particularities, and evidently nothing in between. Babbitt later made much the same observation: "at one extreme of the average English department is the philological mediaevalist, who is grounded in Gothic and Old Norse and Anglo-Saxon; at the other extreme is the dilettante, who gives courses in daily themes, and, like the sophists of old, instructs ingenuous youth in the art of expressing itself before it has anything to express."

In 1915, MLA President Jefferson Fletcher of Columbia noted that whereas one kind of professor tends to "pander to the crowd," the other tends to demand "a full mind rather than an orderly one." The one peddles "a so-called 'broad human appeal,' which keeps its ear to the ground to hear how the cat jumps." The other proceeds "with foot-notiose precision," slavishly imitated by graduate students:

> The most esteemed doctor's examination I ever attended must have sounded from without like a continuous popping of corks, question, answer, question, answer, tic-tac. The candidate was as highly charged with the facts of literary history as a bottle of bock beer with gas. He fairly went to our heads. Among his facts were, of course, formulas and "isms." I don't know whether they meant anything in particular for him or not.

The trouble, Fletcher thought, was that:

> nearly all regarded literary formulas and "isms" as also mere matters of fact. For instance, a Platonist represented to them what Sidney, or Spenser, or Shelley *was. Platonism itself?*—Well, Platonism was a religion of beauty in woman. *Did Plato himself say that?* No, sir, you did. *Yes, but would Plato have said it?*—I . . . I suppose he would have—in principle. *What do you mean by* "in principle"?—Why . . . er . . . the logic of his ideas. *What is that logic?* I never had a course in Plato, sir.

Fletcher added that these students "carry a similar spirit into their research, as their thesis and first drafts of their doctoral dissertations prove."

Such perceptions produced a wave of professional talk about the need for better methods, and a substantial faction recommended various kinds of "criticism" as a way of overcoming the polarity of scholarship and appreciation. Since this early criticism movement did not achieve significant influence until later, I have deferred discussion of it to a later chapter. Suffice it here to say that no method was yet widely available for the kind of aesthetic interpretation that was being urged.

What was needed, in any case, was not merely new methods but some hard thinking and open debate about the larger cultural situation of literary studies. For the conflict between investigators and generalists was finally not simply methodological, but part of the larger crisis of literature and the arts in a mass society, where a gulf had developed between the "highbrow" inheritance of the cultivated and the "lowbrow" democracy around them. Instead of acknowledging the crisis and seeking to make it part of the context of its work—the sort of thing Randolph Bourne had in mind—the literature department acted as if representing the cultural tradition were sufficient, though its diffuse researches could hardly add up to a coherent tradition in the minds of most students or other outsiders. As long as the cultural crisis of literature was not part of the context of literary studies themselves, problems tended to be seen as problems of method, whether critical or pedagogical, and this in turn favored the drift toward positivistic research, seemingly the only pursuit that had direction and therefore commanded the respect of administrators and rival departments.

By the 1890s, disillusionment with the pretensions of linguistic philology for undergraduate—if not graduate—education was widespread, though a few hard-core departments like Johns Hopkins still kept philology at the center of the undergraduate literature program. But even as philology faltered, as it did in the nineties, the research model, with the emphasis shifted from philology to literary history, became more powerful than ever. The generalists remained prominent, and undergraduates crowded their classes, but their very acceptance in the university reflected their marginal relation to the profession as a whole, which did not have to argue with them or respond to their challenge. In an expanding university economy, the generalists could be placated with honored positions in the department, from which they could pursue their interests without interference.

Unexpectedly, the new principles of bureaucracy and the old code of gentility coincided: both discouraged open conflict as unseemly. Lowell and Carter may have avoided conflict for reasons different from those of Santayana's secularized professors—who did not oppose the genteel tradition but ignored it—but the result was much the same. In the structure of "patterned isolation" described by Veysey, the generalists held a place, but on the understanding that conventional scholars did not have to take them seriously.

And yet, what is surprising is how many conventional scholars in this period *did* take the challenge of the generalists seriously. Enough of them to create an interesting literature of professional self-criticism between 1890 and 1915, to which we will turn next.

CHAPTER SEVEN

Crisis at the Outset: 1890–1915

The bell rings and a troop of tired-looking boys, followed perhaps by a larger number of meek-eyed girls, file into the classroom, sit down, remove the expressions from their faces, open their notebooks on the broad chair arms, and receive. It is about as inspiring an audience as a roomful of phonographs holding up their brass trumpets. They reproduce the lecture in recitations like the phonograph, mechanically and faithfully, but with the tempo and timbre so changed that the speaker would like to disown his remarks if he could. The instructor tries to provoke them into a semblance of life by extravagant and absurd statements, by insults, by dazzling paradoxes, by extraneous jokes. No use; they just take it down.

EDWIN E. SLOSSON

Did the members of the Harvard Faculty form an intellectual society? Had they any common character or influence? I think not. . . . I never heard of any idea or movement springing up among them, or any literary fashion. It was an anonymous concourse of coral insects, each secreting one cell, and leaving that fossil legacy to enlarge the earth.

GEORGE SANTAYANA

When Francis A. March observed that, whereas early professors "did not know what to do with" classes in English, modern language scholars had managed to make "English as hard as Greek," his remark must have drawn a laugh from the assembled membership at the 1892 MLA meeting. March's comment was amusing enough, but it was also an early sign of the way the recognition of institutional problems could be harmlessly sublimated into academic humor. Reformers whose vision goes no further than making their subject hard can also be suspected of not knowing what to do with it. Such suspicions were already in the air by the time March spoke. Harsh professional self-criticism went side by side with euphoric boasts of progress. A sense of crisis arose in the very midst of the heroic period of the literature department.

This crisis generated a body of professional self-criticism that can be instructive today, even if its accuracy in diagnosing what was wrong was rarely matched by an imaginative sense of alternatives. In this body of self-criticism, "scholars" were often in essential agreement with "generalists." A more thorough discussion might have led to agreement that the situation required a different kind of literary education from either the old liberal culture or the new philology and literary history. But no such agreement materialized, and the outlook of literary studies in the early professional era was marked by a curious mixture of overconfidence and defeatism.

The Establishment of the Canon

One event that did much to consolidate the study of literature, and particularly "English," as a discipline was the debate over college entrance requirements that developed in the 1890s. As the university grew and became administratively standardized, educators set out to reduce the variations in college entrance policies. This effort led to the formation of bodies such as the Committee of Ten and the National Conference on Uniform Entrance Requirements, which considered the place of English in the college and secondary school curriculum.

At its conference in 1892, the Committee of Ten recommended that "a total of five periods a week for four years be devoted to the various aspects of English studies." Its report recommended literature—"prose and narrative poetry in about equal parts"—for students in the seventh school-year, and it defended "philological and rhetorical studies as 'necessary if the pupil is to be brought into anything but the vaguest understanding of what he reads.' " The committee reasserted what was becoming the popular view of educators, that the study of English could become "the equal of any other studies in disciplinary or developing power." In 1894, representatives to the National Conference on Uniform Entrance Requirements drafted a list of texts to be set for college entrance examinations in English. In Applebee's words, "college entrance requirements were the moving force" in making literature "an important study in its own right" by 1900. The lists of books drafted by the conference not only gave definition to college English as a literary enterprise, but compelled the secondary schools to conform to that definition. The topics for the entrance examinations "were announced in advance and had a way of dictating the preparatory school curriculum for the year."

Yet even as the conferences and committees of the nineties consolidated the power of English, they dramatized the conflict of philosophies that was preventing any stable conception of the new subject from materializing. Significantly, the 1894 conference adopted *two* separate lists, "one for 'wide' and the other for 'deep' study," a compromise between the conflicting viewpoints of "the advocates of disciplined study" and the "proponents of appreciation" and "humanistic goals." This was the very conflict between scholarly and generalist conceptions of literary study that we have looked at in the last two chapters.

English had become a "prescribed" study in schools and colleges, and a canonical set of texts had been established, but this did not make the nature of what was prescribed precisely clear. The fixing of the canon did not guarantee it would be taught in a way that effectively transmitted a coherent body of values. By the turn of the century it was a commonplace among educators that English courses were boring or baffling students rather than successfully acculturating or indoctrinating them. And it was another commonplace that even English professors did not seem able to agree on the core values of English, despite their agreement on the core texts. In 1911 William T. Foster, a shrewd surveyor of American education, was saying that "even the general prescription of English is an agreement in name only; what actually goes on under this name is so diverse as to show that we have not yet discovered an 'essential' course in English."

GERMANITY IN RETREAT: THE 1890S

By the early nineties, a reaction against the narrower Germanic methods pervaded American universities. Its signs are apparent in a series of essays by leading English scholars that were serialized in the *Dial* in 1894, and in 1895 collected in a book, *English in American Universities*, edited by William Morton Payne. The volume is probably the single best source of information about the state of English studies at this time, and the most revealing indicator of the ideological divisions marking the new profession even as its acceptance was ceasing to be in doubt.

Of the twenty departmental programs reported on in Payne's collection, only six required narrowly philological courses of undergraduates, and of these only three made linguistic philology distinctly central. At Lafayette College (still under the sway of Francis A. March), courses were "primarily devoted to the study of the language as it is found in masterpieces of literature." At Johns Hopkins, every undergraduate's "technical introduction to English" was "through the early forms of the language and its literature. Initial courses in Anglo-Saxon and Middle English" were evidently prerequisite to more advanced courses such as Gothic and "the ultimate Indo-European affinities of English." The "major" course at Hopkins was even more intensely language-centered. At the University of Minnesota, English majors gave almost two years to Old and Middle English, the plan being "to devote the two lower years to linguistic training as a foundation of the two upper years in literature. The position is taken that not only are linguistics and literature not inimical to one another, but also that they are necessary and complementary the one to the other." Most of the remaining fourteen reports challenged this necessary complementarity.

The University of Illinois spokesman did so the most bluntly, stating that "it is bad enough to confine ourselves to the grammatical forms of Chaucer; it is little far from criminal to do so with [Shakespeare]. Not that the grammatical and linguistic side shall be ignored; it must, however, be reduced to a minimum, as a means to a greater end." The University of Chicago report stated that "the study of the most charming of the English classics has too often been made a mere starting-point for laborious investigations into antiquities, history, geography, etymology, phonetics, the history of the English language, and general linguistics." At Chicago, the attempt was to study "masterpieces of literature . . . as works of literary art." Cornell, as reported on by Hiram Corson, sought to present literature "mainly in its *essential* character, rather than its historical, although the latter receives attention, but not such as to set the minds of students in that direction." Indiana's program also shifted the emphasis to works of literature, "viewed as art, as transcripts of humanity,—not as logic, not as psychology, not as ethics," and not as illustrations of biography or literary history, "incidentally of vast importance." With the exception of Corson, whose plea for oral interpretation probably seemed outdated to the other contributors, most of the statements agreed that what one contributor called the "sentimental" treatment of literature was "out of date," and that the *study* of literature must not be confused with the *appreciation* of literature. As Indiana's respondent put it, "the professor who tries chiefly to make his students love literature wastes his energy for the sake of a few students who would love poetry anyway, and sacrifices the majority of his class, who are not yet ripe enough to love it."

The clear trend was toward literary history as embodied in the survey course and the coverage model of departmental organization. Illinois devoted "the whole of the first year to a general survey of

English and American literature, dwelling particularly on the great names and the significant periods," and from this course "as a centre all the subsequent courses are made to radiate." At Wellesley, the average student was directed to an introductory course "presenting a bird's-eye view of the field of English literature" followed by a few electives in major periods and authors, while the student specializing in English took "a course in Anglo-Saxon for the Freshman year, followed in turn by the Chaucer course, the Shakespeare course, and a course either in Georgian and Victorian poetry, or in Victorian prose, with a concluding course in the development of English literature." Chicago, where an "aesthetic approach" was in effect, would shift its emphasis to literary history in 1898, when J. M. Manly reorganized the department according to the Harvard model, defining "the basic discipline in six period courses each occupying a quarter, running from the sixteenth century to the nineteenth."

Taken together, the essays in *English in American Universities* suggest that an unexpectedly high degree of sophistication existed at this time. The contributors repeatedly stress the inadequacy of the old textbook approach, in which background information took the place of reading literary texts themselves. But there was also wide recognition that the study of particular texts needs to be integrated with literary and cultural history. Gayley, for example, wrote that the University of California's sophomore courses gave "a synoptical view of English literature as the outcome of, and the index to, English thought in the course of its development." These courses were prerequisite to advanced courses in "rhetoric and the theory of criticism," to sequence courses in periods, authors, literary movements, and the evolution of types, and to a course in poetics which "outlines the theory of art, the theory and development of literature, the relations of poetry and prose, the principles of versification, and the canons, inductive and deductive, of dramatic criticism."

Gayley, who became chairman at California in 1889, had moved the curriculum away from the deadly philological concentration of his predecessors. These men had in the 1870s taught juniors "the comparative study of Anglo-Saxon, Latin, Greek, English, German, and French grammar," and in the eighties they had made the course in English prose style so "heartily despised" that Berkeley students engaged for some years in an annual burning of the textbook, Minto's *Manual of English Prose Literature*. A reviewer of the Payne collection was persuaded that western universities like California had reached a level of "philosophical" planning and organization beyond anything yet attained in the East. As described by Gayley, California's program did seem an attractive attempt to make "the synthesis of the courses and the methods of a department furnish a system."

But impressive as Gayley's talk of "system" sounded on paper, it did not amount to very much, at least if we can believe the account left by Frank Norris, the future novelist, who attended Berkeley from 1890 to 1894. For Norris, Gayley's vaunted system boiled down to little more than a scheme of mechanical classification, imposed by dull textbooks. Norris's description is worth quoting at length, for it gives a detailed, if prejudiced, idea of what the average undergraduate was expected to do in one of the more advanced English programs of the period.

Classification, says Norris, is

> the one thing desirable in the eyes of the professors of "literature" of the University of California. The young Sophomore, with his new, fresh mind, his active brain and vivid imagination . . . is taught to "classify," is set to work counting the "metaphors" in a given passage. This is actually true—tabulating them, separating them from the "similes," comparing the results. He is told to study sentence structure. He classifies certain types of sentences in De Quincey and compares them with certain other types of sentences in Carlyle. . . .
>
> In his Junior and Senior years he takes up the study of Milton, of Browning, the drama of the seventeenth and eighteenth centuries, English comedy, of advanced rhetoric, and of aesthetics. "Aesthetics," think of that! Here, the "classification" goes on as before. He classifies "lyrics" and "ballads." He learns to read Chaucer as it was read in the fourteenth century, sounding the final *e*; he paraphases Milton's sonnets, he makes out "skeletons" and "schemes" of certain prose passages.

By this point, Norris says, the student's "enthusiasm is about dead." He is

> ashamed of his original thoughts and of those ideas of his own that he entertained as a Freshman and Sophomore. He has learned to write "themes" and "papers" in the true academic style, which is to read some dozen text books and encyclopedia articles on the subject, and to make over the results in his own language. He has reduced the writing of "themes" to a system. He knows what the instructor wants, he writes accordingly, and is rewarded by first and second sections.

Naturally, the hard-pressed student resorts to certain shortcuts:

> The young man . . . knows just where he can lay his hands upon some fifty to a hundred "themes" written by the members of past classes, that have been carefully collected and preserved by enterprising students. It will go hard if he cannot in the pile find one upon the subject in hand. . . . Do

you blame him very much? Is his method so very different from that in which he is encouraged by his professor; viz., the cribbing—for it is cribbing—from text books? The "theme" which he rewrites has been cribbed in the first place.

Norris's severe conclusion was that "the literary courses of the University of California do not develop literary instincts among the students who attend them."

It is unfair to condemn a whole program on the basis of one piece of testimony—especially if student evaluations of courses were as savage then as they sometimes are now. Norris was probably already under the sway of the naturalistic prejudice that would influence him as a novelist, according to which whatever was "academic" was by definition out of touch with the harsh realities of life. Norris doubted the efficacy of any analytic literary study, stating that "the best way to study literature is to try to produce literature." He found more red-blooded the advanced course in essay and fiction writing at Harvard, where he enrolled in 1894 after leaving Berkeley without taking a degree. Gayley's biographer gives a more favorable impression than Norris of Gayley's courses, which presumably drew their thousands of students for a reason. Still, allowing for exaggeration, Norris's criticisms ring true and fit the pattern of criticism that was emerging.

"THE OTHER 95 PER CENT"

The criticisms came not only from "generalists" but from "investigators" who, as I noted earlier, often echoed the generalists' arguments on occasions of stocktaking. At the 1904 MLA convention, Alexander R. Hohlfield of the University of Wisconsin, chairman of the MLA Central Division, wondered "whether the swing of the pendulum has not carried us too far." Hohlfield declared that "the older college ideal, in our Association, has been almost entirely superseded by the modern university ideal as it has developed in our strongest institutions," and he encouraged his hearers to look back with satisfaction at the "ascendancy and final victory of scholarship" over the outmoded ways of the college. Yet, Hohlfield asked, "with our present strength as a strictly scholarly body assured, can and should we not give some more attention than we now do to the broader educational and practical interests of our profession?" (Ten years later, Hohlfield must have felt the problem was still just as acute, for he repeated his criticisms in his address as president of the association.)

In a similar tone of reassessment, Frank Gaylord Hubbard observed in a 1912 MLA address, "it is no wonder that an educational system whose main purpose had been intellectual and spiritual directed to social ends has been thrown into confusion and bewilderment and brought sadly out of balance. No wonder, too, that it has caught the spirit of the business and industrial world, its desire for great things—large enrollment, great equipment, puffed advertisement, sensational features, strenuous competition, underbidding." Two interrelated complaints appear in these statements: scholarship has become an industry, valuing bulk in production over higher goals, and "broader educational and practical interests" are being neglected.

We saw earlier that in 1892 a former president of MLA had asked what was to be done with "the other 95 per cent" of students not likely to be interested in the special investigations pursued by most members of his audience. The other 95 percent was now different from what it had been in the old college. The university was dealing with a new kind of student, ill prepared to make sense of the more diversified literary education that was now presented to him. The growth in college enrollments between 1880 and 1910 had coincided with "a change in the social and intellectual life of the college." The reasons for attending college were becoming unashamedly opportunistic, as popular manuals urged that "schools that pay good wages want college graduates," and promised that during the four years a student "will become personally acquainted with hundreds of young men and young women who will become leaders in their communities." In Earnest's words, "a smaller percentage of students came to prepare for the ministry, law, and teaching; they came to prepare for entrance into the business community. . . . And it was the sons of big business, finance, and corporation law who dominated the life of the campus. . . . The clubs, the social organizations, the athletics—even the clothes and the slang [of Harvard, Yale, and Princeton]—were copied by college youth throughout the nation." In Randolph Bourne's succinct description of the prevailing code, "the socially fit take the fraternities, the managerships, the publications, the societies; the unpresentable take the honors and rewards of scholarship."

The college novel is a good index to the snobbery, conformism, and unabashed anti-intellectualism that became the mark of student life after the turn of the century. In Owen Wister's 1903 Harvard novel, *Philosophy Four*, for example, the protagonists, Bertie and Billy, are depicted as admirable for their easygoing delight in the pleasures conferred by their wealth and their disdain for hard study. "Money filled the pockets of Bertie and Billy," Wister writes, "and therefore were their heads empty of money and full of less cramping thoughts." Passing up a cramming session for their final philosophy examination

in favor of a lark in the countryside around Cambridge, the two still manage high grades in the course when their professor judges that their casually improvised answers capture the "*spirit* of the course rather than pedantic adherence to the letter." After graduation, Wister tells us, Bertie and Billy will become wealthy businessmen and administrators, in contrast to their working-class tutor, presented as an unimaginative drudge destined for the despised occupation of book reviewer.

By contrast with Wister, Owen Johnson expresses doubts about the code in *Stover at Yale* (1912). Stover is ostracized for entertaining doubts about the value of the Yale club system and fraternizing with men who "don't count." Yet in the world of *Stover*, as in that of *Philosophy Four*, it remains a given that the function of college is primarily social, and that only students from disadvantaged backgrounds need to take studies seriously. One character in the novel observes that "in a period when we have no society in America, families are sending their sons to colleges to place themselves socially. Some of them carry it to an extreme, even directly avow and hope they will make certain clubs at Princeton or Harvard, or a senior society there. It probably is very hard to control, but it's going to turn our colleges more and more, as I say, into social clearing houses." One symptom of the change reflected in *Stover at Yale* was the transfer of college prestige from literary and debating societies to purely social clubs and athletics. A student debating club, we are told, "which had started with a zest, soon showed its limitations. Once the edge of novelty had worn off, there were too many diverting interests to throng in and deplete the ranks."

In *This Side of Paradise*, a work steeped in the conventions of the college novel, Fitzgerald's Amory Blaine takes *Stover at Yale* as his "text-book." Blaine is drawn to Princeton by "its alluring reputation as the pleasantest country club in America," but his eventual disillusionment and vague dissatisfaction with the superficialities of college life echo those of Stover. John Peale Bishop, Fitzgerald's fellow student and the model for the novel's jaded poet, Thomas Parke D'Invilliers, wrote that "many an arrival [at Princeton] . . . has based his success on brilliantine and a gift for silence. For at times it seems as if nothing matters much but that a man bear an agreeable person and maintain with slightly mature modifications the standards of prep school. Any extreme in habiliment, pleasures or opinions is apt to be characterized as 'running it out,' and to 'run it out' is to lose all chance of social distinction."

It was between 1880 and 1917, according to Earnest, that there "developed the philosophy of 'the gentleman's grade' " of C. We saw earlier that at Yale in the 1860s, "skinning" was accepted practice for everyone except "high stand men," but after the turn of the century high stand men were evidently becoming scarce. A faculty committee in 1903 reported that "in late years the scholar has become almost taboo at Yale" and hard study "*unfashionable*." "The use of purchased themes at Yale had become so common that the price fell from five dollars to two dollars. On three floors of one large dormitory, not a single student wrote his own themes," and younger instructors felt it "undesirable for them to report cases of cheating to the faculty." It was in the eighties and nineties that "football became synonymous with Yale" and soon with college life everywhere, pulling "into its orbit the whole college, from freshman to college president."

Irving Babbitt said that in the large universities of the Middle West especially,

> the men flock into the courses on science, the women affect the courses in literature. The literary courses, indeed, are known in some of these institutions as "sissy" courses. The man who took literature too seriously would be suspected of effeminacy. The really virile thing is to be an electrical engineer. One already sees the time when the typical teacher of literature will be some young dilettante who will interpret Keats and Shelley to a class of girls.

Fred Lewis Pattee could joke about the type of student who "comes to me now and says: 'Lissun, Prof, how is this dope going to help a guy get a job and pull down a good salary? See?' " But Pattee had to admit that "deep inside of me it hurts," and he noted the irony that the younger literary intellectuals were acting as if ridicule of professors were a form of iconoclasm when that very ridicule had become popular among students. "The professor," Pattee wrote, "enters his own best-of-regulated classes now and finds them freely supplied with this new-school criticism which calls all professors nincompoops, 'gelatinous asses,' and pornographic perverts."

It seems to have been a virtual commonplace of this period that college students were impervious to humanistic education. Pattee said that even in attempting to teach, the professor knew "in his heart that there can be no real teaching of value without mutual definitions, mutual respect between teacher and pupil, mutual confidence, mutual desire for the best results possible," and that these had ceased to exist. Ludwig Lewisohn, who taught at Wisconsin and Ohio State from 1910 to 1918, described looking out at "dull faces, vacant faces. Not one that expresses any corruption of heart and mind. I look about me again and watch for one face that betrays a troubled soul, a yearning of the mind, the touch of any flame. There is none." "It is, as a matter of fact, considered rather bad form among them to show any stirring of the mind. It is considered 'high-brow,' queer, that is to say—different, personal, and hence, by a subtle and quite mad implication consoling to stupidity and emptiness—undemocratic." Lewisohn said that "it was practically impossible, in studying literature, to get an emotional response."

Like Frank Norris's ridicule of academic pedantry, Pattee's and Lewisohn's despair at the indifference of students may have been dictated as much by literary convention as by reality, but the reports of more detached observers suggest that their views were not wholly false. In his perceptive survey of "great American universities," Edwin Slosson observed that college students had, "without knowing anything about physiological psychology, devised an automatic cut-off which goes into operation as they open their notebooks and short-circuits the train of thought from the ear directly to the hand, without its having to pass through the pineal gland or wherever the soul may be at the time residing and holding court."

Yet it might have occurred to these writers that the student torpor they described was in some degree a result of the system's failure to make the rituals of the intellectual life intelligible to those who did not already presuppose them. To an even greater extent than in the old college, higher education could no longer take for granted the tacit understanding that polite literature was the natural form of acculturation for gentlemen. Randolph Bourne argued that "the old college education was for a limited and homogeneous class. It presupposed social and intellectual backgrounds which the great majority of college students to-day do not possess." Bourne added that "the idea of studying things 'for their own sake,' without utilitarian bearings, is seductive, but it implies a society where the ground had been prepared in childhood and youth through family and environmental influences." By contrast, the modern student comes to college "ignorant even of the very terms and setting of the philosophy and history and sociology studied there." Bourne thought that "now, when all classes come to college, the college must give that active, positive background which in former generations was prepared for it outside," must in short become "the field for working out a background for the contemporary social world."

The college curriculum still seemed to presuppose a society in which this background had been already inherited. The literature program offered a series of periods and movements and left the student to provide the context for them. Oliver Farrar Emerson observed in an MLA address of 1908 that English had been broken up into so great a "number of subdivisions" that a student "may take one or even two such subjects thru several terms of his course, and yet get no connected idea of the literature in his mother tongue." Emerson said that such fragmentation might do no harm if the class "were already thoroly grounded in essentials of literary study, knew the greater periods fairly well, and already appreciated the greater masterpieces. But such could scarcely be the case except with the most advanced undergraduates, or with students of the graduate school."

A similar point was made by Bliss Perry, who was appointed at Harvard in 1907. Speaking of "the steel core of the English work at Harvard . . . in the solid linguistic and historical courses covering the period from the earliest Anglo-Saxon writers to the decline of the Elizabethan Drama," Perry said that "for all but a small minority of ambitious undergraduates, incoherence in the choice of courses and the mechanical accumulation of course-credits were still the order of the day. There were popular 'snap' courses for miscellaneous good-natured auditors; but for the student who had got beyond that, neither guidance nor encouragement." Like the scholar's accumulation of research facts, the student's gathering of period courses was of itself expected to add up to a significant whole, but nothing made this very likely.

All the critics agreed that there was a glaring contradiction between the research fetish and the needs of most students. In his 1904 MLA address, Hohlfield speculated that "thousands upon thousands of teachers must be engaged in presenting to their students elements which, in the nature of things, can have only a rare and remote connection with the sphere of original research," and he doubted the wisdom of requiring all members of the now-expanding department faculties to engage in such research. To maintain that every college instructor "could or should be an original investigator is either a naive delusion concerning the actual status of our educational system or, what is more dangerous, it is based on a mechanical and superficial interpretation of the terms 'original scholarship' or 'research work.'" Nor was it merely a question of one pedagogical method versus another, Hohlfield emphasized, but a "far broader and deeper problem of the exact function of modern language study in the intellectual training of the student." Stuart Sherman, who took a Harvard Ph.D. in 1906, blamed scholars like Kittredge for turning students into "zealous bibliographers and compilers of card indexes," calling Kittredge himself "a potent force in bringing about the present sterilizing divorce of philology from general ideas." Sherman wrote that, with the exception of the drama, there were long intervals when "there was almost no instruction in English offered at Harvard that an intelligent graduate student could take seriously in the period from the Sixteenth to the Nineteenth Century." He added that conditions at Harvard had "affected more or less seriously the teaching of English throughout the country."

One can see from statements such as these that the early critics of the profession had a keen awareness that their problems were institutional in nature. Yet in diagnosing the causes of these problems, they tended to blame conditions not likely to change, such as the specialization of the disciplines, the laziness or selfishness of individual professors, or the loss of a cultural common ground. When all else failed, the critics blamed the inherent laziness of students or the inherent vulgarity of American culture. These diagnoses only made the problems seem insoluble.

PERSONAL FAILINGS AND LOSS OF COMMUNITY

One of the most popular diagnoses blamed the new profession's problems on a deficiency of professorial fervor. Fred Lewis Pattee, visiting Harvard in 1909 and witnessing the same student apathy that Perry experienced there around that time, noted that he "visited classes of Barrett Wendell, Professor Kittredge and others and was bored rather than inspired. Everywhere education by the pouring-in process, the students sitting as passive buckets. In Copeland's classes there was humor enough and enthusiasm enough to keep the students awake, but I saw nowhere an awakening touch between the desk and the desks that impressed me."

This lack of "awakening touch" was traced by many to the irresponsible selfishness of professors who paid more attention to their research specialities than to the general culture students needed. With O. F. Emerson these critics condemned the "sacrifice of the student's good to the pleasure of the instructor," who "offers the course in which he has specialized, or in which he wishes to carry on special study." With Bliss Perry they attacked the professional for his "cupidity" and "clannish loyalty to his own department only" and complained that departments (as Perry said of Harvard's) acted like "a brilliant array of prima donnas, each supreme in a chosen role."

All the critics saw a prime cause of the profession's ills in the loss of cultural and disciplinary common ground. As early as the turn of the century, MLA addresses start to bewail the disappearance of the sense of solidarity and shared goals that had supposedly marked the first generation of modern language scholars of the eighties and nineties. It is then that we hear the first complaints of the members that they can no longer understand their own colleagues. At the 1902 convention, Hohlfield observed that "the increasing specialization of the papers" delivered at the annual meetings "is rapidly decreasing the number of occasions when a considerable proportion of those present are capable of joining in a discussion. . . . There is danger that the meetings of the future will offer fewer and fewer subjects of general interest." In 1912, MLA president Frank Gaylord Hubbard expressed the fear that "modern education with its increasing specialization seems more and more to narrow the amount of common intellectual interest."

Bliss Perry echoed this theme when he observed of the Harvard department that

> it was difficult for a stranger to discover any common denominator of their activities. What was the underlying philosophy of the Department, its ideal aim, its relation with liberal studies as a whole? . . . Fundamental questions were avoided in our meetings; the precious time was consumed in the discussion of wearisome administrative details. The separate parts of the English machine seemed to be in competent hands, but how were the parts related?

Perry may have fathomed that these arrangements were perpetuated by the very mechanism that made it so easy to avoid confronting problems, namely, the field-coverage principle of organization, which enabled the "English machine" to go on functioning smoothly without having to establish either agreement or debate over what it was doing.

As John Erskine put it,

> When a sufficient number of specialists are assembled on a college faculty, the subject of which each knows only a small part is said to be covered, and the academic department to which they all belong is regarded as fully manned. In ancient Ireland, if legend is to be trusted, there was a tower so high that it took two persons to see to the top of it. One would begin at the bottom and look up as far as sight could reach, the other would begin where the first left off, and see the rest of the way.

As Erskine's parable neatly suggested, by granting each professor sovereignty over his assigned terrain, the coverage principle left no one responsible for the totality, which was trusted to compose itself for the student on its own. The principle appeased competing interests, including even the interest of the totality upheld by Erskine and Perry, but it reduced that interest to one part of the machine among many.

There was certainly much truth in the attacks on specialization and individualism. In the early ethos of the profession, the scholar was seen as a kind of entrepreneur who virtually owned "his" students and "his" field, and research was a form of private property that, it was naturally assumed, any sensible scholar jealously guarded from potential competitors. Henry Seidel Canby recalled that the professor at Yale in the nineties "resented even the interest of an outsider in his subject. Having taught himself with infinite pains to be cautious in handling of his facts, he avoided like fire any opinion on the facts of his neighbor." For Albert S. Cook, according to Canby, "you were either *his* student, or someone else's, and if someone else's, beware! No mercy, no help."

But as justifiable as the complaints about such behavior may have been, the form they took left no apparent alternative and the result tended to be defeatism and resignation. What was the point of attacking research scholars for selfishness when the incentives under which professors operated would have penalized them for behaving otherwise? It may have been true that "modern education with its increasing specialization" inevitably narrowed "the amount of common intellectual interest" and left humanists without a "common denominator" for their activities, but was this not after all simply an inevitable condition of a democratic culture? To make specialization as such the cause of the institution's problems was merely to echo the futile complaints of the classicists of the 1870s, who had objected to the dissolution of the "common life" of the college by the corrosive forces of modern life.

Instead of decrying the inevitable divisiveness of modern culture, the critics of literary studies might have acted more constructively had they accepted that state of affairs as a given and gone on to work out some means by which disparate specializations and ideological conflicts might be brought into some visible correlation or contrast. Instead of bewailing the disappearance of "mutual definitions, mutual respect between teacher and pupil, mutual confidence, mutual desire for the best results possible," as Fred Lewis Pattee had done, the critics might have set about confronting the conflicts of definition and principle, bringing these conflicts out into the open where students might learn from them, take part in them, and perhaps be moved from their much-discussed lethargy. What was needed, it might be argued, was a way of making the conflicts of literary studies part of the subject matter of literary education itself.

Erskine and Perry were right to see that the field-coverage principle enabled the department to evade the issue of its own intellectual coherence, but in conceiving the desired coherence as a "common denominator" of the department's activities they defined their goal in a way that could not have been realized without turning the clock back to the predemocratic conditions of the old college. What the critics of the profession needed was a way of conceiving coherence without consensus. They needed a conception of coherence not based on an intellectual and cultural common ground, a conception that did not presuppose a unified humanistic culture, which no longer existed, but based itself on the very conflicts that now existed inside and outside the university over the place of culture in America.

The ideal of a coherence of conflict may seem utopian, but it appears actually to have been achieved at this time by Harvard's Department of Philosophy, where the dissonant views of James, Royce, Munsterburg, Santayana, and Palmer were exploited as an educational resource rather than treated as a source of trouble to be neutralized. The department chairman, George Herbert Palmer, said that "differences of opinion were always openly acknowledged. In our lectures we were accustomed to attack each other by name. . . . Our students were not misled by these attacks on each other. . . . Truth was sacred; and criticism, the surest way of approaching it, was a friendly, not a hostile, process." Palmer's picture may have been somewhat idealized, but it was not wholly false according to Veysey, who credits the Harvard philosophers with achieving a balance of "lively intellectual conflict without concomitant disintegration."

Why did the Harvard philosopers succeed in achieving this balance while their counterparts in literary studies, given a seemingly equal degree of eminence and talent, did not? Veysey speculates that the Harvard philosophers shared tacit social and cultural assumptions that enabled them to criticize each other's positions publicly without arousing ill feeling: their disagreements were "held within bounds, more than anything else, by the gentlemanly atmosphere that still permeated Cambridge." Yet the English faculty presumably shared the same "gentlemanly atmosphere" without achieving any comparable community of debate. Whatever the case, the moral seems to be, if instructors cannot be made to talk *to* one another, talking *about* one another can accomplish the same end.

The Jeremiads of the MLA

The profession might have had less difficulty converting self-criticism into constructive reform had it been able to exploit the contradictions in its sense of its relation to American society. On the one hand, early professors of literature tried hard to convince themselves that their enterprise was an expression of a larger national will. Officially, the literature department not only represented a coherent and unified humanistic culture, but a culture that legitimately claimed an important role in the leadership of the nation. On the other hand, the everyday facts of the department's situation made this faith increasingly difficult to maintain. In the absence of any way of making positive use of these conflicting self-images or even of airing them, the resulting ambiguities were disabling.

In 1902, repeating what was by now a commonplace of MLA oratory, MLA president James Wilson Bright of Johns Hopkins declared that "the philological strength and sanity of a nation is the measure of its intellectual and spiritual vitality." The philologist, Bright said, must share in "the work of guiding the destinies of the country." Yet nowhere did Bright explain just how philologists or other kinds of literary scholars were helping to guide the nation's destinies. Assertions like Bright's of the cultural importance of literary scholarship and its harmony with national aspirations coexisted alongside complaints of the neglected or despised status of scholarship amidst "the great ocean of American commercialism" and "the ruthless, cynical, destructive competition" of a "brutish age."

These words were spoken only the year before Bright's address, and it was characteristic that Bright saw no reason to refer to them, even though they posed a direct challenge to his optimism. Their speaker was the MLA Central Division president, James Taft Hatfield, a colorful Germanist from Northwestern University, who carried his scorn for philistinism into town-gown disputes with the local gentry. In his 1901 address, Hatfield lamented that "the tender plant of pure humanism" was drying up, and that "America's choicest minds" had no more "direct and fruitful scope for their activities than the reading of Phi Beta Kappa orations and commencement addresses." Like Bright, Hatfield thought that literary scholars ought to partake "in the direct service" of the country. But as far as he could see, they were "largely shut out" from that service, if not by the businessman, then by "the assertive political boss—our American *Ubermensch*." Hatfield perceptively added that "The practical man would hardly conceal his amusement at the assumption of a company of mere philologists that they were identified with the true progress of the community, and were the custodians of its higher fortunes; he would see some vanity in this belief, and yet we cherish it."

Between 1900 and 1920, this kind of lament crystallized into a species of oratory so conventionalized in its basic gestures that it deserves a generic name such as "the jeremiads of the MLA." In this genre, elegaic recollections of the lost serenities of the old college alternated with bitter denunciations of the spiritual degradation of democratic times. Like their seventeenth-century New England prototypes, the jeremiads of the MLA had about them the ritualistic aura of the Sunday rebuke, which is satisfying in direct proportion to the recognition that nobody will be expected to put its exhortations into practice. Larzer Ziff describes the New England jeremiad as "a stylized denunciation of the evils of the time, especially those brought about by prosperity," and observes that it came

> repeatedly to be uttered as a formula rather than practical teaching because its utterers were men whose rhetorical relationship to their audience had changed. From being the chosen leaders of a select band speaking to that band about common problems, they were becoming hired professionals doing a special job from a special position that could be regarded as incontrovertible so long as it was also aloof from practical consequences.

"As the literary class of the community," Ziff says, it was "instructed . . . in sentiment because the truths were Sunday truths," which were not expected to be acted on. Rather like Ziff's Puritan ministers, MLA officials delivered the lofty humanistic rhetoric that was expected of them on ceremonial occasions, even as they seemed no longer to believe that their own colleagues would be moved by them, much less anyone on the outside.

Scholars spoke of "the complacent attitude of the contented Philistine toward the scholar, as though the latter were not more than a half-man, and by no means to be taken seriously." They regretted the time they had to endure between annual meetings of the association as a time of "exile among the alien hosts of Philistia." They deplored the "vast and growing ignorance" that is not peculiar to school and college but "pervades society," and they feared that "men of note are losing the power to speak or write their own language." They asked themselves, "if even the highly cultured are thus to be numbered among the transgressors, what can be expected of the comparatively uneducated?" and they answered that what could be expected was "little less than linguistic anarchy, which the rapid perusal of journalistic headlines only tend [*sic*] to intensify" and that would only get worse as "an unbroken stream of immigration floods our cities with the confusion of Babel." They worried that "enormous quantities of inferior 'current literature,' in place of literature of the highest type, cannot fail to have a deleterious effect upon both thinking and speech."

The vulgarity of American culture accounted for the hopeless ignorance of the students, and it was that ignorance which finally absolved the department of all failings. Emerson blamed the students' lack of knowledge and intellectual preparation, the new campus atmosphere of hedonistic anti-intellectualism, and, ultimately, the general collapse of intellectual standards in democratic America. He asserted that "lack of seriousness in the student body" was unfortunately "characteristic of the times," and noted with defensive acerbity that literature can hardly compete with "the more serious business of athletics, the rushes and the rushing, the many social pleasures, and a good time generally." Before blaming the times for "lack of seriousness," Emerson might have asked whether the literature departments did not lack seriousness in their own way. If it was true that, as Emerson said, few students now studied the modern languages "because of their necessity to the highest culture," it was also true that the language faculty had done little to make that necessity seem obvious. Emerson himself conceded as much when he observed that "a certain narrowness of German culture" pervaded the new departments, and that "with all the improvement in our professional training of the teacher, it is a question whether breadth of culture has not been frequently sacrificed."

The scholars thundered that "self-complacency," born of "an ignorance so absolute as to be unaware of the existence of anything to learn," may be called "the dominating spirit of our time." Among students, "snap courses" are sought and "amusement is looked for, rather than instruction." Study has come to seem "hard and distasteful," for students have "never been used to mental concentration; any other activity, whether it be athletics or 'social service,' seems to them less painful, hence more profitable. You are all aware how dangerous it is to assume, on the part of our college classes, any definite knowledge of any subject." The arts, it was said, had been overcome by a spirit of nihilism and destruction that says "Down with everything!" "By our neglect of the past we have cut ourselves off from standards of all kinds."

On occasion, a blunt warning was issued that only by restoring humanistic culture to prominence could America hope to keep the lower orders of society in their place. In his 1919 address, MLA president E. C. Armstrong predicted that without the "spiritual checks and balances" provided by the humanities, "sordid material gains will be swept away by a society where those who have not will remain more numerous than those who have, and where that majority will bring down in ruins the whole structure in the effort to seize in their turn the lion's share." But such statements were couched in a tone of impotence, bespeaking a recognition that the cultured classes were no longer in control. Armstrong bewailed the fact that "material civilization" was now "out of proportion to the intellectual and spiritual leadership we have been able to develop." Charles Hall Grandgent complained that though "the aggregate of knowledge, at the present day, is greater than ever before," it was "equally true that the large share-holders in this knowledge are no longer in control. Leadership has been assumed by the untrained host, which is troubled by no doubt concerning its competence and therefore feels no inclination to improve its judgment."

Reduced to pious exhortations, men like Armstrong could only remind their audience of the importance of "spiritual checks and balances" and "the life of the spirit," and wonder "what shall it profit a man even materially if you show him how to gather wealth and are not furnishing the spiritual checks and balances?" With similar ineffectuality, others urged "the inculcation of that high idealism which must ever be the chief glory of the educational institutions of a great nation." They reasserted that "a public-spirited scolarship has been the ideal of our intellectual leaders from Ticknor to Gilman, Angell, Eliot, and Hadley," and that "the object of the University . . . is to develop character, to make men." They exhorted the university to recapture the old denominational college's "ideal of public spirit" and said that because "the religious temper is the best available source of public spirit, something of the religious temper should not be absent in the scolar and teacher." After 1918, they affirmed that "the overwhelming waste of war, and the formidable moral slackening that is following in war's track, are giving rise to a materialistic current which demands united and aggressive action if we are to stand up against it."

Even those who seemed to know better could not avoid falling back on nostalgia. Hubbard in 1912 went so far as to argue that in times such as these, "one who is actively engaged in the work of education is impelled to look beyond his own field, to make inquiry concerning his own relation to all this change, his own position in all this turmoil, his own contribution to the activities with which he is most closely bound, the relation of these activities to the social strivings of the times." But rather than ask how literary studies might confront these new social circumstances, Hubbard could only decry the way "peace and quiet seem to have departed from academic halls; meditation, 'the sweet serenity of books,' seem to grow rarer and rarer. . . . More than one gentle soul in a moment of irritation has sighed for the seclusion of the medieval monastery."

The jeremiads exhorted the literary scholars that only they could rehumanize American culture, but shadowing that lofty commission was the troubling recognition that literary studies were far from having humanized themselves, that their present state was marked not by "public spirit" and idealism but "a more or less narrow professionalism" to which "breadth of culture" had "been frequently sacrificed." As "breadth of culture," "high idealism," and "the life of the spirit" became ritualistic expressions, their use only diverted attention from the literature department's real conflicts and made it all the easier to ignore them.

Scholars versus Critics: 1915–1950

CHAPTER EIGHT

Scholars versus Critics: 1915–1930

Progress in knowledge, in mastery, in the substitution of sound learning for amateur conjecture and the fine-spun theories of critics has been in spite of the complaints of the incompetent but vociferous exponents of the good old times.

EDWIN GREENLAW

Between 1915 and 1930, neither the overall configuration of the literature department nor its basic methods changed fundamentally. Linguistic philology ceded further prominence to literary history, the new fields of comparative literature and the history of ideas emerged, and American literature achieved respectability in the wake of wartime patriotism. But the research model of literary studies became in some ways more entrenched than it had been before the war. In 1902, *PMLA* had discontinued the "Pedagogical Section" of the journal, giving indication that, in William Riley Parker's words, "the MLA had become so absorbed in the advancement of research in its field that it was ready to leave to others all talk about teaching and enrollment." In 1916 a clause in the MLA constitution describing the object of the Association as "the advancement of the *study* of the Modern Languages and their literatures" was amended to read, "the advancement of *research* in the Modern languages and their literatures" (emphasis mine). In 1929, the president of the association declared with finality that "henceforth, our domain is research."

At the same time, "criticism" had begun to emerge as a common cause of diverse groups who sought an alternative to the research model that would close the yawning gap between investigators and generalists. The cause of criticism attracted generalists, who initiated great books programs after World War I, but it also attracted the advocates of systematic aesthetic approaches to literature, who, like the scholars, wanted to purge literary studies of the sentimentality and amateurism of the nineteenth-century. Polemics on behalf of criticism begin to show up in professional literature as early as the 1890s, at which time we can already detect most of the disciplinary and pedagogical themes of what would later be called the New Criticism.

Yet the growth of the idea of criticism did not heal separations so much as create new ones, in part because of the way that idea was conceived by both its proponents and enemies. It is in this period that scholar and critic emerge as antithetical terms, and the gulf further widens between fact and value, investigation and appreciation, scientific specialization and general culture.

BEFORE THE NEW CRITICISM

In 1891, John Fruit of Bethel College published an essay in *PMLA* entitled "A Plea for the Study of Literature from the Aesthetic Standpoint." Like the philologists, Fruit regretted the lack of systematic method that had retarded the progress of the profession, but Fruit went on to argue that it is not by philological analysis but by comprehending "the significance of a work of Art" that the teacher of literature "will be clothed with a newer and finer dignity." In an article on Tennyson in the same number of the journal, Henry E. Shepherd of the College of Charleston complained that "the trend of the Modern Language Association has been, thus far, almost exclusively in the direction of grammatical criticism and philological exegesis. The literary side of language has been subordinated or retired until it is almost faded out of memory in the confusion of tongues and the strife of phonetics. Nearly all of the illustrating power, the aesthetic brilliance of literary culture, is lost upon the philological devotee."

Neither Fruit nor Shepherd gave much of a clue how the "significance" of literature and "the literary side of language" might be attended to. "Criticism," as they used the word, included both evaluation and close scrutiny of literary language, but in Shepherd's analysis of "In Memoriam" criticism came out looking more like old-fashioned source-study than what we would now call interpretation. In fact, Shepherd's discussion contains a hint of gentlemanly disdain for interpretation as a process the cultured reader would presumably find superfluous. He says, for example, that since "the general intent" of "In Memoriam" "is thoroughly understood, detailed explanation would be manifestly a work of supererogation."

In 1895, the case for criticism in the university was sharply formulated by the newly appointed chairman of the English department at Indiana University, Martin Wright Sampson. In a contribution to the *Dial* survey of American English programs, Sampson con-

demned as an "obsolescent notion" the habit of "harping on the moral purposes of the poet or novelist." Conceding that the British historian E. A. Freeman's aphorism that "English literature is only chatter about Shelley" was unfortunately "four-fifths true," Sampson warned that until instructors "draw the line between the liking for reading and the understanding of literature," they will make themselves "ridiculous in the eyes of those who see into the heart of things." Once again, neither philology nor literary history were the systematic methods that were needed, for they merely "fill the student full of biography and literary history."

Instead, Sampson thought, the aim should be to place "the student face to face with the work itself." The idea should be to make him

> systematically approach the work as a work of art, find out the laws of its existence as such, the mode of its manifestation, the meaning it has, and the significance of meaning—in brief, to have his students interpret the work of art and ascertain what makes it just that and not something else.

It is interesting that much of the program of the latter-day New Criticism had already been formulated by the mid-nineties:

> the study of literature means the study of *literature*, not of biography nor of literary history (incidentally of vast importance), not of grammar, not of etymology, not of anything except the works themselves, viewed as their creators wrote them, viewed as art, as transcripts of humanity,—not as logic, not as pyschology, not as ethics.

Sampson said that his ideas were already "the commonplaces of to-day—truisms among a certain class of teachers," yet he added that they are as yet only "truisms of theory," "not yet of practice—the difference is profound."

Sampson's program faced several obstacles. First, no model yet existed for the kind of critical practice and pedagogy he was looking for. The program Sampson described at Indiana encouraged students "to read in the class, with the greatest attention to detail, one or more characteristic works of the authors chosen" along with "as outside work, a good deal of collateral reading." Such a plan may have been ahead of its time in the emphasis it put on "close reading," but otherwise it was hard to distinguish from the other programs described in the *Dial* collection. Indiana had the standard coverage of periods, genres, and major figures, with the occasional topical course such as metrics. It all sounded very much like the "steel core" of "solid linguistic and historical courses" that Bliss Perry would find at Harvard in 1907 and by that time was established everywhere.

Second, men like Sampson were up against a scholarly attitude of doubt that criticism could ever rise above whimsical impressionism. Typical was the view of the scholar who in 1901 stated flatly that "the personal element plays too large a part in rhetorical study for anything like accurate or scientific results to be obtained."

> Why then waste time and brains in thrashing over again something which is after all only subjective opinion? Mere aesthetic theorizing should be left to the magazine writer or to the really gifted critic who feels himself competent to tread in the footsteps of Lessing.
>
> My view has always been that the college (university) is a place for research, for scholarship, for finding out something hitherto unsuspected. Such is the object of our libraries and our seminary methods. The outside world hasn't the time to investigate; *we* must do the investigation.

So much, according to this scholar, for "the debatable questions of style."

CRITICISM AND MODERN LITERATURE

The campaign for criticism in the university frequently went along with efforts to legitimate modern literature as an object of study. In his *Autobiography*, William Lyon Phelps tells of initiating an undergraduate course in "Modern Novels" at Yale in 1895, including in the reading such works as *Jude the Obscure*, *Almayer's Folly*, *Pudd'nhead Wilson*, and *Trilby*. Phelps believed his was "the first course in any university in the world confined wholly to contemporary fiction," and he noted that the event was so unusual that it occasioned newspaper editorials in the United States and England. It was also unusual enough to draw the attention of Phelps's senior colleagues, who threatened to dismiss him unless he dropped the course at the end of the year. He did not, and they relented, but in 1910, when Phelps published a book entitled *On Modern Novelists*, he says that reviewers "were amazed that a book of essays on contemporary writers should come from a university professor."

Phelps may not have been so far ahead of other professors as he implied. Brander Matthews claimed to have initiated a course at Columbia in "the evolution of the modern novel" in 1891. Bliss Perry was writing on contemporary fiction, if not teaching the subject, at Williams in the 1890s, and in the same decade several *PMLA* contributors were advocating "that the English teacher push his class work into recent centuries." Still, the hostile reaction to Phelps's course at Yale was characteristic, and academic interest in the literature of the present or recent past was at best hesitant and sporadic.

The more *popular* kinds of recent literature remained outside the pale for scholar and critic alike. John Fruit, the advocate of "aesthetic" criticism, dismissed "the popular literature of the day in the form of novels" as "journeyman literature, . . . made, not created—made to sell." Perry, who in 1896 published a *PMLA* essay recommending "fiction as a college study," conceded that "the vast fiction-reading public into which these [college] classes are so soon to merge is sceptical about the very existence of standards of judgment." Perry worried that "this lawless and inconstant public, craving excitement at any price, journalized daily, neither knowing nor caring what should be the real aim and scope of the novel, has the casting vote, after all, upon great books and little books alike." But for Perry, it was precisely the debased condition of popular taste that argued for making modern fiction a college subject. The point was to "send into this public, to serve as leaven, men who know good work from bad, and who know why they know it."

Perry was in the minority among his colleagues in thinking there was good contemporary literature to be distinguished from bad. Though "contemporary literature" was coming to mean two different kinds of things depending on whether "highbrow" or "lowbrow" taste was at issue, most professors distrusted both kinds—popular entertainment literature for its superficiality, the more serious literature for its immorality, materialism, and pessimism. The issue was not whether the literature was contemporary so much as whether it reinforced traditional literary idealism—as less and less current literature seemed to do. Albert S. Cook wrote in 1906 that there seem no longer to be any poets "with a message, that is, none who announce with decision and persuasiveness a doctrine, or view of the moral universe, such as has power to stir men's souls and lift them above their customary and commonplace moods."

Charles Hall Grandgent in 1912 approvingly cited the judgment of the British critic Frederic Harrison that new artistic and cultural movements (he mentioned Post-Impressionism, Cubism, and Futurism) represented "the cult of the foul," a "worship or admiration of the Ugly, the Nasty, the Brutal. Poetry, Romance, Drama, Painting, Sculpture, Music, Manners, even Dress, are now recast to suit popular taste by adopting forms which hitherto have been regarded as unpleasing, gross, or actually loathsome. To be refined is to be 'goody-goody'; gutter slang is 'so actual.' "

Once again, however, the apparent traditionalism represented by the scholarly attitude could be deceptive. Had the scholars who fulminated against the nihilism of avant-garde art inspected their own practices closely, they could have detected a kinship with the clinical objectivity being cultivated by naturalistic novelists and Cubist painters. Conservative scholars and avant-garde artists subscribed to different versions of a "breakthrough" ethic that had the effect of subverting traditional idealisms even when it attempted to serve them. As Babbitt had pointed out, the most up-to-date "Baconian" scientism in research could go hand in hand with old-fashioned "Rousseauistic" sentimentalism in literary taste—all the more easily because research and literary taste had no visible connection.

THE UNITED CRITICAL FRONT

Calls for aesthetic criticism continued to punctuate professional literature between 1900 and 1915. They urged the teacher to "reveal the generic idea of the book as a work of literature, the proportion and symmetry of the organic parts, and the constructive plan by which artistic unity is attained." Or they recommended that "the quest of literary relations, sources, influences, developments of theme or form" be replaced or supplemented by "a renewed emphasis on interpretative criticism" and on evaluation. Criticism was becoming a common rallying cry for a diffuse number of interests and attitudes not always having much in common except dissatisfaction with the alternatives of pure science and pure impressionism.

At one extreme of the critical spectrum were proponents of aesthetic formalism like Joel E. Spingarn of Columbia, a Renaissance scholar with a reformer's passion for a systematic philosophy of art. Spingarn had divided his graduate studies in the mid-1890s between Harvard and Columbia, where the respective influences of Lewis E. Gates and George Edward Woodberry stimulated his interest in the impressionistic view of art for which he found a systematic underpinning in the work of Benedetto Croce. Spingarn said that Croce gave him "a philosophical explanation for those things which have been implicit in the thought of Woodberry." His Columbia dissertation led to his *History of Literary Criticism in the Renaissance*, published in 1899 when Spingarn was only twenty-four, and hailed by scholars "as a pioneer work of first-rate importance." It was reprinted as late as 1963.

Lewis Mumford called Spingarn "*the* brilliant young man of the university." Yet he was summarily dismissed by Nicholas Murray Butler in 1911 when he opposed Butler's firing of the classicist Harry Thurston Peck for immoral conduct. After his dismissal, Spingarn went into publishing and became a founder of Harcourt, Brace in 1919. A fiery and passionate man, a political liberal, an outspoken defender of academic freedom, and later an official of the National Association for the Advancement of Colored People, Spingarn clashed instinctively with Butler, in whom he saw the embodiment of "the restless gods of Administration and Organization," the men who had "made mechanical efficiency and administrative routine the goal of the university's endeavor."

Spingarn was the prototype of the sort of professor who thinks of "administration" as beneath the calling of the spirit, an attitude which does not usually endear one to colleagues. He told John Erskine that "he found it impossible to conform to meaningless academic routine," he neglected students, and limited his duties "to giving the courses which he himself chose to give, and to guiding the work of the students whom he himself permitted to take a doctor's degree under him." In this disdain for administration, Spingarn was living out his Crocean aesthetic theories: according to his biographer, Marshall Van Deusen, art for Spingarn "was the antidote for American practicality, and artists were to challenge those 'restless Gods of Administration' who threatened even the scholars in their classrooms and libraries."

In *Creative Criticism* (1917), Spingarn developed the theory that works of art were unique acts of self-expression "whose excellence must be judged by their own standards, without reference to ethics." "To say that poetry, as poetry, is moral or immoral," Spingarn wrote, in a passage which pleased the merciless professor-baiter, H. L. Mencken, "is as meaningless as to say that an equilateral triangle is moral and an isoscles triangle is immoral, or to speak of the immorality of a muscial chord or a Gothic arch." Spingarn found American criticism guilty of "a want of philosophic insight and precision." "Golden utterances there have been aplenty," he said, but a "disconnected body of literary theories" and "mere practical programmes" have taken "the place of a real philosophy of art." Spingarn's desire to clean up the disorderly conceptual situation of criticism anticipated the project I. A. Richards would shortly initiate at Cambridge in the twenties. Like earlier critical reformers, Spingarn saw that in the academic climate, where the mere suspicion of amateurism was fatal, criticism would need to develop an ordered, comprehensive system if it hoped to compete with philology on even terms.

At the other extreme from Spingarn were the New Humanists—Babbitt of Harvard, Sherman of Illinois, Norman Foerster of North Carolina, later of Iowa, and Paul Elmer More of Princeton (after 1919). The Humanists had no use for Spingarn's aesthetic formalism and little interest in putting criticism into philosophic order. They accused Spingarn of escapism and exclusivism, or, evidently having his politics in mind, they depicted him as an anarchist or libertarian. Whereas for Spingarn criticism meant isolating the element in literature that distinguished it from everything else in the world, for the Humanists criticism was most valuable when it concentrated on the qualities literature shares with philosophy, ethics, and those "general ideas" that were so lacking in academic literary scholarship and education. These contrasting views of literature would eventually become opposing tendencies in the New Criticism, which would vacillate between the effort to purge literature of social and moral impurities and to promote it as a form of knowledge that could save the world from science and industrialism.

As long as the research scholars remained the common enemy, however, the latent conflicts in the critical camp did not lead to a complete break. The scholars were vulnerable to attack from aesthetic formalists and humanistic moralists alike, since, arguably, they managed to sin in both the antithetical ways that offended each: that is, they confused literature with nonliterary forms of discourse and they divorced it from social and ethical concerns. Against this common adversary, which respected neither the morality nor the aesthetics of art, moralists and aesthetes could for the moment feel part of a loosely united front.

Perhaps the uneasiest allies in this front were those among the "generalists" for whom criticism was not an alternative method to research but an alternative to method itself. Middlebrow critical popularizers like Perry, Phelps, Matthews, and Erskine distrusted the pedantry of the scholars, but they were no less wary of Spingarn's methodological purity or the Humanists' programmatic morality. Erskine spoke for them when he said that a work should speak for itself, with no elaborate "screen of historical and critical apparatus" to come "between pupil and book." The pedagogical expression of this outlook was the great books course Erskine conceived in 1917 and after the war put into effect at Columbia under the name "General Honors."

THE WAR CLIMATE

World War I provoked a general reassessment of educational values that eventually advanced the cause of criticism. In *Mars and Minerva: World War I and the Uses of the Higher Learning in America*, Carol S. Gruber has told the story of the widespread acceptance among American professors of the Wilsonian view of the war as a holy crusade and their consequent conclusion "that their social function should be to offer themselves without reservation to the state's pursuit of military victory." In the anti-German atmosphere of the war, traces of scholarly "germanity" and of "mania teutonica" were rooted out with a fury. At the University of Illinois, for example, public pressure was exerted in 1918 to have German courses discontinued. From his position there, Stuart Sherman, it was said, warned the country against the "Prussianism streaming into Anglo-Saxon communities through the forty volumes of Carlyle." The chairman of the philosophy department at Vanderbilt, who had "absorbed the spirit and technique of German scholarship" and was "an outspoken German sympathizer," was warned by the chancellor that "all members of his faculty were patriotic Americans." Malcolm Cowley recalled that at Harvard "during the winter of 1916–17 our professors stopped talking about the international republic of letters and began preaching patriotism." Robert Morss Lovett was hanged in effigy by his Hyde Park neighbors in Chicago for taking part in a 1917 peace rally.

The war provoked an official mobilization of higher education. In 1917, a National Bureau of Education Bulletin "called upon university professors throughout the land to instruct their audiences in the principles for which the country was fighting." Campuses were transformed into troop training centers, and existing courses were redefined as courses in "War Issues." At Illinois, for example, "history, politics, economics, and literature were taught with a view to inculcating the moral superiority of the Allies." At the University of Michigan, the course lecturer asserted that "the German people do not have the humanitarian spirit of fair play, which the English, American and French do have," and added that the "subject people of France love their masters," as proved by the fact that the "people of Madagascar, Tunis, and Algiers sent their troops voluntarily and these troops fought gladly beside the French." Charles Mills Gayley of Berkeley in 1917 turned his course in great books into a course in "Books on the Great War," which he taught to classes of "from 3,000 to 7,000 students and visitors" in the Greek Theatre behind the university. Gayley in that same year also published a book entitled *Shakespeare and the Founders of Liberty in America*, "interpreting . . . Shakespeare's utterances as a sort of prophecy of the universal war," and proving "that Shakespeare's political philosophy . . . was that of the founders of liberty in America, was that of the Declaration of Independence."

Erskine recollected that "the spirit of pacificism which [Columbia] had encouraged until the threat of war appeared, suddenly became as abhorrent to conservatives" as Communism. In 1917 the Columbia trustees "published their intention of investigating the entire professorial group to make sure that no improper doctrines were promulgated at Columbia and that no bad examples were set to the students." A Columbia professor of English, Henry W. L. Dana, was fired by Nicholas Murray Butler for making antiwar speeches, and Charles Beard, the eminent American historian, resigned in protest of similar actions. A modern language scholar in 1917 referred to "Romance colleagues who declared (and this long before the war) that they would never admit to their staffs any one with a degree from a German university." This scholar said he "heard other colleagues declare since the war began that every instructor under them must be pro-Ally. . . . the student body caught [this] noxious spirit and interpreted us to a large extent in terms of interdepartmental rivalry based upon political conditions in Europe."

American literature studies (to be treated separately in a later chapter) owed its founding in large degree to the impetus of wartime superpatriotism. Fred Lewis Pattee observed that "a kind of educational Monroe Doctrine" became established whose maxim was, "for Americans American literature." In an introduction to a school text of 1919, Pattee said that

> The recent manifestation of American patriotism, the new discovery by Europe of the soul of America, and the new insistence on the teaching of Americanism in our schools and colleges, especially in those that for a time were under government control, has brought the study of American literature into the foreground as never before. More and more clearly is it seen now that the American soul, the American conception of democracy,—Americanism, should be made prominent in our school curriculums, as a guard against the rising spirit of experimental lawlessness which has followed the great war, and as a guide to the generation now molding for the future.

As Pattee's reference to "experimental lawlessness" ominously suggested, the teaching of American literature promised finally to awaken academic literary studies to those responsibilities of national "leadership," which they had so far been sluggish in living up to.

In the same year that Pattee's text was released, Edwin Greenlaw and James Holly Hanford of North Carolina edited a college anthology, *The Great Tradition*, comprising *Selections from English and American Prose and Poetry, Illustrating the National Ideals of Freedom, Faith, and Conduct*. The editors described the selections as "landmarks in the march of the Anglo-Saxon mind from the beginning of the modern period." In another college textbook of English and

American literature he coedited, *Literature and Life* (1922), Greenlaw spoke frankly of the American selections as illustrating "the successive interpretations of American thought and ideals that make the story of American literature a powerful adjunct to training for citizenship." "The meaning of our democratic institutions," Greenlaw wrote, "is best understood by those who add to patriotic emotion and acquaintance with the machinery of government a training in the history of the ideals that underlie our faith, and especially a training in the ideals themselves as interpreted in literature. . . . The study of literature, therefore, is not a by-product, an occupation for leisure hours, but is made the heart of the school."

We should not ignore the fact that checking "experimental lawlessness" and promoting "training for citizenship" were central motives shaping the conception of literary studies in this period. But neither should we forget that these aims probably worked more effectively at the level of the schools than of the colleges. And again, even though a certain ideology of citizenship obviously determined the canon, the existence of a canon does not guarantee that it will be taught in an ideologically consistent way. It seems significant, for example, that though Greenlaw's college text, *Literature and Life*, included a selection from the by now canonical *Silas Marner*, it justified doing so not on the grounds of that citizenship and idealism that were the ostensible theme of the anthology, but because it was a realistic work and thus "especially desirable on account of the vogue of realism represented in the enormous popularity of *Main Street* and other books of its type," the kind of reading the student "will do when he leaves school." Civic uplift has certainly been a persistent and recurring motif in college textbooks and anthologies of American literature, and it resurfaced in the 1950s, in response to the Cold War, but since the mid-1920s it has tended to be one motif among others.

American literature continued to be interpreted according to the old Aryan racial theories, as in Bliss Perry's *The American Mind* (1912) and *The American Spirit in Literature* (1918), but the formulations now tended to be distinctly more hesitant and qualified than they had been before the war, the racial generalities touched with a certain scholarly caution. Perry, for example, warned that "no one can understand America with his brains. It is too big, too puzzling. It tempts and it deceives." To be sure, Perry only meant that it was through emotional intuition that one had to feel the essential American "sentiment," which he described as a set of "vaguely felt emotions of admiration, of effort, of fellowship and social faith." But Perry added that "no one can present a catalogue of American qualities as I have attempted without realizing how much escapes his classification. Conscious criticism and assessment of national characteristics is essential to an understanding of them; but one feels somehow that the net is not holding."

John Erskine, in "The Moral Obligation to Be Intelligent" (1913), could still trace "the beginnings of our conscience" to "the German forests," where it "gave its allegiance not to the intellect but to the will." But Erskine added that "to America, much as we may sentimentally deplore it, England [and therefore Germany] seems destined to be less and less the source of culture, of religion and learning. Our land assimilates all races; with every ship in the harbor our old English ways of thought must crowd a little closer to make room for a new tradition."

What seems surprising is not how much blatantly jingoist ideology was in the academic air but how frequently that ideology was attacked. Even at the peak of war hysteria, the idea of an "international republic of letters," transcending national chauvinism, held its own remarkably well. Although they were no doubt ignored by the country at large, the Modern Language Association addresses between 1914 and 1919 tended to be cosmopolitan, antinationalist, and even overtly scornful of what one scholar called "the insidious introduction into our scholarly relations of the political propaganda of a wholly narrow, selfish, and vicious nationalism and false patriotism." "Today, more than ever before," it was said, "the spirit which inspires the study of modern languages and literatures is the idea of universality, the idea which inspired Leibniz, Herder, and the Romanticists." Kant, Herder, and Lessing were invoked in their hope "for the gradual approach of all the nations toward the ideal of common humanity." Goethe was repeatedly singled out for his "keen, broad mind . . . kept pure and free from national prejudice" with "unfailing interest in every cultural movement, no matter what its origin."

This defense of Western culture against narrow particularism promised to restore an older sense of cultural mission to the historical study of literature. Yet it was criticism rather than historical study that gained, since criticism was associated with the skeptical dissection of destructively chauvinistic arguments, and with distinguishing between politically partisan and disinterested interpretations. In a time of social turmoil, it was said, academic literary studies had to become more conscious of their position in the world. And the vehicle of that heightened consciousness was criticism.

Criticism, Great Books, and the Crisis of Culture

The role of criticism in a time of upheaval was spelled out by MLA president Jefferson Fletcher of Columbia, who at the 1915 meeting said

> it is easy, especially in a time of extreme partisanship, to misinterpret great writers to partisan ends. The written word is indeed potent, yet nothing is more helpless. . . . During the past year, both sides in the conflict have called upon Goethe to attest the right of each. Is the great poet really so Janus-faced? Or has the letter on which his spirit set its seal been blurred by hot prejudice? Who shall answer unless the scholar, armed with the facts, a trained mind, and a judicial conscience?

Here the scholar armed with the "judicial conscience" of criticism is made the arbiter of whether Goethe was properly interpreted as a partisan or as a poet who transcended sides. A similar view of criticism as therapy for ideologically based miscommunication and misunderstanding would shortly inspire Richards's manifestos for criticism in the twenties and thirties as well as the semantics movement associated with such figures as Alfred Korzybski, S. I. Hayakawa, and Charles Morris. The early appeal of interpretive pedagogy was bound up with the hope that linguistic analysis would check the excesses of ideological bias and propaganda.

It was Fletcher whom I quoted earlier on the gulf that had come to separate scholars trying to be "right" and men of letters seeking to be "interesting." Fletcher saw criticism as the means of finally healing this long-standing disparity and making literary studies "both right and interesting," which was to say, "interesting to others besides ourselves." Fletcher suggested that since "nations are fighting for their ideals of life," for most people "the interest of literature is more than ever in its evaluations of life." And it was "a renewed emphasis on interpretative criticism" that was to guide those valuations and reestablish a connection with "others besides ourselves."

Perhaps the interpretative criticism Fletcher had in mind was the kind practiced in Erskine's great books course, which Erskine had in fact first developed as an adult education course for American soldiers in France. Adopted only in the face of "great opposition from many powerful colleagues," the curriculum of Erskine's General Honors "was the classics of the Western World, the Great Books, beginning with Homer and coming down through the nineteenth century—in those days there were as yet no recognized twentieth-century classics."

Erskine's idea was to treat the classics as if they were contemporary documents. He devoted one long evening per week to each work (philosophical and theological treatises as well as imaginative literature were included) and encouraged the fifteen or so students in each class to read the books as "the best sellers of ancient times," experiencing them "as spontaneously and humanly as they would read current best sellers" and forming "their opinions at once in a free-for-all discussion."

Erskine said that when he was "told by angry colleagues that a great book couldn't be read in a week, not intelligently!" he replied that "when the great books were first published, they were popular," and the public who first liked them read them quickly, perhaps overnight, without waiting to hear scholarly lectures about them." In Trilling's words, "to some scholars who had spent a lifetime in the study of certain authors or certain books it seemed sacrilegious that undergraduates should be presumed able to read them with understanding in a single week. Erskine replied that every book had to be read at some time for the first time, that there was a difference between a reading acquaintance with great authors and a scholarly investigation of them. In answer to the assertion that to read a great work in translation was not to read it at all, he remarked that if this were so, very few of his colleagues had read the Bible."

Erskine did not invent the great books idea so much as formalize a set of practices that had earlier been initiated by such men as Woodberry (Erskine's mentor), Phelps, Perry, and Gayley, who at Berkeley had been teaching a course called "Great Books" since 1901. But as Trilling says, it was from Erskine's course "that the movement of General Education in the humanities took its rise and established itself not only in Columbia College but in numerous colleges throughout the nation." Having begun as a two-year course for selected junior and senior honors students, by the mid-twenties General Honors was a multisectioned required course in Columbia College, and similar courses were being established elsewhere. One of Erskine's students and fellow instructors in the twenties was Mortimer J. Adler, who went on to the Philosophy Department at the University of Chicago, where he convinced the young president, Robert Maynard Hutchins, that the great books course could be the model for a general education curriculum which would counteract the entrenched forces of scientific positivism and vocationalism. Erskine, who did not admire the Thomistic metaphysics that Adler and Hutchins proceeded to graft onto the course, dissociated himself from the Chicago enterprise, saying that he had been "concerned with no philosophy and no method for a total education; I hoped merely to teach how to read."

There was a "primitive simplicity," as Trilling called it, about the classroom format of General Honors that came to seem the natural setting for "critical" study and, by extension, any teaching dealing with broad issues rather than the inert information of the historical survey. Here was a dramatic turnabout, for we may recall that when lecturing had been introduced in the nineteenth-century college, it was associated with German *Lehrfreiheit* and seen as a liberation from pettifogging ritual. As disillusionment with the research model spread, however, lectures took on the stigma of mechanical learning formerly attaching to classical recitations, and the aura of intellectual authenticity passed to the discussion course.

It was not till the forties, however, that such trends showed themselves on a large scale. For one thing, the small discussion classes called for by the General Honors model were expensive, especially when, as at Columbia, they were "team-taught" by two instructors. Large-scale implementation would require a level of economic expansion well beyond the universities of the twenties and thirties. For another, the opposition of research scholars, who suspected discussion courses of dilettantism and who saw general education programs as impediments to teaching their specialities, was able to keep such experiments marginal until after World War II.

As the idea for General Honors had arisen during the first war, so had that for the other famous and widely imitated Columbia general education course entitled Contemporary Civilization. "C.C.," as it came to be called, evolved directly from the Columbia War Issues course established in 1917. Gruber notes that after the war was over, the course reinstated "the theme of absolute good versus absolute evil . . . simply by putting the Bolshevik in place of the Hun as the menace to democracy everywhere." At Michigan, for example, in 1918 the course lecturer spoke of "the wild excesses of the revolutionaries," a "surprising number" of whom were Jews, and warned that the Bolshevik friends and sympathizers "are everywhere—in Germany, in France . . . in Italy, in Holland, in England, in the United States—they are on the campus of the University of Michigan." Gradually, however, the integration of "history, politics, economics, and literature" that had been brought about in the war issues courses became a model for a kind of interdisciplinary teaching not so crassly tied to nationalistic purposes.

Unfortunately, Contemporary Civilization and General Honors

were never themselves integrated, as originally they were planned to be, so that "literature" remained separate from "history, politics, and economics." Though General Honors and Contemporary Civilization were considered complementary, they remained without any correlation except whatever students in the two courses might contrive to make on their own. This was a crucial weakness, for, contrary to Erskine's assumption, students could not read the great books as their original readers had unless something of the historical circumstances of those books and readers were recreated for them. It is pleasant to think of Plato and Shakespeare as contemporary writers, and some success can be had teaching them as such, but as the gulf between their world and ours widens, the problem of mediating between different ages becomes acute. Precisely because the great books were *not* contemporary documents, to teach them as if they were was to bypass the whole problem of historical and cultural change.

The distance General Honors maintained from sociology and history suggests how proponents of criticism could in their own way reinforce the separations they hoped criticism would heal. General Honors expressed Erskine's prewar literary idealism, the "flame" that his student, Randolph Bourne, credited Erskine with keeping alive but thought had little relation to the modern world. The course presented itself as an alternative to the social and political world rather than a way of making sense of it. Contemporary Civilization, on the other hand, was as uncritically historicist and liberal-social-scientific as General Honors was timelessly humanistic. C.C. expressed the influence of John Dewey's pragmatism and the "new history" of James Harvey Robinson and Charles Beard, the emphasis of which "was on social change and the novelty of the times." The theme of C.C. was "the social evolution of man" and the concept of "history as social process." The antipathy felt to exist between the two courses was exemplified by Erskine's student, Mortimer Adler, who expressed his hostility to pragmatism "in long, argumentative letters slipped under Dewey's office door." Lionel Trilling's later critique of "the liberal imagination" expressed, among other things, the perspective of General Honors against that of C.C., though as it turned out, Trilling was himself almost too sociological (and too Jewish) for Columbia's English Department.

The Scholars Dig In

Research scholars after the war tended to concede in principle that criticism had a valid place. They now said that what they objected to was not criticism as such, but only premature criticism, criticism attempted before the scholarly "groundwork" had been laid. But these concessions were hollow as long as most scholars still conceived of criticism as an affair of subjective impressions opposed to certifiable facts. As long as that assumption prevailed, there was little chance that criticism could become accepted as part of a literature student's necessary concerns.

The tenor of scholarly conservatism can be gauged from a standard guide for graduate students, published in 1922, *Problems and Methods of Literary History*, by a French scholar, André Morize. According to Norman Foerster, Morize's handbook "commended itself to teachers of those courses in Bibliography and Methods which show the serious student whither he is bound and what road he must travel." Morize conceded the value of "impressionistic criticism," observing that "literary history asks [the critic] only to base his personal reaction on facts that have been historically verified." "Those who have faith in literary history," he added, "ask merely that the critic, before constructing systems, before praising or blaming, worshipping or scoffing, be sure that he knows exactly what he is talking about. They ask that before criticizing he be sure to criticize established facts, indisputable chronology, correct texts, exact bibliographies." The message must have been clear enough to students: indulge your taste for criticism if you must, but do not confuse it with genuine knowledge or thought.

Morize made the customary bow to the heroic ideal of Boeckh and Taine. He dusted off Taine's triad of race, milieu, and moment, arguing that the individual book was a reflection of "the history of 'social transformations'" and that by studying writings of all kinds besides the purely belletristic "we may hope to extract the general cast of mind or moral consciousness of a given period." He warned students never to be content "to collect anecdotes or isolated facts, no matter how interesting and pointed," he urged them to "seek the general, the average, the normal—the ensemble of the social, moral, worldly life of the place or period studied," and he recommended that "every investigation of a source should tend toward a definite end: a wider and truer acquaintance with the author, his thought, the evolution of his art, his working-methods, his character, his originality."

But Morize's application suggested that the methods he was promoting were suited only to such tasks as preparing editions, establishing a critical bibliography, investigating and interpreting sources, and solving problems of authentication and attribution. Morize thought of "scientific consciousness and spirit" as "the determination to leave nothing to guesswork, and, without stifling subjective impressions, to keep them entirely apart from substantiated facts." Once again the assumption seemed to have been that the cultural context into which such work supposedly fit could be taken for granted.

Wellek later commented that Morize's book created "the impression that literary history is almost confined to questions of editing and authorship, sources and biography." "However indispensable all this preliminary work, an overemphasis on it results frequently in trivialities and useless pedantries which justly evoke the ridicule of the layman and the anger of the scholar at wasted energy. Such work has all too much attraction for minds indifferent to the values of literature." Foerster had earlier observed that "however expert its methodism," Morize's book "fails lamentably to convey a clear notion of the nonscientific aspects of scholarship."

The book in which these strictures of Foerster's appeared was *The American Scholar* (1929), an all-out humanistic polemic against the scholarly establishment, in the tradition of Churton Collins, Corson, Babbitt, and the Emersonian essay from which it drew its title. Foerster (pronounced FIRST-er) was a student of Babbitt's and a convert to the New Humanism, yet one who overcame sectarianism to embody in his long career a remarkably large number of the emergent professional tendencies of his day. One of the early spokesmen for the critical movement against the research scholars, and a link between the Humanists and the New Critics, Foerster was also a principal founder of American literature studies, which endeavored to close the gap between research and criticism. He published books on *Nature in American Literature* (1923), *Emerson* (1924), and *American Criticism: A Study in Literary Theory from Poe to the Present* (1929), and he edited the important collection of essays, *The Reinterpretation of American Literature* (1928), a turning point in the maturation of American literature as a field. In addition, Foerster was one of the pioneers in making an academic discipline of "creative writing," whose interests he and others in the thirties saw as closely allied with those of criticism. In 1931 he left the University of North Carolina to assume the directorship of the University of Iowa's School of Letters, where his first step was to establish a graduate program in creative writing that later evolved into the Iowa Writers' Workshop. This is an instructive story in itself (though it cannot be pursued here), for Foerster did not foresee that creative writing programs would quickly be detached from their initial synthesizing purposes and become autonomous enterprises—as would criticism itself.

In *The American Scholar*, Foerster began by attacking the philologists for "confusing means and ends, emphasizing the instrument of language instead of the literary result, neglecting the higher tasks that alone can justify scholarship," and thus cooperating "with the forces hostile to the humanities" and betraying their own cause. He then took on the historians, who in their preoccupation with mere description were "just as much interested in a really bad book as in a good book," and who gave "themselves up to a blind pursuit of facts, an aimless accumulation of small additions to the sum of knowledge." Foerster attacked the mania of " 'keeping up with' other scholars immersed in literary history" and urged that "we must set about restoring the traditional alliance of scholarship and criticism, the divorce of which has worked injury to both and played havoc with education."

Yet Foerster himself seemed at times to encourage that divorce, possibly because he accepted the severe separation the Humanists made between the human and natural orders, "law for man" and "law for thing." Though deploring the separation of scholarship and criticism, Foerster sometimes defined these entities as if they could have no possible relation. "We have too often forgotten," he said, "that art and science are two distinct spheres, that the inwardness of art and the externality of science are essentially alien." Such a doctrine left no connection between the function Foerster ascribed to the scholar, "the task of rendering our knowledge more and more exact and thorough," and that of the critic, "of rendering our standards of worth more and more authoritative and serviceable."

Foerster himself collaborated with literary historians in *The Reinterpretation of American Literature*, at Iowa he saw to it that literary history was part of the graduate writing program, and at the end of *The American Scholar* he briefly outlined a model for an alternative program "in which literary history would be employed to illuminate rather than obscure the literature itself." Yet Foerster had an alarming tendency to speak as if the split between literary history and literature were a result not merely of bad or narrow literary history, but of an irrevocable disjunction. He called the "transfer of allegiance" by certain scholars from literature to literary or general social history "an act of treason." It was one thing to chastise the historians for abandoning "literary history in favor of isolated groups of facts." It was another to suggest that even history more capaciously conceived would be treason against literature. In this latter voice, Foerster was not so distant from the historical scholars themselves, who also disjoined history and criticism.

The scholars' reply to Foerster's manifesto was Edwin Greenlaw's 1931 book, *The Province of Literary History*. Greenlaw was a scholar of Spenser, editor of *Studies in Philology*, and one of the imposing figures of early twentieth-century scholarship. ("Don't buck the Greenlaw trust," a correspondent reports having been warned when he was a graduate student in the late twenties.) Greenlaw had hired Foerster at North Carolina in 1914, and the two were colleagues there until 1925, when Greenlaw moved to Johns Hopkins, remaining there until his death in 1931. It says something about the social homogeneity of the profession at this time that such fierce intellectual antagonists could be close colleagues and friends.

In *The Province of Literary History*, Greenlaw seemingly took the challenge of criticism more seriously than Morize had a decade earlier. He conceded that "we shall always need the literary criticism which tries the masterpiece by comparing it with other masterpieces" and determines "its relation to fundamental conceptions of the meaning of tragedy, or of epic, or of any other great literary form, and which defines its author's genius and his outlook on life in such terms." Greenlaw said his "only point is that such a method, interesting and valuable as it is, is not the only method. The literary historian does not merely gather facts, to be used or not by the critic; his method, carried to its logical end, also issues in criticism, is a basis for criticism, is incomplete otherwise."

There was a hint here of a potential reconciliation of methods: literary explication and judgment could be situated within broad cultural history. Yet, finally, Greenlaw fell back on the old defensive argument: there was no reason to try to broaden the scope of literary studies, for literary history was already sufficiently inclusive when conceived properly, in the broad way in which Taine had conceived it. The detractors of literary history were judging not the true practice of the method but only the abuses into which it had occasionally degenerated.

To be sure, Greenlaw conceded, "the study of sources and parallels may lead to foolishness," and "the product of the learned journals may be redolent with pedantry." But properly conceived, literary history was not a mere accumulation of data, it was grounded in "the desire to know the history of civilization as a whole." The scholar "may gain inspiration and vision if he understands that he is helping to write the history of human culture." He participates in Keats's "grand march of intellect." Why then was literary history under attack? Because those who disliked it were victims of nostalgia—"incompetent but vociferous exponents of the good old times."

In the abstract, of course, Greenlaw's argument was sound enough: it was unfair to judge literary history by its weaker manifestations, as the critics sometimes did, and some of literary history's detractors were indeed incompetent exponents of the good old times. Judged properly, literary history was not incompatible with Foerster's humanistic ideal. Greenlaw's own scholarship possessed considerable scope, and whatever one may say about the patriotic textbooks he edited, they reflected a broad idealism not unlike Foerster's own. But Greenlaw never asked himself how much of his broader conception of literary history was actually represented by existing literature departments. How much of the grand march of intellect was getting into professional journals, graduate seminars, and undergraduate courses?

At other moments in his book, Greenlaw changed course and adopted an even more disarming tack: instead of continuing to claim a broadly educational value for literary-historical research, he conceded that most of that research was indeed irrelevant to the cultural and pedagogical aims of the humanities, and argued that no one should expect otherwise. Greenlaw could then accuse New Humanists like Foerster of failing to "distinguish between the course of study proper to the college and the program of the graduate student," inappropriately expecting the cultural and educational ends of the one to be met by the research practices of the other. From the height of their lofty idealism, Humanists like Foerster could not see that the ends of pedagogy are "collegiate and theological" and "have nothing to do with learning."

> The critics of research [said Greenlaw] suffer from a singular unwillingness to recognize that in the graduate department, as distinguished from the college fitting school on the one hand, or the school of education on the other, the purpose of our work is not the production of creative literary artists, or the production of teachers, or even the diffusion of culture, but the discovery and propagation of a learning.

Here Greenlaw seemed to abandon his claim that the kind of learning he was defending had anything to do with "the diffusion of culture." But if learning had nothing to do with diffusing culture, what did? How was the diffusion of culture to occur when the agency to which it was entrusted was admittedly organized for other purposes? Greenlaw conceded that "not all college teachers should be research men," yet he could hardly have failed to notice that university administrators thought and acted otherwise.

Once again, the division of labor separating undergraduate and graduate study justified the pretense that all interests were being satisfied. Graduate education, one could claim, had not been disfigured by the lack of humanistic content in research, for had not graduate students already as undergraduates acquired a humanistic context for their research? And undergraduate study could not be threatened by research since it had nothing to do with research in the first place. But on this point Greenlaw's position was actually not far from that of a hostile critic like Foerster at moments when Foerster separated the critical from the scholarly functions. If, as Foerster had said, "the inwardness of art and the externality of science" are essentially alien, then each could inhabit its own institutional sphere untouched by the other; all interests would be satisfied, and nothing need change.

Not that the only source of resistance to change was the realm of ideas. Conservatism was certainly strengthened by the tacit assumption that the senior professor virtually owned his field, including the right to monopolize its graduate seminars and upper-division courses, direct its dissertations, and control its junior appointments—though this paternalism at least carried the responsibility when the time came of getting one's students jobs, as a later, more democratized system has not. In the face of attempts to change these baronial arrangements, older professors tended to feel that if *they* had had to work their way up in this system, why should not others as well. (Departmental folklore at one university records the anguished response of one senior man in the early fifties when "his" seminar was opened to junior colleagues: "I fought tooth and nail to control that course," he is said to have protested, "and now you want to give it away.") Then, too, echoing the old theory of mental discipline, scholars tended to plead that, especially at the graduate level, most of the work necessarily had to be the dreary grind that it was. Howard Mumford Jones may not quite have put it that way in 1930–31, writing of "Graduate English Study: Its Rational[e]," but that seemed almost the implication of his statement that "no conscientious teacher of graduate students but realizes with regret that his days and nights are practically given over to the teaching of obvious and necessary information and technique; and though he would gladly push on to higher matters, practically he is unable to do so."

DOUBTS FROM WITHIN

The scholars were at their point of highest confidence in the postwar years, yet divisions continued to appear in their ranks. It was not just New Humanists like Foerster who made fundamental criticisms of the research model, but scholars of unimpeachable standing. The editor of Sidney's works, Albert Feuillerat of Yale, wrote in 1925 that though the scientific method was "a salutary reaction against the vague and unsupported constructions of those who, in an age of inductive analysis, still believed in the haphazard inspirations of mere subjectivism," research had degenerated into a pedantry that converted the means into an end and accumulated "facts, still more facts" without using them "for some purpose beyond them." Formerly, Feuillerat said, scholars "were poets, professors, and critics. But now the divorce between academic criticism and literary criticism" is so nearly complete that "for a literary critic to be called a scholar is an insult calculated to destroy his reputation as a man of brains; and for a scholar to be mistaken for a literary critic is a thing sufficient to fill one with confusion and shame." In divorcing itself from criticism, scholarship had abandoned the "ambition of playing a part in the education of the nation at large." "Let us frankly acknowledge that we have made a mistake," Feuillerat pleaded, and "retrace our steps to the cross-roads where scholarship and criticism began to separate."

In his 1927 presidential address to the MLA, John Livingston Lowes of Harvard also regretted the severance of research from its justifying purposes. Lowes's famous study of Coleridge, *The Road to Xanadu* (1927), seemed the epitome of source-study (though it was more than that). At Harvard he engaged in lively public combat with Babbitt, defending the values of scholarship. Yet anyone who heard Lowes's MLA address might have thought it was Babbitt himself speaking. "More and more," Lowes said, "our interests are becoming special, minute, discrete. In fifty years our emphasis has gone far towards passing from scholarship for larger ends to scholarship for scholars." "Some day somebody may use our accumulations to constructive ends—but why in Heaven's name not more often *we*?"

Even more damaging than such overt self-criticisms were the admissions that slipped unobtrusively into attempts at self-vindication. In his 1929 MLA presidential address, William A. Nitze congratulated the scholars, disparaged the critics, and—anticipating Greenlaw's attack on Foerster—wondered somewhat querulously why "people continue to measure scholarship in this country by other than scholarly aims"? Nitze declared that the "Victorian Age of our scholarship," that "applied itself to individual sources" and emphasized "separate and unconnected units," had happily ended, giving way to "the history of mankind in cross-sections and, especially, to the 'integration' of that history in all of its varied aspects." For evidence, he cited such works as *The Road to Xanadu*, J. M. Manly's *Some New Light on Chaucer*, Root's edition of *Troilus*, and Bedier's "brilliant pages on the 'unity' of the *Chanson de Roland*."

Yet Nitze went on to imply that little of the synthetic influence to be gained from these works was reflected in the association as a whole. He revived the old lament, dating back to the turn of the century, of a lack of relatedness in the diverse activities of the Association.

The problem was now intensified by the division of the membership into Research Groups in 1920. By 1929 there were thirty-nine such groups—"five in General Topics and Comparative Literature each, fourteen in English, five in French and German each, two in Spanish, one in Italian, Scandinavian, and Slavonic respectively." Nitze observed that not only did these various groups have little to do with one another, but even the discussion within groups lacked conceptual focus. A "sound policy," Nitze suggested, would

> bar the miscellaneous type of paper from the Research Groups. For example, I cannot see that a Note on *che si chiamare*, however admirable in itself, makes a suitable group-companion for a paper on *Croce's System as a Theory of Error*, if, as I imagine, the reason for this misalliance is merely that there happens to be a Research Group in Italian or that Italian desires to have a Research Group. . . . The logic of the situation would require that we reserve the Research Groups for specific, cooperative work.

By the end of his address, Nitze was saying that "we have too many papers, too many groups, too many separate interests represented in each group—certainly, too many meetings scheduled at one and the same hour; and the time that may have been intended for discussion never comes round." (What would Nitze have made of the MLA conventions of the 1980s?) Nitze recommended that one meeting be set aside as "the clearing-house of our ideas," bringing topics "out into the open, from the corners in which they are hidden, and occasionally [setting] them into relation with each other for the significance that they may contain." Perhaps then the Association "might be able to estimate whither our researches are tending."

Nitze had unwittingly answered his own question: Why do "people continue to measure scholarship in this country by other than scholarly aims?" The obvious answer was that scholarship had determined the educational and cultural direction of the department, and therefore could not be judged by technical criteria alone. When universities had been small, the failure of scholarship to "play a part in the education of the nation at large," in Feuillerat's phrase, had no great consequences, and scholars might plausibly protest that mass education was not their business. But as the universities expanded, such a failure became magnified, and such disclaimers seemed irresponsible. The case for criticism had been clinched by the scholars themselves.

CHAPTER NINE

Groping for a Principle of Order: 1930–1950

The professors are in an awful dither trying to reform themselves and there's a big stroke possible for a small group that knows what it wants in giving them ideas and definitions and showing the way.

JOHN CROWE RANSOM

From its inception in the thirties, the loosely affiliated group that became labelled "New Critics" was beset by pressures that pulled it in conflicting directions. I have elsewhere suggested that the need to combat a bewildering variety of different factions helps account for the frequently contradictory nature of New Critical theory. There was a tendency to shift the emphasis depending on the enemy in view—now, for example, minimizing the referential and humanistic values of literature in answer to moralistic Humanists, Marxist propagandists, and historical reductionists, now asserting the importance of those same referential and humanistic values against positivist philosophers and philistines. Not the least of the external pressures on the New Critics, however, was the pressure to measure up to the institutional criteria set by its scholarly opposition, which was still in control of literature departments.

The scholars had established a certain conception of methodological rigor as a condition of professional respectability. This conception, the critics could and did argue, implied the isolation of literature as an autonomous mode of discourse with its own special "mode of existence," distinct from that of philosophy, politics, and history. It also put a premium on methods that seemed systematic and could easily be replicated. As the university increased in size, the need arose for a simplified pedagogy, encouraging the detachment of "close reading" from the cultural purposes that had originally inspired it.

Several other factors favored the emergence of the narrower aesthetic and methodological potentialities latent in the New Criticism, but these have received more attention than the institutional ones and will therefore get less notice here. One such factor was the political situation of the 1930s, which generated theories of art so crudely propagandistic that they made the separation of art from politics seem an attractive or even a necessary position. Another factor—to be deferred to later chapters—was the hostile academic climate surrounding the modernist revolution in literature for which the New Critics were spokesmen.

For a confluence of independent reasons, then, after the mid-1930s, the more aggressive partisans of criticism in the university began to dissociate themselves from the motley of "generalist" groups with which they had previously coexisted. One might say that it was a condition of becoming institutionalized that the New Criticism sever its ties with the social and cultural criticism of which first generation New Critics were a part. Eventually, the very term "New Critical" would become synonymous with the practice of explicating texts in a vacuum. This is what it became in institutional practice, but decidely not what it was for the founding generation.

THE COLLAPSE OF THE UNITED CRITICAL FRONT

Greenlaw's scorn, in *The Province of Literary History*, for "incompetent but vociferous exponents of the good old times" permits us to infer that in 1931 it was still not necessary to take the critical opponents of research very seriously. To scholars like Greenlaw, none of the schools of criticism possessed the rigorous methodology needed to qualify for academic acceptance. Nitze of Chicago made the point bluntly in his MLA presidential address of 1929: "Our literary critics are a cheerless lot," Nitze said. "Either . . . they are still groping for a principle of order, or they have an axe to grind that is sociological or journalese rather than literary." Such a comment made clear that if criticism was ever to accredit itself in the university, it would have to undergo a purification, acquiring a principle of order and dispensing with any axe to grind that was sociological or journalese rather than literary.

By the mid-1930s, the ranks of the generalists were thinning out: Sherman and Erskine had left the profession in the mid-twenties, and Sherman died in 1926. Babbitt died in 1933. Perry, Phelps, Vida Scudder, and Fred Lewis Pattee retired during the thirties. The New Humanists remained a force in several of the eastern universities and in a few western outposts such as the University of Nebraska English Department, which harbored a humanist coterie and journal under the leadership of Prosser Hall Frye. But, ironically, the same heavy-handed moralism that made it so easy for the research scholars to dismiss the Humanists as incompetent caused the younger generation of academics to see them as "professors" rather than "critics." Recalling his thoughts in the twenties and thirties, Yvor Winters said that he and other younger writers of the period thought of Babbitt as the archprofessor, even though they recognized that for his colleagues, "Babbitt was a professor largely on sufferance: he was really a dangerous innovator. . . . he was a critic and had defended criticism as an academic discipline and had attacked the colleges and universities for neglecting it." For Winters and other younger academics, Babbitt was still a professor, since "he held the title at Harvard, he had obviously read a great deal, he was quite obviously imperceptive in writing about poetry," and of course he had nothing but scorn for contemporary literature.

Many of the younger critics with generalist inclinations gravitated toward journalism and bohemia—options still open in an economy that permitted a living to be eked out on book reviewing, translating, and occasional editorial work. A distinctly antiacademic class of literary journalists took shape in the twenties, enlisting figures such as Van Wyck Brooks, H. L. Mencken, Edmund Wilson, and Malcolm Cowley. When this type did teach, as Bernard DeVoto did at Northwestern and Harvard, it was usually in temporary positions, and then only until an alternative presented itself. Others, however, began to fit their generalist interests into the methodological mold of the New Critics, and some began to dissociate themselves entirely from the generalists' moral and social interests. The need to meet those standards of methodological purity and order set by positivistic scholars like Nitze, the need not to have "an axe to grind that is sociological or journalese rather than literary," meant divesting criticism of its encumbering moral and social attachments.

R. S. Crane of Chicago, advocating a reformed literature program in 1935, wrote that "men of the type of the older impressionists we could hardly use, and as for the remnants of the Humanists, there is little to be hoped for from the kind of principles—essentially political and ethical rather than esthetic in character—for which they have mainly stood." That political and ethical principles now disqualified one from contributing to the academic critical program was a token of what was to come. Crane's defense of criticism was clearly aimed at historians like his colleague Nitze, yet the terms in which Crane defended criticism seemed curiously to accede to Nitze's standard of measurement.

John Crowe Ransom welcomed Crane's support in 1938, calling

Crane "the first of the great professors to have advocated [criticism] as a major policy for departments of English." In a pivotal essay significantly entitled "Criticism, Inc.," Ransom wrote that "the university teacher of literature . . . should be the very professional we need to take charge of the critical activity." In its present state, Ransom observed, the English department had so little to do with "literature, an art," that it might "almost as well announce that it does not regard itself as entirely autonomous, but as a branch of the department of history, with the option of declaring itself occasionally a branch of ethics." The Humanist "diversion" had been little help, Ransom said, having "in the long run . . . proved to be nearly as unliterary as the round of studies from which it took off at a tangent." And of course the proletarian critics were but another set of "diversionists," with concerns no less extraliterary than those of the Humanists.

Ransom certainly had a point in noting the limitations of these groups, but he simplified a potentially complex issue by flatly asserting, as if it were self-evident, that "criticism is the attempt to define and enjoy the aesthetic or characteristic values of literature." Once it was assumed that there were "aesthetic or characteristic values of literature" that could be isolated from other values, it had to follow—as it might not under some other definition of criticism—that an autonomous literature department was naturally more desirable than one which would see literature as inseparable from history, philosophy, psychology, and social thought. The autonomy of poetic language demanded the autonomy of departments to teach it as a matter of territorial rights. As Ransom put it, "Strategy requires now, I should think, that criticism receive its own charter of rights and function independently."

RECOIL FROM POLITICS

Yet New Critics like Ransom did not think they were turning their backs on the moral and social function of literature. For them, rather, the point was to define these social and moral functions as they operated within the internal structure of literary works themselves—something the generalists had grossly neglected to do. It was not a question of purging moral and social significance from literature, but of showing how that significance became a function of the formal texture of the work itself rather than something external or superadded. The morality and politics of literature would thus be recognized in a way that would not entail crudely reducing poems and novels to their instrumental or doctrinal content. In this way, the

interests both of generalist humanism and of methodological rigor would be met—critical methodology being precisely the means of reconciling the two. But in practice these interests were not reconciled.

The rupture in the previously united critical front was not just between New Critics and New Humanists or New Critics and literary journalists, but between conflicting impulses within the New Criticism itself. Whatever one may think of their predominantly conservative politics, the fact remains that first-generation New Critics were neither aesthetes nor pure explicators but culture critics with a considerable "axe to grind" against the technocratic tendencies of modern mass civilization. Even when they minimized the social aspect of their work, their very way of doing so bespoke a social concern; for emphasizing the aesthetic over the directly social was a way of counteracting what the New Critics saw as the overly acquisitive and practical tenor of modern urban society. It was not merely that the taste of Eliot and the Southern New Critics for organically complex, overdidactically "Platonic" poetry reflected their admiration for organic, hierarchical societies over the abstractions of mechanistic industrialism, though this was in fact the case. These critics' very insistence on the disinterested nature of poetic experience was an implicit rejection of a utilitarian culture and thus a powerfully "utilitarian" and "interested" gesture.

The charge of formalism against the New Critics was popularized by disgruntled nonacademic critics like Van Wyck Brooks, who spoke in 1953 of the school's "excessive concentration on questions of form" and charged that its "sole criterion is technical expertness." Brooks said that this criticism "stimulates the cerebral faculties at the expense of the feelings upon which the normal growth of the writer depends," and he blamed it for having "stopped the circulation of the blood in both novels and poems." It bespoke an "excess of the academic" that had turned its back on the social and cultural functions of literature. But even at its most "formalistic" (or especially then), the New Critical view of poetry made a social and cultural point, rejecting the allegedly vitiated language of "a dehumanized society," as Allen Tate put it, in which men may "communicate, but they cannot live in full communion." As Tate saw it, "the battle is now between the dehumanized society of secularism, which imitates Descartes' mechanized nature, and the eternal society of the communion of the human spirit." Again, whatever one may think of such a view, to label it formalist, aesthetic, or apolitical is misleading.

Nor did the early New Critics explicate literature in a vacuum, as has so often been charged. Eliot did not much like explication at all, longing as he did for a culture in which poetry would be so instinctively part of the common consciousness that it would not need to be explicated, and he ridiculed what he called "the lemon-squeezer school of criticism." As for Richards, who did promote poetic explication through his practical criticism program, we have already seen that this program was part of a wider conception of semantic therapy aimed at mitigating the destructive effects of science and nationalism. First-generation New Critical explications of literature were rarely explications only: they were cultural and philosophical essays, in which texts like "The Canonization," "Sailing to Byzantium," and the poems of Poe became allegorical statements about the dissociation of sensibility, technological rationality, the collapse of the Old South, or some other equally large theme. Reuben Brower's *The Fields of Light* (1951) was probably the first major work of the New Criticism that explicated poems without an accompanying cultural thesis.

Richard Ohmann, one of the school's severest critics, seems to me right in arguing that "the pages of the New Criticism are bound together with moral fibre, almost strident in urging a social mission for literature." But by the end of the thirties—the Hitler-Stalin Pact of 1939 was an embarrassment to left and right both—social missions for literature had become compromised. The argument that the politics of literature should be seen as part of its form modulated subtly into the idea that literature had no politics, except as an irrelevant extrinsic concern.

One can see the turn taking place in R. P. Blackmur's 1935 essay "A Critic's Job of Work," which attacked Granville Hicks's Marxist study of American literature, *The Great Tradition*, for its "tendentiousness," its initial "hortatory assumption that American literature ought to represent the class struggle from a Marxist viewpoint, and that it ought thus to be the spur and guide to political action." Blackmur said that Hicks's approach was "concerned with the separable content of literature, with what may be said without consideration of its specific setting and apparition in a form." Blackmur privately described himself as "still something of that smelly thing an independent liberal," but he agreed with the conservative critics that "the fine object of criticism," which Hicks's approach could not encompass, should be "to put us in direct possession of the principles whereby works move without injuring or disintegrating the body of the works themselves," and this object could be achieved only by "sustained contact . . . with the works nominally at hand."

Critics on the left retorted that "the principles whereby works move" are inseparable from matters of belief and ideology. This valid argument was compromised by crude application, as in Hicks's dismissal of Henry James in *The Great Tradition* on the grounds that for the most part his novels and tales "seem completely remote from the lives of the majority of men." "It is all very well to praise James's technique," Hicks said, "but could not one fairly characterize the literary processes we have been describing as a game?" Passages like this one, or like the embarrassingly Stalinist call to arms with which Malcolm Cowley ended the 1934 edition of *Exile's Return* (quietly deleted from the 1951 reprint most readers know today) made it easy to reject any form of ideological criticism as inherently crude.

Increasingly the failings Ransom, Blackmur, and others charged against the proletarian school came to be adduced against any approach to literature which took politics and ideology seriously. Consider the reaction provoked by Edmund Wilson's 1931 study of modernist literature, *Axel's Castle*, a work which reflected the influence of Marxist criticism. Wilson's book was by no means an attack on modernist decadence—from some points of view it was a defense of the modern poetic revolution. Christian Gauss congratulated Wilson for showing the importance of the new literature to "an academic group whose minds and sympathies have lost flexibility and are usually closed to the new." But Wilson's study took Eliot and Valéry to task for encouraging "a conception of poetry as some sort of pure and rare aesthetic essence with no relation to any of the practical human uses for which, for some reason never explained, only the technique of prose is appropriate." Wilson accused modern poets of a point of view that was "absolutely unhistorical—an impossible attempt to make aesthetic values independent of all the other values." He disputed Eliot's pronouncements on the separability of poetry and beliefs and detected in Eliot's poetry "a kind of reactionary point of view" hiding behind the pretense of disinterestedness. Wilson said that "when we read Lucretius and Dante, we are affected by them just as we are by prose writers of eloquence and imagination—we are compelled to take their opinions seriously."

Cleanth Brooks replied to Wilson's arguments in *Modern Poetry and the Tradition* (1939), setting out what would become the standard New Critical response to socially minded critics. Brooks charged that Wilson had confused poetry with its beliefs, proceeding as if "the poet might state [ideas] plainly if only he chose to." The poet, Brooks argued, does not make statements that can be separated from the whole of the poem. "The experience which he 'communicates,'" Brooks writes, "is itself created by the organization of the symbols he uses. The total poem is therefore the communication, and indistinguishable from it." Brooks was right in suggesting that Wilson had not dealt sufficiently with the way Eliot's beliefs had been deflected, ironized, and otherwise modified by the poetic structure of his works, yet he might have made his point without leaping to the conclusion that "embodiment" in a poetic structure necessarily negates the force of a poet's beliefs as beliefs. Indeed, Eliot had argued not that Dante put forth no beliefs in his verse (as both Brooks and Wilson took him to say), but that Dante had been able to presuppose agreement about beliefs in the culture in which he wrote, and therefore did not have to assert them explicitly or didactically.

Instead of correcting Wilson's oversimplification of the ideas in Eliot's poetry, Brooks chose to deny that poems could assert ideas at all, an argument that had the effect not only of neutralizing in advance the ideological questions Wilson was raising, but of pushing Brooks into a more extreme position than he wanted to hold. If literature was incapable of "saying" anything, or if what it said was too complex for reformulation, then literature could not speak, and what could not speak was in principle immune from liability. This "limited liability" theory of literary assertion, as I have called it elsewhere, was becoming a pervasive view, and not just among conservative critics. The crucial years in which criticism was becoming established in the university, then, were the very years in which intellectuals were moving away from political concerns.

"FOUNDING" CRITICISM: 1937–1940

It is possible to fix 1937–41 as the turning point for the consolidation of criticism in the university. 1937 was the year Ransom moved from Vanderbilt to Kenyon, where he shortly became founding editor of the *Kenyon Review* and later director of the Kenyon School of English. In 1938, Cleanth Brooks and Robert Penn Warren, two former students of Ransom's at Vanderbilt, published their influential textbook, *Understanding Poetry*. In 1935 Brooks and Warren had cofounded the *Southern Review* at Louisiana State University, where they were joined by Robert B. Heilman. In 1939 came Brooks's *Modern Poetry and the Tradition*, synthesizing the disparate ideas and judgments of Eliot, Richards, and Ransom into a usefully compact revisionary theory of the history of poetry. In 1939 Allen Tate, another former student of Ransom at Vanderbilt, left the Women's College of North Carolina to become Resident Fellow in Creative Writing at Princeton, and when Tate went on leave in 1940 he was able to arrange for R. P.

Blackmur to take his place. Delmore Schwartz became an instructor at Harvard in 1940.

In 1939 René Wellek, who had emigrated from Prague in 1927 at age twenty-three and served as an instructor at Princeton and Smith between 1929 and 1930, returned from Europe to take a position at the University of Iowa, whence he would move to Yale in 1946. In 1940 William K. Wimsatt came to Yale, having taught for a decade in Catholic schools and colleges, and Austin Warren, who had studied with Irving Babbitt at Harvard in the early twenties, joined the faculty of the University of Iowa. Yvor Winters had been teaching at Stanford since 1927. Kenneth Burke was working at temporary teaching positions, before taking a permanent one at Bennington in 1943. The book by Ransom that gave "the New Criticism" its name (though Spingarn had coined the term in a somewhat different sense in an essay of 1910) was published in 1941. As this list of names suggests, many of the first critics to achieve a foothold in the university did so on the strength of their poetry rather than their criticism. It is worth pondering the probability that the critical movement would not have succeeded in the university had it not been tied to creative writing, from which it was soon to part company.

By the early forties, then, critics were in powerful enough positions and sufficiently in agreement with one another on general principles to make a concerted move. Not that they had ceased to be vulnerable to persecution from their scholarly superiors, who still regarded them as amateur intruders. Tate had only a B.A., Burke had only two years of college, and Blackmur had not been to college at all. Though most of the others had taken conventional advanced degrees, almost all were vulnerable to the suspicion that they were not qualified scholars. According to Blackmur's biographer, Russell Fraser:

> the older men in the department thought Richard's presence at Princeton absurd, and were horrified to discover "a Blackmur cult" springing up around them. They warned their students to keep away. . . . To Robert K. Root, Richard walking on Cannon Green below his windows in Nassau Hall seemed a desecration. Friends were alarmed when this eminent Chaucer scholar, having moved from Department Chairman to Dean of the Faculty, did his best to expel the offending presence.

At Stanford, Winters's chairman, A. G. Kennedy, like Root a medievalist, kept him teaching freshman composition for many years. Winters said Kennedy warned him "that criticism and scholarship do not mix, that if I wanted to become a serious scholar I should give up criticism. He told me likewise that poetry and scholarship do not mix, and that he had given up the writing of poetry at the age of twenty-five. And he added that my publications were a disgrace to the department. Fortunately for myself, he was the only one of the four department heads to hold these views, but one was almost enough. And he was far from an exception so far as the profession as a whole was concerned."

At Harvard, Delmore Schwartz and John Berryman took consolation in drink for the uncertainty in which they were kept by the senior faculty about their future: "Both of us felt crushed," Berryman said, "but gradually we drank more and more and talked about Shakespeare and verse and in the end we were as happy—in the context of despair & humiliation—as I ever expect to be." When Schwartz came up for review, though the departmental committee had presumably read his published work, one member asked "if I had ever written any short stories," another "declared that he knew nothing at all about literature, and it was obvious that one impression was that I was a Dadaist. It was decided to recommend me without reservation, but to suggest that these appointments ought not to be given to the kind of author that I was."

Prejudice against critics was occasionally reinforced by prejudice against Jews and any other group suspected of bohemian leanings. Karl Shapiro notes that "the present generation has forgotten the moral constraints of the academy of the Forties, the monogamic imperative, the lofty anti-Semitism of English professors, the prudishness, the watchfulness, the conformity." Before World War I, Ludwig Lewisohn had been told by a member of the Columbia English faculty—whose "cool and kindly smile" Lewisohn well described—that he had not got a graduate fellowship because "it seemed to us . . . that the university hadn't had its full influence on you." It becomes clear in published excerpts from Lionel Trilling's notebooks how little this attitude had changed at Columbia by the mid-thirties. Several of Trilling's colleagues saw his Jewishness, his interest in criticism, and his "emphasis on 'Sociology' " as part of the same complex, stamping him as one of those men who "didn't fit" and would not be "happy" at Columbia. The English department chairman warned Trilling that his teaching "irritated many freshman students by talking about literature as sociology and psychology," and another colleague, Emery Neff, told him that his "sociological tendencies had hidden [his] literary gifts in the thesis [the doctoral dissertation on Matthew Arnold on which Trilling was then working] as in the classroom." The suspicion was that Trilling had "involved himself with Ideas"; he was "too sensitive"; he "doesn't fit in because he is a Jew." When Trilling was finally promoted, Neff expressed the hope that "now that Lionel was a member of the department, he [Neff] hoped that he would not use it as a wedge to open the English department to more Jews."

Despite such persecutions from various quarters, conditions had begun to favor the critics, quite apart from the genuine merits of their cause. American universities had been growing steadily since 1900, with the percentage of the eligible population attending college rising in forty years from 4 to 14 percent, and from 1940 to 1964 enrollments making a quantum leap to 40 percent. It was in the late forties, according to Veysey, that "the proportion of the overall American population receiving some form of higher education suddenly mushroomed. The war veterans made up only one segment of this dramatic increase, which more broadly reflected an awareness within a greatly enlarged sector of the middle and skilled working classes that some version of college was necessary in order to keep economically afloat."

Though the great explosion in graduate programs would not come till the fifties and sixties, figures indicate the beginning of an upswing a decade earlier. By 1938, Indiana University had awarded only seven doctorates in English, whereas between 1938 and 1950 it awarded twenty. Between 1920 and 1929, twenty students took Ph.D's at the University of North Carolina, whereas between 1930 and 1939 thirty-six did so, and between 1940 and 1949 fifty-two. The effect of this growth, combined with the effect of the war itself, was to inspire a mood of rethinking favorable to educational experimentation. As Robert Fitzgerald recalled, "the critical movement in the colleges . . . antedated the war, but the war had made it more earnest." And the postwar student body, swelled by numerous beneficiaries of the G.I. Bill, was a peculiarly serious one—according to Kenneth Lynn, one of their number, "the oldest, most experienced students the university had ever known."

If there was a single critical career whose personal trajectory perfectly coincided with the institutional fortunes of criticism, it was that of John Crowe Ransom. Born in 1888, Ransom received a traditional classical education in Nashville schools and at Vanderbilt (class of 1909), after which he taught Greek and Latin in secondary schools and studied classics and philosophy as a Rhodes Scholar at Oxford. In 1914 Ransom joined the Vanderbilt English faculty, which had recently been reorganized on historical principles with required courses in "the development of English literature from Beowulf to Kipling." In these courses, students had to "become acquainted with the names, titles, and facts of English literature" and, in the section taught by the department chairman, "to memorize the five thousand or so lines that in the opinion of their instructor were most representative of their literary heritage."

Ransom ignored such methods and, in the words of his biographer, Thomas Daniel Young, "began almost immediately the practice of teaching literature in the manner later made popular by Robert Penn Warren and Cleanth Brooks in *Understanding Poetry* and *Understanding Fiction*." This approach to teaching may have been prompted by Ransom's speculations on the "theory of poetics" inspired by his reading of Kant and Bergson at Oxford. Ransom had already worked out, in rough essays and personal letters, the antithesis between the imaginative and the logical or practical dimensions of experience on which his mature theory of poetry would be based. For whatever reason, Ransom did not attempt to "lecture on all, or nearly all, of Shakespeare's plays," as his colleagues did, but "concentrated on four or five plays, reading those closely and analytically and emphasizing particularly the poet's use of language."

In the twenties Ransom and a group of his students formed the Vanderbilt Fugitives and began developing the program for poetic and cultural renovation of the South that would culminate in the publication of *I'll Take My Stand* at the end of the decade. For a brief period, Ransom became a traveling propagandist for agrarianism around the South. But in the early thirties, deciding that the agrarian program had no chance of practical realization, he stopped participating in politics in order to concentrate on poetry and criticism. Whether Ransom ever actually believed that agrarianism had a realistic chance seems doubtful. Irony was an attitude Ransom cultivated early in his life, and knowing this one is led to wonder if he saw his political experience as an instance of it—the promoting of a political cause in whose future one only half believes.

Whatever the case, Ransom by the early thirties had concluded that "the form of art is as important to a traditionalist as his religion, or his state, or his values anywhere." But as long as Ransom remained at Vanderbilt, he was blocked from putting his ideas into practice on an institutional scale. Only with the offer from Kenyon in 1937 did that opportunity present itself. That two students who followed Ransom from Vanderbilt to Kenyon were Robert Lowell and Randall Jarrell makes the move seem all the more portentous. Anthony Hecht, who went to Kenyon on the G.I. Bill, recalled how he and other students felt themselves part of a "happy few" under Ransom's tutelage: "To have become one of that little group of Kenyon students in the mid-forties was not merely to have joined them under Mr. Ransom's remarkable tuition; it was also to have been assimilated into a hieratic tradition, a select branch in the great, taxonomic structure of the modern intellect. . . . Let it be said that Mr. Ransom was altogether innocent as well as ignorant of our fatuities."

The newly formed *Kenyon Review*, whose editorship Ransom assumed, was one of the journals that, with the *Southern Review* (founded in 1935) and the *Sewanee Review*, would be most instrumental in disseminating the new kind of university-based criticism that Ransom and others were starting to write. It was a criticism that resembled neither the scholarship published by *PMLA* nor the cultural and political criticism published by the *New Masses*, the *New Republic*, and the *Partisan Review*. As editor of the *Kenyon*, Ransom emphasized, in his biographer's words, "the need for professional literary critics who would insist upon the necessity of an approach to literature that is primarily concerned with formal and aesthetic values, one always centered upon the world of art itself."

The opening number of the *Kenyon* (January 1, 1939) contained an editorial statement that the journal hoped "to carry on literary and aesthetic discussion in language of a rather severer economy than is usual, provided no sacrifice is required in warmth of style, or literary quality." The "severer economy" also meant that politics would be de-emphasized. As Ransom wrote to Tate in 1937, seeking to interest him in the associate editorship of the journal, "our cue would be to stick to literature entirely. There's no consistent, decent group writing politics . . . [and] in the severe field of letters there is vocation enough for us: in criticism, in poetry, in fiction." The regionalism of the Agrarians would be replaced by professionalism, for attaining "a professional level of distinction" meant making "no reference to local setting whatever." As professionalism had earlier conflicted with the humanistic traditions of the scholars, it now began to come into conflict with the social interests of the critics.

Ransom added, in his letter to Tate, "I have an idea that we could really found criticism if we got together on it." For "the professors are in an awful dither trying to reform themselves and there's a big stroke possible for a small group that knows what it wants in giving them ideas and definitions and showing the way."

The School of English and the Gauss Seminars

In 1948, Ransom became involved in another enterprise that would prove an important step in the "founding" of criticism in the university. Aided by a grant of $40,000 from the Rockefeller Foundation, Ransom established the Kenyon School of English, a summer institute at which graduate students and junior faculty would study under such leading critics as Ransom, Tate, Brooks, Empson, Winters, and Austin Warren. (In 1951 the school moved to the University of Indiana, rechristening itself the School of Letters.) This was not the first instance in which foundation money assisted the cause of one academic literary faction against another. The hiring of Tate and Blackmur at Princeton had been made possible by a grant from the Carnegie Foundation to Dean Gauss in 1939 to establish a Creative Arts Program that would bring writers to the Princeton Faculty—another case of the unity of interest, in this period, of criticism and creative writing.

In his application to the Rockefeller Foundation, Ransom proclaimed the advantages of criticism over the established scholarly methodologies. He wrote that existing English courses did "not have a proper regard either for the literary interest of their maturing students or for the possibilities of their subject." He said that the more spirited students "are not content with the recital of facts which are important but largely sub-literary, and which are not being consistently employed with intelligent purpose." Such students know that "critics have a deeper and more enlightened interest in the creative process as a human adventure." Therefore the School of English would "bring literary criticism into the academy more rapidly, by teaching it to those who are going to be teachers."

The School of English thus came into existence for the express purpose of training and retraining a new professional cadre to displace, or at least supplement, the already established groups. Like the later School of Criticism and Theory of the seventies, which would come into being for the purpose of retraining critics and scholars as theorists, the School of English was attended by a bracing, if slightly deceptive, sense of iconoclasm and risk. As an early enrollee, George Lanning, recalled, he and the other students felt that they had come

> to help make order in the wilderness of literary criticism. Perhaps we were like the early Beats—as improbable as that yoking may at first appear. But I mean that we possessed the kind of exhilaration that they had to start with. And we knew, too, that on every side, even in our midst, was the Enemy, the wooly headed Beast of primitive criticism in whose territory we proposed to settle. He was fighting back hard—very hard, just then. Vigorously, we "explicated" in and out of class; we got so we could spot a Precious Object at a thousand yards; and where we couldn't find an ambiguity we made one.

The Beast might be fighting back hard, but $40,000 had been bet that it would be tamed.

If we look at the board of senior fellows at the School of English and the School of Letters, most of whom taught a stint at one or the other, we can see that the models of criticism conveyed were by no means as monolithically fixated on pure explication as George Lanning's remarks quoted above may suggest. The roster included such wide-ranging critics as Eric Bentley, Richard Chase, F. O. Matthiessen, Lionel Trilling, Jacques Barzun, Kenneth Burke, Alfred Kazin, Arthur Mizener, Philip Rahv, Mark Schorer, Delmore Schwartz, and Yvor Winters. Yet the academic situation favored the pure explicators to a degree that some of the critics would later regret.

One who was already having misgivings was Blackmur. According to Robert Fitzgerald in his informative memoir, *Enlarging the Change*, Blackmur feared that the critical movement was "grinding into a self-centered methodology in Ransom, in Empson, and particularly in the 'grammars' of Kenneth Burke." (Burke and Empson, however, would probably have shared his fears.) The Princeton Seminars in Literary Criticism, the famous "Gauss Seminars," begun under Blackmur's leadership in 1949, were originally conceived as a means of airing the larger cultural and political concerns that Blackmur himself never fully clarified in his later critical work.

Like the Kenyon School of English, the Princeton Seminars had foundation support, first by Carnegie, later by the Rockefeller Foundation. But in appealing for support, Blackmur tied the mission of criticism not, as Ransom had, to the reform of literary studies, but to the reassessment of the place of the humanities in American life. In Blackmur's vision, as reported by Fitzgerald (who assisted him in running them), the seminars would contribute to a national project of stock-taking afforded by postwar affluence, in which "the citizenry," in Fitzgerald's words, "might take thought, if they cared to and were capable of it, about the significance of the life of which they found themselves still in possession." Blackmur assumed that Americans after the war now had "the money and the leisure that are held propitious to the arts," and thus the incentive to "make use of the sources of wisdom." It was Blackmur's idea that

> during the breaking of nations certain substructures of tradition had been laid bare for the United States to take account of. . . . Circumstances in the world at large appeared to demand a certain centering, grounding, and girding up—hence the new attention the universities were giving to human-

istic studies on their own grounds, not as adjuncts of social or other sciences, and not as adornments of the politely educated.

Superseding the two earlier models of humanistic education—adornment of the politely educated and adjunct of science—the critical movement would instruct the nation on how the humanities could be something more than a superfluous decoration. Blackmur thought "Princeton fitted in with this effort, and the seminars should instruct it . . . so, at least, ran his first speculations."

As Fitzgerald's account makes clear, the Gauss Seminars of the early fifties did bring together an unusually large-minded group of literary figures. It mixed "scholars" like Jacques Maritain and Ernst Robert Curtius with "critics" like Mark Schorer and Francis Fergusson and others who crossed these boundaries—Wellek and Erich Auerbach and the poet-critic Blackmur. On another level, the seminars brought together native Americans and those European masters of comparative literature who were part of the great foreign influx after the war. Though it has been omitted from my account, it should be noted that the development of comparative literature at this time established an alternative to the old scholarship and the New Criticism, out of which grew phenomenological criticism and later deconstruction. The seminars' combination of old scholars, New Critics, creative writers, and European intellectuals could hardly fail to produce interesting exchanges. But finally witnesses seem to agree that these fell short of helpful definition or even coherence, and the relations between positions were not clarified or worked through. Wellek, a speaker at the seminars in 1950, "confessed himself 'often puzzled' by the questions which Blackmur addressed to the room." Others thought the fault lay with the speakers and praised Blackmur for taking up "the scattered bits of gristle that our symposiac had served us for an unending hour" and contriving "to have understood him as saying something that was actually interesting."

Heroic as their synthesizing ambitions were, the Gauss Seminars gave early evidence of a new division beginning to replace the old one between positivistic investigators and dilettante generalists. This was a division between an explicative criticism that was precise, orderly, and claustrophobic and a cultural criticism that was broadly inclusive but lacking in clear shape. Criticism, which had promised to close the gap between vapid generality and pedantic investigation, was vulnerable to its own internal conflict.

The critics had responded to the challenge thrown down by the scholar who in 1929 charged that they were either "still groping for a principle of order" or had "an axe to grind that is sociological or journalese rather than literary." As the Kenyon School alumnus said, those assembled there had come "to help make order in the wilderness of literary criticism," and they had largely succeeded in making that order. What troubled Blackmur was the feeling that the wrong kind of order had been made, but he did not have a clear alternative.

In 1953, René Wellek said that having abandoned "the old philology with its definite methods and body of knowledge," critics would "have to replace it with a new body of doctrines, a new systematic theory, a technique and methodology teachable and transmissible and applicable to any and all works of literature." It is easy to see why making its way in the university required criticism to have a "systematic theory" and a methodology "teachable" and "transmissible" and "applicable to any and all works of literature," but it is difficult to think of any other justification. How and in what terms criticism became teachable and transmissible we shall examine later on, but it should be clear by now that in streamlining itself to meet academic specifications, criticism sacrificed some of its own more interesting preoccupations. Like Ransom before him, Wellek did not seem to notice that in outlining the program for criticism as he did, he was letting the opposition dictate the terms.

CHAPTER TEN

General Education and the Pedagogy of Criticism: 1930–1950

There is implicit in every assertion of fixed and eternal first truths the necessity for some *human authority to decide, in this world of conflicts, just what these truths are and how they shall be taught.*

JOHN DEWEY

If this is an extract we ought to have more of it *to judge from. If not, there is probably* some biographical information needed. *I frankly don't understand it.*

PROTOCOL WRITER, *I. A. Richards's "Practical Criticism"*

No development had more influence in securing the fortunes of criticism in universities and secondary schools than the movement for general education revived and restated by Robert Maynard Hutchins of Chicago in the 1930s and institutionalized after World War II. The general education movement was a response to two kinds of fears: that because of increasing disciplinary specialization and emphasis on vocational training, knowledge was becoming fragmented, and that because of deepening conflicts of ideology, the unity of Western culture was disintegrating into a chaotic relativism. General education expressed a desire to restore common beliefs and values, and the humanities were seen as central to this goal by endowing the student with the sense of a common cultural heritage.

World War II brought the crisis of education to a head. In James Sloan Allen's words, "the aftermath of war had again breathed new life into educational idealism. Just as the end of World War I had seen the rise of General Education—including the Great Books idea—the end of World War II had brought a resurgence of similar curricular reforms." The general education ideal was given influential formulation in the 1945 Report of the Harvard Committee, *General Education in a Free Society*, the celebrated Harvard "Redbook." A look at the Redbook's recommendations on literary education in the high school and college is particularly pertinent here, because these recommendations coincided in striking ways with the direction academic literary criticism was taking at the time. The conjuncture of general education and criticism was no accident: I. A. Richards, who had left Cambridge for a visiting appointment at Harvard in 1931 and, after an interval spent in China, became professor of English at Harvard in 1943, was appointed by James Bryant Conant to the Harvard Committee. Richards's hand is evident in the portions of the report dealing with the teaching of literature.

Critical pedagogy answered the needs of general education by providing access to the unified cultural tradition that was felt to be latent in the great literary texts beneath or above the merely fragmentary and incoherent flux of history and historical knowledge. Through the new pedagogy of explication, it was felt, tradition and cultural unity could thus be inculcated without providing elaborate historical contexts.

The Great Conversation: The Chicago Plan

Robert Maynard Hutchins, who became president of the University of Chicago in 1929, had given the philosophy of general education its most influential prewar formulation in the early 1930s. Many of Hutchins's central ideas had come from his young professor of philosphy, Mortimer J. Adler, who we recall had been a graduate and fellow teacher of John Erskine's General Honors course at Columbia. Adler persuaded Hutchins that the Western intellectual tradition constituted "a Great Conversation among Great Thinkers on universal themes" and that by putting this Great Conversation at the center of education, in the form of courses in the great books, educators could stem the demoralizing tides of modern materialism, vocationalism, specialism, departmentalism, empiricism, and relativism. The assumption behind the concept of the Great Conversation—the term had been invented by Erskine—was that "despite variations of time, place, and language, the thinkers of the Western tradition shared a common human experience which they have debated by means of common themes . . . across the ages."

The large-scale institutional expression of these ideas was the so-called Chicago Plan that Hutchins proposed in the early thirties calling for the consolidation of the seventy-two departments of the university into four upper-level divisions (Biological Science, Physical Science, Social Science, and Humanities) and at the base a preparatory College, totally committed to general education, where students would spend two years before proceeding to one of the divisions. "The College instituted year-long lecture courses supplemented by discussion groups concentrating on the broad conceptual issues fundamental to the four divisions." The College faculty was conceived as an autonomous group of teachers unconnected with the divisions, chosen for the generality of their interests and commitment to teaching and freed from expectations of research. In 1930 Hutchins and Adler themselves began teaching the first great books courses at Chicago, under the title General Honors, or "Readings in the Classics of Western European Literature" from Homer to Freud, and a few years later they gave the course in the university's high school.

Yet the Chicago Plan was not fully implemented for a decade, partly because "Hutchins's willfulness and Adler's abrasive manner set too much opposition against them," partly because many members of the research faculty were so set against the threat the plan posed to their specialties that they would have refused to cooperate with it under any conditions. Adler had warned Hutchins at the outset of their experiment that "organized departments and departmentally minded individuals don't understand [the program], resent it, distrust it," and that specialized scholars think that "the work must be sloppy because it isn't their type of scholarship." The Chicago Plan was most successfully realized at other colleges such as St. John's of Annapolis, where Hutchins's former associates, Stringfellow Barr and Scott Buchanan, took over as president and dean in 1937, and at Notre Dame, St. Mary's of California, and the University of Kansas.

Hutchins greatest influence came through the series of books he published in the thirties, notably, *The Higher Learning in America* (1936). There Hutchins argued that "the times call for the establishment of a new college or for an evangelistic movement in some old ones which shall have for its object the conversion of individuals and finally of the teaching profession to a true conception of general education." Such a conception required "a course of study consisting of the greatest books of the western world and the arts of reading, writing, thinking, and speaking, together with mathematics, the best exemplar of the processes of human reason." The idea was "to frame a curriculum which educes the elements of our common human nature," which would teach "what has been done in the past, and what the greatest men have thought," and provide "a common stock of ideas and common methods of dealing with them." The effect would be to overcome "the disorder of specialization, vocationalism and unqualified empiricism" as well as the rampant love of money which had inspired these forces, and to unite the disciplines "by a rational principle" through which "professors and students will all be pursuing the truth for its own sake; they will know what truths to pursue and why."

Though much of the resistance to Hutchins's program came from faculty vested interests, some of it came from the recognition that Hutchins's ideas were fundamentally incompatible either with professionalism or democracy. One of Hutchins's shrewdest critics was Harry Gideonse, an economist at Chicago and later president of Brooklyn College, who wrote, in answer to *The Higher Learning in America*, a brief tract entitled *The Higher Learning in a Democracy*. Gideonse argued that Hutchins's position left unclear not only what his unifying "rational principle" would be, but how it would be implemented. "If the higher learning is to be unified," Gideonse asked, "is the unity to be voluntary or mandatory?" If it was to be voluntary, would it not have to arise out of "the community of scholars" itself and rest "upon the multiplicity of contemporary data and methods of attaining insight"?

Gideonse reasonably wondered "how much more consistency a country's educational institutions can have than the society in which they exist." He argued that the kind of unity Hutchins wanted could only be imposed by authority, in comparison with which a state of "chaos and disorder" might seem preferable. For chaos and disorder "at least maintain a field that is widely open to new truth and new methods of gaining insight." Gideonse saw, quite correctly in my view, that however much diversity a general education program might incorporate, as long as it was grounded in the idea of a unified truth or culture it would have either to marginalize or to exclude reasonable points of view.

In this, Gideonse showed a sense of history from which the self-styled traditionalist Hutchins could have learned. Gideonse pointed out that "within a single generation . . . an academic curriculum, designed for a relatively small group with well-understood social and intellectual 'backgrounds,' has been put through a shift in personnel that threatens to make it a complete misfit for the great majority of students now in the colleges." Yet educators assumed "that the position of the school with respect to the whole of society is still identical with that same position of an earlier period." The fact had to be faced that it was hopeless to try to restore an earlier stage of unified knowledge (if indeed there had ever actually been such a stage), as Hutchins was trying to do.

An even more influential critic of Hutchins in the late thirties was John Dewey, who, like Gideonse, charged that Hutchins had "conveniently ignored" the problem "of who is to determine the definite truths that constitute the hierarchy" of learning. For there was "implicit in every assertion of fixed and eternal first truths the necessity for *some* human authority to decide, in this world of conflicts, just what these truths are and how they shall be taught." Dewey conceded Hutchins's point that many of the present ills of education had come from a surrender to the immediate social pressures of vocationalism and material interest, but he argued that Hutchins's "policy of aloofness" from such pressures was no solution.

Here Dewey added a shrewd political point: Dewey said that Hutchins's policy really amounted "to acceptance of a popular American slogan, 'Safety first.' " To divorce education from the immediate vocational world, as Hutchins did, was merely to leave the world of business and power to flourish unexamined. Dewey on the other hand wondered why "the facts stated about the evil effects of our love of money" should not legitimately invite attention from "institutions devoted to love of truth for its own sake," attention, that is, "to the economic institutions that have produced this overweening love, and to their social consequences in other matters than the temper of educational institutions; and attention to the means available for changing this state of things." Dewey reminded Hutchins and other traditionalists that involvement in "the science and social affairs of their own times" rather than withdrawal had been the policy of Plato, Aristotle, Saint Thomas, and other sages Hutchins constantly invoked.

By the time their plan was finally implemented at Chicago in 1942, Hutchins and Adler had become tired of struggling with unsympathetic professors and began to look to new fields for the application of their ideas. The field of adult education was one in which no departments or specialists stood in their way, and in the early forties Hutchins and Adler established their great books discussion groups, which quickly became "the country's most popular program of adult education," with "a network reaching from coast to coast and incorporating over 5,000 people." Forming a connection with the *Encyclopaedia Britannica*, Adler compiled and with Hutchins merchandized the multivolume series, *The Great Books of the Western World*, supplemented by Adler's *Syntopicon*, which reduced the Great Conversation to its constituent topics, neatly cross-referenced. Hutchins's interests moved increasingly away from the university (he left the chancellorship of Chicago in 1951), and toward adult education—and the cause of world government, which he took up after 1945.

Hutchins's program had failed to achieve its objectives of unifying the higher learning, at Chicago at any rate. Ironically, it probably had its greatest success in becoming a target for vehement opposition, thus generating a climate of campuswide debate that gave Chicago its reputedly lively intellectual life during this period. For once, students and professors were forced to argue openly "over the very character of knowledge," and "quarrels about the purpose, form, and content of education so stirred a college campus" that according to Adler they affected everybody "from the President down to the janitors."

Tradition without History: The Harvard Redbook

For Hutchins, the world-political counterpart of the general education ideal was an internationalist concept of universal political order. But others who developed the theory and practice of general education after the war embraced a more nationalistic conception of cultural unity. In *Education in a Divided World* (1948), a book on American high school education, Harvard's President James Bryant Conant put the case bluntly:

> A set of common beliefs is essential for the health and vigor of a free society. And it is through education that these beliefs are developed in the young and carried forward in later life. This is the social aspect of general education, one might say. The future citizens we desire to educate should have strong loyalties and high civic courage. These loyalties ought to be to the type of society we are envisaging and to the United States as the home of this society. Such emotional attitudes are in part the product of a common knowledge and a common set of values.

Conant's appeals to "common beliefs" and "a common set of values" were a frank expression of Cold War anti-Communism. They had been necessitated, as Conant put it, by "the impact of the European radical doctrines of the nineteenth-century based on the notion of class struggle." These radical doctrines, he said, had "diverted the attention of forward-looking men and women from the social goals implicit in our native American traditions" and had put the American "type of political, social, and economic system . . . on trial in the grim world of the mid-twentieth century." The general education movement was connected with an attempt to think "of the system of universal education as an instrument of national policy."

Conant had given these themes a more circumspect expression three years earlier in his introduction to the Harvard Redbook that he commissioned, *General Education in a Free Society*. There Conant declared that "the war has precipitated a veritable downpour of books and articles dealing with education. In particular the future of the liberal arts colleges has been a subject of widespread discussion both within and without the academic walls. There is hardly a university or a college in the country which has not had a committee at work in these war years considering basic educational questions and making plans for drastic revamping of one or more curricula." Among the reasons for this concern, according to the Harvard Committee itself, were "the staggering expansion of knowledge produced largely by specialism and certainly conducing to it; the concurrent and hardly less staggering growth of our educational system with its maze of stages, functions, and kinds of institutions; and not least, the ever-growing complexity of society itself."

The question was, "what then is the right relationship between specialistic training on the one hand, aiming at any one of a thousand different destinies, and education in a common heritage and toward a common citizenship on the other? It is not too much to say that the very character of our society will be affected by the answer to that question." Central to the report's analysis was the need to reconcile diversity—"even a greater diversity than exists at present in the still largely bookish curriculum"—with that sense of "common heritage" and "common citizenship." This meant reconciling vocational "competence in a particular lot" with "preparation for life in the broad sense of a human being." Though conceding that the "dispersion and dividing of work" were desirable and inevitable, the report emphasized the "need for some principle of unity, since without it the curriculum flies into pieces and even the studies of any one student are atomic or unbalanced or both." None of these problems were new, but in an expanding system of higher education they seemed more urgent than ever.

What did all this entail for literary education? Though the committee began by warning that "there is not one best way of introducing people to Homer or Plato or Dante," it did favor one way over others; namely, the great books philosophy:

> the course in the area of the humanities which will be required of all students [would] be one which might be called "Great Texts of Literature." The aim of such a course would be the fullest understanding of the work read rather than of men or periods represented, craftsmanship evinced, historic or literary development shown, or anything else. These other matters would be admitted only in so far as they are necessary to allow the work to

speak for itself. Otherwise they should be left for special, not general education.

Though the committee here conceded that the "other matters" it referred to might sometimes be "necessary to allow the work to speak for itself," it assumed these other matters would normally be negligible. The aim of the basic general education course was a restatement of the old vision of disencumbering the great works from excrescences in order to allow them to speak for themselves. As the committee put it, "the instructor can only seek to be a means by which the authors teach the course."

The committee explicitly discouraged "emphasis on literary history, on generalizations as to periods, tendencies and ready-made valuations—in place of deeper familiarity with the texts." It discouraged "use of critical terms (Romanticism, Realism, Classical, Sentimental) as tags, coming between the reader and the work." It seemed to the committee "entirely undesirable to have a course of the block-survey type which would include portions of all, or nearly all, of the humanities." After all, the report asked, "what principle of synthesis would bring together in one, or even in two courses, the subject matter of philosophy, the fine arts, music, and literature?" Not staying for an answer to this question, the committee concluded that "such a broad survey of the superficial aspects of fields which have relatively little in common" was productive only of "a smattering of information." The assumption seemed to be that history could be made the context of the humanities only if there was agreement on a synthesis of it.

Granted, a mere smattering of information is precisely what the old-fashioned survey course had usually amounted to, but did that justify abandoning historical principles altogether? The committee bordered on recognizing the need for history when it warned that "if the books read do not seem to the student to have any bearings one on another, we are losing endless educational chances." But what it hoped would give the books a "bearing one on another" was not historical continuity or context but what it called "a common body of tradition," something very different from history, as it turned out. The implication was that the great works themselves formed a coherent and unified order by being a repository of "the greatest, most universal human preoccupations."

Here a curious discrepancy begins to show up between the urgency of the committee's appeal to a unified cultural heritage and the poverty of its suggestions about just what the content of that heritage actually was. The committee's very assertion of the need to restore cultural unity all but conceded that such unity was a thing of the past that could hardly be expected to materialize in and of itself:

> Ours is at present a centrifugal culture in extreme need of unifying forces. We are in real danger . . . of losing touch with the human past and therefore with one another. The remedy is not in more knowledge about the past. That has been piled up as such knowledge never was for any former generation. Its sudden, all but overwhelming, increase is one of our chief difficulties. . . . The humanities have become so diffuse that "not even the great scholar can see the human store steadily or whole."

This statement strikingly echoes the discussion, in earlier works by Richards such as *Science and Poetry*, of the crisis precipitated by the scientific "neutralization of nature," which renders history, among other things, meaningless. Such a crisis prompted the very question Hutchins had avoided: If a unified heritage had not already grown organically out of "a centrifugal culture" and its academic disciplines, what could cause it to reconstitute itself?

The answer was that if the *greatest* literature is taught, the fragmentation, discontinuity, and lack of meaning of modern history can be overcome. It was the modern condition of fragmentation, the committee wrote, that was "the root argument for using, wherever possible, great works in literature courses." The committee's working assumption was that coherent tradition had disintegrated—otherwise, why call for its restoration? Yet it trusted that the tradition would reconstitute itself if only the "great works" were taught—or, rather, if only they were freed from historical contexts and allowed to teach themselves:

> It is through the poetry, the imaginative understanding of things in common, that minds most deeply and essentially meet. Therefore the books—whether in verse or prose, whether epic, drama, narrative, or philosophy—which have been the great meeting points and have most influenced the men who in turn have influenced others are those we can least afford to neglect, if ways can be found of opening better access to them. It is a safe assumption that a work which has delighted and instructed many generations of ordinary readers and been to them a common possession, enriching and enriched, is to be preferred to a product which is on its way to limbo and will not link together even two school generations.

Everything here is made to depend on the power of the great works to overcome disparities of time, place, and cultural circumstances. But again, if the great works really could overcome these disparities in and of themselves, why had they not already done so? The success of the plan really depended not on the works themselves, but on whether "ways" could be found of "opening up better access to them."

Designed to accomplish this were the methods of practical criticism, which Richards and other New Critics had been refining since the twenties. Practical criticism promised access to the timeless, universal tradition embodied in the great works without the need for that historical knowledge, which, as the committee had made clear, could provide no coherent context for literature. "History" was not part of the solution but part of the problem, being merely that "more knowledge of the past," which was already "piled up as such knowledge never was for any former generation" and had been packaged in "the course of the block-survey type." By recovering the past as eternally present, practical criticism would rescue tradition from the jaws of history.

Here was a restatement of the dream of the generalists before and just after World War I: if only literature itself could be allowed to work its potential magic, all would be well. Far from needing to think through the problem of how to provide literature with a context, instructors needed to decontextualize literature as much as possible. As the introductory humanities courses at Harvard, Chicago, and Columbia became the prototypes everywhere for general education courses in literature, the general education program and the New Critical program gradually merged, and a new kind of division became institutionalized between literature and history. As Daniel Bell observed in *The Reforming of General Education* (1966), general education courses in literature tended toward "an extreme 'New Criticism,' of reading the work *in se*, without reference to any external context." The historical survey did not disappear from the curriculum any more than literary historians disappeared from the faculty. But the survey now often became a curious compromise between history and criticism—a course in which students read texts New Critically in chronological order.

At Columbia, as we have seen, the humanities requirement, descended from Erskine's General Honors course, had initially been meant to parallel and complement the historical and social thought emphasized in Contemporary Civilization. In theory, the humanities course supposedly provided "in the realm of ideas and imagination a concurrent sense of the movement of thought with events." But according to Bell, the humanities courses "never realized this formal intention," a failure he attributed to the "lack of any direct relationship *between* the Humanities and Contemporary Civilization readings." This nonrelation contributed, "for many students, to a bewilderment about the courses. The great works of the Western mind, which are read in Humanities, arise as singular experiences of individual imaginations, but often the historical or social context which could relate these ideas and changing sensibilities (and modes of expression) to institutional and social developments is lacking." One discerns more or less the same lack of correlation in the University of Chicago College, where the intellectual traditions embodied in the courses in humanities and sociology never came into contact.

Bell's book, which was commissioned as a report by Columbia, was a sign of a renewed wave of interest in the old problems of general education aroused by the campus upheavals of the 1960s. By that time, however—or perhaps in that superheated atmosphere—such problems no longer stirred much interest in the faculty. Looking back at the episode ten years later, Trilling remarked on the Columbia faculty's "sad and significant" lack of interest as "to the questions [Bell's] report raised and sought to answer. . . . Through some persuasion of the Zeitgeist, the majority of the faculty were no longer concerned with general education in the large and honorific meaning of the phrase."

Trilling rightly regretted his colleagues' indifference, for Bell had said things they ought not to have ignored. Yet Trilling conceded that "it was in some part the seriousness with which they took their teacherly function that led them to withdraw their interest from the large questions of educational theory," for "periodically the answers to these questions become platitudinous and boring, mere pious protestations, and at such times a teacher might naturally and rightly feel that he does most for his students not by speculating about what shape and disposition their minds ought eventually to have, but by simply pressing upon them the solid substance and the multitudinous precisions of his own particular intellectual discipline."

What Trilling did not seem to recognize (or at least did not say) was the point Bell had made in suggesting that the general education idea needed "reforming": that in a complex and diverse culture, where there might be many different and contested views of "what shape and disposition" a student's mind "ought eventually to have," any attempt to abstract some *single* "shape and disposition" as the one to aim at will necessarily be so attenuated as to be "platitudinous and boring." The vacuity that Trilling sadly but accurately detected in the rhetoric of general education was itself a result of the fact that there was no longer a tacitly shared culture in which the presuppositions of that rhetoric were taken for granted. Arguably, in such a culture the old universals can recover their interest only by being thoroughly historicized. In deciding that the monuments of the humanities had to be abstracted from their history in order for their power to be recovered, the theorists of general education had removed the one condition under which the great works had a chance to recover that power.

It is customary to attribute the stalling of the general education experiment not to its conceptual contradictions, but to its inability to draw faculty from the specializations on which their professional incentives depended. Though accurate up to a point, such an analysis implicitly revives the old argument that blames educational problems on the "selfishness" inherent in specialism, departmentalization, research, and, ultimately, professionalism itself, and thus renders any solution hopeless from the start. It might be more realistic to assume that the chronic inability of general education programs to compel faculty support is itself a symptom of the impossibility of superimposing unity or coherence on an inherently refractory and ideologically conflict-filled professional and cultural setting.

To put it another way, any program will fail that does not arise out of the contingent activities of professional work and cultural conflict. What kind of coherence could ever arise out of the collision of disparate and conflicting viewpoints and activities may be hard to fathom, but what seems certain is that any program organized around a unitary idea of culture is doomed from the beginning. The assumption that coherence must involve agreement about first principles, or a shared intellectual and cultural tradition, will inevitably make the very idea of general education in a democratic society seem a contradiction in terms.

The Text Itself

The new pedagogical concentration on the literary "text itself" was designed to counteract the large problems of cultural fragmentation, historical discontinuity, and student alienation. But putting the emphasis on the literary text itself also had a more humble advantage: it seemed a tactic ideally suited to a new, mass student body that could not be depended on to bring to the university any common cultural background—and not just the student body but the new professors as well, who might often be only marginally ahead of the students. The explicative method made it possible for literature to be taught efficiently to students who took for granted little history by professors who took for granted a little more history.

Obviously there was a danger that the larger objectives of the explicative method would be lost sight of and that the method would become merely a way of making a virtue of necessity, a line of least resistance to a predicament that had been forced on students and teachers alike. Reading the text itself in a vacuum was an all too inviting expedient in an institution where no contexts could be taken for granted because nobody could be assumed in advance to know any one thing, where nobody knew what anybody else knew, and where nobody talked to others on a consistent enough basis to find out.

Some of the partisans of criticism themselves foresaw the problem very clearly. In *Theory of Literature*, for example, Wellek and Warren observed that "the study of isolated 'great books' . . . may be highly commendable for pedagogical purposes," but they argued that such a study "makes incomprehensible the continuity of literary tradition, the development of literary genres—and indeed the very nature of the literary process—besides obscuring the background of social, linguistic, ideological, and other conditioning circumstances. In history, philosophy, and similar subjects, it actually introduces an excessively 'aesthetic' point of view." But it is difficult, to say the least, to see how an approach that makes "the very nature of the literary process" incomprehensible could be considered "commendable for pedagogical purposes."

The trouble, as Wellek and Warren all but said, was that concentrating on "the text itself" in a vacuum left students without any means of making sense of the text itself, unless they already took for granted appropriate contexts for understanding literature, as very few did. Here was the fatal flaw in Richards's otherwise heroic attempt to think through the problems of literary pedagogy in *Practical Criticism*. When Richards there demonstrated that even relatively cultured Cambridge undergraduates had difficulty making out the plain "sense" of a poem, much less its more complex nuances, he thought he had proved the need for a more intrinsic literary pedagogy. Richards's experiment was eye-opening, and it exposed glaring inadequacies in the received methods of instruction, but hindsight suggests that the conclusions he drew from his data were the very opposite of the ones he should have drawn. For what Richards's experiment unwittingly showed was that though students may have needed more "direct" contact with literature, if one's way of providing that contact is to withhold information from them about a poem's period, authorship, and circumstances of composition, they will not be able to grasp the poem successfully.

In their agony, Richards's protocol-writers sometimes sent up distress signals trying to point this out, but Richards invariably ignored them or drew the wrong conclusions from them. The protocol-writers said things like, "I suppose, really, I do not understand the lines, and certainly wish I had some context, some 'co-ordinates' which might furnish an invaluable clue." Or they said, "*if this is an extract we ought to have more of it* to judge from. If not, there is probably *some biographical information needed*. I frankly don't understand it." Richards dismissed these requests for more information as "excuses," even though he obliquely seemed to acknowledge their legitimacy when he observed of one reader's trouble in understanding Donne's poem "At the round earth's imagined corners" that it seemed to stem from his being "unacquainted with the rules of attendance at the Day of Judgment." To be unacquainted with the Day of Judgment is to lack sufficient contextual information, not to lack sensitivity to poetic meaning in itself. In any case, it was more probable that this reader did not recognize that the context *was* the Day of Judgment—as he might have had Richards not withheld the information that the poem was written by an Anglican divine and entitled "Holy Sonnet."

Among the most prominent of the protocol-writers' various "stock responses" that Richards deplored was the tendency to fabricate wildly hypothetical historical circumstances for poems. For Richards, this habit only showed the writers' inability to confront poetry on its own terms. But it is only by conjecturing *some* contextual circumstances for an utterance that any interpreter can make inferences about meaning (as Richards and Ogden had in fact pointed out in *The Meaning of Meaning*). If you deprive readers of the information needed to infer the probable relevant circumstances of a text, you force them to do the the next best thing and construct an improbable set of circumstances, which is what Richards's hapless protocol-writers persistently did. Deprived of the information needed to make an appropriate response, they quite naturally grasped for—what else?—a "stock" one.

A recent speech-act theorist, Marilyn M. Cooper, concisely points out what went wrong:

> When Richards asked his students to respond to and comment on unidentified poems, the students continually attempted to make sense of the poems by providing the missing contexts. They guessed at the authorship: "a spinster devoted to good works, and sentimentally inclined, or perhaps Wordsworth. . . ." They guessed at the literary period: "Reminded of the pitched-up movement or strong artificial accent of post-Elizabethans. . . ." They guessed at the author's pragmatic intentions by projecting the purpose the poem fulfilled for them.

Richards's failure to see this point made his reactions to the protocol-writers' flounderings sometimes seem downright callous—as when he placed in derisive italics the desperate conjecture of one protocol-writer that what must be going on in Hopkins's sonnet, "Spring and Fall, to a Young Child," is that "Margaret *has apparently been jilted* and is, very sensibly, *finding solace* in the autumn tints of golden grove." Stock response? Perhaps, but what other kind of response was likely when the reader did not know the title of the poem, or that it was written by a Jesuit known for an obsession with change and mortality?

Perhaps one reader in twenty will read perceptively enough to infer the requisite information from the text of "Spring and Fall," but to expect an average group of readers to be able to do so seems unrealistic and merely sets up yet another excuse for formulary lamentations—themselves a kind of stock response—about how dreadfully ill prepared and inattentive the students are.

Richards professed to be scandalized that "without further clues (authorship, period, school, the sanction of an anthology, or the hint of a context) the task of 'making up their minds about it,' or even of working out a number of possible views from which to choose, was felt to be really beyond their powers." But nobody can read anything accurately without the help of some of the "clues" Richards mentioned, not even Richards himself. I find that in rereading cold the protocol poems in *Practical Criticism,* I am myself able to make out very little of the plain "sense" of most of them. The two or three I can read successfully are the ones whose background I know something about. The reading habits of Richards's subjects were no doubt bad, but we do not know just how bad because Richards's way of setting up the experiment did not give them a fair chance. The condition of the experiment guaranteed at least a measure of the "overtone of despairing hopelessness" that Richards found haunting the protocols. But even if we grant Richards that the protocol responses were appalling, it does not follow that the cure for the problem lay in a less historical mode of pedagogy.

In a recent analysis, Paul Bové depicts Richards's practical criticism as a "fundamentally conservative, even reactionary" project, an instrument for inscribing the literacy of high culture "within new students coming into the university," a literary counterpart to the panoptic prison classically described by Foucault. Practical criticism for Bové is an extension of the "hegemonic discourse and practices of Western disciplinary capitalism," "part of the disciplinary machine of that advanced capitalist society." Similarly, "Richards' insistence on the need to produce a single theory of language that will provide a *unitary* explanation of all linguistic and literary phenomena typifies humanism's inability to tolerate difference." Bové concludes that the effect of practical criticism has been to obscure "criticism's own position within the empowered network of knowledge production and its relation to the dominant forces in American culture."

The "hegemonic discourse and practices of Western disciplinary capitalism" is such a broad category that it is hard to imagine anything that could not be plausibly said to be in complicity with it. But the alleged nexus between practical criticism and "the dominant forces in American culture" seems merely asserted, mostly on the basis of a facile conflation of very different kinds of totalization and discipline. That Richards sought a "unitary explanation" of language and literature does not in itself convict his project of "inability to tolerate difference" in the social sphere, any more than reducing interpretation to a "discipline" really resembles disciplining subjects of confinement. Richards's politics were indeed more technocratic and "functionalist" than "oppositional," as Bové argues, but a more dialectical assessment of his project would have to consider its apparently progressive role in breaking up the "hegemony" of the genteel criticism that preceded it. Nevertheless, there is truth in the charge that practical criticism obscured the relations between culture and politics and furthered the general depoliticization of academic discourse in the fifties and since. Indeed, it was that depoliticized discourse that seems to have produced as a kind of reflex the hyperpoliticized discourse of Bové and other recent critics.

The link between *Practical Criticism* and the theory of literary education presented in *General Education in a Free Society* was the assumption that great literary works are independent of history and culture and that literary education must henceforth base itself on "direct" experience of those works, unmediated by history. The report, we recall, stated that it was "a safe assumption that a work which has delighted many generations of ordinary readers and been to them a common possession" would naturally have a greater prior tendency to induce enthusiasm anywhere than works which had no such wide appeal. This had been Erskine's assumption in the twenties in proposing that the great books could be read by students as if they were contemporary best sellers. But it was not a safe assumption at all—it was, in fact, a wrong assumption.

It took a sociologist, Daniel Bell, to put his finger on where the error lay, namely, the premise that "the young should approach the work directly so that they could experience directly the bracing impact of greatness." Bell pointed out that

> while any particular young man may come upon a great work afresh, as an experience for *himself*, the way in which he will respond will be signifi-

cantly influenced by a general mode or convention of the time. . . . The problem for the course is not only to make a student aware of a text, but of the scholarly context in which it arose. . . . In sum, the successive histories of mind and sensibility are as integral to the interpretation of a text as the student's (and the instructor's) own "naive" responses.

Again, the attempt to preserve a residue of "the greatest, most universal human preoccupations" by isolating them from their history had only made those preoccupations seem more inaccessible.

Some autobiographical remarks by Irving Howe seem to back up Bell's observations. Howe recalled that he "used a loosened version of the New Criticism almost as a matter of course" when he started teaching at Brandeis in 1953 and at Stanford and the City University of New York in the sixties. Howe discovered that "the techniques for close reading that Brooks and Warren developed in their famous textbook could succeed only if students already had some modest stores of literacy and historical reference." "With the indifferently trained but alert students at Brandeis, this method worked well, forcing them to a certain discipline and checking their fondness for grand talk." But "the well-trained but largely unteachable students" at Stanford "quickly turned the method into just another routine for churning out papers." And at CUNY, "where the problems of mass education are acute," he had to "drop whatever of the New Criticism" he had used earlier, since the undergraduates there "were fearful of critical abstraction, as if all the talk about irony and ambiguity, structure and diction was a luxury they could not afford." The CUNY students lacked the context to make New Critical methods work, whereas the Stanford students made them "work" all too well: "so the New Criticism worked best with students partly educated, responsive but ill-disciplined; it usually failed, at least in my experience, with brilliant elite students who didn't need it, and with the mass of untrained students who couldn't abide it."

It was perhaps the instructors who needed the New Criticism the most. From my own experience as one of those "trained" in a stepped-up Ph.D. program of the early sixties, I can testify that usually I was lucky to be one evening ahead of my undergraduate classes. I remember the relief I experienced as a beginning assistant professor when I realized that by concentrating on the text itself I could get a good discussion going about almost any literary work without having to know anything about its author, its circumstances of composition, or the history of its reception. Furthermore, as long as the teaching situation was reduced to a decontextualized encounter with a work, it made no difference that I did not know how much the students knew or what I could assume about their high school or other college work—just as it made no difference that they had no more basis for inferring anything about me than I had about them. Given the vast unknowns on both sides of the lectern, "the work itself" was indeed our salvation.

It is easy today, with the advantages of hindsight, to see what was wrong with the assumption of postwar educational theorists that the saving power of the humanities could be rescued only by divorcing the humanities from history. The model of "history" to which almost everyone in universities had become accustomed did seem not merely irrelevant to any culturally useful appropriation of the humanities but, as the Harvard Report put it, one of the "chief difficulties" obstructing such a goal. It is not surprising that the educators of this period failed to consider that the concept of "history" represented by the positivist historiography—the standard model—was not the only available or possible model of history.

In other words, the idea did not emerge that the remedy for bad historical teaching of literature might be *better* historical teaching, not the reduction of history to something so ancillary that readers were better off without it.

Scholars versus Critics: 1940–1965

CHAPTER ELEVEN

History versus Criticism: 1940–1960

The charge to be made against much traditional academic scholarship is not that it was historical, but that it was not historical enough or it had a narrow view of what "historical" meant.

IRVING HOWE

That the New Criticism was "ahistorical" in its theory and practice has become a commonplace, but it would be more accurate to say that the New Critics accepted and worked within the view of history held by most of the literary historians of their time. This was a view that reduced history to atomized "background" information and saw only an "extrinsic" connection between history and literature. The New Critics followed the historians in thinking of literary history as at best a body of preliminary information that, however indispensable, could be set aside once the would-be explicator had done a minimal amount of homework. Instead of challenging this narrow view, the critics echoed the historians in thinking of history as a preliminary activity from which one moved on to something more literary.

Even so, critics and scholars in the forties and fifties reached an understanding that reconciled their conflict at a certain level: critics dealt with literary works "in themselves" in an "intrinsic" fashion, while historians dealt with their "extrinsic background." More precisely, criticism and history were but aspects of a total activity of literary understanding, so that potentially any professor was both critic and scholar, and the sense of a necessary antagonism between these functions began to wane. Though the words "scholar" and "critic" continued to denote different principles and methods (as they still do at times), it was increasingly understood that the difference was one of emphasis rather than an inherent conflict in principles. Criticism and history, it was agreed, were complementary, and no sound literary education could forgo either.

But what were the theoretical, practical, and pedagogical terms in which the desired merger would be effected? So long as the dualism was accepted between intrinsic and extrinsic, the work itself and its historical background, there remained a tension at the conceptual level that mirrored unresolved institutional tensions.

WELLEK'S CRITIQUE OF LITERARY HISTORY

The most thorough diagnosis of the inadequacies of the established historical scholarship was offered in a 1941 essay by René Wellek, which would be incorporated in Wellek and Warren's influential *Theory of Literature* (first edition, 1949). By this time, attacks by critics on the old scholarship were not new, but here was a more detailed critique than any yet made, by someone who clearly knew the old scholarship from the inside. Wellek was himself a scholar, the author of books on Kant's influence in England and English literary history, but one who had acquired a "critical" way of thinking through his association with the Prague Linguistic Circle before emigrating to America in 1939.

"Most histories of literature," Wellek wrote, "are either social histories or histories of thought as mirrored in literature, or a series of impressions and judgments on individual works of art arranged in a more or less chronological order." On the one hand, one group of literary historians "treat literature as mere document for the illustration of national or social history." This group, in which Wellek included Thomas Wharton, Hallam, Morley, Stephen, Courthope, Taine, Jusserand, Cazamian, and Greenlaw, had failed to write history that was specifically *literary.* On the other hand, another group "recognizes that literature is first and foremost an art. But they seem to be unable to write history. They present us with a discontinuous series of essays on individual authors, linked together by 'influences' without any conception of real historical evolution." In this group Wellek included Saint-Beuve, Gosse, Elton, and Saintsbury. Contemplating these twin failures, Wellek wondered whether it was even "*possible* to write literary history, that is, to write a history of literature which will be both literary and a history."

The apparent irreconcilability of the literary and the historical was nowhere better exemplified for Wellek than in the elaborate edifice of A. O. Lovejoy's historiography of ideas. In the mid-thirties Lovejoy's method had looked to many literary historians like the long-awaited path to that synthesis they were always being reproached for not having achieved. In his preface to *The Great Chain of Being* (1936), Lovejoy proposed that the history of ideas could provide that "unifying background to many now unconnected and now, consequently, poorly understood facts" that the proliferation of intellectual disciplines had generated. Lovejoy added:

> It would help to put gates through the fences which, in the course of a praiseworthy effort after specialization and division of labor, have come to be set up in most of our universities between departments whose work ought to be constantly correlated. I have in mind especially the departments of philosophy and of the modern literatures.

Lovejoy repeated this plea in his 1948 *Essays in the History of Ideas*, arguing that the need for a "*liaison*" between "primarily distinct disciplines" was now "much more apparent and more urgent than it has ever been before."

In outlining his case, however, Lovejoy had incautiously stated that "the ideas in serious reflective literature are, of course, in great part philosophical ideas in dilution." Pouncing on the figure of speech—he quoted it in his essays of 1941 and 1953 and again in *Theory of Literature* —Wellek argued that Lovejoy saw literature merely as "the water added to philosophy." That is, for Lovejoy "the history of ideas imposes purely philosophical standards on works of imagination." Lovejoy had at least qualified his unfortunate chemical analogy with "in great part" and implied that he was talking only about "reflective" literature, yet Wellek was not unfair in suggesting that Lovejoy characteristically treated literary works as vehicles for "unit-ideas," and R. S. Crane reinforced Wellek's point at length in a 1954 critique of Lovejoy. Lovejoy did at times hint at a relation between "what is distinctive" in Milton's style and both Milton's ideas and "manifestations of the same ideas elsewhere." But he tended to assert that such a relation existed without explaining what it might be.

But if Lovejoy's history of ideas did not satisfactorily reconcile criticism and history, it at least dramatized some of the historians' dissatisfactions with older methods. By the late forties the fight had not yet gone out of the historians, but the terms of their opposition to the critics had crucially softened.

The Search for Compromise

The last defiant roar of the old historical scholars was Douglas Bush's 1948 presidential address to the Modern Language Association, "The New Criticism: Some Old-Fashioned Queries." In this celebrated polemic, Bush, president of the MLA, Harvard professor, and expounder of Renaissance "Christian humanism," lit into the critics with a fury. He indicted them for "the invention of unhistorical theories and the reading of modern attitudes and ideas into the past." "In emphasizing complexity and ambiguity, " he argued, "the critic has often been unwilling to accept anything else." For "when complexity and ambiguity have become a fetish, there seems to be no check upon interpretative irresponsibility except the limits of the critic's fancy." This irresponsibility only pointed up the fact that "poets and critics" had cut themselves off from "the common reader"—who still "might go so far as to think that poetry deals with life"—and "decided to write for one another," thus turning criticism into "a circumscribed end in itself." Bush defined his own "creed" as a restatement of the traditional humanistic "conception of poetry which reigned for some 2,500 years, through the greatest periods of literature—the conception which the new aesthetes call the didactic heresy."

By now the conventions of such attacks had become as ritualized as the passes of a bullfighter, and Bush's address rehearsed all the familiar *topoi* long ago established by the Morizes, the Nitzes, the Greenlaws: the initial concession that, rightly practiced, criticism was an indispensable activity that had been deplorably neglected; the judicious warning that no good, however, could come from premature criticism, attempted before the groundwork of scholarship had been laid; the inexorable conclusion that, regrettably, such prematurity was the condition of virtually all criticism being written today. (Frederick Crews has expertly parodied both argument and tone in the final chapter of *The Pooh Perplex*.)

Yet what made Bush's speech interesting was that its concessions were no longer quite so hollowly rhetorical as they may have looked:

> The scholar starts with the attempt to see a piece of writing through the minds of its author and his contemporaries, in the belief that, if we understand the work as it was conceived under the conditions of its own age, we allow, consciously and unconsciously, for altered conditions and distinguish between temporal and permanent significance. The critic may start with the author in the act of composition or with the modern reader in the act of reading, but in either case he is likely to analyze the work *in vacuo* as a timeless autonomous entity. Both the historical and the critical methods are essential and, pursued by themselves, inadequate.

In seemingly assigning "temporal" significance to the scholar and "permanent," "timeless" significance to the critic, Bush was conceding in principle that criticism had a rightful place in the literature department. Furthermore, unlike earlier scholarly attacks on criticism,

Bush's did not characterize criticism as a subjective activity. On the contrary, an analysis of "the work *in vacuo* as a timeless autononous entity" was something clearly very different from the subjective impressionism that had been dismissed by Morize and Greenlaw. The terms of the controversy were shifting, as the critic Eliseo Vivas noted when he wrote in 1951 that though "one hears disparagement, sometimes peevish and usually patronizing, of the so-called, 'new criticism' among the scholars, the established academic research journals have begun to open their pages very tentatively and gingerly to criticism." Vivas predicted that "an interpenetration by both sides" would heal the "specious split" between the little magazine and the research publication.

And yet, certain issues remained unresolved. If Bush was willing to grant that critics did not need to be concerned with the "temporal" meanings of literature, then why did he go on to attack them for "unhistorical theories" and anachronistic misreadings? Bush's distinction left unclear what the relation might be between temporal and permanent significance, and what was to be done when these conflicted. Was "Christian humanism," for example, to be understood as the "temporal" significance of Renaissance poetry, while the paradox and irony the New Critics found in that poetry were its "permanent" significance? And if Bush's interpretation of Renaissance poetry committed "the didactic heresy" in the eyes of the critics, where was the supposed ground for compromise? To say that criticism dealt with "a timeless autonomous entity" was apparently to give it no possible connection with history.

The critics about this time were also beginning to make conciliatory gestures, but without clarifying the relation of criticism to history any more than the scholars had done. The critics now conceded the indispensable importance of literary history to criticism. In the second edition of *Understanding Poetry* (1950), Brooks and Warren made what they described as "certain shifts of emphasis" from the first edition a decade before, at which time, they said, they had felt they could afford to leave "to implication" the relation of the poem "to its historical background, to its place in the context of the poet's work, and to biographical and historical study generally." The subsequent years, they now said, "have indicated that these relationships could not safely be left to implication and needed to be spelled out rather than merely implied." As Brooks and Warren added, it was "not a matter of putting in two pounds of biographical study or three slices of literary history to go with so much poem. *The problem is, rather, to see how history, literary and general, may be related to poetic meaning.*" Accordingly, the revised edition included extensive historical discussions of Marvell's "Horatian Ode" and *The Waste Land.*

Yet, much like Douglas Bush, Brooks and Warren and other New Critics did often continue to speak as if literary history were a matter of "pounds or slices of data" rather than a rich historical process. Irving Howe seems right in saying the real charge that should have been made against much traditional scholarship was "not that it was historical, but that it was not historical enough or had a narrow view of what 'historical' meant."

HISTORY AS "BACKGROUND"

Brooks, for example, presupposed a typically diminished concept of history when he wrote in 1941 that

> almost every English professor is diligently devoting himself to discovering "what porridge had John Keats." This is our typical research: the backgrounds of English literature. And we hopefully fill our survey textbooks with biographical notes on the poets whose poems are there displayed. But one may know what the poet ate and what he wore and what accidents occurred to him and what books he read—and yet not know his poetry.

Once history is conceived as an affair of porridge and wearing apparel, it certainly does become only of marginal relevance to criticism, but the question should have been whether a more capacious view of history was possible.

At times it almost seemed as if the only type of literary history New Critics could imagine was gossip, amorous or otherwise. When Wellek, in 1953, declared that "biographies of literary figures" are "frequently of very little relevance to an understanding and evaluation of the works themselves," he thought of biography as "information" about "the movements, quarrels, and love affairs of authors." At such times it was hard to see how Wellek's conception of literary history was much more interesting than that of André Morize's old handbook of graduate study, which Wellek rightly said gave "the impression that literary history is almost confined to questions of editing and authorship, sources and biography." Similarly, when Wimsatt and Beardsley, in their celebrated attack on the intentional fallacy, minimized the importance of external evidence for literary interpretation, their examples of external evidence were "letters or reported conversations" about "how or why the poet wrote the poem—to what lady, while sitting on what lawn, or at the death of what friend or brother."

Brooks, too, spoke as if history were something that might "enhance for us the meaning of the poem as a personal document of [the poet's] life" but presumably could not enhance its meaning as a poem. Brooks conceded that there are "poems which do depend for their basic meaning upon some knowledge of the historical characters mentioned in them," but, again, the implication of a phrase like "historical characters mentioned in them" was that history is chiefly a matter of footnotes identifying local allusions.

Then too, even when the critics thought of history in more capacious terms than these, a further problem arose from the consideration that such history still seemed insufficiently literary. For Wellek the trouble with Greenlaw's vision of literary history as a comprehensive study of "civilization" was finally not, as one might have thought, that scholars were not actually writing such history, but that the conception itself was inherently wrong. Wellek argued that Greenlaw's "study of everything connected with the history of civilization" would only "crowd out strictly literary studies. All distinctions will fall and extraneous criteria will be introduced into literature." Wellek therefore had to conclude that the historian "should perhaps restrict attempts to account for literature in terms of something else." (The year 1941 seems to have been particularly bad for the interests of "something else." John Crowe Ransom declared that "in strictness the business of the literary critic is exclusively with an esthetic criticism. The business of the moralist will, naturally and properly, be with something else.")

Again Wellek's point was not to reject literary history as much as to rescue it from its burden of nonliterary reference. His solution was an "internal history" that would trace "the history of literature as an art in comparative isolation from its social history, the biographies of authors, or the disjointed appreciation of individual works." This internal history would "look for the essence of a work of art in a system of signs and implicit norms existing as social facts in a collective ideology just as, for instance, the system of language exists." The major product of this idea has been Wellek's multivolume *History of Modern Criticism* (volume 1 published in 1955), in which the story of criticism follows an "inner logic in the evolution of ideas," independent even of the evolution of the works of art to which criticism refers. Martha Woodmansee has pointed out that, "fortunately . . . in practice Wellek does not invariably abide by these principles." For example, he attributes the collapse of neoclassical criticism to "the shifting interests of poets and their audiences."

I cannot pause here to pursue the elusive problem of historical explanation (I have tried elsewhere). But I would argue that even if a purely internal literary history were possible, it would lack explanatory power, because changes in literary forms and theories cannot be satisfactorily accounted for without reference to social and philosophical states of affairs. Definitions of literature, for example, can be seen to have been strongly colored by reactions to specific cultural circumstances. It is only since the coming of industrial, commercial, and utilitarian culture that literary theorists in large numbers have thought it must be the essence of literature (or art) to be nonpractical, nonpurposive, and nonreferential. The abrupt swing toward this view away from traditional instrumentalist and mimetic theories of literature may have only partly been in reaction to such changes in sociohistorical circumstances, but no purely internal logic of ideas can hope to explain why it happened just when and how it did.

EXTRINSIC AND INTRINSIC

This is not to argue, however, for extrinsic rather than intrinsic literary history, but to suggest that the very distinction needs to be reconsidered, as in fact many recent historians and theorists have done. In objecting to the historians' alleged reliance on extrinsic information, the critics failed to ask what it means to call a reading intrinsic or extrinsic. Their appeal to the poem itself against extrinsic or secondary information about it was deceptive. For as Richards had unwittingly demonstrated in *Practical Criticism*, any reader's comprehension of a poem (or any other text) inevitably depends on information that cannot be inferred from the text itself.

Brooks was thus begging the key question when he said that "even where we know a great deal about the author's personality and ideas, *we rarely know as much as the poem itself can tell us about itself*" (emphasis mine). The trouble is there is no telling how much a poem or any other text "can tell us about itself," since that will be relative to how much requisite background information its reader already possesses. It is impossible to specify in advance the extent to which any text is independent of contextual information, since this will depend on who reads the text, when, and in what circumstances.

There is, then, no saying in general what evidence is internal or external to a text, because what is internal for one reader may be external for another. If I already know before I read "The Canonization" that for Donne's contemporaries the word "die" could refer to sexual intercourse, then that meaning of "die" will be intrinsic for me as I read the poem, whereas for someone who does not possess this information it will be extrinsic and have to be supplied. In this sense of the terms, there is no meaning that cannot be potentially either intrinsic or extrinsic, which is to say, intelligible with or without the aid of additional information.

This was a point Wimsatt and Beardsley overlooked in "The Intentional Fallacy," an essay that might have occasioned less confusion had it been entitled "The Extrinsic Fallacy." A careful reading suggests that Wimsatt and Beardsley did not really mean to say that authorial intention *cannot* be the object of literary interpretation, though at one point at least they did say just that. What Wimsatt and Beardsley were chiefly attacking was not the practice of looking for authorial intention, but the practice of determining that intention only from biographical information, hypothetical constructions of the *Zeitgeist* such as "the Elizabethan world-picture," or extratextual statements by the author about what he or she had "really meant," without ever asking whether the interpretations prompted by these forms of evidence squared with ones that could be inferred from the text without them. The objection was well taken, for some literary historians seemed hardly to bother with literary texts at all in arriving at interpretive conclusions. But it did not follow that even in inferring interpretations from the text without consulting works of biography or history, readers were remaining within the orbit of the text.

Consider Wimsatt and Beardsley's chief exhibit of misconceived historical-intentionalist interpretation, Charles M. Coffin's reading of the phrase "trepidation of the spheres" in Donne's "A Valediction Forbidding Mourning" as an allusion to the new Copernican science:

> Moving of th' earth brings harmes and feares,
> Men reckon what it did and meant,
> But trepidation of the spheares,
> Though greater farre, is innocent.

Wimsatt and Beardsley objected that in construing the lines as a reference to the new science, Coffin had preferred "private evidence to public, external to internal." The trouble was that Coffin had found the new science not in the poem itself, but in "external" evidence, "private" to Renaissance scholars, about the Renaissance intellectual climate. Whereas if you stuck to the poem itself, Wimsatt and Beardsley argued, you could take the lines to be more plausibly a reference to earthquakes than to the new science.

But Wimsatt and Beardsley's earthquake-interpretation was no less (or more) private or external than Coffin's new science-interpretation, since decoding a reference to an earthquake depends just as much on background knowledge as does decoding a reference to the new science. Earthquakes may be more familiar to nonscholars than the new science and therefore in a sense less "private," but this fact has no bearing whatever on whether Donne may have meant the one or the other—unless one could argue that we know from other contexts that Donne was the sort of poet who liked esoteric references, and that in his time also the new science would have been more esoteric than earthquakes. Whether Donne was in fact alluding to the new science, earthquakes, or something else, we probably do not have enough evidence to guess, but in any case there is no privileged "internal" evidence that we can use, evidence not dependent on information we at some point have to learn.

The critics' hesitation to accept the private evidence of specialized scholars seemed to come from an unreasonable fear that if a poem's meaning is allowed to depend on such evidence its universality and hence its value will have been diminished. The fear was that to refer a text to a historical context implies relativism and the consequent extinction of values. The critics assumed that their own approach gave privileged access not only to intrinsic meaning, but to intrinsic value as well. For Brooks, criticism had "to be distinguished from scholarship of the history of ideas, for the obvious reason that the historian of ideas may find just as much to explain in a poor and unsuccessful poem as in a good poem." For "a mere round-up of the sources will never in itself tell us what the poet has done with them." It may be true, as far as it goes, that a roundup of a poem's sources is not sufficient to account for why it should be valued, but then neither is an analysis of its structural paradoxes and ironies. After all, the same ironies and paradoxes may appear in a bad poem or a nonpoem as well as in a good poem.

R. S. Crane made this point when he adduced Einstein's energy equation $E = mc^2$ and argued satirically that, "judging it solely by Brooks's criterion for poetic structure," it was "the greatest 'ironical' poem written so far in the twentieth century." Crane's point was that logical structures such as paradox and irony are no less "external" (or "internal") to poetry than are biographical data or unit-ideas. Like the fear of "private" interpretation, the fear of a relativism of values bespoke once again the feeling that the power of literature was somehow compromised if it were felt to be rooted in history. The danger of relativism was real, but it was hardly to be warded off by drawing a circle around an intrinsic realm allegedly immune from it.

Unresolved Conflicts

By the early fifties scholars and critics formally agreed that their methods were complementary, but neither group was sure how criticism and scholarship might combine theoretically or institutionally. A practical resolution was quietly achieved after the war by a new professional generation that had no vested interest in the earlier quarrels and was eager to merge history and criticism in its own work. Scholar and critic began to fuse in the same individuals, doubtless to the great enrichment of all the fields, the quality of whose work can be seen to have made marked advances over most of the work before the war. But what did not make any comparable improvement was the degree of correlation or contrast between history and criticism on the level of departmental organization and curriculum. Instead of trying to think through the relation and connect departmental factions accordingly, departments tended to assume that as long as scholars, critics, and scholar-critics were sufficiently represented, and as long as courses in explication supplemented survey courses, a decent balance would inform the experience of students. The more progressive the department, the more it left individual instructors to work out their integration of criticism and history for themselves, trusting that diverse faculty biases would naturally even out and give the curriculum overall breadth.

As Jonathan Culler remarks, the result was "not so much a synthesis" of history and criticism as "a curious overlay" in which "introductory courses employing *Understanding Poetry* might avoid historical considerations . . . but advanced courses divided literature according to periods, and critics, like scholars, were expected to be experts in a period." In many cases, what resulted was the symptomatic compromise I mentioned in a previous chapter: the course or sequence of courses in which masterpieces of literature were studied New Critically in chronological order. The field-coverage principle remained unquestioned and continued to determine the curriculum, keeping the department self-regulating and relieving old scholars and new critics alike of the need to discuss their differences and agreements and to see how these might be infused into the literature program.

Had scholars and critics had to thrash out their differences in order to determine how they would organize the literature program, they would no doubt have left many issues unresolved and perhaps only illustrated the incommensurability of their outlooks. Yet even this result might have been more instructive than the silent tradeoffs and negotiated settlements that actually ensued. Not that there was any absence of vigorous debate, which enlivened the professional periodical literature throughout the forties with intense controversies over such issues as the problem of the intrinsic and extrinsic, "the problem of belief," and the various "heresies" and "fallacies" of modern criticism. Yet none of these controversies achieved enough prominence to become accessible to more than an inner circle of theoretically initiated professors and graduate students. If my experience in the mid-fifties was representative, these controversies hardly registered at all on undergraduates. The English major I completed, though respectable and up to standard in every way, managed to keep me innocent of issues that, as I learned only years later, were then being fought over with unprecedented intensity, issues that might have given my study the context it lacked. I was later fascinated to discover that several of my teachers held exemplary positions in these debates that in retrospect illuminated their ways of teaching; but all this had passed me by at the time.

Thus a set of conditions that might have created an atmosphere of edifying disputatiousness became assimilated in the polite congeniality wherein old antiquarians and new critics, insofar as they continued to think of themselves as opposing types, tactfully left each other alone. The senior "Renaissance man" might fulminate privately about the obstreperous young "modernist" in the office down the hall with his impertinent opinions about Milton and Shelley and his pretentious and incomprehensible cant about textures, structures, and objective correlatives. But his more tolerant department chairman had only to remind the old scholar that he personally need have nothing to do with the offensive young man, whose courses in any case were drawing so many students into the department that the dean might soon be ready to meet the department's request for another medievalist. When the Renaissance man retired, his replacement was most likely somebody who had quietly assimilated the critical methods, with the offensive prejudices smoothed away.

CHAPTER TWELVE

Modern Literature in the University: 1940–1960

The literature of the youth's own century is more easily understood by him. He can read it rapidly without being perplexed by historical background or outmoded style.

COLLEGE TEXTBOOK (1948)

I have come to think it inadvisable to attempt to teach modern British and American literature to large groups of poorly prepared students. A great deal of this literature is interesting, and some of it is brilliant; but much of it deals with modes of thought and action so alien to the majority of students that they remain passive, or become bewildered, or resentful, or, worst of all, titivated by the least admirable in what they read.

NORTHWESTERN UNIVERSITY INSTRUCTOR, PRIVATE CORRESPONDENCE (1943)

I noted earlier that the critical movement was connected with the movement to make modern and contemporary literature objects of university study. Most scholars who resisted the entry of criticism into the university also resisted the modernization of the canon, partly because they resented the incursion of any literature that had not been sanctified by the test of time, but also because historical method, in the antiquarian terms in which both they and their critical opposition understood it, could have no application to recent literature. As Ransom pointed out in 1938, contemporary literature "is almost obliged to receive critical study if it receives any at all, since it is hardly capable of the usual historical commentary."

It is always tempting to believe that the literature of one's own time requires no history for its comprehension. As the textbook editor quoted in my epigraph said, "the literature of the youth's own century is more easily understood by him. He can read it rapidly without being perplexed by historical background or outmoded style." If this were actually the case, then an apparent solution presented itself to the problem of apathetic students. The hope that reading the literature of their own time would awaken students was a powerful force in dissolving professorial resistance.

That resistance has so thoroughly crumbled that it is hard to believe it ever existed at all, though at what exact point it gave way has not been precisely determined. As early as 1925, Fred Lewis Pattee was saying that "more and more contemporary authors are made subjects of university courses. Within a year 'The Novels of Hergesheimer' has been allowed as a dissertation subject in a leading university. Columbia has at least a dozen doctorate theses in process with subjects drawn from later phases of American literature. . . . Twenty-five years ago this attitude toward American literature would have been inconceivable." Pattee wondered if the change was for the best: "that the colleges," he said, "entrenched behind a thousand years of conservatism, should have surrendered so completely in so short a period, is little less than amazing. It leads us to wonder if the foundations have not been too rudely shaken. Are our professors not yielding too much? Can education be democratized to such a degree as this with entire safety?"

Though a more systematic review of offerings and enrollments would be needed to prove it, Pattee seems to have exaggerated the extent of the surrender. My impression, based on limited evidence, is that though *courses* in the literature of the recent past became frequent in colleges as early as the 1890s, it was not till well after World War II that it became possible for any large proportion of study to be devoted to modern literature. To take the arbitrary example of Northwestern University, as early as 1895–96, according to its catalog, Northwestern was offering a course in "English Literature since 1850," including "The Modern Novel," "The Short Story," and "Some Recent Poets and Essayists." This course evolved into English B7, a sophomore-level survey with average enrollments of about one to two hundred through the fifties. But up to then modern literature offerings were limited to this and two other upper-division courses, and enrollments remained distributed evenly across the major periods of English literature since *Beowulf*.

It is not till the early sixties that a new pattern begins to emerge whereby, though the *number* of twentieth-century courses increases only moderately, the *enrollment* in them goes up disproportionately. In 1974–75, for example, of the sixty-three undergraduate courses offered in English and American literature at Northwestern, eighteen could be classified as concentrating on literature of the twentieth century. These eighteen courses drew an enrollment of 783, by comparison with the total of 789 enrolled in *all* the courses in the earlier periods combined. In other words, some one-half of the average student's literature coursework was devoted to twentieth-century literature, and the enrollment in the average twentieth-century literature course (43.5) amounted to between two and three times that of the other courses (17.5).

Before the fifties, even had literature departments wanted to increase their commitment to modern literature, they would have been hard pressed to find instructors competent to teach the subject, because the emphasis in doctoral programs was still overwhelmingly antiquarian. Those who did teach modern literature tended to be recruited from earlier periods, and their versatility did not always earn them the respect they hoped for. At Northwestern, the sophomore survey and the two upper-level courses in modern literature were handled, beginning in 1932, by a man with a Northwestern Ph.D. in the medieval period who volunteered to teach them in the hope of earning a permanent place in the department. Ten years later he complained to his department chairman that the survey course had "absorbed all my interests," leaving him no time "to publish articles derived from my Ph.D. Thesis and in related subjects," and he asked to be given "definite assurance of promotion" if he returned to teach the modern courses. He was not invited back.

Ancients versus Moderns

The interesting issue in the controversy over the place of modern literature in the university was not whether or how much modern literature should be studied, but what status should be accorded to the modern *view* of literature. A frequent complaint of literary historians in the 1940's was that the New Critics were interpreting and judging the literature of all periods according to what the historians took to be tendentiously and anachronistically modern presuppositions. Behind all the quarrels of these years over alleged "heresies" and "fallacies"—for example, the personal heresy, the heresy of paraphrase, the didactic heresy, the intentional fallacy, the problem of belief, and so forth—was the question of how far earlier works of literature could properly be read according to postromantic poetic theories.

At issue, in other words, was a dispute over the very definition of "literature." Philologists and literary historians had replaced nineteenth-century conventions of literary commentary with a new ideal of scientific rigor, and they had purged a good deal of Victorian moralism and sentimentalism, but they had not seriously challenged the traditionalist poetics that viewed literature as a form of elevated rhetoric. We have seen Douglas Bush's boast that his creed rested on a "conception of poetry which reigned for some 2,500 years." To be sure, the New Critics also claimed to be "traditionalists" in their own way, but this was a way that challenged the adequacy of Bush's didactic poetics, and not just in its application to postromantic literary works. Had the critics been content merely to praise modernist writers for attempting to "wring the neck of rhetoric" and for writing poems which aimed not to "mean" but simply to "be," that would have been scandalous enough, but probably would not have called the scholars' wrath down on their heads. But instead of restricting their ideas to the authorized literature of their own field, the critics presumptuously insisted on meddling with everybody else's.

The critics reinterpreted and reevaluated earlier literature in the light of a modernist poetics that said poetry is neither rhetorical persuasion nor self-expression but an autonomous discourse that cannot be reduced to its constituent concepts or emotions. In Eliseo Vivas's words, a poem or other work of art was "an entity which must be considered as isolated, must be considered as capable of embodying intransitively its own universe of discourse fully within its own confines, for the apprehending mind." More often than not, this conception of art caused poets like Spenser, Milton, Wordsworth, and Shelley to be rejected for philosophical or emotional discursiveness, while it elevated the metaphysical poets, who allegedly most resembled the moderns in their imagistic complexity. It was almost worse, however, when the older poets were not rejected, for then they were reread in ways that to the scholars made them no longer look familiar. Traditionalist poetics was simply effaced, as when New Critics misappropriated Sidney's line "the poet nothing affirms, and therefore never lieth," as if Sidney had meant that poetry should not mean but be.

Pedagogical contingencies played a role here, for the student body was infected with the "message-hunting" approach to literature that was still the standard way of reading for most Americans, for whom "poetry" still meant James Whitcomb Riley and Longfellow's "A Psalm of Life," if not Edgar Guest. Cleanth Brooks recalled that when he first started teaching at Vanderbilt in the thirties, the students there "actually approached Keats's 'Ode to a Nightingale' in the same spirit and with the same expectations with which they approached an editorial in the local county newspaper or an advertisement in the current Sears, Roebuck catalogue." Such a statement goes a long way toward explaining why critics like Brooks and Vivas felt it necessary to insist that poetry embodied "intransitively its own universe of discourse fully within its own confines, for the apprehending mind."

Much of the bewilderment and anger this view evoked in the scholars betrayed their simple refusal to see that fundamental changes had taken over literature, literary culture, and criticism. Instead of trying to understand and argue with the modernist movement on its own terms, they dismissed it as an elitist conspiracy in which, evidently from sheer perversity, "poets and critics," in Bush's words, "have decided to write for one another" and to turn their backs on the "plain student of literature, not to mention a scientist or a businessman." There was more than a grain of truth in Bush's charge, but it called for understanding and analysis rather than mere condemnation. The "plain student," the scientist, and the businessman themselves were no longer part of the kind of society that had sustained an uplifting conception of literature and the common reader.

It was not just modern critics and poets who spoke in a specialized professional vocabulary and claimed "autonomy" for their discourse, but virtually all other professionals as well. As Harold Rosenberg pointed out in a searching essay of the late fifties, it was characteristic of professionalism "to detach itself from the social will and to ignore every other form of thought except as it can absorb it into its own technical apparatus." "Pure art, physics, politics, is nothing else than art, physics, politics, that develops its procedures in terms of its own possibilities without reference to the needs of any other profession or of society as a whole." Rosenberg imagined a "Dictionary of Puristic Ideas" that would plausibly "transmigrate from poetry into, say, military science, back into painting, over again into city planning, sideways into political agitation and party life." "Since its first appearance, 'pure' art has been attacked as nihilistic," Rosenberg said. "If, however, all the high professions are nihilistic in the identical way, the accusation becomes pointless, though not necessarily untrue."

The scholars were most out of their depth when rehearsing the old middlebrow complaints about the irresponsibility of modern poetry and criticism. But they were likely to know what they were talking about when they objected to anachronistic misreadings of earlier literature. The effort to refute the spread of anachronistic critical interpretations kept many scholars busy during this period. In essay after essay they tried to beat back what they took to be spuriously attributed ambiguities and paradoxes by reconstructing an allegedly probable historical context.

The most sustained and powerful single work to be produced in this genre was probably Rosemond Tuve's *Elizabethan and Metaphysical Imagery* (1947). This was a polemic of notable ferocity and learning that indicted Eliot in particular for ascribing to seventeenth-century English poetry a modern concern with the dissociation of sensibility and a consequent antithesis between rationality and imagination. According to Tuve, such an antithesis would have been "inconceivable" to earlier poets, "with their very different conception of poetic belief" and their lack of embarrassment about "the intrusion into poetry of the methods of reasonable discourse." Tuve argued that what had undoubtedly for modern poets become an all-important distinction between artistic and scientific truth "was not one to which the earlier period gave much concern." Renaissance writers and theorists had no reason to avoid conceiving poetry as rhetoric, with a "necessary core of conceptual meaning."

Tuve seemed not to see that in a way she was only making Eliot's own point—that poets like Donne (or Dante) had fewer worries about unity of sensibility or metaphysical belief and could thus achieve them without the self-conscious struggle forced on the modern poet. But Tuve's attack was still a pertinent corrective to much of the cant then in the air about the metaphysical poets' alleged ability to "feel" their thought "as immediately as the odor of a rose." In *A Reading of George Herbert* (1952), Tuve made a similar case against Empson's interpretation, in *Seven Types of Ambiguity*, of Herbert's "The Sacrifice," arguing that recognizing the probable Christian context of certain passages eliminated most of the celebrated ambiguities Empson had found in them.

In "The New Criticism and *King Lear*" (1949), W. R. Keast attacked Robert B. Heilman's reading of *King Lear* in *This Great Stage* (1948), in which Heilman argued that Shakespeare "had got hold of the modern problem" of "the conflict of old and new orders." In Heilman's interpretation, Shakespeare seemed almost to have presciently anticipated the agrarian critics' hostility to the functional rationality of northern urban industrialism. Thus Goneril and Regan became symbols of "the spirit of calculation," as if Shakespeare could have had the same animus toward "calculation" as did so many later writers who associated it with technocratic management. Keast argued that Heilman had imposed an alien conception of Shakespeare's methods as well as his themes: he had been misled by "the tendency of such modern writers as Kafka, Brecht, and Broch to write symbolic works" into taking it "as self-evident, or requiring only passing justification, that a symbolic reading is appropriate to any work."

In 1951 J. V. Cunningham revived the quarrel with Heilman,

disputing the latter's reading of the line "ripeness is all" in *King Lear* as an expression of the modern perspectivist view that "one moment's mood does not close off all the perspectives available." Cunningham argued that when read as the commonplace of Christian resignation Shakespeare most likely intended it to be, Edgar's line closed off a good many perspectives. "The difference in meaning is unmistakable," Cunningham said: "ours looks toward life and [Shakespeare's] toward death; ours finds its locus in modern psychology and his in Christian theology." Taking up poems by Nashe and Marvell, Cunningham argued in another essay that Eliot and his followers had ignored the Aristotelian logical exposition on which the poems had been constructed in order to extract a symbolist *frisson* from them. For example, Eliot had praised the vividness of images in "To His Coy Mistress" such as:

> My *vegetable* love should grow
> Vaster than empires, and more slow.

Cunningham suggested that, contrary to Eliot, who had inappropriately visualized "some monstrous and expanding cabbage," "vegetable" was probably not a visual image at all but a reference to the Renaissance doctrine of the generative lower level of the tripartite soul.

One of the most fascinating collisions of historical and modernist interpretations occurred over Nashe's line, "Brightness falls from the ayre" in the lyric "In Time of Pestilence." Cunningham cited a textual note by Nashe's editor, who said that while "it is to be hoped that Nashe meant 'ayre,' " it seems more probable "that the true reading is 'hayre,' which gives a more obvious, but far inferior sense." Cunningham inferred that the editor's taste for symbolist suggestiveness, reminiscent of Stephen Dedalus's rhapsody over Nashe's line in *Portrait of the Artist as a Young Man*, had caused him to rewrite the poem without any textual warrant. Wesley Trimpi, however, subsequently argued that "ayre" becomes the more plausible historical reading once one knows that in the Renaissance the image of brightness falling from the air often referred to lightning and that lightning was considered an omen of plague—a set of associations that Trimpi persuasively demonstrated by adducing relevant parallel passages. Strengthening the probability of this reading was the fact that Nashe's lyric was part of a play set during the London plague. At the same time, Trimpi defended Cunningham's point in principle, that whatever we take Nashe to have meant, that meaning is not subject to change—and it cannot depend on what later readers might like Nashe to have meant.

In response to these attacks, critics countered by questioning whether the "original intentions" of authors are in fact recoverable, or if we need to rule out later-accruing meanings even if they are. Recent commentators have missed this point when they have assumed, as for example Catherine Belsey does, that New Criticism was "compelled by its own logic to argue that the text . . . means now what it has always meant." Wellek and Warren maintained in *Theory of Literature* that "the meaning of a work of art is not exhausted by, or even equivalent to, its intention. As a system of values, it leads an independent life." It cannot "be defined merely in terms of its meaning for the author and his contemporaries. It is rather the result of a process of accretion, i.e., the history of its criticism by its many readers in many ages." Concerning the interpretation of Marvell's "vegetable love," they asked "whether it is desirable to get rid of the modern connotation and whether, at least, in extreme cases, it is possible." Wimsatt and Beardsley took the same position when they said that "the history of words *after* a poem is written may contribute meanings which if relevant to the original pattern should not be ruled out by a scruple about intention."

Without entering into an extensive discussion of the still much-disputed issue of intention, I would argue that the scholars, on the whole, had the better of this argument. True, they sometimes conceived "intention" too narrowly, failing to allow a place for half-intentions, blurred and contradictory ones; or they assumed that intentionalist interpretations precluded other kinds; or they forgot that intentions might be so elusive that to speak of intention in some cases might be merely a formal or hypothetical gesture. But the historians were more theoretically consistent than their critical opponents and showed a firmer sense of what might count as an argument for or against their position. The critics often confused two quite different arguments against intention (the two have remained confused in subsequent attacks on intentionalist theories). One argument (let us call it the "unknowability argument") held that an author's intention was essentially unknowable, and therefore could not control or limit the meaning of a text. The other (which we could call "the undesirability argument") held that that even if an author's intention could be discovered, it should not be allowed to control or limit the interpretation, since such a limitation will only impoverish the meaning.

The confusion of the two arguments is seen in Wimsatt and Beardsley's statement that "the design or intention of the author is neither available nor desirable as a standard for judging the success of a work of literary art." If the author's intention were really not "available," then what was the point of adding that it was not "desirable" to bring it in? On the other hand, Wellek and Warren invited a different kind of objection when they said, "if we should really be able to reconstruct the meaning which *Hamlet* held for its contemporary audience, we would merely impoverish it." To this point the historians might have replied, "True, perhaps, but so what?" The historians, after all, claimed only to be telling us what the author had probably meant, not whether that meaning was the richest or most interesting that could be attributed to his or her words.

Indeed, the historians who took up the issue were perfectly willing to concede that a meaning acquired by a work after it had been written might be "rich and important in itself," as Cunningham put it, and that it need not be given up. That is, they acknowledged the importance of present relevance, what E. D. Hirsch has subsequently called the "significance" of a text, as distinct from its "meaning." The historians urged only that interpreters be clear about the logic of their own claims, clear about whether they assumed they were talking about intentions or something else. Such clarity would have meant recognizing that when one spoke of meaning as a "process of accretion," one had already presupposed a distinction between originally intended meanings and later-accruing ones. For it may be true, as a matter of psychological fact, that it is impossible "to get rid of the modern connotation" of "vegetable" when we now read Marvell's line. But the pertinent question is not whether we can erase our own feelings but whether we can recognize them as our own, whether we can recognize the modern connotation *as* modern. Wellek and Warren themselves seemed to think they could do so when they designated certain meanings as "the modern connotation."

Wellek later wrote (in reply to criticisms of my own) that the historians' ideal of reconstructing original intentions "excludes a proper dialogue between past and present and postulates a concept of history divorced from present-day interests and concerns." (This in a nutshell was Hans-Georg Gadamer's phenomenological answer to E. D. Hirsch.) Again, the historian's reply might have been that in order to speak coherently of a "dialogue between past and present," one has to be granted a hypothetical chance to identify "the past" as such—nor should this be confused with entering a time capsule and reexperiencing it. The better historians never forgot that any reconstruction of the past is always problematic and open to challenge, that historical interpretation is not simply a matter of accumulating facts, but a hermeneutical weighing of inferences and hypotheses whose results are conjectural, tentative, and subject to refutation. Unfortunately, few historians elaborated their theoretical assumptions as assiduously as the critics did theirs, and, with the notable exception of the later R. S. Crane, as theorists few historians were in a class with the critics. An uncompleted work by Crane that might have brought about a reconciliation of criticism and history was not published until 1967.

FROM EVALUATION TO RATIONALIZATION

As criticism was becoming institutionalized, then, unresolved conflicts persisted between the claims of past-centered historical recovery and present-centered reinterpretation. But these conflicts like others were muffled in the departmental atmosphere of opportunistic cooperation and the longing for a truce between scholars and critics. What is more, as the New Criticism achieved academic respectability, its position underwent a subtle change that mitigated the earlier discrepancy between traditional and modernist literary taste. Here is a point which, so far as I know, has not been noticed.

This change is exemplified in the difference in outlook between two of Brooks's books published eight years apart, *Modern Poetry and the Tradition* (1939) and *The Well Wrought Urn* (1947). In the earlier book, Brooks echoed Eliot's account of the history of poetry since the seventeenth century as the story of a more or less uninterrupted decline from the unified sensibility of the Renaissance into the long interregnum of dissociation, only recently reversing itself in the symbolists and the poets of Eliot's own generation. "The" in Brooks's title boldly claimed an exclusivity about "the Tradition" that was not lost on the book's scholarly readers. As Douglas Bush complained, "in *Modern Poetry and the Tradition*, Mr. Brooks gave the impression that nearly all poetry betwen Marvell and Pound was a mistake." Other scholars—including Herbert J. Muller, Donald Stauffer, Richard Fogle, and Darrel Abel—also objected to Brooks's narrowness, Stauffer for instance charging that Brooks "is unfair to poetry as a whole" because "his position excludes from the reader's enjoyment great areas of poetry."

Yet, even in the earlier book, Brooks had actually softened many of Eliot's more severe judgments, and in *The Well Wrought Urn* he pretty much abandoned them altogether. The very aim of this later book seemed to be to allay the many objections to the New Criticism's exclusivity by showing through a series of explications that, if examined closely, representative poems by Milton, Gray, Pope, Wordsworth, Keats, and Tennyson would prove just as rich in irony and paradox and therefore just as acceptable to New Critical taste as the best poems of Donne, Shakespeare, Herrick, and Yeats.

Perhaps the most dramatic sign of Brooks's deviation from Eliot was his defense of Keats's line, "Beauty is Truth, Truth Beauty" against Eliot's caustic observation that the line was "a serious blemish on a beautiful poem; and the reason must be either that I fail to understand it, or that it is a statement which is untrue." As early as the first edition of *Understanding Poetry*, Brooks and Warren had argued that Keats's line "grows intimately out of a special context . . . and does not come merely as a kind of disconnected comment on life or as an adage." Brooks now elaborated the implications of this idea, arguing that Eliot's objections were disarmed if one read the line not as an assertion about truth and beauty but as a speech "in character," and thus "dramatically appropriate."

Interestingly, Brooks compared Keats's line to Shakespeare's "Ripeness is all," which he said was also "a statement put in the mouth of a dramatic character and thus governed and qualified by the whole context of the play. It does not directly challenge an examination of its truth because its relevance is pointed up and modified by the dramatic context." The problem Cunningham had raised about Heilman's attempt to turn "Ripeness is all" into a statement of modern perspectivism had now become unnecessary, since the line was not a statement at all but a dramatic utterance to which the canons that apply to statements are irrelevant. The conflicting views of literature that had divided traditionalists and modernists over the problem of belief were now smoothed over, for neither traditional nor modern literature had anything to do with belief.

The Well Wrought Urn illustrated how the New Criticism had imperceptibly shifted its claims in a way that put earlier conflicts to rest while flattening literary history into a repetition of the same motifs. Eliot did say that "a degree of heterogeneity of material compelled into unity by the operation of the poet's mind is omnipresent in poetry." But he made clear enough that unity-in-heterogeneity was not a *definition* of poetry but a historically situated preference, indeed a tactical response to what Eliot called the "material at hand" of that "panorama of futility and anarchy" that was contemporary history. In a late essay, Eliot admitted that both in the "general affirmations about poetry" of his early criticism and in the comments about writers who had influenced him, "I was implicitly defending the sort of poetry that I and my friends wrote." Eliot's very attacks on major figures in the history of poetry presupposed that important poetry had been written in modes wholly different from the ones he was recommending. He never confused the kind of poetry he liked or thought was needed by the modern age with a definition of poetry as such.

For this reason, when Eliot later moderated his early severities, he did not have to weaken his criteria but simply acknowledged the claims of different ones. Eliot concluded his 1947 revaluation of Milton by saying that poets now seem "sufficiently liberated" from Milton's grandiloquent manner to profit from him. In other words, Eliot did not now maintain that Milton had not actually been a grandiloquent stylist after all, but had really written in the manner of the metaphysicals—Eliot merely said that grandiloquence could no longer do much harm; he did not try to reread Milton so as to make him square with other criteria. This, however, was precisely Brooks's tactic in *The Well Wrought Urn*, where he exonerated "L'Allegro" and "Il Penseroso," as well as Pope, Gray, Keats, and Tennyson, by so widening the categories of "paradox" and "irony" that these poets now fit them. Paradox and irony were suddenly no longer the poetic qualities admired by a partisan school admittedly promoting one kind of poetry over others. They were the defining characteristics of poetry in general.

The "tradition" had been stretched to cover almost all the poets anyone in the university liked, which is to say, one could now accept New Critical poetics without renouncing the poets in one's field. There was after all no conflict between the old and the new poetics, for "the language of paradox" vindicated all true poems, ancient and modern. And make no mistake that it did indeed vindicate them; for, given the convenient elasticity of terms such as paradox and irony, not many poems could fail to reveal these qualities somehow, under the right kind of close inspection. The difficult choices that Eliot had forced on readers no longer had to be faced.

After the war, the literature department seemed abruptly to have changed sides in the cultural quarrel over modern literature. An institution that had once seen itself as the bulwark of tradition against vulgar and immoral contemporaneity was now the disseminator and explainer of the most recent trends. One might imagine that such a transformation could not have taken place without open violence and confrontation. Yet the assimilation of modern literature had been accomplished so quietly and with so little open discussion of its cultural or ideological implications outside the pages of the journals specializing in that sort of controversy that most students and perhaps most professors hardly noticed what had happened.

Eliot, Joyce, and Faulkner were miles away ideologically from Sidney, Johnson, and Tennyson, but once they had become acceptable they took on the status of another "field." In the separate but equal segregation of the curriculum, Dr. Johnson and James Joyce each occupied an honored place—Did not each represent "literature"?—and therefore the ideological differences between them did not need to arise as a subject. In the department, as in the case of "Ripeness is all," the problem of belief did not need to be confronted. In what was by now a familiar pattern, the institutionalization of a movement had been accomplished by the erasure of its more interesting cultural implications.

Occasionally, to be sure, exponents of the old and the new poetics confronted one another before the students in a lively after-hours symposium such as those that occurred at Johns Hopkins under the aegis of the History of Ideas Club or at the Gauss Seminars at Princeton. But such confrontations were too infrequent and occasional to provide the sustained discussion that was needed. By the 1960s, as we have seen, students had come to study more modern literature than any other kind; yet because they rarely studied it in conjunction with earlier literature they did not acquire the contrastive perspective that would have enabled them to see what was "modern" about modern literature. Though an individual instructor might do so, nothing in the system encouraged students in either the modern or the earlier literature classes to ask how either body of work ought to be read or what the competing ways of reading them entailed.

All this was disabling, for it turned out not to be true, as the textbook editor had said in 1948, that students found it easier to read the literature of their own century and not be "perplexed by historical background." Ransom had not been wrong when he said that contemporary literature was "hardly capable of the usual historical commentary," but this was only because "the usual historical commentary" was historical only in a narrow sense, reducing history to "background" data that obscured the more useful historical contexts. Modernity, after all, was a historical concept, having no meaning unless studied in relation to premodernity.

After 1960, the new generation of academic critics would no longer be much interested in fighting over whether Eliot's or Yeats's poetry deserved the same kind of attention as Milton's—such questions had now been settled in a manner advantageous to all parties. The old fierce battles pitting the school of Milton against the school of Donne, Tennysonians against Yeatsians, those who thought poetic beliefs mattered against those who did not, now seemed professionally counterproductive. Why force anyone to choose between Tennyson and Yeats when both could be enjoyed and when so much work still "needed to be done" in advancing both fields? To be sure, curmudgeons like Winters and Leavis intensified their rude challenges to major reputations, but there was no point even dignifying these with counterargument (though it seems symptomatic that Leavis's work became a public issue in England in a way that Winters's did not in the United States). Such attacks had been sufficiently "answered" by the accumulated explications surrounding the works they had impugned, making counterargument superfluous.

By the late fifties, the antagonism between scholars and critics seemed antiquated, an expression of the passions and prejudices of a less flexible era. Quarreling over the intentional fallacy or the problem of belief was all well and good in its place, but progress called for setting old hostilities aside and mobilizing the resources of scholarship and criticism to exploit those "research opportunities" which were described in the evolving professional Fieldspeak used to announce them in the journals. Large portions of the literary canon still had not been interpreted, and those that had been cried out for reinterpretation.

An opportunity had been missed, for like the earlier conflict between generalists and investigators, the struggle between critics and scholars might have enabled literary studies to clarify what they stood for, even if this should prove to be nothing more coherent than the manifest divisions within a literary culture that no longer agreed on what "literature" was or on its social function or on how it should be read.

CHAPTER THIRTEEN

The Promise of American Literature Studies

Again the role of the national literature in shaping the nation's identity became a subject for debate.

RICHARD RULAND

American studies has not had the influence on other disciplines that one might expect and has produced an interdisciplinary subfield rather than a reorganization of knowledge.

JONATHAN CULLER

Because the New Criticism has been the most discussed of the postwar academic methodologies and the one that has had the most influence on pedagogy, we are prone to forget that it was never more than one among many. The direction of postwar academic literary studies was interdisciplinary as much as it was intrinsic. Yet even observers who clearly know better can say that "there was hardly a movement" from the late twenties to the late fifties "that did not subscribe to the tenet that such 'extrinsic' disciplines as psychology, sociology, and philosophy represented a threat of contamination to the contextual purity of serious literature." That this is not wholly the case is implied by this very commentator, who quotes Northrop Frye's complaint in *Anatomy of Criticism* (1957) about proliferating "determinisms in criticism . . . Marxist, Thomist, liberal-humanities, neo-Classical, Freudian, Jungian, or existentialist, . . . all proposing, not to find a conceptual framework for criticism within literature, but to attach criticism to one of a miscellany of frameworks outside it."

As Frye's statement negatively suggests, though "interdisciplinary" is a latter-day term, what it denotes was well under way by the late forties and perceived to be so. In his 1948 survey, *The Armed Vision*, Stanley Edgar Hyman actually characterized "modern criticism" (if only "crudely and somewhat inaccurately") as "*the organized use of non-literary techniques and bodies of knowledge to obtain insights into literature.*" Hyman's exemplary critics were those who borrowed systematically from extraliterary disciplines: Richards (linguistics and psychology), Maud Bodkin (anthropology), Kenneth Burke (sociology and rhetoric), Christopher Caudwell (Marxism); and even in his chapters on Richards and Empson what interested Hyman was their importation of concepts from linguistics and psychology. In the offing was Frye, whose system of myths, modes, and genres would make it possible to blur distinctions among literature, religion, popular entertainment, and advertising as expressions of common patterns of mythic identification.

So far had the interdisciplinary trend penetrated criticism by the late forties that by then the counterreaction against it had already begun. The attraction to the New Criticism for some came from the concern that interdisciplinary methodology was becoming so powerful as to obscure the integrity of literature itself, a concern that does not first date from reactions against poststructuralism or neo-Marxism. Randall Jarrell worried in 1952 that, judging from Hyman's title and other indications in *The Armed Vision*, "the ideal modern critic" would "resemble one of those robots you meet in science-fiction stories, with a microscope for one eye, a telescope for the other, and a mechanical brain at Harvard for a heart." "Critics," Jarrell observed, "are so much better armed than they used to be in the old days: they've got tanks and flame-throwers now, and it's harder to see past them to the work of art—in fact, magnificent creatures that they are, it's hard to *want* to see past them."

Though one can appreciate Jarrell's alarm at the implications of an "armed" criticism, the problem arguably lay not in the presence of new weaponry, to retain the figure, but in what it might be used to do or not do. Given the advances in interdisciplinary method that Hyman had described, and given the widespread agreement by now that criticism and history should seek to merge, it might at last have been possible to situate the work of the literature department in a larger study of cultural history without simply reducing literature to a "reflection" of sociological conditions or the history of ideas. Implicit in the new interdisciplinary methods was a redefinition and reorganization of literary studies that promised finally to confront some of their chronic problems.

Yet this redefinition and reorganization did not take place, and some of the reasons why not are suggested by the trajectory of one field, American literature studies, that from its inception was peculiarly tied to the project of overcoming the gulf between literature and its sociohistorical contexts. Jonathan Culler has argued that the field of "American Studies," which arose after World War I, has aimed at "a major reorganization of knowledge around what it takes to be the central question: what is American culture and how did it get to be the way it is?" Yet Culler observes, rightly in my view, that the promised reorganization of knowledge failed to occur. Why, when conditions seemed ripe for the creation of a study of culture that would overcome the old compartmentalizations and fragmentations, did such a study not materialize?

American Literature Studies

College courses in American literature existed before World War I—quite a few, in fact—but they were sporadic and their emphasis usually was on history rather than literature. According to Fred Lewis Pattee, surveying the history of the college study of American literature in 1925, the first course "distinctively marked 'American Literature' " was offered at the University of Michigan in 1875 by Moses Coit Tyler, whom Pattee credits as "the first to make the history of American literature a separate academic subject in an American university" and "the first to study American literature against the background of American history." Yet, in Tyler's classes at Ann Arbor, "according to the testimony of his students, it was hard sometimes to determine whether the subject they had just heard lectured upon was history or literature." When Tyler went to Cornell in 1881, "he announced at the start that in all his courses he intended to 'use American literature as a means of illustrating the several periods of American history.' He was ahead of his times even for the new and radical Cornell. It was not till 1897 that his college caught up with him and added to its curriculum an unattached course in the history of American literature."

Pattee credited the women's colleges as pioneers in introducing American literature—noting courses that appeared in the 1880s at Smith, Wellesley, and Mount Holyoke. Dartmouth and the University of Wisconsin initiated courses in 1883, under C. F. Richardson (with whom Pattee studied) and J. C. Freeman. These courses—and the concurrently appearing American literature textbooks and histories—aroused protests, for the very idea of "American literature" was to many minds a laughable contradiction in terms. Properly speaking, it was said, "there is no such thing" as American literature, "unless the pictorial scratchings of aborigines on stones and birch bark are to be classed as literary productions. Every piece of literary work done in the English language by a man or woman born to the use of it is a part of that noble whole which we call English literature."

When this sort of academic prejudice was overcome, it was because "some member of the English department in some way became interested in [American literature] and had influence enough to secure what he desired." This occurred often enough that by 1900, according to Pattee, "American literature as an independent subject had been introduced into practically all of the American colleges" (I shall pass over the exceptions here). They could hold out, he observes, only until the World War, when the "demands upon the colleges for patriotism-inducing subjects" caused American literature to be added to the curriculum everywhere. By 1925, according to Pattee, the battle had "been so completely won now that many of the younger generation of American literature teachers even have never heard of it."

Early teachers of American literature tended to adopt an apologetic view of their subject. Like Barrett Wendell in his *Literary History of America* (1900), they defended American literature with faint praise or apologized for it, but they did not question the assumption that whatever was of value in it was a product of New England and therefore predominantly British in spirit. In a celebrated witticism, Pattee remarked that the title of Wendell's book should have been "A Literary History of Harvard University, with Incidental Glimpses of the Minor Writers of America." Textbooks still treated American literature as an expression of traditional New England idealism, much as Rufus Griswold and Clarence Stedman had treated it in the mid-nineteenth century.

A typical attitude was expressed by Reverend Henry Van Dyke of Princeton, who, in his 1910 book *The Spirit of America* (reissued in 1922), argued that American literature characteristically approached "life from the point of view of responsibility" and gave "full value to those instincts, desires, and hopes in man which have to do with the unseen world." Van Dyke acknowledged that there were American writers "who are moved by a sense of revolt against the darkness and severity of certain theological creeds," but he added that even in such cases "the attempt is not to escape from religion, but to find a clearer, nobler, and more loving expression of religion." The "characteristic note of the literature of America," Van Dyke said, was to take "for granted that there is a God, that men must answer to him for their actions, and that one of the most interesting things about people, even in books, is their moral quality."

Bliss Perry expressed a similar view in 1912, arguing that "our

American literature . . . is characteristically a citizen literature, responsive to the civic note." Perry detected a Puritanical "thinness or bloodlessness" in Cooper and Poe and argued that the most valuable American literature lay not in fiction and poetry but in public writings such as the *Federalist* and in town-meeting oratory and sermons. Even America's preachers seemed to deserve more attention than its novelists and poets, for they had "performed the function of men of letters without knowing it" and had been "treated with too scant respect in the histories of American literature." For Perry, as for Van Dyke, James Whitcomb Riley was a major American poet.

This view that civic uplift was the defining quality of American literature was initially intensified by World War I and its aftermath. I quoted in an earlier chapter Pattee's remark that an "educational Monroe doctrine" had appeared after the war, declaring "for Americans American literature." And I quoted Pattee's own comment in 1919 that "the American soul, the American conception of democracy,—Americanism, should be made prominent in our school curriculum, as a guard against the rising spirit of experimental lawlessness which has followed the great war." Textbooks like the one this remark appeared in still presented American literature much as Brander Matthews had in the nineties, as an exemplification of the march of the "English speaking race . . . as this race is steadily spreading abroad over the globe."

But freeing itself from such overt patriotic uplift was virtually a condition of the constituting of American literature as a professional field. Academic Americanists tended to be more sensitive than their antiquarian colleagues to critical trends outside the university, and they could not but be aware that patriotic uplift was on the defensive in those circles, as it was becoming irrelevant in professional quarters. Since Van Wyck Brooks's call for a "usable past" before the war, nonacademic critics had been developing a heterodox criticism of American culture, attacking the genteel canon of Longfellow and Riley, endorsing the naturalists, reviving unpopular writers like Melville, Dickinson, and Thoreau, and scorning everything "academic." Academic Americanists bridled under such criticism, but they tended to modify their own tastes accordingly. Pattee, for example, whose career spanned the preprofessional and the mature period of American literary studies and whose tastes reflected the conflicts between the two, wondered in 1925 whether the typical "old professor" whom the young intellectuals were assaulting had not become obsolete.

By the late twenties, such defensive resignation had given way to a positive sense of corporate mission, most dramatically illustrated in the manifesto published in 1928, *The Reinterpretation of American Literature*. The new sense of mission drew its energy from the nationalist pieties released by the war, but with a crucial difference. For though the contributors to the *Reinterpretation* urged the need to revitalize the concept of an American national literature, their immediate interest was not in shoring up patriotic ideals but in overcoming the fragmentation of the academic disciplines. It is significant that the editor of the *Reinterpretation* was the New Humanist and scourge of the research specialists, Norman Foerster, whose previously discussed polemic against the research industry, *The American Scholar*, appeared the following year.

Both Foerster in his introduction and other contributors to the *Reinterpretation* expressed impatience with the kind of scholarship which still assumed that "facts of any sort are worthy of blind pursuit," and they explicitly connected the cause of American literature in the university with the cause of criticism. The essays in the *Reinterpretation* did not oppose criticism to literary history but emphasized the need to integrate the two, to merge history and criticism in a larger cultural study that would bring literary studies into more intimate connection with American society. It was this impulse toward synthesis and integration more than anything that gave the new field an iconoclastic and populist aura that continued to be part of its image for decades to come. The very sites that became known as centers of American literature study bespoke a break with the traditional eastern and New England universities: Pattee's Penn State; V. L. Parrington's University of Washington; the University of North Carolina, one of the first to emphasize work in American literature and the home of such first-generation Americanists as Foerster, Howard Mumford Jones, Floyd Stovall, and C. Hugh Holman.

American patriotism, then, was the force that initially reawakened the old concern with nationality as an organizing category of literary study, but as American literature studies became professionalized the reassertion of nationality had less to do with exclusionary piety about the national spirit than with transcending positivistic specialization, embracing diversity as part of the whole, and even bridging the gap between high and popular American culture. In a passage reminiscent of one of Whitman or Emerson's democratic catalogs, Harry Hayden Clark predicted that

> the literary historian of the future will have to widen his vision and take into proper account such factors as the invention of the rotary press, the

state of general education and enlightenment, the constant cheapening of the processes of printing, the increasing ease of travel and communication, the distribution of surplus wealth and leisure, the introduction of the typewriter, the distribution of bookstores and circulating libraries, the popularization of the telephone, motor car, movies, and radio, and legislative attitudes toward such questions as censorship, international copyright, and a tariff on foreign books.

Emphasizing the "parallelism" of "cultural phenomena" in their "interaction and interdependence," Clark warned that "the student of literature is under a constant temptation to keep his eyes so close to the particular specimen under examination that . . . he often forgets that the plant has roots, a stem, a system of life, and is affected by changes in temperature, soil, and other incidental conditions." The product of such efforts is "literature studied in a vacuum, without relation to anything but itself." Such statements suggest how closely the initial aspirations of American literature studies were tied to a quest for cultural synthesis not unlike what Van Wyck Brooks and the young radical intellectuals were calling for. But unlike Brooks's impressionistic talk of a usable past, this project would combine synthetic vision with precise scholarship.

The figure who at first most influenced the shape of that combination was V. L. Parrington, whose three-volume *Main Currents in American Thought* (1927–30) reinforced the link between the academic study of American literature and the progressive social outlook of the nonacademic critics. Howard Mumford Jones recalled "the tingling sense of discovery" with which he and his generation first read Parrington, following "this confident marshalling of masses of stubborn material into position, until book, chapter, and section became as orderly as a regiment on parade!" According to Lionel Trilling, Parrington's ideas were still in the late forties "the accepted ones wherever the college course in American literature is given by a teacher who conceives himself to be opposed to the genteel and the academic and in alliance with the vigorous and the actual."

But Parrington's influence was no sooner established than it began to be attacked, and it would soon become a casualty of the reaction against progressive criticism at the end of the thirties. As the title of his major study suggested, Parrington was a historian of ideas rather than of literature, a member of the generation of Greenlaw, Nitze, and Jones, that still thought of scholarship as a science and of criticism as inherently subjectivist or, in Parrington's favorite term of condescension, "belletristic." Accordingly, critics in the thirties attacked Parrington's conception of literary "thought" as an instance of the reductionism they found in Lovejoy's history of ideas, compounded by Parrington's thoroughgoing economic determinism.

In an essay of 1940 that turned out to be decisive, "Parrington, Mr. Smith, and Reality" (reprinted in revised form as "Reality in America" in *The Liberal Imagination*), Trilling charged that Parrington's conception of culture as a set of "currents" betrayed his "characteristic weakness as a historian," his inability to see that "a culture is not a flow, nor even a confluence; the form of its existence is struggle, or at least debate—it is nothing if not a dialectic." Parrington might well have retorted that "currents" could be dialectical—as his history in fact might have been thought to to show. But what was at issue for Trilling was Parrington's allegedly uncritical conception of "reality" as "always material reality, hard, resistant, unformed, impenetrable, and unpleasant." It was this crude materialism that had led Parrington to dismiss Poe, Melville, and Henry James as escapists, while excusing writers like Dreiser for writing badly as long as they were properly, as Trilling put it, "impatient of the sterile literary gentility of the bourgeoisie." Yvor Winters echoed Trilling's judgment, writing in 1943 that Parrington had been "almost brutally crude" in distinguishing the ideas in a work of art from its "belletristic" aspect. By the end of the thirties, those searching for a synthesis of American literature and culture had to look for an alternative to Parrington.

THEORIES OF AMERICAN LITERATURE

They tended to find the alternative in the study of cultural motifs and symbols, which, from the end of the 1930s, has produced an outpouring of theorizing about the "American" element in American literature that is one of the distinctive achievements of academic literary studies. Over the ensuing twenty-five years, the theoretical synthesis of American literature achieved a flowering as a critical genre. A partial list of the major works would include Yvor Winters, *Maule's Curse* (1938); F. O. Matthiessen, *American Renaissance* (1941); Henry Nash Smith, *Virgin Land: The American West as Symbol and Myth* (1950); Charles Feidelson, *Symbolism and American Literature* (1953); R. W. B. Lewis, *The American Adam* (1955); Richard Chase, *The American Novel and Its Tradition* (1957); Harry Levin, *The Power of Blackness: Hawthorne, Poe, Melville* (1958); Leslie Fiedler, *Love and Death in the American Novel* (first edition, 1960); Marius Bewley, *The Eccentric Design* (1963); A. N. Kaul, *The American Vision: Actual and Ideal Society in Nineteenth Century Fiction* (1964); Leo Marx, *The Machine in the Garden* (1965); and Richard Poirier, *A World Elsewhere* (1966).

It was this generation of theorists that was the first to apply the methods of the New Criticism to American literature, and in their hands—more than in other fields, I believe—the New Criticism became a historical and cultural method. This was accomplished by reviving the latent cultural dimension of organicist poetics that, for Coleridge and the Southern New Critics, had connected the literary with the social organism. The theorists of American literature conceived the organic structure of a literary work as a microcosm of collective psychology or myth and thus made New Criticism into a method of cultural analysis.

Their first step, however, was to overturn and revise the simplistically negative interpretation of American Puritanism that had come down from Parrington and Mencken. In the work of Perry Miller and of Winters, the Puritans suddenly achieved a new and complex relevance to later American writing. Miller, in studies of Puritanism in the thirties such as *The New England Mind: the Seventeenth Century* (1939), rejected Parrington's picture of the Puritans as reactionaries out of step with the ultimately progressive direction of American history. Miller located in Jonathan Edwards's thought the sources of a visionary tradition of perception that anticipated the symbolist methods of later poets, and he charted a continuity "from Edwards to Emerson" in the conflict between antinomian and Arminian theological impulses.

In *Maule's Curse: Seven Studies in American Obscurantism* (1938), Winters extended certain implications of Miller's work—though Winters was influenced less by Miller than by the intellectual historian H. B. Parkes. Winters argued that Melville, Hawthorne, Dickinson, Jones Very, and Henry Adams had inherited a Puritan obsession with allegorical meanings even as they no longer fully believed such meanings could be based in experience. These writers retained the Puritan allegorical habit of perception at the same time as they no longer accepted the dogmatic theology that might have legitimated it, and they were therefore thrown back on private sources of belief. This "curse" Winters suggestively likened to the one visited by Hawthorne's Matthew Maule on the descendants of the House of the Seven Gables: "God will give him blood to drink."

What was striking in Winters's argument was the suggestion that American literature comprised a conceptual unity, that it could be read as a kind of debate of American writers among and within themselves. The debate was not a "Great Conversation" above or outside history, as John Erskine had used that phrase in shaping his Great Books concept, but a collective struggle to interpret American

historical experience. It assumed that American literature was a series of efforts, continuing still in the present day, to come to terms with the ambiguous and self-destructive legacy of Puritan ancestry. In this vision, the national literature—or at least a major part of it—made sense as a life and death debate over a common set of issues. Such a vision had already been suggested by Brooks and D. H. Lawrence, but developed only in an impressionistic way.

It was probably because the turn Winters gave his interpretation was so pejorative (a later book in which he extended it was called *The Anatomy of Nonsense*) that he has received less credit than others as a pioneer figure. Already well developed in *Maule's Curse* are the themes that would shortly come to define the widely expounded "romance" interpretation of American literature: the central role of the Puritans; the continuity from Puritan to Transcendentalist to modernist; the cultivation of symbolic perception and of intensity of experience divorced from society; the primacy of Manichean dualism and unresolved moral and epistemological conflict in the American imagination. Into the largely moral dualisms emphasized by Winters and Miller, later theorists would inject a social dimension through various permutations of the themes of escape and evasion of social experience.

Here the predominant oppositions became "Adamic" innocence versus tragic experience (Lewis); frontier versus city (Smith); pastoral "middle landscape" versus industrial machine (Marx); and male fellowship versus acceptance of social and sexual experience (Fiedler). These thematic dualisms were seen to correspond to a formal dualism between American romance, symbolism, and preoccupation with a "world elsewhere" of art (Chase, Feidelson, Poirier) over against socially grounded European realism. The theory of the American symbolic romance made a kind of virtue of the perennial complaint leveled at America by nineteenth-century American writers that the country's inherent poverty of social experience had put them at a disadvantage. Cushing Strout has pointed out that one reason Tocqueville became such a central authority for critics in the forties was that he lent support to this myth of the peculiarly impoverished state of social experience in America, as for instance in his prophecy that in democratic nations literature diverts "the imagination from all that is external to man and fixes it on man alone," man as such, rather than man as localized in a specific society. As Strout observes, Tocqueville's vision of "a poetic subject disengaged from society" appealed to critics who already thought of American literature as an "escape from the world and society." The idea of the romance permitted critics to "account for the qualities in American writing that distinguished it from English social realism," making "something positive out of the lack of social density in the American novel in terms of English social class."

The symbolic-romance theory, stressing as it did the inability of American narratives to resolve their conflicts within any social form of life, provided expression for disappointments left over from the thirties toward a society that had failed to fulfill its ideal image of itself but evidently could not be righted by social action. The "tragic vision" of American writing bespoke a sense of innocence betrayed, of pastoral hopes disappointed, a conviction, as Leo Marx summarized it at the end of *The Machine in the Garden*, that "the aspirations once represented by the symbol of an ideal landscape have not, and probably cannot, be embodied in our traditional institutions." As Irving Howe later argued, a kind of "apolitical politics" was at stake here, "not the usual struggle among contending classes nor the interplay and mechanics of power, but a politics concerned with the *idea* of society itself, a politics that dares consider whether society is good and—still more wonderful question—whether society is necessary." To read the American canon as a tragic romance was to see it as a critique not just of "traditional" institutions, as it was for Leo Marx, but of any institutions.

The one theorist of the group whose politics were most conspicuously not apolitical was F. O. Matthiessen, whose *American Renaissance* (1941) managed to transform the organic social conservatism of Eliot and the Agrarians into a celebration of the democratic spirit. Matthiessen's book comprehensively fused cultural criticism and academic literary history with the New Criticism's method of explication and its themes of complexity, paradox, and tragic vision. It combined a feeling for national literary identity with scrupulously thorough—if sometimes needlessly prolix—explications of individual texts. Like the work of Miller and Winters, *American Renaissance* stood above the routine studies of its time by confronting American literature not only as an academic field but as a problem of cultural destiny. Matthiessen set out to overcome the "inordinate cleavage between fact and theory" that had troubled earlier academic and nonacademic critics and to challenge "the usual selfish indifference of our university men to political or social responsibility." Matthiessen said American culture's greatest weakness "has continued to be that our so-called educated class knows so little of the country and the people of which it is nominally part."

Unfortunately, the very comprehensiveness of Matthiessen's book set a limit to the fusion he was attempting and in the process dramatized the obstacles to making the academic setting the basis of a revived cultural criticism. After Matthiessen, no critical generalization would seem worth taking seriously unless supported by pages of voluminous textual explication, and after him the old public-spirited criticism to which Matthiessen was trying to restore respectability looked all the more like an unprofessional anachronism that academics could safely ignore. And as Jonathan Arac has pointed out, Matthiessen's work was immediately appropriated by academic critics in ways that were contrary to his democratic socialist intentions: "recall the irony that his work produced specialists of a sort that he himself considered 'hopefully obsolescent.' "

ACCOMPLISHMENTS AND LIMITATIONS

Historical scholars were quick to protest that the "American culture" and "American history" grandly invoked by the theorists of American literature were frequently so tendentiously described that they were unrecognizable. As often as not, the history in question rested on little more than bold assertions, buttressed by the occasional quotation from Tocqueville, Lawrence, or Frederick Jackson Turner. What Warner Berthoff said in a 1967 review of Poirier's *A World Elsewhere* can be said about the critical genre as a whole: "America," Berthoff said, figured "as an almost completely unanalyzed historical integer." About the same time, Howard Mumford Jones complained that "once it is granted that the only parts of a usable past for Americans of the mid-twentieth century are those that are precisely like the values and anxieties of the twentieth century," it seems evident that "the cultural purpose of historical studies weakens or vanishes." It was the old scholarly charge of anachronism once again, and again the charge had some validity. The dualism and paradox that New Critics somewhat questionably attributed to poetry *as such* had a suspect way of reappearing in the work of Americanists as the supposedly unique characteristics of *American* literature and culture. Work after work of American literature was said to be uniquely American because of those qualities of tragic vision, moral ambiguity, psychological duplicity, and other "existential" traits that New Critics attributed to great literature irrespective of nationality. All literature was New Critical, it seemed, but American literature was somehow a bit more so. The danger Ruland noted in Van Wyck Brooks's work came to roost in the academic theorists, who seemed able to create mythical usable pasts at will.

Nor did it escape notice that the theorists' generalizations about

"American literature" rested on a very limited number of works. As Berthoff suggested, nearly all the theorizing was based on "the same limited number of authors and titles—the contents of a year's course in the American classics." Jones charged that most of the theorizing "ignored or naively misconstrued" kinds of American literature that did not conform to its presuppositions—for example, the "obviously non-symbolic prose of the Revolutionary Era and of the founding fathers." He added that "those who read American literature in terms of unconscious imaginative process, racial memory, symbolical expression, and hidden *Angst* have concocted in many cases a language that at its best is cultist and at its worst is jargon."

As Berthoff put it, what the theorists of American literature had not sufficiently considered was the possibility that "American literature is, very simply, *not* an organic or dialectical whole." Berthoff acutely suggested that the "inflation of limited evidence to the end of selling some comprehensive package-conception of the order of things, the evasiveness as to real historical causes and parallels," was a result of the "accidental separation in most universities of the study of American literature from the rest of the curriculum" and the need to legitimate "a field for professional inquiry and advancement." Berthoff pointed out that such a need had been very remote from the minds of the preacademic generation of Van Wyck Brooks and Constance Rourke, whose reinterpretations of American literature had been inspired by "new movements in art and letters, during the *anni mirabiles* of high modernism, and from the related surge of progressivist hopefulness in politics and social action." According to Berthoff, just as the university had turned the New Criticism into a narrowly intrinsic form of explication, it had turned the historical study of American literature into an equally reductive form of theorizing.

Still more recently, the theorists of the forties and fifties have become targets of a "new historicism" that has offered a revisionary reinterpretation of American literary history. The ideological implications of the official American literature canon are exposed, the opposition between romance and realism is deconstructed, and the "valorization" of romance as a means of transcending politics gives way to an analysis of romance as a site of political conflict. To take one example, in *Subversive Genealogy* (1983), a study of Melville, Michael Paul Rogin argues that "the critics most sensitive to the symbolic power of American fiction still separate it too far from American historical experience. They still protect American literature from contamination by the 'petty interests' of American society."

Rogin sets out to provide a corrective by reading Melville's romances for their bearing on "the distinctive American social facts of mobility, continental expansion, and racial conflict."

Part of the new historicist challenge to the dominant pattern of theorizing has come from feminist critics, who argue with Nina Baym that "if one accepts current theories of American literature," one accepts "a literature that is essentially male." Not only that, one also accepts a myth that defines that literature as a set of "melodramas of beset manhood," in which male protagonists are ever in flight from the destructive pressures of an overcivilized, artificial society identified with women. Baym rightly reminds us that the same myth is used by women writers in inverted form, with the main character as a woman and "the socializer and domesticator . . . a man." But when this happens these writers are felt "to be untrue to the imperatives of their gender, which require marriage, childbearing, domesticity. Instead of being read as a woman's version of the myth, such novels are read as stories of the frustration of female nature. Stories of female frustration are not perceived as commenting on, or containing, the essence of our culture, and so we do not find them in the canon."

Such challenges are related to those protesting the exclusion of American popular literature from the dominant theories. In promoting romance over realism, the postwar theorists quietly substituted an academic tradition for a popular (and populist) one, taking the side of "high" art over "masscult." They overthrew the naturalistic canon of the twenties and thirties that had itself only a short time before displaced the genteel canon of Bliss Perry and Henry Van Dyke. When the postwar theorists mentioned popular literature at all it was only to contrast the "sentimental" versions of romance and pastoralism they represented (e.g., *Gone with the Wind* and *Anthony Adverse*) with their "complex" counterparts in the highbrow tradition. And when they did embrace writers in the popular tradition such as Cooper, Hawthorne, and Twain, they did so in ways that depopularized their work, emphasizing the elements of ambiguity, obliquity, and unresolved conflict. Richard Brodhead makes the point well when he says that "the academicization of American literature in the twentieth century proceeded by delegitimating the popular portion of the previous canon, and constructing a new canon that was thoroughly unpopular (hence the final arrival of such writers without audiences as Melville, Dickinson, and Thoreau)."

In this process Emerson and Whitman underwent a devaluation that had the curious effect of enhancing their importance, for though these writers were criticized for their "innocence" and lack of "tragic vision," they remained figures to reckon with in a way that the naturalists did not. They could be related to the symbolist viewpoint that was now said to be centrally American, and they remained presences later writers had to wrestle with. Dreiser, by contrast, whose work had been concerned with a specific form of society rather than with the "idea" of society, could be safely neglected. Though Matthiessen published a book about him and he remained a "field," Dreiser was in some departments demoted to such inferior status that (I can testify from experience) graduate students risked the scorn of certain faculty members if they admitted even to having read his work. Fiedler and Chase made a place for Dreiser and other naturalists in their theories, but only by exploiting what traces of symbolic romance they could find in them.

Valid though they are, these criticisms should be put in perspective. The progressivist view of American literature against which these theorists were reacting had been barely more adequate than the genteel view it had replaced. As Leslie Fiedler observed in the late fifties, the symbolist-romance interpretation of American literature provided "a long overdue counterbalance to the never-satisfactory view of our literary history as a slow struggle upward from darkness toward realism."

Whatever their political failings, there is something misplaced in the recent tendency to assimilate the postwar theories of American literature, along with much other criticism of the period, to a "social control" model that makes Cold War ideology, "disciplinary power," and "surveillance" so pervasive that it empties these concepts of useful content. In a curious kind of academic competition in which each critic tries to establish himself by "out-lefting" all others, the very concept of an "American Renaissance" is reread as a mere rationalization of the Cold War, and particular classics are reread accordingly. To take just one example, the interpretation of *Moby Dick* "in which Ishmael's freedom is opposed to Ahab's totalitarianism" is interpreted as an apology for American anticommunism—a statement about " 'our' freedom versus 'their' totalitarianism."

Despite their undeniable lack of interest in what would now be called the socially produced nature of American writing, the theorists of American literature did show a readiness to move from explication of particular works to larger statements about American culture as a whole, and this trait distinguishes them from many other scholars and explicators of their time. To talk about American literature as an escape from society was at least to revive questions of literature and society, as few academic scholars and critics were doing. And the kinds of questions that were raised—Berthoff notwithstanding—did have meaning beyond the confines of an academic field. The postwar theorists' fusion of history and explication may not have added up to a convincing "usable past," but it provided a potentially usable context for students of American literature. Though sweeping assertions about loss of innocence and the machine and the garden can become examination clichés just as cheaply arrived at as any close readings of isolated works, some clichés are more productive than others, particularly when the alternative to a simplistic overview is usually no overview at all.

To see the point, one need only compare the theoretical syntheses of American literature with the monumental *Literary History of the United States*, edited by Robert E. Spiller, Willard Thorp, Thomas H. Johnson, and Henry Seidel Canby, first published in 1948 and reprinted in several subsequent editions. As Spiller's prefatory "Address to the Reader" shows, the *History* aimed again to revive the question of national literary identity. Spiller harked back to Taine in his characterization of American literature as "an organic expression of [American] experience." But René Wellek was probably right to say that the Spiller *History* only demonstrated "the impasse which literary history has reached in our time." The volume made an attempt at thematic coherence (Matthiessen and Henry Nash Smith were among the contributors whose chapters attempted overviews), but the fragmentary structure of the work, perhaps inevitable in any collaborative history of this kind, belied its claim to make organic sense of American experience. A student seeking a context for American literature study will probably get more from a handful of the theoretical studies than from the whole of the *History*.

To return to the original question, then, why did so promising an attempt to revive questions of national culture fail to exert the influence one might have expected? Why did it, in Jonathan Culler's words, produce "an interdisciplinary subfield rather than a reorganization of knowledge"? For perhaps outside of a few American studies programs at their best moments (that is, the rare occasions when the teaching of literature in the English department was even affected by the American studies program), probably few of the best students in American literature courses over the past three decades even heard of the issues being raised by the theorists of American literature, much less used these issues as a context for their studies. They constituted at most a "special topic" for those interested in presumably rarefied subjects, and that is what they remain today, along with the new political critiques, which, for all their excesses, are at least an attempt to keep larger issues alive. The old debate over the national letters has not ceased, but it goes on increasingly behind the backs of almost everyone except those for whom it is a field.

Why this happened has to do, again, with that dynamics of "patterned isolation" with which we have been concerned before in this book. This is a pattern that has welcomed innovations, but so isolated them that their effect on the institution as a totality is largely nullified. American literature and culture studies were merely *added* to the existing departments and fields, which did not have to adapt to them, quarrel with them, or recognize their existence to any sustained degree. Their influence has finally been assimilated, but quietly and in uncontroversial fashion.

But this fate was little different from that of other postwar literary fields that harbored enlivening debates—the Renaissance, for example, where a debate between medieval Christian and modern secular interpretations of the period became a central issue, or the Romantic period, where instructive controversies arose over how or whether the term "romanticism" could be defined and whether it was continuous or discontinuous with modernism. A similar marginality overtook other postwar programs organized around cultural history, such as the Committee on Social Thought at the University of Chicago, the Modern Thought Program at Stanford, and the History of Consciousness Program at Santa Cruz. All these programs have generated excitement and produced unusually good students, but "the reorganization of knowledge" implicit in their approaches has yet to become central in the university.

The failure of cultural history to become a centralizing context created a vacuum that was readily filled by an attentuated New Criticism of explication for explication's sake. This explains why criticism had no sooner triumphed in the university after the war than it began to be routinized.

CHAPTER FOURTEEN

Rags to Riches to Routine

[William Blake] is still not an acceptable subject for a dissertation or tenure-winning essay in many American art history departments. These opinions must change if the institutional art world is ever going to clasp Blake to its corporate bosom.

This opening up of determinate structures, penetrating beyond tropological inventiveness and into the most basic elements of language, should offer opportunities for investigation by those schools of modern criticism founded on linguistics and semiotics.

I am more than happy to admit that we have most of the scholarly tools that we need to support some serious efforts at credible interpretation from now to the turn of the century.

CONTRIBUTORS TO "INSIDE THE BLAKE INDUSTRY" SYMPOSIUM

In 1943, Cleanth Brooks stated that the New Critics "have next to no influence in the universities." A decade later, René Wellek quoted Brooks's remark and observed that it was "apparently outdated," for "among the younger members of the staff, critical interests are so widespread that it seems merely a matter of time when (and not whether) the graduate teaching of literature will pass into the hands of those who have broken with the ruling methods." But only a decade after that, Wellek remarked that the New Criticism "has, no doubt, reached a point of exhaustion. . . . It has not been able to avoid the dangers of ossification and mechanical imitation." And in 1962 Brooks complained of the "mechanization" of "certain critical 'methods'—for example, heavy-handed and witless analyses of literary works, often pushed to absurd limits and sometimes becoming an extravagant 'symbol-mongering.' " With remarkable speed, the fortunes of the New Criticism in the university had gone from rags to riches to routine.

Wellek in 1961 was moved to wonder if "there may be something in the very nature of institutional academic life which will lead again to mechanization, ossification, to Alexandrianism in the bad sense." We have seen that the tendency to blame problems on institutionalization as such is one to which the traditions of the profession have long been prone. This helps explain why pedagogical problems have frequently been viewed not as issues of institutional structure but as technical matters to be worked out at the level of the individual course—through the introduction of new courses or improved incentives. In the end, it tends to be assumed that whether a critical method gets used creatively or mechanically depends less on institutional organization than on whether good teachers or poor ones are using it.

It is probably true that no critical method is immune to routinization, but to carry the analysis no further than such commonplaces only promotes a fatalism that absolves the institution of responsibility—something Wellek certainly had no intention of doing in the remarks quoted just now. Reducing the problem of routinization to one of good or bad individual teaching (or criticism) begs the question not only of what is meant by good and bad teaching, but of whether the effectiveness of teaching can be fairly measured apart from the institutional forms that shape it. Institutional success may not be merely the sum total of the activities of disparate individuals, for how individuals are systematically connected or disconnected can make a difference. "Routinization" in the sphere of pedagogy and criticism has hardly begun to be analyzed, and this chapter and the next can be seen as a preliminary effort.

Explication as a Protection Racket

It was the hope of explication's proponents that by shifting the pedagogical emphasis to critical explication, they would heal the old crippling divisions between history and literature, professional publication and undergraduate teaching. Explication claimed to be as rigorously "professional" as any of the methods of philology or history, yet unlike those methods it also claimed to meet the rudimentary needs of students, who could finally be put in touch with literary texts themselves rather than their backgrounds and genetic conditions. These had been among the aims Wellek had in mind when he urged critics to develop "a technique and methodology teachable and transmissible and applicable to any and all works of literature." But how were intellectual concerns to be made systematic, teachable, and transmissible in a culture where there was disagreement about what the primary concerns should be? What was relatively easy to make systematic, teachable, and transmissible was not these controversial concerns but the technique of explication.

Before the war, we have seen, the complaint had been that scholars turned their backs on interpretations and accumulated "facts, still more facts," without regard "for some purpose beyond them." In the wake of the critical revolution, critics could now accumulate interpretations without regard for any purpose behind them. It soon became obvious, that is, that criticism was open to the same abuses that the old scholarship had been. It was not immune to becoming an industry in which the routines of production obscured the humanistic ends production presumably served. Here was the burden of the complaints that began to appear soon after the war. As F. O. Matthiessen put it in 1949, "the trouble is that the terms of the new criticism, its devices and strategies and semantic exercises, can become as pedantic as any other set of terms if they are not handled as the means to fresh discoveries but as counters in a stale game." In the most celebrated of the alarms, the 1952 essay, "The Age of Criticism," Randall Jarrell said that the New Critic was "but old scholar writ large. . . . The same gifts which used to go into proving that the Wife of Bath was really an aunt of Chaucer's named Alys Perse now go into proving that all of Henry James's work is really a Swedenborgian allegory." Jarrell predicted that "criticism will soon have reached the state of scholarship, and the most obviously absurd theory—if it is maintained intensively, exhaustively, and professionally—will do the theorist no harm in the eyes of his colleagues."

Less obvious but possibly in the long run more demoralizing than the fact that many explications were farfetched, however, was the way they subtly and unintentionally worked to protect literature from criticism. Critical explication was, if anything, even more prone than the old scholarship had been to a kind of guild mentality where it is assumed as the natural course of things that any specialist in a writer or period will be a *promoter* of that writer or period (an assumption illustrated by the epigraphs to the present chapter). Whereas scholarly accumulations of sources, influences, and other information had functioned as a silent endorsement, explication seemed to be an even more authentic endorsement, claiming as it did to lay bare the innermost structure of the work. Then too, the very stockpiling of competing explications came to seem a prima facie proof of a work's complexity and therefore of its value. Doubtless it was a valid proof in some cases, but the effect might be to intimidate none-too-confident students and instructors into passivity.

The assumption of the organic nature of poetry was surely a condition of progress in the analysis of literary works, which had long been hampered by the preestablished canons of style and content so rigidly applied by the traditional rhetorical and moralistic aesthetics. Once critics began looking at a poem as an autonomous entity responsible to laws generated from within its own structure rather than to fixed rules of beauty or taste, patterns began to be perceptible that had not been noticed before. Yet methodological advances in one area may be paid for by blind spots in another. It soon became clear that an explicator using the conventions of analysis developed by the New Critics could hypothetically justify almost any feature of a literary work as an organically harmonious part of the total structure. We saw earlier how Cleanth Brooks had been able to neutralize Edmund Wilson's criticism, in *Axel's Castle*, of certain kinds of ideology in modernist poetry, by arguing that the poetic "organization of symbols" limits the liability of what the poem "communicates," turning it into something other than a propositional statement. In the late thirties Brooks's limited liability theory of poetics was still on the defensive, but after the war that was no longer clearly the case.

The issue arose most urgently in the 1948 controversy over the Bollingen award to Ezra Pound's *Pisan Cantos*. In a study of Pound's anti-Semitism, Robert Casillo points out that the Bollingen judges were able to dismiss the poem's fascist and anti-Semitic doctrines as poetically irrelevant by applying the New Critical principle that poetry is impervious to assertion. Casillo remarks that when Allen Tate said that the *Cantos* are "not about anything," what he probably meant was "that they were not propositional or dogmatic, that as 'dramatized' experience they made no isolatable truth claims or assertions, and that those parts of *The Cantos* which did make such claims might therefore be viewed as less than poetry and thus discounted." By this assumption, the central ideological problems posed by modern literature could hardly be raised, much less debated. As Casillo says, "there could be little meaningful debate between the New Critics" and critics like Irving Howe and Karl Shapiro, who argued, in Shapiro's words, that Pound's "political and moral philosophy ultimately vitiates his poetry and lowers its standards as a literary work."

Pound's case was only the most spectacular instance of the way academic literary explication tended to explain away problems of doctrine. If poems were "organizations of symbols" to be judged strictly by intrinsic criteria, then the kinds of ways a poem could go wrong were in principle reduced. For by this doctrine the prospective evaluator was logically restricted to questions of formal coherence. And since what counted as the formal criterion was presumably whatever the poem itself was organically trying to be, even formal criticism was disarmed, in principle if not in practice. As Irvin Ehrenpreis later remarked, "modern criticism is not so clumsy that it cannot dispose of the judgment that a poem is badly written. There are two approved techniques for smothering literary fault finders. First, one says the author meant to do what he did. Second, one says the style is mimetic or expressive, and it peculiarly suits the meaning."

Brooks and Warren never went that far, but postwar textbooks modelled on *Understanding Poetry* sometimes prescribed tactically evasive formulations for students. They pointed out that terms like "theme" and"persona" would help one avoid getting caught making the claim that a poet or poem actually says something. One text warned against attributing a bald *assertion* to Wordsworth's "Composed upon Westminster Bridge" such as "The city is as beautiful a place to live in as the country," which "comes perilously close to giving advice." Instead, the shrewd student was advised to speak of the theme of "*the natural beauty of the city*," as if such a circumlocution kept the integrity of poetry intact. As the editors put it, "the danger of regarding theme as message or moral decreases when a noun with appropriate modifiers replaces the complete sentence."

More recently, similar textual rationalizations have been packaged for use in the many handbooks designed to help the student to write essays on literature. In one of these entitled *Writing Themes about Literature*, the student is told that "what might appear to be a problem [in a literary work] can often be treated as a normal characteristic, given the particular work you are studying." For example, "you may find a problem about an 'unreal' occurrence in a work. But if you can show that the work is laid out as a fantasy or a dream, and not as a faithful representation of everyday reality, then you can also show that the 'unreal' occurrence is normal *for that work*." This of course is eminently sensible advice as far as it goes and would be absolutely necessary for the type of student who objects to "an unreal occurrence" on the grounds that good literature is always realistic. What the author fails to mention, however, are those occasions when a student's naive skepticism may be justifed: an unreal occurrence that fails to harmonize with the purpose of a work, say, or an occurrence that harmonizes with purposes that are puerile. Readers may be safe in assuming an intention of coherence in a text until they have evidence of a contrary intention, but there is something patronizing about assuming a priori that coherence is always achieved or—as in deconstructionist readings—always undone.

Like the *Cliffs Notes* study guides (a phenomenon that cries out for attention from sociologists of criticism), these handbooks are easy enough to deplore as a prostitution of the values of literary study. But no doubt because they are strictly commercial ventures, these guides tend to be based on a more realistic assessment of the actual conditions of literary education as students experience them than what one finds in the official pronouncements of educators. The guides recognize that literary education typically presupposes a context of discussion that it fails to articulate clearly. They recognize that students do not normally talk the way the average literature assignment asks them to talk and thus need to find out how to ape that sort of talk in the quickest way possible. "Good" students rapidly master a more or less professorial style of talk without needing to know why they are doing so, but less facile ones need the ready-made models that the guidebooks and cribs provide. Like the many students who are forever asking what the literature instructor "wants," these students are walking proof that the institution is failing to transmit its rituals.

The essay-writing guides are predicated on an assumption that tends to be tacitly conveyed to students from high-school English on; namely, that when one encounters an apparent anomaly in a literary work—especially if it is a canonized work—one can be fairly sure it will not be a real anomaly. Students quickly catch on that the "critical problems" posed in literature classes exist chiefly for the purpose of enabling explicators to dispose of them, and much of the current malaise of literary education is summed up in the twin cases of the student who has not learned how to locate the coherence of a literary work and the one who has not learned how *not* to locate it. Both are symptoms of the narrowing of reading to the explication of texts in a vacuum.

Of course when it comes to modern literature, this protective way of dealing with literature was initially necessitated by a cultural climate in which that literature was ignored, despised, and persecuted. The ease, however, with which modern literature has become assimilated into the curriculum suggests that changes in the culture may have lessened the need for protection. As academic critics were honing their weapons against philistine hostility, that hostility was in the process of being replaced, either by an attitude of acquiescence before experts or by a consumerlike receptivity.

In one of the best statements about this shift as it has affected teaching, the 1961 essay "On the Teaching of Modern Literature,"

Lionel Trilling described his odd sensation on realizing that as a teacher of the modern classics he was in effect a licensed agent of alienation, whose job was to shatter every comfortable assumption his students had inherited. Trilling then described the even odder sensation of realizing that his project was not meeting the expected resistance. Trilling found himself in the position of having to *inform* his students about those complacent pieties that modern literature was supposed to disabuse them of. If complacency was a problem, it was so in a new way: "I asked them to look into the Abyss," Trilling wrote, "and, both dutifully and gladly, they have looked into the Abyss, and the Abyss has greeted them with the grave courtesy of all objects of serious study, saying: 'Interesting, am I not? And *exciting*, if you consider how deep I am and what dread beasts lie at my bottom. Have it well in mind that a knowledge of me contributes materially to your being whole, or well-rounded men.'"

The experience Trilling described took place at Columbia in the late fifties, and one might speculate that if Trilling had been teaching then at Mississippi State—or perhaps at any number of places now—he might have complained less about receiving so much respectful attention for the Abyss. Since the sixties, uncritical acceptance of modernist art and ideas among certain segments of the urban middle class has been matched by a return of traditional provincial suspicion and pressure for censorship. Then or now, solicitous exposition of the ideology of modernism may have been just what Mississippi State needed while being too much of what Columbia already had. Rationalizing strategies may be a defensible means of combatting aggressive philistinism in some colleges or communities, but in those where strong literary prejudices have never been acquired in the first place, such strategies will only be duly recorded in student notebooks and recited back on the final examination.

Organic Unity or Bust

As explication became a primary enterprise in university literature departments, a set of conventions developed that took on the ritualized character of a competitive sport. The fact that a previous commentator had taken some feature of a text to be a defect was a challenge to the determined explicator to demonstrate that the feature in question harmonized with the text's internal structure. In *Flawed Texts and Verbal Icons*, Hershel Parker deals with several fascinating cases in which interpreters of American fiction have attributed thematic unities to texts that, if Parker's work on the composition of these texts is correct, had been flawed to the point of incoherence by a carelessly revising author or an insensitive editor. Among the many curious features of the academic critical scene pointed up by Parker's unusual angle of vision, one of the most striking is the sheer determination to rationalize that seems to be built into the dynamics of the explication industry.

As Parker puts it, "confident that their aesthetic goosebumps are authorially planned [or perhaps simply indifferent to whether they are authorially planned or not], critics are lured into seeing authority where the passage they are reading contains nonsense." One of Parker's exhibits is Mark Twain's *Pudd'nhead Wilson*, a text so spectacularly botched by Twain's carelessness in revising, according to Parker, that it is patently unreadable as a thematically coherent whole. Yet the novel's interpreters "approach the text as the most trusting of New Critics, and what they find is unity. They find the book 'a far more unified, more balanced novel than many of its critics have been willing to grant,' they find a 'unity of theme and general organization,' unity from themes and images, unity from 'the concern with property,' 'artistic and philosophical unity,' 'unity of vision,' and unity from 'metaphors.' " The interpreters of *Pudd'nhead Wilson* see "the slavery theme" and "the heredity *vs.* training theme" as informing "brief passages or longer units of the book which were written before Mark Twain introduced these themes into the manuscript (and which were not later revised to contain those themes)." They talk about characterization "throughout" the novel in which "chapters survive from stages when a character was white and a stage when he was part black," and in which some chapters "date from a stage when that character had not been invented." They see a "major structural device" in the cynical "affyisms" that Twain composed independently and later "placed at the chapter heads more or less casually." It is not impossible for genuine order to come about fortuitously or for a writer, in the act of revising, to notice a previously unseen order and let it stand. Parker's point, however, is that Twain's critics do not see the burden of proof of the unity of the text as their affair. They "define their role as bringing order out of a chaos which they insist is only apparent, not real. The order *must* be there, awaiting the sufficiently attentive and unbiased reading which the present critic is always the first to supply."

Crane and the High Priori Road

This tendency of academic interpretation to become a kind of self-validating promotion operation received its most trenchant analysis in R. S. Crane's later writings. Crane was no sociologist, but in retrospect it is possible to see his work after the war, and his influence in the so-called Chicago school, as a critique of the routinization of criticism in this period. We saw earlier that Crane had been one of criticism's more aggressive advocates in the thirties, praised by Ransom as "the first of the great professors to have advocated [criticism]as a major policy for departments of English." By the mid-fifties, however, Crane was having second thoughts. In an essay of 1957, he expressed surprise at "the relative ease with which the political victory of criticism was brought about" and wondered if this was not an indication that something had gone wrong. Crane now regretted that critics still maintained the antithesis between criticism and history, "which perhaps had some rhetorical or political justification two decades ago, but surely no other justification then or since." He confessed he was embarrassed by René Wellek's and Austin Warren's commendation of the Department of English at Chicago for having " 'boldly reoriented' its whole graduate program 'from the historical to the critical.' "

Not that Crane had changed his mind about the inadequacies of the old literary history, which, he reiterated, had been best suited to "problems that turned rather on the material contents and the historical circumstances of literary works than on their distinctive character as works of art." One of Crane's most devastating later essays was his 1961 attack on the "historical criticism" of D. W. Robertson's school of patristic interpretation of medieval literature. But Crane's quarrel with the historicism of the Robertsonians was very different from that of the New Critics—in fact Crane accused both critics and scholars of much the same mistaken approach to interpretation, and in an extended essay that was never finished and was published only at the end of his life, Crane worked out a set of "critical and historical principles of literary history" that went further than any theory of its time toward a theoretical synthesis of critical and historical methods.

Both the scholars and critics of his time, according to Crane, had invested heavily in an a priori method of interpretation—the "high priori road," as he called it—that employed critical concepts not as "working hypotheses," to be tested against the facts of the text, but as all-embracing propositions or "privileged hypotheses" that could not but be "confirmed" by the facts, since these hypotheses tautologically predetermined "the facts" in advance. Crane did not tackle the elusive problems of hermeneutic circularity that would subsequently emerge in controversies over interpretative theory, and had he written a few years later he would have had to defend the distinction he took for granted between "the facts of a given case" or text, which he called "independent of theory," and interpretive hypotheses about the facts. He would also have had to give a fuller defense than he did of the concept of the falsifiability of interpretive hypotheses that he borrowed from Karl Popper. Even so, Crane's arguments had a powerful corrective potential.

The Robertsonians, Crane observed, started with a conception of "medieval thought 'as a whole,' " which they then wielded as "a principle of explanation applicable to all medieval poetic texts." They assumed that medieval poets "would deliberately compose their works in a way calling for . . . allegorical or symbolic interpretation" and that, "being Christians, they would write, literally or allegorically, on only one great theme—the Christian message of charity." Robertson, for example, had argued that "Medieval Christian poetry, and by Christian poetry I mean all serious poetry written by Christian authors, even that usually called 'secular,' is always allegorical when the message of charity or some corollary of it is not evident on the surface." What bothered Crane in such statements was the categorical "always," which meant that even the *absence* of an explicit "message of charity" evident "on the surface" could be taken as "evidence" that the message was there, since presumably medieval readers and writers would take it for granted. In principle, Robertson's procedure was not different from the one by which Freudian interpreters like Ernest Jones "proved" that Hamlet must desire revenge against his father precisely because he gives no indication of desiring such revenge.

Crane conceded that Robertson's assumptions might be sound enough as working hypotheses, for mere statistical probability dictated that any medieval poem figured to invite a Christian allegorical interpretation. But Crane argued that there was a crucial difference between starting with an expectation based on assumption about the period that one proceeds to test as rigorously as one can, and using that expectation to guarantee predetermined conclusions about the text's meaning. For even if the historical interpreter's estimate of the general characteristics of the period were correct, the burden would rest with that interpreter to show that those period-characteristics were in fact exemplified by the text at hand. In other words, unless historical interpreters could adduce evidence independent of their conception of the period, "historical criticism" became trivially circular. Crane here anticipated later critiques of historicism's circularity, but he did not draw the conclusion that such circularity could not to a greater or lesser degree be overcome.

Logically speaking, Crane's quarrel with the New Critics was much the same as his quarrel with the Robertsonians, except that a different set of a priori assumptions was at issue. Whereas the Robertsonians wielded a privileged conception of "the medieval world," the New Critics wielded a privileged theory of the nature of "all literature" or "all poetry, present, past, and future." At times, to be sure, Crane himself spoke as if there existed some autonomous poetic function, as the New Critics said there did, and that is why he and the Chicago school could be labeled "formalist." He argued that "what a poet does as a poet is not to express himself or his age or to resolve psychological or moral difficulties or communicate a vision of the world or to use words in such-and-such ways, and so on—though these may all be involved in what he does—but rather, by means of his art, to build materials of language and experience into wholes of various kinds to which, as we experience them, we tend to attribute final rather than merely instrumental value." Whether any uniquely poetic or artistic ends could be distinguished, however, from other kinds of ends, social, ethical, and psychological, remained an unresolved problem in Crane's work. At times Crane seemed to suggest that there might not be any one thing that "a poet does as a poet" beyond the various quite different, historically contingent, and finally unpredictable ends that poems have served or might serve, and it was on that basis that he attacked the critics for arbitrarily restricting the concept of "poetry" to those ends that they happened to value.

Critics talk habitually, Crane noted,

> of "poetry" or of "the poem" as if these were names of eternal ideas or of simple homogeneous elements in nature. . . . They set down such all-embracing propositions as the following: that "literature is ultimately metaphorical and symbolic"; that "the language of poetry is the language of paradox" or, in a variant formulation, an "alogical" or "counterlogical" language, based not on "the principle of discreteness" but on a principle of creative interaction diametrically opposed to that. All this is far above what the historical student of literature, even if he is prone to theorizing, can honestly pretend to know. How is it possible, he is bound to ask, so easily to reduce to a single formula the overwhelming variety of aims, subjects, moods, views of life, forms, methods, uses of language he has encountered in past and present writings which have gone under the names of "literature" or "poetry," and how can anyone be so sure of what will be included under these names in the future?

I quote at length because Crane's questions seem to me fundamental and because so far as I know they were never answered.

That they were not was partly Crane's fault, for his key points were often obscured by a style so elephantine and scholastic that it became a target of parody. But even had he spelled them out more incisively, Crane's arguments would probably have been ignored for several reasons. In the first place, Crane was ahead of his time in worrying about the problem of the interpretability of literature when most literary theorists were still preoccupied with the problem of its truth. Until the mid-seventies, the great debate was over whether poets told the truth, not interpreters. It was not until later, under the influence of Continental theory, that attention shifted from the question of the authority of literature to that of the authority of criticism. Recognizing before most other theorists the urgency of what would come to be called "the problem of the text" and "the conflict of interpretations," Crane saw that concepts like "literature" and "text" could no longer be taken for granted, that they were problems of theory, open to debate.

In the second place, Crane was raising problems few people wanted to hear about at a time when academic literary studies had finally won their institutional autonomy and achieved that "technique and methodology teachable and transmissible and applicable to any and all works of literature" that Wellek had called for. Critics hardly relished being told that no method was a priori "applicable to any and all works of literature" and that indeed there might be no such thing as "literature" or "poetry" in general, only "an overwhelming variety" of unpredictable and historically contingent activities. Having established unprecedented levels of scholarly and critical productivity, departments did not want to hear that there might be no one uniquely literary mode of language, susceptible to infinite reexamination in text after text. An industry on the move, generating "fruitful new approaches," does not want to be told that its major successes may have been rigged. In a period that produced, it almost seemed, a catchphrase for every conceivable critical fallacy, "the high priori road" was one that did not catch.

Crane's positions were at once too archaic and too advanced to be understood easily in his time. Certainly Crane was archaic in the suspicion he cast on the very idea of a critical "approach," when that word denoted a methodology that told an interpreter what to say about a literary work before having read it. Crane thought that interpreters should try to *dis*prove rather than prove their interpretations, for only an interpretation that had stood up to a rigorous attempt at refutation deserved to see print. But Crane was ahead of his time (and perhaps ours also) in recognizing that an interpretation can fail not just by being disproved but by being all too irrefutably immune to disproof—that the usefulness of an interpretive hypothesis paradoxically depends on its capacity to be refuted. If there are no conceivable conditions under which an interpretation can be shown to be mistaken, its results will be of little value. An interpretive method needs to have some way of putting on the brakes, of producing counterexamples as well as examples—otherwise it condemns itself to turning all texts into monotonous illustrations of the method's infallibility. A method that assumes axiomatically that all poetry is the "language of paradox" will find no great difficulty subsuming a more or less gratifying number of examples under it, especially when there are institutional rewards for doing so.

A subtle change was taking place in the ethics of criticism, as the scientific positivism of the generation of Greenlaw and of Crane's old adversary Nitze was coming to seem as superstitious as the moralistic impressionism it had long ago replaced. Crane's view that critics had an obligation to try to destroy their own pet hypotheses seemed a throwback to that positivism, a curiously masochistic survival of a more austere age. In fact, Crane's view did no doubt reflect an earlier scarcity-economy of criticism, now giving way, in an era of academic affluence and disciplinary expansion, to an age of stepped-up production and built-in methodological obsolescence. This is not to say that professors began looking for easy ways to publish books and articles without responsibility to truth or evidence. Intensified competition among interpreters has probably had contradictory effects, causing standards of interpretive proof to become more stringent in some ways as they have become more relaxed in others. What one can say is that new uncertainties about what counts as valid proof have made questions of verification seem more debatable, and this has opened the way for new criteria in criticism that have coincided with increased production requirements.

The correctness or cognitive plausibility of an interpretative "hypothesis" (the very scientistic aura of Crane's terminology would soon seem quaint) was becoming a less urgent matter than whether it was "interesting," "provocative," "fruitful"—words that denoted, in professional Fieldspeak, whether it helped to generate more criticism. The point of criticism was no longer subtractive but additive, the idea being to produce more criticism, not less. This view dovetailed nicely with the growing view that literary meanings were in and of themselves aesthetically desirable, so that the more of them that could be attributed to a literary work, the more the work's value was presumably enhanced and the more the interests of literature and of humanism were therefore served. The most sensitive reading was the one that showed awareness of the greatest richness of possible meanings. (This view would later assume quasi-political form in the belief that unlimited semiosis was "transgressive" of humanism and therefore socially emancipatory.)

The assumption became tacitly established that when it comes to literature, sensible readers will naturally *wish* to maximize ambiguity wherever possible, just as in nonliterary communication they will naturally wish to minimize it. This view was rarely stated in so many words—though Philip Wheelwright came close when he argued in *The Burning Fountain* (1954) that it was of the very nature of literature to obey a "principle of plurisignation." But it was not necessary to state the point explicitly, because in an unspoken way the principle of plurisignation already defined what counted as the "literary" way of looking at the world and thus what distinguished sophisticated from naive or retrograde critical practices. To the extent this was so, there ceased to be a real argument between the critics and the historians who attacked them for anachronistic readings, since the two were seeking different goals. It was not the critics' misreadings so much as their cheerful indifference to the whole question whether the ambiguities they detected could conceivably have been intended by the author that infuriated scholars.

Richard Levin is at least partly right, I think, that

> the prevailing attitude in much of the critical arena today seems to be "live and let live"—a kind of intellectual laissez-faire in which each entrepreneur minds his own business of turning out new readings and expects his competitors to do the same, so that any disputes among them are kept within narrow bounds and do not raise the sort of basic issues that might hold up production.

Though the attitude Levin describes takes itself to be a "subversive" position, it is also an entrepreneurially practical one, amounting to a suspension of protectionism or a "decontrol" of the market. Here was the trouble with Crane's line of argument, just as it would be a serious stumbling-block to E. D. Hirsch's theories of interpretive validity, which Crane lived long enough to endorse. Hirsch's arguments may have had philosophical difficulties, but I doubt that these sufficiently account for the animus directed against them, which animus seems to have been rooted in an inveterate resistance to any argument that threatened to subtract from literature any meanings that could otherwise be attributed to it. On the other hand, the alarms that interpretation is being swept away in an orgy of permissiveness seem overstated. Not only has competition among interpreters intensified as well as relaxed standards, but the vogue of transgressive interpretations is an ambiguous phenomenon. These readings are as much a testimony to the security of commonsense readings of literature (which are usually presupposed by them) as an assault on them.

Without trying to be sociology, Crane's work laid bare the interpretive logic that governed the new marketplace of explications. To this extent it provides one of the best commentaries extant on the routinization of the New Criticism from within. Crane analyzed the logical means by which the New Criticism neutralized in advance the kinds of critical checks that could be placed on it and thus made the world safe for its explications. But in a more constructive way, Crane's work looked forward to the later growth of "theory" that would advance the investigation of the interpretive issues these problems posed.

By the early sixties the feeling was in the air that the heroic age of criticism, in effect the second heroic period of academic literary studies, was over. Then, in the sixties, literature departments and universities suddenly came under attack for political complicity or irrelevance. The New Criticism was caricatured as an extension of technological domination, explication being now seen as at best an evasive activity, at worst a form of manipulation whose resemblance to technocratic modes of reasoning was no coincidence. Yet as crude as cries for relevance often were and as paranoid as were the denunciations of complicity, they did point to real problems.

In fact, many of the educational problems underlying the protests of the sixties were the same ones conservatives like Irving Babbitt had pointed out a half-century earlier. The politics of the literature department's critics had changed, but much that the critics were protesting had not. The kinds of relevance demanded by New Humanists and New Leftists may have had little in common, yet both groups were reacting to the university's failure to examine its relation to its social surroundings or to bother justifying its routines of production.

A conspicuous symptom of the routinization of criticism was the rash of attacks on interpretation that began to appear in the late sixties and continue to the present day. These began with suppressed undergraduate mutterings at forever having to hunt for "hidden meanings" in literary works, evolved later into stylish polemics "against interpretation" on behalf of an "erotics of art," and culminated in deconstructive transgressions of those conventions of interpretive closure that, according to Derrida, "the police" were "waiting in the wings" to enforce. From another angle, it was said that acts of interpretation were "textual strategies" that inscribed a will to power, "that all criticism is strategic" in the sense of "a violent and bloody act," so that New Critical interpretive techniques were not innocent but part of a larger technology of control.

The New Critics were now the whipping boy of everyone, including some who had actually read their work. The surviving old historians, who had once denounced the New Critics for playing fast and loose with authorial intentions and for reading Shakespeare as if he were Kafka, were now confronted with theories and interpretations that made those of the New Critics seem tame and respectable by comparison. It was at this point that allegiances began to shift, and old historian and New Critic set aside their antagonisms to make common cause against deconstructionism and other new theories and methods. New Criticism had not merely become routine, it was suddenly a branch of "traditional literary studies," as presumably it had always been.

Soon enough the New Critics would have their revenge, however: for with astonishing speed indeterminacy, transgressive interpretation, and even the analysis of discursive power became routinized, emerging as yet another set of self-protected methodologies, fully insured against error, backed by its own Fieldspeak, its own journals, conferences, and old-boy/old-girl network, and immune to criticism from outsiders. Paul de Man went so far as to predict that "the whole of literature would respond" to deconstructive techniques of reading, for there was no reason why the techniques de Man applied to Proust "would not be applicable, with proper modifications of technique, to Milton or to Dante or to Hölderlin. This will in fact be the task of literary criticism in the coming years." Though to de Man and his followers such pronouncements only bespeak the fact that the whole of literature is deconstructive, to more jaded observers of the profession's history they merely prove once more that "the whole of literature" can all too readily be made to "respond" to techniques that validate themselves tautologically.

Like the New Critics' prior knowledge that all literature is paradoxical, the deconstructionists' foreknowledge that all texts are allegories of their own unreadability (or that they necessarily foreground the problematic of representation, mask and reveal their rhetorical conditions of possibility, undo their claims of reference by their figurality, metaphoricity, and so forth) is made suspect by its monotonous universality of application. This is not to say that deconstructive readings are invariably groundless, any more than New Critical readings were or are. But there needs to be some criterion for differentiating interesting, nontrivial cases of rhetorical self-undoing of the process of representation from cases that merely exemplify an alleged condition of all discourse. To assume that, by some structural necessity of discourse or desire, all literature or all texts undo the logics of significations on which they operate only tends to make the revelation of that process in any particular text a foregone conclusion. This is no doubt why voices within the deconstructionist camp itself have begun to complain about the way deconstruction has functioned as yet another gimmick for the production of explications.

A less widely noted effect, however, is the way deconstructive textual transgressions have obliquely served to patronize literature and keep it on its cultural pedestal, just as much as New Critical organic-unity readings did—and not just because deconstructionists have tended to deal with canonized texts. Deconstructive readings seem iconoclastic in removing texts from the sovereign control of their authors, but then a post-Freudian culture finds a rich state of decontrol more interesting than one of puritanical control. Literature worship survives, even though the object of worship is no longer timeless, static perfection, but terroristic, defamiliarizing, transgressive otherness, what de Man calls "vertiginous possibilities of referential aberration." Since such vertigo long ago became a respected cultural value, the exposure of its presence (or its absent traces) in a text functions as organistic readings once did to normalize the text and render it a supercomplex object, immune to criticism. The New Critical fetish of unity is replaced by a fetish of disunity, aporias, and texts that "differ from themselves," but criticism continues to "valorize" that complexity in excess of rational reformulation that has been the honored criterion since the forties. Indeed, on the complexity scoreboard, an ostensible unity that unravels into a self-undoing heterogeneity naturally sets off more rockets than any merely complex unity.

If this account seems too pessimistic, it should also be noted that, like the New Criticism, these very tendencies have generated their own self-critique, a theoretical awareness of themselves whose ultimate direction, philosophical and institutional, has yet to become clear. The age of theory that seems to be superseding the age of criticism has stimulated a promising critique of the very routinizing processes to which it has been prone. In a kind of cycle, routinization generates theoretical awareness, whose terms and concepts are themselves routinized, generating further theoretical awareness in turn. Whether the cycle can be broken in a way that maximizes the theoretical awareness and minimizes the routinization may well depend on matters of institutional organization. For as I have been suggesting and will argue in my final chapter, the routinization of critical discourses is a function of institutional arrangements that do not require these discourses to confront one another.

Problems of Theory: 1965–

CHAPTER FIFTEEN

Tradition versus Theory

The modern languages have had so much practical success in supplanting Greek and Latin that they have hardly felt the need as yet of justifying themselves theoretically.

IRVING BABBITT (1908)

Theory, which is expectation, always determines criticism, and never more than when it is unconscious. The reputed condition of no-theory in the critic's mind is illusory.

JOHN CROWE RANSOM (1938)

Literary theory, an organon *of methods, is the great need of literary scholarship today.*

WELLEK AND WARREN (1949)

It is obvious that random patching of the existing curricula, though it may have a practical look, is no longer practical. The only thing that is practical now is to gain a new theoretical conception of literature.

NORTHROP FRYE (1963)

These statements by distinguished humanists should help make the point that it is only very recently that the term "literary theory" has come to be associated with an assault on tradition. At the turn of the century, traditionalists like Irving Babbitt spoke of the need for theory to combat the unreflective empiricism of research scholarship. So did the New Critics later on, for much the same reason. Today, defenders of theory tend to equate the New Criticism itself with unreflective empiricism, but in its time the movement stood for theoretical reflection against the primitive accumulation of data. In their joint preface to the 1941 survey, *American Literary Scholarship*, Norman Foerster, René Wellek, and others complained that most scholars have left "virtually uninspected the theory upon which their practice rests," or have proceeded "as if that theory were an absolute good for all time."

On the other hand, there is no doubt that traditional humanists have felt ambivalent about theory, fearing that theoretical abstractions were a threat to literature itself. Today not only have theory and traditional humanism parted company, they define the polar extremes of the literary-critical spectrum. Like the earlier disciplinary conflicts we have examined in this book, this one, instead of being worked through, has tended to be resolved in an armed truce, with corresponding curricular trade-offs. Thus literary theory has become accepted as a useful option for graduate students and advanced undergraduates, but something to be kept at a distance from the normal run of students. This division of spoils between theory and tradition not only effaces the history of the two terms, but prevents the theoretical impulse from exerting a coordinating role and diverts it toward its own brand of isolationism.

INITIATION RITES

From the vantage point of the history we have surveyed in this book, we can now see that the charges current traditionalists make against theorists are similar to those of an earlier generation against what is now taken to be traditional literary history. Back in 1931 in *The Province of Literary History*, Edwin Greenlaw defended literary-historical research against the objection "that it apes scientific methods, that it is against ancient standards, that it is immersed in subjects of no possible use, that it destroys the ability to teach. It is neglectful of culture. It stifles creative art. It looks at facts rather than at the soul." With very modest updating of the vocabulary, the attack on research described over fifty years ago by Greenlaw could pass for any number of recent attacks on literary theory. So could Douglas Bush's 1948 attack on the New Criticism for its "aloof intellectuality," its "avoidance of moral values," its "aping" of science, its reduction of literary commentary to "a circumscribed end in itself," and its "rejection of the common reader," who still fancied that "poetry deals with life."

That Greenlaw could characterize the resistance to historical research as a throwback to the incompetence of "the good old times," as he put it, suggests that at that moment research was still in its heroic phase, continuing to see itself as the vanguard of enlightenment, progress, and sophistication against a motley rearguard of moralists, provincials, and gentlemen amateurs. He did not see that a new vanguard was on the horizon that would soon make historical scholars like Greenlaw look as if *they* were the ones blindly resisting change and clinging to the good old times. When this happened, the charges of subverting tradition and humanism that had been hurled against research scholars during their upstart phase were redirected at upstart critics.

It was as if, now that the critics had finally come to occupy a prominent role in the department, it was their turn to be made the scapegoat of the perennially nagging recognition that literary studies were falling short of their humanistic pretensions, while the "scholarship" that had so long taken the blame for that condition could finally become identified with the traditions that had been betrayed. The sins of which scholars like Bush accused the New Critics were precisely the ones for which New Humanists and other generalists had earlier attacked research scholars—scientism, preference for nit-picking analysis over direct experience of literature itself, and favoring the special interests of a professional coterie over the interests of general readers and students.

And now today, when the words "scholarship" and "criticism" no longer denote incompatible or even necessarily distinguishable activities, critical explication has in its turn become a "traditional" method, and it is forgotten how recently explication was thought to be almost as much a threat to traditional literary studies as literary theory is felt to be today. When current traditionalists urge that we put theory behind us and get back to studying and teaching literature itself, their program sounds curiously reminiscent of the one scholars like Bush in the forties denounced as an antihumanistic innovation.

In an institution with a short memory, evidently, yesterday's revolutionary innovation is today's humanistic tradition. It is as if charges of antihumanism, cerebralism, elitism, and coming between literature and students are a kind of initiation rite through which professional modes must pass before they become certified as traditionally humanistic. Though the terms by which the profession has defined treason against humanism never change, the activities that the terms refer to change every generation. This is not to say that history repeats itself, but only that it may do so if the institutional arrangements that encourage repetitive patterns are not recognized and altered.

If history runs true to form once more, then we can expect literary theory to be defused not by being repressed but by being accepted and quietly assimilated or relegated to the margin where it ceases to be a bother. Something of the sort seems already to be happening, as forward-looking departments rush to hire theorists, who form a new ghetto alongside those occupied by the black studies person hired several years ago and the women's studies person hired yesterday. (Marginalization may affect women's studies and black studies less, however, since they have outside political ties.) Once literary theory is covered in the department's table of areas, the rest of the faculty is free to ignore the issues theorists raise—though a certain number may colonize theory in order to spruce up a shopworn methodology. Instead of being used to bring the different ideologies and methods of the literature department and the university into fruitful relation and opposition, literary theory becomes yet another special field—a status that encourages it to be just the sort of self-promoting and exclusionary activity its enemies denounce it for being.

The point is not that innovation is inevitably isolated and prevented from affecting the established methodologies, but that even when innovation has such effects the educational potential of the conflicts occasioned by it tends to be lost. Whenever cross-factional conflict threatens to break out, it tends to be muffled by the expedient of *adding* another unit to an aggregate that remains unchanged or silently adapts. In either case, pressures are relaxed all around: the innovators are appeased, having become insiders with their own positions or programs, while the university gets to congratulate itself for its up-to-dateness and tolerance without having had to ask the established insiders to change their behavior significantly or to confront their critics.

Let us not ignore the fact that such a system works very well at a certain level and for certain purposes. It unquestionably avoids the chronic stagnation that resulted from merely rejecting innovation, as the nineteenth-century college did; it turns the university into a center of immense intellectual resources; and it confers on scholars a bracing degree of independence that is good in the short run for professional productivity. Unfortunately, these gains are paid for at a high cost in intellectual community, educational effectiveness, and professional morale. The recent intensity of interest in humanities conferences of various kinds is a symptom: the conferences have obviously become substitutes for the type of general discussion that does not take place at home.

A major reason for this condition is that the need to avoid duplication in the selection of faculty can have the unintended effect of systematically screening out commonalities. If the interests of candidate X overlap too much with those of faculty member Y, this is an argument for not hiring X—"We already have Y to do that." The principle on which departments are organized thus tends to preselect those who have the least basis for talking to one another. Hiring instructors with the same interests will not be the answer for most departments (though a critical mass of like-minded people can be provocative and helps to achieve visibility), but departments could still begin to consider other things besides field-coverage when they take stock of departmental strengths and weaknesses. In addition to reviewing the periods, genres, and approaches it covers, a department might ask itself what potential conflicts and correlations it harbors and then consider what curricular adjustments might exploit them.

Theory can supply the conceptual vocabulary for such correlations, but not as long as it remains an isolated field whose relation to the rest of the department is left to the student to puzzle out. It is largely the institutionalization of literary theory as a special field that lends truth to the complaint that literary theory has become a private enclave in which theorists speak only to one another. But in this respect, literary theory only exemplifies to a heightened degree the tendency of all professional literary fields to define their interests parochially and to close ranks against outsiders. It is easy to disparage theorists for being ingrown and esoteric, but it is hard to think of any field from Chaucer to Pynchon studies that is not ingrown and esoteric if viewed from the lay point of view. To most lay observers, the difference between the publications of deconstructionists and of orthodox historical scholars and explicators would probably be hardly discernible. The controversies of theorists are only the latest in a long line of professional disputes whose potential cultural relevance has remained invisible to outsiders. It is symptomatic that, in a period when literary studies have gone through the most fundamental conflict of principles in their history, that conflict has informed very little of the average student's study and is still generally regarded as little more than a tempest in a teapot.

If any headway is to be made, the terms of the discussion need to be shifted. The question can no longer be whether we are going to be deconstructionists or humanists, theory specialists or Chaucer scholars or Pynchon explicators, for "we" as a unified body, doing some one kind of thing, do not exist. The question is how the many different kinds of things professors of literature do may be so organized as to begin providing a context for one another and take on a measure of corporate existence in the eyes of the world.

It is not a matter of somehow elevating the curriculum above intradepartmental political trade-offs and bargaining, things that are unavoidable aspects of institutional life. Rather than try to insulate the curriculum from political conflicts, a more realistic strategy would be to recognize the existence of such conflicts and try to foreground whatever may be instructive in them within the curriculum itself. If the curriculum is always going to be determined by trade-offs, why not try to let students in on whatever matters of principle are at issue in them?

HUMANISM AS THEORY

As I use the term here, "literary theory" is a discourse concerned with the legitimating principles, assumptions, and premises of literature and literary criticism. Contrary to the stipulation of recent pragmatist arguments "against theory," literary theory may but need not be a *system* or *foundational discourse* that aims to "govern" critical practice from some outside metaphysical standpoint. When literary theory is attacked, this systematic or foundational conception of theory is usually the target, whether the opponents be disgruntled humanists, deconstructionists, or pragmatists. But it is at least as legitimate, and more in line with normal usage, to think of literary theory not as a set of systematic principles, necessarily, or a founding philosophy, but simply as an inquiry into assumptions, premises, and legitimating principles and concepts.

Thus, another way of describing literary theory is as a discourse that treats literature as in some respect a problem and seeks to formulate that problem in general terms. Theory is what is generated when some aspect of literature, its nature, its history, its place in society, its conditions of production and reception, its meaning in general, or the meanings of particular works, ceases to be given and becomes a question to be argued in a generalized way. Theory is what inevitably arises when literary conventions and critical definitions once taken for granted have become objects of generalized discussion and dispute.

When literary theory is understood in this way, then it becomes easier to see that "traditional humanistic" criticism is theoretical, even when—or especially when—it is overtly hostile to theory, as it often has been. Modern hostility to theory first originated in the romantic critique of industrial society, a critique which associated abstract modes of thought with the nihilistic and corrosive rationalism that had supposedly destroyed the earlier organic unity of culture. Most of the major culture critics of the last hundred and fifty years have doubted the value of abstract principles and avoided explicitly formulating those that operated in their own work.

Yet the very fact that a unified culture no longer existed placed these culture critics in a contradictory position. The only way they could hope to restore that unified culture was to propagandize about its desirability; that is, to theorize. This contradiction underlay all the romantic and postromantic attempts to hold up preindustrial societies as alternatives to modern science and industrialism; for example, Carlyle and Ruskin's Middle Ages, Arnold's Hellenism, Eliot's Europe before the dissociation of sensibility, Lawrence's Mexico, Leavis's England before "technologico-Benthamite civilization," and so forth. Each of these conceptions advanced or presupposed theories of modern civilization and the breakdown of continuity between literary and everyday social communication.

Eliot saw the increasingly theoretical tendency of modern culture very well, though he refused to be reconciled to it, when he said that "the important moment for the appearance of criticism seems to be the time when poetry ceases to be the expression of the mind of a whole people." For Eliot this loss of consensus stemmed from a breakdown of political authority:

> When the poet finds himself in an age in which there is no intellectual aristocracy, when power is in the hands of a class so democratised that whilst still a class it represents itself to be the whole nation; when the only alternatives seem to be to talk to a coterie or to soliloquize, the difficulty of the poet and the necessity of criticism become greater.

What Eliot called "criticism" is what we have come to call "theory"—the self-consciousness generated when consensus breaks down. Were we to follow Eliot's point that the breakdown of aristocratic culture forced poets "to talk to a coterie or to soliloquize," we would be led into the questions of communication-theory and hermeneutics that have lately become associated with academic literary theory.

My point is that traditional cultural criticism is unavoidably theoretical in that its starting point and condition of existence is that "culture," literature, and communication have become a problem that has to be theorized. Cultural criticism can hardly avoid theorizing itself, though it can resist making its theories systematic or even explicit. Arnold could avoid explicit theorizing by repeating critical catchphrases such as "high seriousness" and "criticism of life," and resorting to ostensive "touchstone" passages in order not to have to define "what in the abstract constitutes the characters of a high quality of poetry." And Leavis, on being challenged by Wellek to spell out his critical principles, could refuse on the ground that critics were better off not spelling out their principles. Yet what has kept Arnold and Leavis in the forefront of current discussion is surely not their contributions to understanding particular authors and texts, but their theorizing on the relations of poetry to culture and education.

THE RETURN OF "LITERATURE ITSELF"

In a culture without much consensus, debate on matters of theory cannot be avoided; it can only be prevented from coming to the forefront where outsiders might have a chance to learn from it. Yet today, many humanists have decided that the literature department can right itself only if it desists from theoretical chatter and puts literature itself back at the center of its concerns. As the present history has tried to show, these humanists are echoing a way of thinking that has animated disgruntled teachers since the dawn of the professional era: let literature speak for itself so that we do not need a theory of how to organize it institutionally. Of course those who revive the Literature Itself argument today do not claim that there ought to be no organization of literary studies. But they invoke literature itself as if the problem of what that organization is to be will somehow take care of itself.

Consider, for example, Helen Vendler's 1980 MLA presidential address, which began in time-honored fashion with an exhortation to the assembled membership to think back to that primordial experience of literature that had led them to take up the study of the subject in the first place and that their entanglements with the secondary discourses of scholarship and criticism had caused them to forget. Vendler urged her audience to recall "that early attitude of entire receptivity and plasticity and innocence before the text, . . . before we knew what research libraries or variorum editions were, before we had heard any critical terms, before we had seen a text with footnotes." Vendler declared that "we prize not something we call 'Renaissance literature' but *King Lear*, not 'the Victorian Temper' but *In Memoriam*, not modernism but *Ulysses*." She concluded by stating that "a general interdisciplinary Poloniuslike religious-historical-philosophical-cultural overview will never reproduce that taste on the tongue—as distinctive as alum, said Hopkins—of an individual style," and she thus urged the literary scholars to maintain "our own separateness from other disciplines."

One can only share Vendler's wish that the New Critics' fight against substituting a picture of the Renaissance for *King Lear* not have been fought in vain. But the choice Vendler offers between prizing literature for itself or for its historical contexts is misleading. Of course an interdisciplinary "religious-historical-philosophical-cultural overview" *may* kill "the taste on the tongue" of a literary work, but recent experience shows that bare, unmediated contact with the work itself does not necessarily inculcate that taste either.

Vendler herself concedes that "a piece of literature yields different insights depending on the questions put to it," that "we all love different things in literature or love literature for different reasons," that "literature is a dense nest of cultural and linguistic meanings, inaccessible to the casual passerby." It seems to me that once that is granted then the need for a contextual and cultural study of literature has been conceded, and there is no point pretending we can revert to a core experience of literary bliss prior to all contexts. Vendler can afford to disparage cultural "overviews" as "Poloniuslike" since she takes such overviews for granted. Students do not have this luxury, especially those who are not sure who Polonius is.

In appealing to the precritical experience of literature supposedly underlying her own sense of literary vocation, Vendler must surely underrate the extent to which her initial literary excitements (like anybody's) were made possible only by the prior acquisition of cultural and literary preconceptions, ones that were not explicit in the works she read but that she had to bring to the works before they could become interesting or intelligible. One salutary lesson of current theory is that though the experience of reading a text may *feel* like a pretheoretical, precritical activity, that feeling can arise only because the reader has already mastered the contexts and presuppositions necessary for the texts's comprehension.

Having experienced the taste on the tongue may be an indispensable qualification for teaching literature, but it cannot dictate what a teacher is to *say* about a literary work, something that hinges on matters of purpose, context, and situation that are not pregiven either in literary works themselves or our experience of them. If works of literature "speak for themselves," they do so only up to a point, for their authors were not aware, and could not have been aware, of the kinds of situations in which their works would later be read and taught and the different problems of comprehension and appreciation these situations might occasion. The initial questions we decide to ask in teaching a literary work, the questions that delimit what we will say about it, are always dictated in some part by the pressures of our time, our culture, and our sense of history: what is it in Shakespeare or Keats or Beckett that an age like ours—and whatever may be meant by "an age like ours" is part of what has to be considered—needs to relearn, consider imaginatively, or fight against? To suppose such controversial questions can be left to sort themselves out as a random result of an aggregate of courses is simply to assume that literary education has to be out of control. As I suggested at the start of this book, the remedy for bad contextualizing of literature has to be better contextualizing, not no contextualizing or random contextualizing.

TEACHING THE CULTURAL TEXT

In invoking the efficacy of literature itself against Polonius-like cultural overviews, Vendler revives the diminished view of history that underlay the New Critical critique of historical reductionism. Current literary theory constitutes a sustained effort to overcome the disabling opposition between texts and their cultural contexts that attended that kind of critique. If there is any point of agreement among deconstructionists, structuralists, reader-response critics, pragmatists, phenomenologists, speech-act theorists, and theoretically minded humanists, it is on the principle that texts are not, after all, autonomous and self-contained, that the meaning of any text in itself depends for its comprehension on other texts and textualized frames of reference. Current schools of criticism disagree over whether anything like an objective reconstruction of the relevant context of any text is possible, just as they disagree over how much real-world referentiality and authorial agency can be ascribed to any text and how broadly the "relevant context" should be defined—whether it should include popular and uncanonized texts or not. But despite these substantive and important disagreements, there is considerable agreement on at least one point: that meaning is not an autonomous essence within the words of a text but something dependent for its comprehension on prior texts and situations.

For example, Jonathan Culler writes that "the problem of interpreting the poem is essentially that of deciding what attitude the poem takes to a prior discourse which it designates as presupposed." Robert Scholes says that "the supposed skill of reading is actually based upon a knowledge of the codes that were operative in the composition of any given text and the historical situation in which it was composed." Ross Chambers argues that "meaning is not inherent in discourse and its structures, but contextual, a function of the pragmatic situation in which the discourse occurs." Culler, Scholes, and Chambers are all spokesmen for structuralist or poststructuralist positions, but E. D. Hirsch makes much the same point when he writes that "every writer is aware that the subtlety and complexity of what can be conveyed in writing depends on the amount of relevant tacit knowledge that can be assumed in readers."

In this instance, the structuralists and poststructuralists are more "traditional" than the traditionalist who rejects theory entirely: they are giving reasoned accounts of something the best of the old literary historians knew in their bones but did not know how to formulate adequately—that the historical circumstances that must be inferred in order to understand any text are not a mere extrinsic background, as positivist historians and New Critics supposed, but something presupposed by the work and thus necessary to intrinsic comprehension.

From another angle the same point is made by recent work in "dialogics" influenced by Mikhail Bakhtin. As Don H. Bialostosky observes, "dialogics recognizes each discourse as an actual or potential response to other discourses." Bialostosky notes that all narratives make reference to opposing voices whether these voices are discernible in them or not: "Whether they pointedly ignore opposing voices, co-opt them, diminish them, or answer them, the narratives I have cited take shape in response to one another in a virtual space between narratives, and they change that space itself by their responses." The worst vice of formalism, he adds, "is to imagine that what does not appear in the text does not impinge upon it." Insofar as departmental organization and curricula cut away the dialogic relations of texts in order to isolate them for close study, they institutionalize this vice of formalism by effacing the "virtual space" between texts that enables them to be understood. The pedagogical implication of dialogics seems to be that the unit of study should cease to be the isolated text (or author) and become the virtual space or cultural conversation that the text presupposes.

If, as Chambers argues, a text's "indication" of "the narrative situation appropriate to it" depends on the reader's ability to recognize the relevant "situational phenomena," then this establishes "the social fact that narrative mediates human relationships and derives its 'meaning' from them; that, consequently, it depends on social agreements, implicit pacts or contracts, that themselves are a function of desires, purposes, and constraints." Students run into trouble when they have not inherited either the requisite "social agreements" and "implicit pacts or contracts" the text takes for granted, or those other codes taken for granted by the intellectual communities that are constantly recontextualizing and reappropriating texts for various purposes. As Scholes sums it up, "in order to teach the interpretation of a literary text, we must be prepared to teach the cultural text as well." But teaching the cultural text requires a university aware of the history of its own self-divisions.

A university is a curious accretion of historical conflicts that it has systematically forgotten. Each of its divisions reflects a history of ideological conflicts that is just as important as what is taught within the divisions yet is prevented from being foregrounded by the divisions themselves. The boundaries that mark literary study off from creative writing, composition, rhetoric, communications, linguistics, and film, or those that divide art history from studio practice, or history from philosophy, literature, and sociology, each bespeak a history of conflict that was critical to creating and defining these disciplines yet has never become a central part of their context of study. The same is true of the very division between the sciences and the humanities, which has been formative for both yet has never been an obligatory context for either. As I noted earlier, either the conflict of the sciences and humanities is not offered because it is nobody's field—or else it is offered (as an option) because it *is* somebody's field. Falling into the creases as they do, interdisciplinary conflicts go unperceived by students, who naturally see each discipline as a frozen body of knowledge to be absorbed rather than as social products with a history that they might have a personal and critical stake in.

At issue in the teaching of literature, then, and in the formation of a literature curriculum, are how much of the "cultural text" students must presuppose in order to make sense of works of literature, and how this cultural text can become the context of teaching. That there is no agreement over how the cultural text should be understood, or whether it should come into play at all in the teaching of literature, seems to me an argument for rather than against a more explicitly historicized and cultural kind of literary study that would make such disagreements part of what is studied. The important thing, in any case, is to shift the question from "Whose overview gets to be the big umbrella?" in which form it becomes unanswerable, to "How do we institutionalize the conflict of interpretations and overviews itself?" To emphasize conflict over consensus is not to turn conflict into a value, nor certainly is it to reject consensus where we can get it—as would the silly recent argument that identifies consensus with repressive politics. It is simply to take our point of departure from a state of affairs that already exists.

A number of programs that situate the study of literature in cultural history along these lines is already in existence, and still others will be by the time this book appears. An incomplete list of institutions that have developed them would include Minnesota, Brandeis, Duke, Northwestern, Stanford, Johns Hopkins, Cornell, Pittsburgh, Carnegie-Mellon, Yale, Columbia, the Berkeley and Santa Cruz campuses of the University of California and the Albany and Buffalo campuses of the State University of New York, and the number is growing so rapidly that a full list would be much longer. Most are graduate programs, but it is hard to see why their concerns would not be as relevant and as needed in undergraduate study as well. Typically, the organization of these programs is simple, consisting of a small number of required core courses in literary and cultural theory, methods, and exemplary problems, with some six to eight electives in which the principles, methods, and problems dealt with in the core courses are to be applied.

Much of the effectiveness of these programs depends on the ability of the core courses to equip students with contexts they can actually use in other courses, and this does not automatically occur. Unless they are carefully planned, such core courses—and with them the whole program—can easily succumb to interdisciplinary chaos, which results when it is assumed that something constructive will arise merely by mixing a variety of topics and vocabularies from different departments. Interdisciplinary studies are not immune to the temptation to fall back on faith in the net result of a system of uncoordinated individualism, which in the short run is easier to administer than a coordinated system. Being "cultural-historical" in a controlled and useful way takes considerable thinking through and probably much trial and error, and the greater the number of departments and faculty involved, the greater will be the need for thoughtful coordination. Some of the programs I have named are too marginal to the literature departments to exercise much general influence and perhaps will have to prove themselves before they are given a more central role. Whatever the problems, there seems no reason why with only moderate success, such programs cannot be an improvement on present literary education.

To see more concretely what is at issue here, consider a brief example. Everyone knows about the challenge to the traditional humanistic canon that has been mounted by feminist criticism. The editor of a recent anthology asserts, for example, that "feminist critics do not accept the view that the canon reflects the objective value judgments of history and posterity, but see it instead as a culture-bound political construct. In practice, 'posterity' has meant a group of men with the access to publishing and reviewing that enabled them to enforce their views of 'literature' and to define a group of ageless 'classics.'" Other feminists go even further, arguing that the basic frameworks of logic and rationality are not universal but gender specific, that discourse as traditionally conceived is male.

Clearly, feminist criticism challenges some if not all of the most fundamental assumptions of those who call themselves humanists, and not surprisingly the counterattack has been intense. To mention only two recent examples, Gail Godwin, reviewing *The Norton Anthology of Literature by Women* in a recent *New York Times Book Review*, objected that, in choosing its selections to illustrate a theory of literary sisterhood through the ages, the editors, Sandra Gilbert and Susan Gubar, had elevated "the values of feminist interpretation . . . at the expense of literary art and individual talents." The editors' principles of selection and omission, Godwin complained, were "dictated by a stated desire to document and connect female literary experience rather than present a showcase of the most distinguished writing by women in English." In a similar vein, Denis Donoghue writing in the *New Republic* argued that "the criteria adopted by the [anthology] editors are not critical at all. They are political and sociological." They set aside "the questions of crucial concern to literary criticism in favor of documentary value and thematic relevance."

It is obvious that the feminist controversy as it is here typically enacted forces a fundamental choice on the teacher: Literary values or social relevance? The established great tradition or the putative tradition of sisterhood? One of Godwin's complaints is that when she tries to imagine herself "as an apprentice student of literature in a course that had adopted this book," she realizes that as such a student she "would come away judging literature produced by women in English solely by what I had found in this book." She would come away, for instance, judging Jane Austen's work on the basis not of *Pride and Prejudice* or *Emma*, but of Austen's teenage work "Love and Freindship [*sic*]," which Gilbert and Gubar include not just because of its brevity but because it exemplifies "the parodic stance by which some women resisted the sentimental education accorded Regency ladies."

It is certainly true that feminist criticism forces us as intellectuals and critics to choose between antithetical standards. But does it follow that the choice is necessarily posed quite so starkly for the teacher? Do the purposes of liberal education require that the teacher *resolve* this controversy before proceeding with his or her task? One can imagine a teaching situation in which one would not have to decide which side of the feminist controversy one thought was in the right, for one could bring the controversy itself into the classroom and make it part of one's subject matter. I can even imagine a situation in which the teacher is unsure which side of the controversy to side with and arranges the course dialectically in order to form an opinion. My impression is that such courses already exist and have proved successful.

The feeling that we have to decide between the humanist and the feminist positions in order to teach literature stems again from the assumption that students should be exposed only to the *results* of the controversies of their teachers and educators and should be protected from the controversies themselves. It also assumes that since it is out of the question that different courses might be correlated, the issue will need to be resolved in the same way for every course. Godwin's worst-case scenario is a situation in which the only exposure to literature an introductory student gets is a course taught out of *The Norton Anthology of Literature by Women.* But what if that course also used a conventional anthology in order to dramatize conflicting standards. Or what if the students taking that course were also to take another one that not only included *Pride and Prejudice* on its reading list but raised the question of the relative claims for reading the feminist and the nonfeminist text, or for reading either text "as literature" or from a feminist political viewpoint. Brook Thomas has suggested pairing courses this way in order to foreground major conflicts and relations of ideology and method, and the idea does not seem impossible if departments set out to accomplish it.

Some hard-liners, of course, believe that even according the feminist canon the amount of classroom recognition that would be needed to discredit that deplorable notion would constitute a betrayal of humanistic values, or at least a diversion from what teachers of literature ought to be doing. Perhaps they would regard it as equally a sellout or a diversion to pair ideologically acceptable courses with ones that challenge their premises. Such educators are saying, in effect, that it is more important to protect the integrity of the great tradition than to relate that tradition to the cultural controversies of its time. This seems a mistake from a tactical point of view, if no other, for it is doubtful that the traditional canon profits from being insulated against challenges. It seems finally to be in the interests of the traditionalists to help create a situation in which their quarrel with their enemy could be dramatized. For one thing, their traditionalism would suddenly begin to *stand for* something in the eyes of students, as it does not so long as teachers representing opposing positions are structurally isolated by the field-coverage system. For another, if the traditionalists persist in keeping things institutionally as they are, they are certain to lose their battle by attrition or default, as earlier conservative factions in the history of literary studies always have. Of course these traditionalists will be able to console themselves, as their predecessors have always done, by constructing stories of cultural and educational decline that will rationalize their defeat, but such consolation may no longer afford the pleasure it once did.

In any case, though ideological resentment runs high among both the advanced and the rear guards (and divisions between junior and senior faculty reinforce them), my hunch is that the most formidable obstacle to change is structural rather than ideological. The great advantage of the present system of patterned isolation over any system that tried to pair courses and bring different viewpoints into relation and contrast is that in the short run it is easier to administer. It is easier because it does not require students to take many courses in common, does not require faculty to take into account what their colleagues do, and aside from gossip and committee work does not require diverse groups to talk to or about one another. Even so, it is possible that a more coordinated structure would prove easier in the long run, for if it were successful it would eliminate unexploited duplication (something one might think deans would find attractive) and replace some of the present institutional boredom and loneliness with the excitement of collaboration.

A former department chairman, James Kincaid, has eloquently described the new conception of literary studies now emerging:

> Abandoning coverage as an impoverished ideal, we might begin by imagining an ideal course. . . . Wouldn't it seek to define the subject matter, literature, and to discuss the various and competing assumptions about texts, language, meaning, culture, readers, and so forth that we make? Wouldn't it show that these assumptions are themselves constructions, that there is considerable debate about such things as texts, about where meaning resides, about the importance of gender, about the relations of these things to historical situations? Wouldn't it also show that these assumptions were not themselves innocent, that they were value-laden, interested, ideological? You are starting to suspect that this is a course in theory. And so it is. But all courses are courses in theory. One either smuggles it in or goes through customs with it openly. . . . We need to teach not the texts themselves but how we situate ourselves in reference to those texts.

What is most promising about this model is that it places the emphasis squarely at the point where current positions divide—the issue of "how we situate ourselves" in reference to literary texts. Though the framework is based on recent theory, it would require the participation of dissenters, traditionalists and radicals alike, in order to work. There is no guarantee that this model of literary study would escape the cycle of routinization that has caught up all the earlier ones, but I think its chances would be better.

Notes

Chapter 1. Introduction: The Humanist Myth

Page

2 **very much.**—On the dependence of literary studies on composition, see Richard Ohmann, *English in America: A Radical View of the Profession* (New York: Oxford University Press, 1976), and the chapter in Ohmann's book by Wallace Douglas, "Rhetoric for the Meritocracy."

10 **"cultural text"**—Robert Scholes, *Textual Power: Literary Theory and the Teaching of English* (New Haven: Yale University Press, 1985), p. 33; William E. Cain presents a similar analysis in *The Crisis in Criticism: Theory, Literature, and Reform in English Studies* (Baltimore: Johns Hopkins University Press, 1984).

11 **"social practices."**—Terry Eagleton, *Literary Theory: An Introduction* (Minneapolis: University of Minnesota Press, 1983), p. 213.

12 **"working class"**—Eagleton, p. 24; for other interpretations along similar lines, see Chris Baldick, *The Social Mission of English Criticism, 1848–1932* (Oxford: Claredon Press, 1983); Peter Widdowson, ed., *Re-reading English* (London: Methuen, 1982); Jonathan Culler offers a trenchant critique of Eagleton and other recent political analyses of literary studies in "Problems in the 'History' of Contemporary Criticism," *Journal of the Midwest Modern Language Association* 17, no. 1 (Spring 1984): 3–15.

"literary studies"—Eagleton, *Literary Theory*, p. 27.

13 **to change**—For the charge that the university is logocentric, see Jacques Derrida, "Living on/Border Lines," trans. James Hulbert, in *Deconstruction and Criticism* (New York: Seabury Press, 1979), pp. 94–95; other poststructuralist critiques of academic literary studies include Derrida, "The Principle of Reason: The University in the Eyes of Its Pupils," trans. Catherine Porter and Edward P. Morris, *Diacritics* (Fall 1983): 3–20; see also the special issue of *Yale French Studies* entitled "The Pedagogical Imperative," ed. Barbara Johnson, 63 (1982); William V. Spanos, "The Apollonian Investment of Modern Humanist Education: The Examples of Matthew Arnold, Irving Babbitt, and I. A. Richards" (part 1) *Cultural Critique* 1, no. 1 (Fall 1985): 7–72; Paul A.

13 Bové, *Intellectuals in Power: A Genealogy of Critical Humanism* (New Haven: Yale University Press, 1986).
"their history"—Jane Tompkins, *Sensational Designs: The Cultural Work of American Fiction, 1790–1860* (New York: Oxford University Press, 1985), p. 199.

CHAPTER 2. THE CLASSICAL COLLEGE

Page

19 **"not egocentric."**—William Charvat, *The Origins of American Critical Thought: 1810–1835* (Philadelphia: University of Pennsylvania Press, 1936), p. 23.
20 **"the ministry"**—President Oliver Marcy, quoted by Harold F. Williamson and Payson S. Wild, *Northwestern University: A History, 1850–1975* (Evanston, Ill.: Northwestern University Press, 1976), p. 55.
"gentle breeding"—Charles William Eliot, *A Turning Point in Higher Education* (Cambridge: Harvard University Press, 1969), pp. 14–15.
"cultivated gentleman."—Noah Porter, "The Ideal Scholar," in *The Phillips Exeter Lectures, 1885–86* (Boston: Houghton, Mifflin, 1887), p. 170.
"well bred."—Laurence R. Veysey, *The Emergence of the American University* (Chicago: University of Chicago Press, 1965), p. 188.
21 **"not know."**—Carl Becker, quoted by Morris Bishop, *A History of Cornell* (Ithaca: Cornell University Press, 1962), p. 37.
poor backgrounds—Ernest Earnest, *Academic Procession: An Informal History of the American College, 1636–1953* (New York: Bobbs, Merrill, 1953), pp. 127–28.
"their leaders."—Frederick Rudolph, *Curriculum: A History of the American Undergraduate Course of Study since 1636* (San Francisco: Jossey-Bass, 1977), p. 90.
"the professions."—Edmund Wilson, *The Triple Thinkers: Twelve Essays on Literary Subjects* (New York: McGraw-Hill, 1948), p. 162.
"continental countries"—Richard Hofstadter and Walter P. Metzger, *The Development of Academic Freedom in the United States* (New York: Columbia University Press, 1955), p. 226.
"political power"—Francis Wayland, *Thoughts on the Present College System in the United States* (Boston: Gould, Kendall and Lincoln, 1842), pp. 153–54.
"subsequent life."—Wayland, p. 41.
22 **"especially exposed."**—Noah Porter, *The American Colleges and the American Public* (New Haven, Conn.: Charles C. Chatfield, 1870), p. 180.
the effort.—William T. Foster, *Administration of the College Curriculum* (Boston: Houghton Mifflin, 1911), pp. 108–9.
"United States."—Wayland, *Thoughts on the Present College System*, p. 90.

23 **attend prayers.**—John W. Burgess, *Reminiscences of an American Scholar* (New York: Columbia University Press, 1934), p. 58.
"his teacher."—Burgess, p. 180.
"or Princeton."—Earnest, *Academic Procession*, p. 207.
faculty consultation—Hofstadter and Metzger, *Development of Academic Freedom*, pp. 235–36.
"was interested."—Thomas S. Harding, *College Literary Societies: Their Contribution to Higher Education in the United States, 1815–1876* (New York: Pageant Press International, 1971), p. 32; see also Frederick Rudolph, *The American College and University* (New York: Alfred Knopf, 1962), pp. 164–67.
"religious soundness."—Veysey, *Emergence of the American University*, p. 48; see also Hofstadter and Metzger, *Development of Academic Freedom*, pp. 209–74.
24 **"was perfunctory."**—Andrew D. White, in Edward E. Hale, ed., *The How I Was Educated Papers* (New York: D. Appleton, 1896), p. 111.
"professor's pittance."—Bishop, *History of Cornell*, p. 82.
"more extensive."—Wayland, *Thoughts on the Present College System*, p. 136.
"and talent."—Wayland, pp. 69–73.
"great rarity."—William Riley Parker, "Where Do English Departments Come From?" *College English* 28, no. 5 (February 1967):345.
Methodist community.—Williamson and Wild, *Northwestern University*, p. 103.
were ministers.—Douglas MacMillan, *English at Chapel Hill: 1795–1969* (Chapel Hill: Department of English, University of North Carolina, n.d.), pp. 53–54.
25 **"a child."**—Burgess, *Reminiscences*, p. 170; compare Brander Matthews's similar student recollection of this professor, Charles Murray Nairne, in *These Many Years: Recollections of a New Yorker* (New York: Charles Scribner's Sons, 1919), pp. 109–10.
college restrictions.—Wayland, *Thoughts on the Present College System*, p. 145.
"prepared lessons."—Kermit Vanderbilt, *Charles Eliot Norton: Apostle of Culture in a Democracy* (Cambridge: Harvard University Press, 1959), p. 26.
as well.—Earnest, *Academic Procession*, pp. 102–4. On the frequency of misbehavior and violence in the early college, and the "carnival atmosphere and bohemianism," see Burton J. Bledstein, *The Culture of Professionalism: The Middle Class and the Development of Higher Education in America* (New York: W. W. Norton, 1976), pp. 228–36; see also Edwin E. Slosson, *Great American Universities* (New York: Macmillan, 1910), p. 492. In 1882 a Northwestern undergraduate wrote of fraternity chapters' "making no claim to literary improvement, and making their meetings times for general hilarity and fun, not infrequently enhanced by the exhilaration of the 'flowing bowl' "

25 (Williamson and Wild, *Northwestern University*, p. 60).
" 'its care.' "—Andrew D. White, *Autobiography* (New York: Century, 1905), 1:19.
"be drunk."—MacMillan, *English at Chapel Hill*, p. 4.
"so on."—Lyman Bagg ["A Graduate of '69"], *Four Years at Yale* (New Haven: Charles C. Chatfield, 1871), p. 657.
26 **"and contemptible."**—Bagg, p. 650.
"about him."—Bagg, p. 702.
"possible way."—Bagg, p. 697.
was unknown—Veysey, "Stability and Experiment in the American Undergraduate Curriculum," in *Content and Contex: Essays on College Education*, Carnegie Commission on Higher Education Report (New York: McGraw-Hill, 1973), p. 2.
almost 8,000—Oliver Farrar Emerson, quoting Ira Remsen, "The American Scholar and the Modern Languages," *PMLA* 24, no. 4, appendix (1909): lxxvii–lxxix.
"particular fields."—Emerson, xc.
"a week"—Bishop, *History of Cornell*, p. 108.
borrow them.—See Burgess, *Reminiscenses*, p. 175.
27 **"appropriation unused."**—Bishop, *History of Cornell*, p. 108.
be circumvented.—See Burgess, *Reminiscences*, p. 175.
student's mind.—Rudolph, *Curriculum*, p. 69.
"needed more."—Porter, "Ideal Scholar," pp. 157–58; emphasis in original.
"and 'classmate.' "—Porter, *American Colleges and the American Public*, p. 181.
"common life."—Porter, p. 191–92.
"by years."—James Morgan Hart, *German Universities: A Narrative of Personal Experience* (New York: G. P. Putnam's Sons, 1874), p. 45.
the requirements.—Abraham Flexner, *Daniel Coit Gilman: Creator of the American Type of University* (New York: Harcourt, Brace, 1946), pp. 61 ff.
28 **"the century."**—Timothy Dwight, *Memories of Yale Life and Men, 1845–1899* (New York: Dodd, Mead, 1903), p. 62.
"it imparts."—Porter, *American Colleges and the American Public*, p. 139.
"of esthetics."—Fred Lewis Pattee, "The Old Professor of English: An Autopsy," in *Tradition and Jazz* (New York: Century, 1925), pp. 202–3.
29 **"that sort."**—Francis A. March, "Recollections of Language Teaching" (summary of talk), *PMLA* 7, no. 2 (1893): xix.
"the classics."—Fred Lewis Pattee, *Penn State Yankee* (State College: Pennsylvania State University Press, 1953), pp. 84–85.
"the sunshine."—William Lyon Phelps, *Autobiography with Letters* (New York: Oxford University Press, 1939), pp. 136–37.

29 **spiritual value.**—G. W. F. Hegel, "On Classical Studies," excerpted in *German Aesthetic and Literary Criticism: Kant, Fichte, Schelling, Schopenhauer, Hegel*, ed. David Simpson (New York: Cambridge University Press, 1984), pp. 202–4.

30 **"read it."**—Hegel, p. 204; emphasis in original.

linguistic "essentialism"—Hans Aarsleff, *From Locke to Saussure: Essays on the Study of Language and Intellectual History* (Minnesota: University of Minnesota Press, 1982), pp. 36–39.

"rational aspect."—Hegel, "On Classical Studies," p. 205; Nietzsche echoed Hegel both in his high expectations for the possibilities of philology and in his disappointment with actual achievements: "There is a lack of great thought [Nietzsche wrote] in the field of philology and for that reason a lack of drive in the study of philology. Those who work in the field have become factory laborers—a sense of the whole eludes them." Quoted by Hendrik Birus, unpublished essay.

"field bears."—Charles Francis Adams, Jr., *A College Fetich* (Boston: Lea and Shepherd, 1884), pp. 20–21.

31 **"is employed."**—Quoted by Rudolph, *Curriculum*, p. 71.

"mental discipline."—Bagg, *Four Years at Yale*, p. 696.

"for him."—E. H. Babbitt, "How to Use Modern Languages as a Means of Mental Discipline," *PMLA* 6, no. 1 (1891): 53.

"same accuracy."—Porter, quoted by Veysey, *Emergence of the American University*, p. 24.

"and Greek."—Edward E. Hale, in Hale, ed., *How I Was Educated Papers*, p. 7.

"equally unimaginable."—James B. Angell, in Hale, *How I Was Educated Papers*, p. 96.

"for derision."—White, *Autobiography*, 1:362.

"charming literature."—Charles Francis Adams, *An Autobiography* (Boston: Houghton Mifflin, 1916), p. 26.

32 **"been dismissed."**—Bagg, *Four Years at Yale*, pp. 550–52.

"lessons properly."—Vanderbilt, *Charles Eliot Norton*, p. 26.

"own language."—Angell, in Hale, *How I Was Educated Papers*, p. 100.

"of originality."—Wayland, *Thoughts on the Present College System*, p. 83.

to concentrate.—Porter, *American Colleges*, p. 127.

"his powers."—Porter, p. 139.

33 **"and taught."**—White, in Hale, *How I Was Educated Papers*, p. 111.

"loosened tongue."—Porter, "Ideal Scholar," p. 158.

"was accepted."—Rudolph, *Curriculum*, pp. 89–90.

"of him."—Phelps, *Autobiography*, p. 137.

"of superficiality."—Adams, *College Fetich*, p. 21.

"great value"—Adams, p. 17.

"was expected."—Adams, p. 8.

33 **"a language!"**—Adams, p. 16.
34 **"reflective powers"**—Adams, p. 19.
"and theoretical."—Adams, p. 12.
"increasingly remote."—Richard Hofstadter, *Anti-intellectualism in American Life* (New York: Alfred Knopf, 1963), p. 400–401; see also Hofstadter's *The Age of Reform: From Bryan to F.D.R.* (New York: Alfred A. Knopf, 1955), pp. 135 FF.; also Martin Green, *The Problem of Boston: Some Readings in Cultural History* (New York: W. W. Norton, 1966).
35 **culture outside.**—After this book went to press, I encountered Myron Tuman's article "From Astor Place to Kenyon Road: The NCTE and the Origins of English Studies," *College English* 48, no. 4 (April 1986): 339–49. Tuman argues that the decline of the rhetorical conception of writing in the colleges and the influence of "Romantic poetics" was already evident in the colleges by the time of Edward T. Channing's accession to the Boylston Professorship at Harvard in 1819. If Tuman is correct, my argument in this and the following chapter would have to be qualified.

CHAPTER 3. ORATORICAL CULTURE AND THE TEACHING OF ENGLISH

Page
36 **"necessary acquisition."**—Quoted by Rudolph, *Curriculum*, p. 72.
37 **"in this."**—T. R. Lounsbury, quoted in "Extra Session," *PMLA* 11, no. 4 (1896): x.
"and German."—March, "Recollections of Language Teaching," p. xx.
"anything else."—John F. Genung, in William Morton Payne, ed., *English in American Universities*, (Boston: D. C. Heath, 1895), p. 110.
"natural sciences."—Ann Douglas, *The Feminization of American Culture* (New York: Alfred Knopf, 1977), p. 67.
"classical curriculum."—Earnest, *Academic Procession*, p. 194.
38 **"of study."**—Rudolph, *American College and University*, pp. 317–18.
"Greek is."—Quoted by Albert H. Tolman in Payne, *English in American Universities*, p. 89.
"or Greek."—March, "Recollections of Language Teaching," p. xx.
"'one's mind.'"—March, in Payne, *English in American Universities*, p. 76.
Noah Webster.—Arthur N. Applebee, *Tradition and Reform in the Teaching of English: A History* (Urbana, Ill.: National Council of Teachers of English, 1974), p. 40, n. 23. On the careers of March and other pioneering American scholars (George Marsh, George Ticknor, Francis James Child), see Phyllis Franklin, "English Studies: The World of Scholarship in 1883," *PMLA* 99, no. 3 (May 1984): 356–70.
"the class."—March, "Recollections of Language Teaching," p. xx.
"linguistic study"—March, p. xx.
39 **"the predicate?"**—March, *Method of Philological Study of the English*

Language (New York: Harper and Brothers, 1879), p. 8.

39 **"for ourselves."**—Brander Matthews, *These Many Years*, p. 108. The manual Matthews referred to was Thomas B. Shaw's *A Complete Manual of English Literature* (New York: Sheldon, 1873).

"and when?"—Charles D. Cleveland, *A Compendium of English Literature* (Philadelphia: E. C. and J. Biddle, 1857), p. 765.

40 **the 1880s.**—Applebee, *Tradition and Reform*, p. 34.

student papers.—Horace E. Scudder, *James Russell Lowell: A Biography* (Boston: Houghton, Mifflin, 1901), 1:395; on Lowell's teaching, see also the reminiscence of Barrett Wendell, "Mr. Lowell as a Teacher," in *Stelligeri and Other Essays concerning America* (New York: Charles Scribner's Sons, 1893), pp. 203–17.

"a *causerie*."—Scudder, p. 398.

"their thought."—Scudder, pp. 393–94.

41 **"undergraduate compositions."**—Henry James, *Charles W. Eliot* (Boston: Houghton Mifflin, 1930), 2:14–15.

"nothing more."—Charles H. Grandgent, "The Modern Languages: 1869–1929," in *The Development of Harvard University*, ed. Samuel Eliot Morison (Cambridge: Harvard University Press, 1930), p. 66.

42 **"separate laws"**—Hugh Blair, *Lectures on Rhetoric and Belles Lettres* (Philadelphia: Hayes and Zell, 1854), p. 394. On Blair's importance in the nineteenth century "as a model for using literature to teach writing," see James A. Berlin, *Writing Instruction in Nineteenth Century American Colleges* (Carbondale: Southern Illinois University Press, 1984), pp. 25–28.

"he speaks."—Blair, p. 421.

"and disposition"—Blair, p. 378.

"and great."—Blair, p. 15.

"this end."—Blair, p. 421.

"poetry begins."—Blair, p. 422.

"the author."—Editor's Note, Blair, p. 4.

43 **"were essential."**—Walter P. Rogers, *Andrew D. White and the Modern University* (Ithaca: Cornell University Press, 1942), p. 31.

***English Reader*.**—Hiram Corson, *The Voice and Spiritual Education* (New York: Macmillan, 1896), p. 22.

"not done."—White, in Hale, *How I Was Educated Papers*, 105.

own subject.—Bagg, *Four Years at Yale*, pp. 559–62.

"an orator."—Bagg, pp. 567–68.

44 **similar obligation.**—Bagg, p. 615.

"also 'writers.' "—Bagg, pp. 608–9.

entrance examinations.—Applebee, *Tradition and Reform*, p. 30.

"the world."—Earnest, *Academic Procession*, p. 87.

Henry Adams.—Thomas S. Harding, *College Literary Societies*, pp. 8–9; see also Ernest Samuels, *The Young Henry Adams* (Cambridge: Belknap Press, 1967), p. 36.

"college libraries."—Rudolph, *Curriculum*, p. 96.

44 **"student magazines."**—Rudolph, *American College and University*, p. 143.

45 **"in literature."**—Earnest, *Academic Procession*, p. 94.

"future eminence."—Bishop, *History of Cornell*, pp. 138–39.

"to Caedmon."—Earnest, *Academic Procession*, pp. 96–97.

on campuses.—White, *Autobiography*, 1:268–69.

delivery inaudible.—Bliss Perry, *And Gladly Teach* (Boston: Houghton Mifflin, 1935), p. 79.

"of Byron."—Earnest, *Academic Procession*, pp. 92–95.

46 **"in 'nature.' "**—Bledstein, pp. 250–51.

"the day."—Angell, in Hale, *How I Was Educated Papers*, p. 102.

at Williams.—Perry, *And Gladly Teach*, pp. 48–49.

"academic community."—Lynn Miller Rein, *Northwestern University School of Speech: A History* (Evanston, Ill.: Northwestern University Press, 1981), p. 1.

"prize competition."—Bagg, *Four Years at Yale*, p. 619.

optional subject—Grandgent, "Modern Languages," p. 75.

"train elocutionists."—Rein, *Northwestern University School of Speech*, p. 1.

47 **"half-taught scholar."**—Adams, *College Fetich*, p. 11.

any college.—Bishop, *History of Cornell*, p. 115.

"literary scholarship—Bishop, p. 116.

"literature itself."—White, *Autobiography*, 1:429.

48 **"but itself"**—Hiram Corson, *The Aims of Literary Study* (New York: Macmillan, 1895), pp. 42–44.

"*absolute being*."—Corson, *Voice and Spiritual Education*, p. 6.

"moral slovenliness"—Corson, p. 107.

was reading—Corson, p. 23.

young pupils.—Corson, p. 53.

49 **"other world."**—Bishop, *History of Cornell*, pp. 117–18.

50 **"people everywhere."**—Rein, *Northwestern University School of Speech*, pp. 8–22.

CHAPTER 4. THE INVESTIGATORS (1): THE NEW UNIVERSITY

Page

55 **"anti-professionals"**—Stanley Fish, "Profession Despise Thyself: Fear and Self-Loathing in Literary Studies," *Critical Inquiry* 10, no. 2 (1984): 349–64.

56 **"*limiting* them."**—Applebee, *Tradition and Reform*, p. 28.

of knowledge.—Flexner, *Daniel Coit Gilman*, p. 54.

" 'own sake' "—Flexner, p. 9.

57 **"or partisanship."**—Daniel Coit Gilman, "Fundamental Principles," in *The Launching of a University, and Other Papers* (New York: Dodd, Mead, 1906), p. 41.

"scientific treatises."—Flexner, pp. 63–64.

"results attained."—Gilman, in Richard Hofstadter and Wilson Smith,

American Higher Education: A Documentary History (Chicago: University of Chicago Press, 1961), 2:646.

57 **undergraduate college.**—Flexner, *Daniel Coit Gilman*, pp. 50, 55–56.
"and sciences."—Eliot, quoted by Flexner, pp. 108–9.

58 **"ancient truth?"**—Henry Wade Rogers, quoted by William Albert Locy in Arthur Herbert Wilde, ed., *Northwestern University: A History: 1855–1905* (Evanston, Ill.: Northwestern University, 1905), 1:343.
and programs—Bishop, *History of Cornell*, p. 239.
"neighboring departments."—Parker, "Where Do English Departments Come From?" p. 348.

59 **in 1878.**—Flexner, *Daniel Coit Gilman*, pp. 89–90.
"industrial ideal"—René Wellek, "American Literary Scholarship," in *Concepts of Criticism* (New Haven: Yale University Press, 1963), p. 299; first published as "Literary Scholarship," in Merle Curti, ed., *American Scholarship in the Twentieth Century* (Cambridge: Harvard University Press, 1953).
"who can."—Pattee, "Old Professor of English," p. 185.
"to knowledge."—Grandgent, "Modern Languages," p. 99.
"to another."—Veysey, "Stability and Experiment in the American Undergraduate Curriculum," p. 36. Veysey states that the departmental major was virtually universal by 1910.

60 **to 1930.**—Earnest, *Academic Procession*, p. 310.
"and opinion."—Veysey, *Emergence of the American University*, p. 311.
"increasingly ritualistic."—Veysey, p. 258.
"same terms."—Veysey, p. 315.
"shared values."—Veysey, p. 311.
"threateningly serious."—Veysey, p. 308.
"on ignorance."—Veysey, pp. 337–38.
"for jobs."—Rudolph, *Curriculum*, p. 117.
"their differences."—Bledstein, *Culture of Professionalism*, p. 327.

61 **suspected subversives**—On Butler, see Horace Coon, *Columbia: Colossus on the Hudson* (E. P. Dutton, 1947), pp. 93–133; see also Hofstadter and Metzger, *Development of Academic Freedom*, pp. 468–506; for an illuminating account of repression on campus, see James Wechsler, *Revolt on the Campus* (New York: Covici Friede, 1935).
academic tenure.—Hofstadter and Metzger, *Development of Academic Freedom*, pp. 468–506.
"of matter-of-fact."—Thorstein Veblen, *The Higher Learning in America: A Memorandum on the Conduct of Universities by Businessmen* (New York: Hill and Wang, 1975; first published 1918), p. 7.
"least taboos."—T. Atkinson Jenkins, "Scholarship and Public Spirit," *PMLA* 24, no. 4, appendix (1914): cv.
"like Germany."—Ludwig Lewisohn, *Up Stream: An American Chronicle* (New York: Boni and Liveright, 1922), p. 125. Lewisohn secured a

post in German at the University of Wisconsin in 1910, went to Ohio State in 1911, and left teaching in 1919 to work at the *Nation.*

62 **"vote each."**—George Santayana, *Character and Opinion in the United States* (New York: Norton Library, 1967; first published 1921), pp. 142–45.
"forget it."—Santayana, p. 144.
"in dignity."—James McCosh, *The New Departure in American Education: Being a Reply to President Eliot's Defense of It in New York, Feb. 24 1885* (New York: Charles Scribner's Sons, 1885), p. 22.
"with himself."—James Morgan Hart, *German Universities*, p. 264.
"listless reciters."—Hart, p. 268.
"our youth."—Porter, *American Colleges and the American Public*, pp. 129–30.
"scholarly renown."—Hart, *German Universities*, p. 43.

63 **"intellectual giants"**—Hart, pp. 260–61.
"me through."—Fred M. Fling, "The German Historical Seminar," *Academy* 4, no. 3 (April 1889): 219; see also Felix Schelling, "The Unscientific Method," *Academy* 4, no. 9 (December 1899): 594–501.
"and scholarship."—Mattoon M. Curtis, "The Present Condition of German Universities," *Educational Review* 2 (June 1981): 39.
"among nations."—Hart, *German Universities*, p. 260.

64 **"world's knowledge."**—G. Stanley Hall in Hofstadter and Smith, *American Higher Education*, pp. 649–50.
"open society."—Bledstein, *Culture of Professionalism*, p. 87.
social changes.—Bledstein, p. 88.
"technical competence."—Bledstein, p. 90.
"they educated."—Richard Ohmann, "Reading and Writing, Work and Leisure," unpublished essay.

CHAPTER 5. THE INVESTIGATORS (2): THE ORIGINS OF LITERATURE DEPARTMENTS

Page

66 **departmental status.**—Grandgent, "Modern Languages," p. 73.
"and Dryden."—Jo McMurtry, *English Language, English Literature: The Creation of an Academic Discipline* (Hamden, Conn.: Archon Books, 1985), p. 78.
"or slept."—Robert Morss Lovett, *All Our Years* (New York: Viking Press, 1948), p. 37.
"examined me?"—J. Donald Adams, *Copey of Harvard: A Biography of Charles Townsend Copeland* (Boston: Houghton Mifflin, 1960), pp. 227–28.
"stage conditions."—Wellek, "American Literary Scholarship," p. 304; see also Applebee, *Tradition and Reform*, p. 41, n. 27.
"the classics."—Lovett, *All Our Years*, p. 32.

67 **"anyone's satisfaction."**—Grandgent, "Modern Languages," p. 69.
Harvard culture—On the tenor of the Harvard writing courses of this

period, the best sources I have found are Adams, *Copey of Harvard*; Walter Rollo Brown, *Dean Briggs* (New York: Harper and Brothers, 1926), pp. 49–94; and Paul Cohen, "Barrett Wendell: A Study of Harvard Culture" (Ph.D. diss., Northwestern University, 1974).

67 **"of English."**—Richard Ohmann, *English in America*, pp. 245–46. Ohmann's source is Donald J. Gray et al., *The Department of English at Indiana University Bloomington: 1869–1970* (Bloomington: Indiana University, n.d.).

"of philology"—Applebee, *Tradition and Reform*, p. 28.

68 **"any other."**—H. C. G. Brandt, "How Far Should Our Teaching and Text-books Have a Scientific Basis?" *PMLA* 1 (1884–85): 57–60; italics in original.

" 'soft snap.' "—Quoted by William Riley Parker, "The MLA, 1883–1953," *PMLA* 68, no. 4, part 2 (September 1953): 21.

"mutually exclusive."—Theodore H. Hunt, "The Place of English in the College Curriculum," *PMLA* 1 (1884–85): 126. This important essay has been discussed by Michael Warner, "Professionalization and the Rewards of Literature: 1875–1900," *Criticism* 27 (Winter 1985): 4 ff., and Wallace Douglas, "Accidental Institution: On the Origins of Modern Language Study," in *Criticism in the University*, ed. Gerald Graff and Reginald Gibbons (Evanston, Ill.: Northwestern University Press, 1985), pp. 41 ff. See below, pp. 77–78.

"pedagogical tools."—Warner, "Professionalization and the Rewards of Literature," pp. 2–4.

"of vegetables."—Quoted by Warner, p. 25, n. 8.

69 **"modern languages."**—Wellek, "American Literary Scholarship," p. 299.

United States.—Wellek, p. 298.

"a people."—Applebee, *Tradition and Reform*, p. 25.

"of cultures."—Albert S. Cook, "The Province of English Philology," *PMLA* 13 (1898): 200.

"humane disciplines"—Richard Macksey, ed., *Velocities of Change: Critical Essays from MLN* (Baltimore: John Hopkins University Press, 1974), pp. xviii–xx.

"an aggregate."—August Boeckh, quoted by Macksey, p. xix.

"the philologists."—McMurtry, *English Language, English Literature*, p. 150.

"Aryan brotherhood."—Friedrich Max Müller *Three Lectures on the Science of Language* (Chicago: Open Court, 1895), pp. 53, 55.

"Aryan hypothesis"—Max Müller, *My Autobiography: A Fragment* (New York: Charles Scribner's Sons, 1901), p. 104. Müller, "explained" German anti-Semitism as an understandable reaction to Jews' buying of titles and money-making (*My Autobiography*, pp. 69–70); he defended "imperial rule" when "held under proper control" (*Three Lectures on the Science of Language*, p. 55). On the Aryan hypothesis, see the critical account by Isaac Taylor, *The Origins of the Aryans: An*

Account of the Prehistoric Ethnology and Civilization of Europe (New York: Humboldt, 1889).

69 ***Gentleman's Magazine***—Hans Aarsleff, *The Study of Language in England: 1780–1860* (Minneapolis, University of Minnesota Press, 1983), p. 195.

70 **and others.**—Frederic E. Faverty, *Matthew Arnold the Ethnologist*, Northwestern University Studies no. 27 (Evanston, Ill.: Northwestern University Press, 1951); see also Michael S. Helfand and Philip E. Smith II, "Anarchy and Culture: The Evolutionary Turn of Cultural Criticism in the Work of Oscar Wilde," *Texas Studies in Literature and Language* 20, no. 2 (Summer 1978): 200; David Lloyd, "Arnold, Ferguson, Schiller: Aesthetic Culture and the Politics of Aesthetics," *Cultural Critique* 1, no. 2 (Winter 1985): 137–69.

"were isolated"—Hippolyte Taine, *History of English Literature*, trans. H. Van Luan (London: Chatto and Windus, 1897; first published 1863), 1:2.

"a symbol"—Taine, 1:7.

"a race."—Taine, 1:34.

"of states."—John W. Burgess, quoted by Hofstadter, *Social Darwinism in American Thought*, rev. ed. (Boston: Beacon Press, 1955), p. 175; Burgess "designated the Teutonic nations . . . as the bearers of modern political civilization" (*Reminiscences*, p. 248).

71 **"continental nation."**—Theodore Roosevelt, quoted by Alan Trachtenberg, *The Incorporation of America: Culture and Society in the Gilded Age* (New York: Hill and Wang, 1982), p. 13; Burgess's recollections of Roosevelt as a student at Columbia appear in Burgess's *Reminiscences*, pp. 211–14.

"the globe."—Brander Matthews, *An Introduction to the Study of American Literature*, rev. ed. (New York: American Book Company, 1896), pp. 10–11; see also Matthews's presidential address to the 1910 MLA meeting, "The Economic Interpretation of Literary History," which defends "Taine's stimulating book" as an alternative to the "defective" conception of literary development as a mere "chronological collection of biographical criticisms with only casual consideration of the movement of . . . literature as a whole" (*PMLA* 26, appendix, [1911]: lxi).

"as well."—Paul Lauter, "Race and Gender in the Shaping of the American Literary Canon: A Case Study from the Twenties," *Feminist Studies* 9, no. 3 (Fall 1983): 442.

72 **"specialism and Philology."**—John Churton Collins, *The Study of English Literature: A Plea for Its Recognition and Reorganization at the Universities* (London and New York: Macmillan, 1891), pp. 11–12.

"from philology"—Albert H. Smyth, "American Literature in the Classroom," *PMLA* 3 (1887): 239. Smyth's full statement is worth quoting: "We have problems enough in the progress of a nation's thought and literary style to occupy the time of the college class-room and the University Seminary without importing others from philology which can be solved only by far different instruments. Literature can by no possibility render its highest service to the cause of education until it has been divorced from philology. The seminary of the latter must be distinct from that of the former, for the mental equipment of a critic of literature is distinct from that of a student of language and cannot be obtained by the same processes."

73 **"as good."**—Adams, *College Fetich*, p. 18–19.

"and Chaucer"—Brandt, "How Far Should Our Teaching and Text-books Have a Scientific Basis?" p. 61.

"and improvement."—Porter, *American Colleges and the American Public*, pp. 81–82; Porter defended the modern practices of "interpretation and judgment of literature"; see his essay "The New Criticism," *New Englander* 29, no. 111 (April 1870): 295–316.

"to it."—Brandt, "How Far Should Our Teaching and Text-books Have a Scientific Basis?" pp. 61–62.

74 **"as Greek."**—March, "Recollections of Language Teaching," p. xxi.

"receding future."—Norman Foerster, "The Study of Letters," in *Literary Scholarship: Its Aims and Methods*, ed. Norman Foerster et al. (Chapel Hill: University of North Carolina Press, 1941), pp. 11–12.

"and sources."—Wellek, "American Literary Scholarship," 300; see also Wellek's essay "The Concept of Evolution in Literary History," in *Concepts of Criticism*, pp. 37–53.

years later.—Such a conclusion seems to me to be implied by R. Steven Turner's informative essay "The Prussian Universities and the Concept of Research," *Internationales Archiv für Sozialgeschichte der Deutschen Literatur* 5 (1980): 68–93.

"romantic medievalism."—Wellek, "American Literary Scholarship," p. 301.

75 **"future civilization."**—Taine, *History of English Literature*, 1:25.

"of history."—Edmund Wilson, *To the Finland Station: A Study in the Writing and Acting of History* (New York: Doubleday, 1940), pp. 51–52.

"available authors."—W. W. Skeat, quoted by McMurty, *English Language, English Literature*, p. 151.

76 **"their limbs."**—Taine, *History of English Literature*, 1:4.

"than interesting."—Jefferson Fletcher, "Our Opportunity," *PMLA* 31, no. 4, appendix (1916): li.

the South.—MacMillan, *English at Chapel Hill*, p. 17.

"of literature."—C. Alphonso Smith, "Interpretative Syntax," *PMLA* 15, no. 1 (1900): 97–101.

"replacing individualism."—Smith, pp. 101–2.

77 **"the profession."**—Warner, "Professionalization and the Rewards of Literature," p. 4.

"essentially barbarians."—Morton W. Easton, "The Rhetorical Tendency in Undergraduate Courses," *PMLA* 4, no. 1 (1889): 20–21.

77 **"the point."**—E. H. Magill, "Remarks upon the work of the Pedagogical Section," *PMLA* 8, no. 4, appendix (1893): li–lii.

78 **"and style."**—Hunt, "Place of English in the College Curriculum," p. 125.

"the English."—Hunt, p. 127.

"intellectual life."—Theodore H. Hunt, *Studies in Literature and Style* (New York: A. C. Armstrong, 1891), p. 19.

teach literature.—Warner, "Professionalization and the Rewards of Literature," p. 2.

"*Canterbury Tales*."—Warner, p. 17.

79 **"present exigency."**—Albert S. Cook, *The Higher Study of English* (Boston: Houghton, Mifflin, 1906), p. 117.

"adopt it."—Cook, "The Province of English Philology," Presidential Address, *PMLA* 13, no. 1 (1898): 203–4; reprinted in Cook, *Higher Study of English*.

"literary studies."—Henry Seidel Canby, *Alma Mater: The Gothic Age of the American College* (New York: Farrar and Rinehart, 1936), p. 182.

80 **"since intervened."**—Albert S. Cook, *The Artistic Ordering of Life* (Ithaca: Cornell University Press, 1957), p. 13; Cook's lecture was delivered in 1898.

"in Milton."—Canby, *Alma Mater*, p. 184.

of philology—Cook, "Province of English Philology," p. 200.

"of literature."—Cook, p. 200.

professional opportunism.—Wallace Douglas has made this point through a close analysis of the early literature in "Accidental Institution," pp. 35–61.

"felt institutionally."—Wellek, "American Literary Scholarship," p. 300.

CHAPTER 6. THE GENERALIST OPPOSITION

Page

81 **"*limiting* them."**—See above, p. 56.

82 **"earlier chapter."**—See above, p. 40.

"Matthew Arnold."—Lionel Trilling, "Some Notes for an Autobiographical Lecture," in *The Last Decade: Essays and Reviews, 1965–75* (New York: Harcourt Brace Jovanovich, 1979), p. 233.

83 **"and vulgarity."**—Norton, quoted by Alan Trachtenberg, *The Incorporation of America*, p. 155.

"best vein."—Lovett, *All Our Years*, p. 38.

"of EVERYTHING"—Vanderbilt, *Charles Eliot Norton*, p. 138.

"tolerate himself."—Frank W. Noxon, "College Professors Who Are Men of Letters," *Critic* 42, no. 1 (January 1903): 126.

"educated classes."—Barrett Wendell, *A Literary History of America* (New York: Charles Scribner's Sons, 1900), p. 356.

"or America."—Wendell, p. 342; in *The Privileged Classes* (New York:

Charles Scribner's Sons, 1908), Wendell argued that in a democracy it was the *working* class that deserved the title.

83 **"and enduring."**—James Russell Lowell, "Address," *PMLA* 5, no. 1 (1890): 157.

"concentrated wealth."—"Hiram Corson," *Dictionary of American Biography* (New York: Charles Scribner's Sons, 1930), 4:454.

"the boss."—Henry Van Dyke, *Essays in Application* (New York: Charles Scribner's Sons, 1913), p. 57.

84 **"own alienation."**—Trachtenberg, *Incorporation of America*, p. 155.

"found it."—Van Dyke, *The Van Dyke Book: Selected from the Writings of Henry Van Dyke*, ed. Edwin Mims (New York: Charles Scribner's Sons, 1921), p. 181.

"prodigious 'mixer.' "—Adams, *Copey of Harvard*, p. 144.

"[his] purposes."—George Santayana, *The Middle Span* (New York: Charles Scribner's Sons, 1945), 2:177.

kind anywhere.—Vida Duton Scudder, *On Journey* (New York: E. P. Dutton, 1937), pp. 127 ff. Scudder published a book based on her lectures, entitled *Social Ideals in English Letters* (Chautauqua, N.Y.: Chautauqua Press, 1898).

85 **"a polity"**—Trilling, "Notes for an Autobiographical Lecture," p. 233.

"could be."—John Henry Raleigh, *Matthew Arnold and American Culture* (Berkeley: University of California Press, 1957), p. 174.

"intelligent living."—Van Dyke, *The Spirit of America* (New York: Macmillan, 1922), p. 227.

"most intense,"—Scudder, *On Journey*, p. 114.

"would read."—John Erskine, *The Memory of Certain Persons* (Philadelphia: J. B. Lippincott, 1947), p. 164.

86 **"economic forces."**—Erskine, *My Life as a Teacher* (Philadelphia: J. B. Lippincott, 1948), p. 171.

"industrial democracy."—Bliss Perry, *The Amateur Spirit* (Boston: Houghton, Mifflin, 1904), p. 31.

"general readers."—Erskine, *My Life as a Teacher*, pp. 24–25.

"ever rival."—Woodrow Wilson, "Mere Literature," in *The Papers of Woodrow Wilson*, ed. Arthur S. Link (Princeton: Princeton University Press, 1970), 8:244.

"awakening touch"—The phrase is Fred Lewis Pattee's; see below, p. 110.

"are dead."—Edwin Mims, Introduction, *Van Dyke Book*, pp. xvii–xix.

87 **"published articles."**—Warner, "Professionalization and the Rewards of Literature," pp. 22–23.

"same person."—Irving Babbitt, *Literature and the American College: Essays in Defense of the Humanities* (Boston: Houghton, Mifflin, 1908), p. 130.

"personal impressions."—Babbitt, p. 119.

"unctuous voice."—Wellek, "American Literary Scholarship," p. 304.

87 **"mere intellect."**—Warner, "Professionalization and the Rewards of Literature," p. 22.
"a scholar."—Erskine, *My Life as a Teacher*, p. 100.
"college teaching."—Phelps, *Autobiography with Letters*, p. 252.
88 **"producing successors."**—Warner, "Professionalization and the Rewards of Literature," p. 17.
"doctor's degree."—Babbitt, *Literature and the American College*, p. 131.
"at Harvard."—Babbitt, letter to William Roscoe Thayer, quoted by Arthur Dakin, *Paul Elmer More* (Princeton: Princeton University Press, 1960), p. 113.
"have him."—Erskine, *My Life as a Teacher*, p. 112.
"great races."—Wilson, "Mere Literature," p. 252.
"infinite suggestion."—Lowell, "Address," p. 36.
89 **Francis Adams.**—See above, p. 30.
"against mind."—Erskine, "The Moral Obligation to Be Intelligent," in *The Moral Obligation to Be Intelligent and Other Essays* (New York: Duffield, 1915), p. 15.
"themselves theoretically."—Babbitt, *Literature and the American College*, p. 181.
90 **" 'and shallows' "**—Lowell, "Address," p. 21.
"in college."—Lowell, p. 19.
"the pupil."—Franklin Carter, "The Study of Modern Languages in Our Higher Institutions," *PMLA* 2 (1886): 14–15.
"modern tongues."—Carter, pp. 12–13.
91 **"something better"**—Lowell, "Address," p. 21.
"of instruction"—Thomas Henry Huxley, quoted by Flexner, *Daniel Coit Gilman*, p. 86, n. 71.
92 **"give him."**—Felix E. Schelling, "The American Professor," *PMLA* 30 no. 4, appendix (1915): lxviii.
"her bottom."—Harry Gideonse, "Inaugural Address," *Bulletin of the Association of American Colleges* 25, no. 4 (December 1939): 494.
"standardless analysis."—John K. Winkler, *Woodrow Wilson: The Man Who Lives On* (New York: Vanguard Press, 1933), p. 85.
"the students"—Winkler, p. 84.
"ten millions."—Winkler, p. 97.
"classical studies"—The Morrill Act, in Hofstadter and Smith, *American Higher Education*, p. 568.
93 **"in English."**—Pattee, *Penn State Yankee*, pp. 156–67.
its usefulness.—Magali Sarfatti Larson, *The Rise of Professionalism: A Sociological Analysis* (Berkeley: University of California Press, 1977), p. 152.
94 **"dirty game."**—Erskine, *Memory of Certain Persons*, p. 151.
"of life."—Randolph Bourne, "The Professor," in *The History of a Literary Radical and Other Essays*, ed. Van Wyck Brooks (New York: B. W. Heubsch, 1920), p. 94.

94 **less pure.**—Bourne, "Professor," p. 97.
social world.—Bourne; see below, p. 108.

95 **"not interesting."**—Calvin Thomas, "Literature and Personality," *PMLA* 12, no. 3 (1897): 301; along the same lines, see the comments of C. Alphonso Smith in 1899: "It does not avail to cite beautiful definitions of philology, definitions that assert the philologian's equal right to all the slopes of Parnassus; this alienation exists in practice and it has proved hurtful both to the student of literature and to the student of syntax. Literary criticism, lacking the solid basis of language study, has lost the note of authority and becomes mincing and arbitrary; while studies in syntax, divorced from the vitalizing influence of literature, have become mechanical in method and statistical in result" ("Interpretative Syntax," p. 97).
"to express."—Babbitt, *Literature and the American College*, p. 130.
"the crowd"—Jefferson Fletcher, "Our Opportunity," p. xliii.
"orderly one."—Fletcher, p. xl.
"dissertations prove"—Fletcher, pp. xliii–xliv. A similarly amusing portrayal of the trials of the English Ph.D. oral, more sympathetic to the graduate student, is the novel by George R. Stewart, *Doctor's Oral* (New York: Random House, 1939).

Chapter 7. Crisis at the Outset

Page

98 **"as Greek"**—March, see above, p. 74.

100 **"humanistic goals."**—Applebee, *Tradition and Reform*, pp. 30–34.
"in English."—Foster, *Administration of the College Curriculum* p. 174.
"of literature."—Francis A. March, in Payne, *English in American Universities*, p. 76.

101 **"of English."**—James W. Bright, in Payne, *English in American Universities*, p. 150.
"the other."—George E. MacLean, in Payne, *English in American Universities*, pp. 156–57.
"greater end."—Daniel Kilham Dodge, in Payne, *English in American Universities*, p. 72.
"literary art."—Albert H. Tolman, in Payne, *English in American Universities*, p. 89.
"that direction."—Hiram Corson, in Payne, *English in American Universities*, p. 60.
"vast importance."—Martin Wright Sampson, in Payne, *English in American Universities*, p. 96.
"of date."—Charles Mills Gayley, in Payne, *English in American Universities*, pp. 107–8.
"love it."—Sampson, in Payne, *English in American Universities*, p. 97.

102 **"to radiate."**—Dodge, in Payne, *English in American Universities*, p. 71.

102 **"English literature."**—Katharine Lee Bates, in Payne, *English in American Universities*, pp. 146–47.
"aesthetic approach"—For some sense of what the principles may have been at Chicago, see Richard G. Moulton, *Literary Criticism and Theory of Interpretation: Syllabus of a Course of Six Lectures* (New York: D. C. Heath, 1893).
"the nineteenth."—Lovett, *All Our Years*, p. 92.
"its development."—Gayley, in Payne, *English in American Universities*, p. 104.
"dramatic criticism."—Gayley, p. 105.
Prose Literature.—Benjamin P. Kurtz, *Charles Mills Gayley* (Berkeley: University of California Press, 1943), pp. 98–101.
the East.—Quoted by Kurtz, p. 122.

103 **"a system."**—Gayley, in Payne, *English in American Universities*, p. 109.

104 **"attend them."**—Frank Norris, "The 'English' Classes of the University of California," in *The Literary Criticism of Frank Norris*, ed. Donald Pizer (Austin: University of Texas Press, 1964), pp. 6–8; first published in *Wave* 15 (28 November, 1896).
"produce literature."—Norris, p. 8.
a degree.—For an account of Norris's work in English 22 at Harvard, see James D. Hart, *Frank Norris: A Novelist in the Making* (Cambridge: Harvard University Press, 1970), pp. 12–19.
Gayley's courses—Kurtz, *Charles Mills Gayley*, p. 152; see below, p. 129.
"strongest institutions"—Alexander Hohlfield, 'The Teaching of the History of a Foreign Literature," *PMLA* 20, no. 4, appendix (1905): xxxvi–xxxvii.
the association.—Hohlfield, p. xxxvii; for Hohlfield's repeated remarks, see "Light from Goethe on Our Problems," *PMLA* 29, no. 4, appendix (1914): lxxii ff.

105 **"competition, underbidding."**—Frank Gaylord Hubbard, "The Chairman's Address," *PMLA* 28, no. 4, appendix (1913): lxxxi.
"per cent"—E. H. Magill; see above, p. 77.
"their communities."—Waitman Barbe, *Going to College* (New York: Hinds and Noble, 1899), pp. 20–21.
"the nation."—Earnest, *Academic Procession*, p. 204.
"of scholarship."—Bourne, *Youth and Life* (Boston: Houghton Mifflin, 1913), p. 318.
"cramping thoughts."—Owen Wister, *Philosophy Four: A Story of Harvard University* (New York: Macmillan, 1903), p. 36.

106 **"the letter."**—Wister, p. 93.
of book reviewer.—Wister, pp. 94–95.
"clearing houses."—Owen Johnson, *Stover at Yale* (New York: Frederick A. Stokes, 1912), p. 323.
"the ranks."—Johnson, p. 325.

106 **"in America"**—F. Scott Fitzgerald, *This Side of Paradise* (New York: Charles Scribner's Sons, 1920), pp. 38, 40.

"social distinction."—John Peale Bishop, "Princeton," in *The Collected Essays of John Peale Bishop*, ed. Edmund Wilson (New York: Charles Scribner's Sons, 1948), pp. 394–95; Bishop's essay first appeared in the *Smart Set* in November 1921.

107 **"college president."**—Earnest, *Academic Procession*, pp. 219–22.

"of girls."—Babbitt, *Literature and the American College*, pp. 118–19.

"pornographic perverts."—Pattee, "Old Professor of English," p. 183.

"results possible"—Pattee, "Old Professor of English," p. 183.

108 **"emptiness—undemocratic."**—Lewisohn, *Up Stream*, pp. 155–56.

"emotional response."—Lewisohn, pp. 163–64.

"holding court."—Edwin E. Slosson, *Great American Universities* (New York: Macmillan, 1910), p. 162.

"studied there."—Bourne, "Medievalism in Our Colleges," in *The History of a Literary Radical and Other Papers* (New York: S. A. Russell, 1956), p. 157.

"social world."—Bourne, pp. 156–57.

109 **"graduate school."**—Oliver Farrar Emerson, "The American Scholar and the Modern Languages," *PMLA* 24, no. 4, appendix (1909): xcviii–cxix.

"nor encouragement."—Perry, *And Gladly Teach*, pp. 244–46.

" 'research work.' "—Hohlfield, "The Teaching of the History of a Foreign Literature," xxxi–xxxiii.

"the student."—Hohlfield, p. xxxvii.

110 **"general ideas."**—Stuart P. Sherman, "Professor Kittredge," in *Shaping Men and Women: Essays on Literature and Life* (New York: Doubleday, 1928), p. 81. My reading of this essay disputes the claim of Sherman's biographers, Jacob Zeitlin and Homer Woodbridge, that Sherman's criticisms of Kittredge were offered in a spirit of admiration and affection (*Life and Letters of Stuart P. Sherman* [New York: Farrar and Rinehart, 1929], 1:106). Sherman was not an unqualified "New Humanist." He never shared Babbitt and More's distrust of democracy, and late in his career he became an admirer of Dreiser.

"Nineteenth Century."—Sherman, pp. 82–83.

"the country."—Sherman, p. 40.

"impressed me."—Pattee, *Penn State Yankee*, 268; on student passivity in this period, see Edwin Slosson, *Great American Universities*, p. 520.

"special study."—Emerson, "American Scholar and the Modern Languages," p. xcviii.

"department only"—Perry, *Amateur Spirit*, p. 29.

"chosen role."—Perry, *And Gladly Teach*, p. 243.

111 **"general interest."**—Hohlfield, Summary of Central Division Proceedings," *PMLA* 18, no. 1 (1903): cvi.

"intellectual interest."—Hubbard, "Chairman's Address," p. 1xxxv.

"parts related?"—Perry, *And Gladly Teach*, p. 243.

111 **"the way."**—Erskine, *My Life as a Teacher*, pp. 11–12.

112 **"his neighbor."**—Canby, *Alma Mater*, p. 157.

"no help."—Canby, p. 183.

"results possible"—Pattee, "Old Professor of English," p. 183; see above, p. 107.

113 **"hostile, process."**—George Herbert Palmer, quoted in Veysey, *Emergence of the American University*, p. 231; on the Harvard Philosophy Department and its professionalization in this period, see Bruce Kuklick, *The Rise of American Philosophy: Cambridge, Massachusetts, 1860–1930* (New Haven: Yale University Press, 1977).

"permeated Cambridge."—Palmer, quoted by Veysey, pp. 232–33.

114 **"the country."**—James Wilson Bright, "Concerning the Unwritten History of the Modern Language Association of America," *PMLA* 18, appendix 1 (1903): lxii.

"brutish age."—James Taft Hatfield, "Scholarship and the Commonwealth," *PMLA* 17, no. 3 (1902): 391–94.

local gentry.—Hatfield, appointed to a chair in German language and literature at Northwestern in 1889, responded to criticism in the Evanston press of the Northwestern faculty for having "drawn themselves down to narrow limits" and remained aloof from the civic and social life of Evanston. Hatfield replied that "the university was one of the few redeeming features of the town" and certainly "worth more to the community than the custards, high-balls, and ping pong of so called 'social Evanston.' " He ended, "I have long since come to the conclusion that the barrier lies not in the exclusiveness and selfishness of the gown but in a certain vulgarity of standards on the part of the town." (quoted by Williamson and Wild, *Northwestern University*, p. 103).

"cherish it."—Hatfield, "Scholarship and the Commonwealth," pp. 394–95.

115 **acted on**—Larzer Ziff, *Puritanism in America: New Culture in a New World* (New York: Viking, 1973), pp. 199–201.

"taken seriously."—Hatfield, "Scholarship and the Commonwealth," p. 395.

"of Philistia."—Hatfield, p. 408.

"pervades society"—Grandgent, "The Dark Ages," *PMLA* 28, no. 4, appendix (1912): li.

"own language."—Grandgent, p. li.

"of Babel."—Lewis Freeman Mott, "Disrespect for Language," *PMLA* 27, no. 4, appendix (1912): liii–liv.

"and speech."—Mott, p. li.

116 **"time generally."**—Emerson, "American Scholar and the Modern Languages," p. xcvi.

"highest culture"—Emerson, p. xcv.

"German culture"—Emerson, p. c.

"frequently sacrificed."—Emerson, pp. xcv–c.

116 **"our time."**—Grandgent, "Dark Ages," p. xlix.
"than instruction."—Grandgent, p. lxvi.
"any subject."—Grandgent, p. l.
"all kinds."—Grandgent, pp. liii–lv.

117 **"to develop"**—E. C. Armstrong, "Taking Council with Candide," *PMLA* 35, no. 4 (1920): xxxix.
"its judgment."—Grandgent, "Dark Ages," p. lviii.
"and balances?"—Armstrong, "Taking Council with Candide," p. xxxix.
"great nation."—Hubbard, "Chairman's Address," p. lxxxix.
"make men."—T. Atkinson Jenkins, "Scolarship and Public Spirit," *PMLA* 29, no. 4, appendix (1914): cii–ciii.
"and teacher."—Jenkins, p. xxxix.
"against it."—Armstrong, "Taking Council with Candide," p. xxxix.
"the times."—Hubbard, p. lxxiii.
"medieval monastery."—Hubbard, p. lxxxi.

118 **"narrow professionalism"**—Jenkins, p. ciii.
"frequently sacrificed."—Emerson, see above, p. 116.

Chapter 8. Scholars versus Critics: 1915–1930

Page

121 **"and enrollment."**—Parker, "MLA, 1883–1953," p. 32.
"their literatures"—"Constitution of the Modern Language Association of America," *PMLA* 32, no. 4, appendix (1917): ci. The MLA constitution would be amended again in 1951, the objective now being "to promote study, *criticism*, and research in modern languages and their literatures" (emphasis mine). "Constitution," *PMLA*, 67, no. 1 (1952): 107.
"is research."—William A. Nitze, "Horizons," *PMLA* 44, supplement (1930): iv.

122 **"finer dignity."**—John P. Fruit, "A Plea for the Study of Literature from the Aesthetic Standpoint," *PMLA* 6, no. 1 (1891): 29.
"philological devotee."—Henry E. Shepherd, "Some Phases of Tennyson's *In Memoriam*," *PMLA* 6, no. 1 (1891): 41.
"of supererogation"—Shepherd, p. 44.

123 **"collateral reading."**—Martin Wright Sampson, in Payne, *English in American Universities*, pp. 94–97.

124 **"of style."**—W. E. Mead, "The Graduate Study of Rhetoric," *PMLA* 16, no. 4 (1901): xxi–xxii.
"contemporary fiction"—Phelps, *Autobiography with Letters*, pp. 297–98.
"university professor."—Phelps, p. 323.
"modern novel"—Matthews, *These Many Years*, p. 393.
"recent centuries."—Albert H. Smyth, "American Literature in the Classroom," *PMLA* 3, no. 1 (1887): 241.

125 **"to sell."**—John Fruit, "Plea for the Study of Literature from the Aesthetic Standpoint," p. 38.
"know it."—Bliss Perry, "Fiction as a College Study," *PMLA* 11 (1896): 84.
"commonplace moods."—Cook, *Higher Study of English*, p. 110.
" 'so actual.' "—Grandgent, "Dark Ages," p. lv.
126 **literary taste**—See above, p. 87.
"is attained."—Thomas R. Price, "The New Function of Modern Language Teaching," *PMLA* 16, no. 1 (1901): 86.
"interpretative criticism"—Fletcher, "Our Opportunity," p. li.
"of Woodberry."—Joel E. Spingarn, quoted by Marshall Van Deusen, *J. E. Spingarn*, Twayne's United States Authors Series, no. 182 (New York: Twayne, 1971), p. 165, no. 3.
"first-rate importance."—Van Deusen, *J. E. Spingarn*, p. 22.
"the university."—Lewis Mumford, quoted by Van Deusen, p. 32.
127 **"and Organization"**—Spingarn, quoted by Van Deusen, p. 46.
"university's endeavor."—Van Deusen, p. 52. The story of Spingarn's firing by Butler over the Peck case is told by Van Deusen, pp. 47–57. See also Coon, *Columbia*, p. 125.
"under him."—Erskine, *My Life as a Teacher*, pp. 106–7.
"and libraries."—Van Deusen, *J. E. Spingarn*, p. 105.
"to ethics."—J. E. Spingarn, *Creative Criticism and Other Essays* (New York: Harcourt Brace, 1931; first published 1917), p. 130.
"Gothic arch."—Spingarn, p. 28. Mencken praised this remark in "Criticism of Criticism of Criticism," in *Prejudices* (New York: Alfred A. Knopf, 1919), p. 28.
"been aplenty"—Spingarn, p. 123.
"of art."—Spingarn, p. 127.
New Humanists—On the New Humanists and their controversies, the most useful sources I have found are J. David Hoeveler, Jr., *The New Humanism: A Critique of Modern America, 1900–1940* (Charlottesville: University Press of Virginia, 1977), and Richard Ruland, *The Rediscovery of American Literature: Premises of Critical Taste, 1900–1940* (Cambridge: Harvard University Press, 1967), especially chaps. 1–4.
128 **or libertarian.**—Van Deusen, *J. E. Spingarn*, p. 104.
"and book."—Erskine, *My Life as a Teacher*, pp. 24–25.
129 **"military victory."**—Carol S. Gruber, *Mars and Minerva: World War I and the Uses of the Higher Learning in America* (Baton Rouge: Louisiana State Unversity Press, 1975), p. 255.
courses discontinued.—Fred Lewis Pattee, *Penn State Yankee*, pp. 311–12.
"of Carlyle."—Mark Sullivan, *Our Times* (New York: Charles Scribner's Sons, 1933), 5:468.
"patriotic Americans."—Thomas Daniel Young, *Gentleman in a*

Dustcoat: A Biography of John Crowe Ransom (Baton Rouge: Louisiana State University Press, 1976), pp. 88, 93.

129 **"preaching patriotism."**—Malcolm Cowley, *Exile's Return: A Literary Odyssey of the 1920s*, rev. ed. (New York: Viking Press, 1951), p. 36.

"was fighting."—Kurtz, *Charles Mills Gayley*, p. 219.

"the Allies."—Jacob Zeitlin and Homer Woodbridge, *Life and Letters of Stuart P. Sherman*, 1:362.

peace rally.—Lovett, *All Our Years*, p. 143.

"the French"—Quoted by Gruber, *Mars and Minerva*, p. 241.

"of Independence."—Kurtz, *Charles Mills Gayley*, pp. 219–20.

130 **"the students."**—Erskine, *My Life as a Teacher*, p. 111.

similar actions.—Coon, *Columbia*, p. 127.

"in Europe."—Thomas Edward Oliver, "The Menace to Our Ideals," *PMLA* 33, no. 4, appendix (1918): xcvii–xcviii.

"American literature."—Fred Lewis Pattee, *Tradition and Jazz*, p. 206.

"the future."—Pattee, *Penn State Yankee*, p. 314.

"modern period."—Edwin Greenlaw and James Holly Hanford, eds., *The Great Tradition: Selections from English and American Prose and Poetry, Illustrating the National Ideals of Freedom, Faith, and Conduct* (Chicago: Scott, Foresman, 1919), p. xiii.

131 **"for citizenship."**—Edwin Greenlaw, William H. Elson, and Christine M. Keck, eds., *Literature and Life* (Chicago: Scott, Foresman, 1922), 2:v.

"the school."—Greenlaw, Elson, and Keck, 1:iii.

"leaves school."—Greenlaw, Elson, and Keck, 2:iv.

among others.—Patriotic texts revived during World War II and the Cold War aftermath. See, for example, the 1943 anthology edited by professor of English Colonel Clayton E. Wheat of the United States Military Academy, *The Democratic Tradition in America* (Boston: Ginn, 1943). My thanks to Harrison M. Hayford for calling my attention to this and other American literature texts. A full study of college and high-school textbooks of American literature would be most useful. My guess is that such a study would reveal a pattern similar to that described (as I interpret it) by Frances FitzGerald in her work on American history texts, *America Revised: A History of Schoolbooks in the Twentieth Century* (New York: Atlantic Monthly Press, 1979): explicit patriotism, giving way at a certain point to pluralistic incoherence.

132 **"not holding."**—Perry, *The American Mind* (Boston: Houghton Mifflin, 1912), pp. 82–84.

"the will."—Erskine, "Moral Obligation to Be Intelligent," p. 15.

"new tradition."—Erskine, p. 22.

"false patriotism."—William Henry Hulme, "Scholarship as a Bond of International Union," *PMLA* 32, no. 4, appendix (1917): xcix.

"the Romanticists."—Julius Goebel, "The New Problems of American Scholarship," *PMLA* 30, no. 4, appendix (1915): lxxx.

132 **"common humanity."**—Kuno Francke, "The Idea of Progress from Leibniz to Goethe," *PMLA* 33, no. 4, appendix (1918): lxxxv. Julius Goebel (see previous note) came to these universalist sentiments late, probably compensating self-protectively for his earlier ardent glorifications of Wilhelmian nationalism. On the shifting political outlook of German departments in this period, as reflected in the *Monatshefte für Deutsche Sprache und Pädagogik*, an illuminating discussion is that of Henry J. Schmidt, "The Rhetoric of Survival: The Germanist in America from 1900–1925," in *The Grip Report*, unpublished papers of the Group for Interdisciplinary Study of the Professions, second draft, vol. 1.

"its origin."—Oliver, "The Menace to Our Ideals," p. cxii; see also the addresses by Alexander R. Hohlfield, "Light from Goethe on Our Problems," *PMLA* 29, no. 4, appendix (1914): lxv.; Felix E. Schelling, "The American Professor," PMLA 30, no. 4, appendix (1915): lv.; and the frequent wartime contributions by professors of literature to *International Conciliation*, the journal of the American Association of International Conciliation.

133 **"judicial conscience?"**—Fletcher, "Our Opportunity," p. lii.

Charles Morris.—Arthur Applebee, *Tradition and Reform*, p. 157.

be "interesting."—See above, p. 76

"besides ourselves."—Fletcher, "Our Opportunity," p. li.

"twentieth-century classics."—Lionel Trilling, "Notes for an Autobiographical Lecture," p. 232. See also Trilling's detailed essay "The Van Amringe and Keppel Eras," in *A History of Columbia College on Morningside* (New York: Columbia University Press, 1954), pp. 44–47.

134 **"free-for-all discussion."**—Erskine, *Memory of Certain Persons*, p. 343; see also *My Life as a Teacher*, pp. 165–75.

"about them."—Erskine, *Memory of Certain Persons*, pp. 342–43.

"the Bible."—Trilling, "Van Amringe and Keppel Eras," p. 44.

since 1901.—Kurtz, in *Charles Mills Gayley*, says that Gayley's "Great Books" course met for the first time in January 1901 (p. 152).

"the nation."—Trilling, "Notes for an Autobiographical Lecture," p. 232.

and vocationalism.—James Sloan Allen, *The Romance of Commerce and Culture: Capitalism, Modernism, and the Chicago-Aspen Crusade for Cultural Reform* (Chicago: University of Chicago Press, 1983), p. 81.

135 **"to read."**—Erskine, *Memory of Certain Persons*, p. 343.

"primitive simplicity"—Trilling, "Notes for an Autobiographical Lecture," p. 232.

pettifogging ritual.—See above, pp. 32–33.

"of Michigan."—Quoted by Gruber, *Mars and Minerva*, p. 241.

136 **modern world.**—See above, p. 94.

"social process."—Daniel Bell, *The Reforming of General Education: The Columbia College Experience in its National Setting* (New York:

Columbia University Press, 1966), p. 211. For a full account of the history of the Columbia Contemporary Civilization course, see Justus Buchler, "Reconstruction in the Liberal Arts," in *History of Columbia College on Morningside*, pp. 48–135.

136 **"office door."**—Allen, *Romance of Commerce and Culture*, p. 80.

of C.C.—See below, pp. 154–55. For illuminating discussion of the close connections between Trilling's criticism, teaching, and educational views, see Mark Krupnick, *Lionel Trilling and the Fate of Cultural Criticism in America* (Evanston, Ill.: Northwestern University Press, 1986).

137 **"must travel."**—Foerster, *The American Scholar: A Study in "Litterae Inhumaniores"* (Chapel Hill: University of North Carolina Press, 1929), p. 20.

"historically verified."—André Morize, *Problems and Methods of Literary History* (Boston: Ginn, 1922), p. 1.

"exact bibliographies,"—Morize, pp. 2–3.

"given period."—Morize, pp. 283–87.

"period studied."—Morize, p. 130.

"his originality."—Morize, p. 287.

138 **"substantiated facts."**—Morize, p. 3.

"of literature"—René Wellek, "Literary History," in *Literary Scholarship: Its Aims and Methods*, ed. Norman Foerster et al. (Chapel Hill: University of North Carolina Press, 1941), pp. 94–95; reprinted (with revisions) in René Wellek and Austin Warren, *Theory of Literature*, 1st ed. (New York: Harcourt Brace, 1948).

"of scholarship."—Foerster, *American Scholar*, p. 54, n. 1.

Writers' Workshop.—D. G. Myers, "Creative Writing as an Academic Discipline," unpublished chapter of a Northwestern dissertation in progress to which I am indebted here and elsewhere.

139 **own cause.**—Foerster, *American Scholar*, pp. 7–8.

"good book."—Foerster, p. 12.

"literary history"—Foerster, pp. 16–17.

"with education."—Foerster, p. 42.

"essentially alien."—Foerster, p. 13.

"and serviceable."—Foerster, pp. 32–33.

writing program—Myers, "Creative Writing as an Academic Discipline."

"literature itself."—Foerster, *American Scholar*, p. 59.

"of treason."—Foerster, *American Scholar*, p. 21.

140 **and friends.**—On the Foerster-Greenlaw friendship, see "Norman Foerster's Recollections of Edwin Greenlaw," in MacMillan, *English at Chapel Hill*, pp. 44–46.

"incomplete otherwise."—Greenlaw, *The Province of Literary History*, Johns Hopkins Monographs in Literary History no. 1 (Baltimore: Johns Hopkins Press, 1931), pp. 145–46.

"with pedantry."—Greenlaw, p. 110.

140 **"a whole."**—Greenlaw, p. 152.
"human culture."—Greenlaw, p. 176.
"of intellect."—Greenlaw, p. 126.
"old times."—Greenlaw, p. 4.

141 **considerable scope**—See the posthumous collection by Greenlaw, *Studies in Spenser's Historical Allegory*, Johns Hopkins Monographs in Literary History no. 2 (Baltimore: Johns Hopkins Press, 1932).
Foerster's own.—See above, pp. 130–31. Foerster himself coedited a patriotic anthology, *American Ideals* (New York: Houghton Mifflin, 1917), that was similar to Greenlaw and Hanford's *The Great* Tradition.
"graduate student"—Greenlaw, *Province of Literary History*, p. 8.
"with learning."—Greenlaw, p. 21.
"a learning."—Greenlaw, p. 8.
"research men"—Greenlaw, p. 30.

142 **"do so."**—Howard Mumford Jones, "Graduate English Study: Its Rational[e]," *Sewanee Review* 38 (October–December 1930) and part 2, 39 (January–March 1931): 205.

143 **"mere subjectivism"**—Albert Feuillerat, "Scholarship and Literary Criticism," *Yale Review* 14, no. 2 (January 1925): 312.
"beyond them."—Feuillerat, p. 320.
"and shame."—Feuillerat, p. 316.
"to separate."—Feuillerat, pp. 317–20.
source-study—One such confrontation is described by James Luther and J. Bryan Allin in *Irving Babbitt: Man and Teacher*, ed. Frederick Manchester and Odell Shepard (New York: G. P. Putnam's Sons, 1941), pp. 274 ff.
"for scholars."—John Livingston Lowes, "The Modern Language Association and Humane Scholarship," *PMLA* 48, suppl. (1933): 1402.
"often we?"—Lowes, p. 1404.

144 **"are tending."**—Nitze, "Horizons," pp. vii–xi.

CHAPTER 9. GROPING FOR A PRINCIPLE OF ORDER: 1930–1950

Page

145 **and philistines.**—Gerald Graff, *Literature against Itself: Literary Ideas in Modern Society* (Chicago: University of Chicago Press, 1979), p. 140.

146 **"old times"**—See above, p. 140.
"than literary."—Nitze, "Horizons," p. v.
Hall Frye.—R. D. Stock, *The New Humanists in Nebraska: A Study of the Mid-West Quarterly (1913–1918)*, University of Nebraska Studies, new series no. 61 (Lincoln: University of Nebraska Press, 1979).

147 **"about poetry."**—Yvor Winters, "Problems for the Modern Critic of Literature," in *The Function of Criticism: Problems and Exercises* (Denver: Alan Swallow, 1957), pp. 11–12.
presented itself.—On De Voto's career, see Wallace Stegner, *The*

Uneasy Chair: A Biography of Bernard De Voto (New York: Doubleday, 1974).

147 **"mainly stood."**—R. S. Crane, "History versus Criticism in the Study of Literature." in *The Idea of the Humanities and Other Essays Critical and Historical*, ed. Wayne C. Booth (Chicago: University of Chicago Press, 1967), 2:23.

148 **"of literature."**—John Crowe Ransom, "Criticism, Inc.," in *The World's Body* (New York: Charles Scribner's Sons, 1938), pp. 330–36.

"function independently."—Ransom, p. 346.

149 **"interested" gesture.**—See Graff, *Poetic Statement and Critical Dogma* (Evanston, Ill.: Northwestern University Press, 1970; reprinted, Chicago: University of Chicago Press, 1980), and Graff, *Literature against Itself*. For other studies of the social contexts of the New Criticism, see John Fekete, *The Critical Twilight: Explorations in the Ideology of Anglo-American Literary Theory from Eliot to McLuhan* (London: Routledge and Kegan Paul, 1977); Grant Webster, *The Republic of Letters: A History of Postwar American Literary Opinion* (Baltimore: Johns Hopkins University Press, 1979); and Frank Lentricchia, *After the New Criticism* (Chicago: University of Chicago Press, 1980).

"excess of the academic"—Van Wyck Brooks, "On Certain Critics," in *The Writer in America* (New York: E. P. Dutton, 1953), pp. 9–28.

"human spirit."—Alan Tate, "The Man of Letters in the Modern World," in *The Man of Letters in the Modern World: Selected Essays, 1928–1955* (New York: Meridian Books, 1955), p. 12.

150 **"of criticism."**—T. S. Eliot, "The Frontiers of Criticism," in *On Poetry and Poets* (New York: Farrar, Straus and Giroux, 1957), p. 125.

and nationalism.—See above, p. 133.

cultural thesis.—Reuben Brower, *The Fields of Light: An Experiment in Critical Reading* (New York: Oxford University Press, 1951).

"for literature."—Ohmann, *English in America*, p. 71.

become compromised.—One professor, now just retiring, who was a graduate student in the fall of that year, describes feeling at the time that the pact was the one event that signaled "the end of it all" for the politics of literature. "You could feel it in the air after all—the Fellow Travellers and the Agrarians were both embarrassed and made a tacit agreement to call the whole thing off. The people who had previously been talking about literature from a Left or Right position climbed up a rope and pulled it up after them, saying that one had to stick to the poem itself" (Harrison Hayford, Northwestern University, private communication).

"a form"—Blackmur, "A Critic's Job of Work," in *Language as Gesture: Essays in Poetry* (New York: Columbia University Press, 1980), pp. 384–85.

"independent liberal"—R. P. Blackmur, letter to Malcolm Cowley, quoted by Daniel Aaron, *Writers on the Left* (New York: Avon Books, 1965), p. 274n.

"at hand."—Blackmur, "Critic's Job of Work," p. 385.

151 **"a game?"**—Granville Hicks, *The Great Tradition: An Interpretation of American Literature since the Civil War* (Chicago: Quadrangle Books, 1969; first published 1933), p. 121.

know today—Cowley, *Exile's Return: A Narrative of Ideas* (New York: W. W. Norton, 1934).

"the new."—Christian Gauss, letter to Edmund Wilson, January 31, 1931, in *Papers of Christian Gauss*, ed. Katherine Gauss Jackson and Hiram Haydn. (New York: Random House, 1957), pp. 273–74.

"other values."—Edmund Wilson, *Axel's Castle: A Study in the Imaginative Literature of 1870–1939* (New York: Charles Scribner's Sons, 1931), p. 119.

"of view"—Wilson, p. 136.

"opinions seriously."—Wilson, p. 119.

152 **"chose to."**—Cleanth Brooks, *Modern Poetry and the Tradition* (Chapel Hill: University of North Carolina Press, 1939), p. 58.

"from it."—Brooks, p. 59.

153 **"offending presence."**—Russell Fraser, *A Mingled Yarn: The Life of R. P. Blackmur* (New York: Harcourt Brace Jovanovich, 1981), pp. 188–89.

154 **"was concerned."**—Winters, "Problems for the Modern Critic of Literature," p. 13.

"to be."—John Berryman, quoted by James Atlas in *Delmore Schwartz: The Life of an American Poet* (New York: Farrar, Straus and Giroux, 1977), p. 209.

"I was."—Delmore Schwartz, letter to Karl Shapiro, in *Letters of Delmore Schwartz*, ed. Robert Phillips (Princeton, N.J.: Ontario Review Press, 1984), p. 157.

"the conformity."—Karl Shapiro, Foreword, in *Letters of Delmore Schwartz*, p. xii.

"on you."—On Lewisohn, see above, p. 61.

Trilling's notebooks—"From the Notebooks of Lionel Trilling," *Partisan Review* 51 (1984): 500; see also Diana Trilling, "Lionel Trilling: A Jew at Columbia," *Commentary* 67, no. 3 (March 1979): 40–46.

155 **"a Jew."**—Trilling, "From the Notebooks," pp. 499–502.

"more Jews."—Edward Le Comte, "Dinner with Butler and Eisenhower: A Columbia Memoir," *Commentary* 81, no. 1 (January 1986): 59.

40 percent.—Veysey, "Stability and Experiment in the American Undergraduate Curriculum," p. 15.

"economically afloat."—Veysey, p. 15.

1949 fifty-two.—Gray et al., *Department of English at Indiana University*, pp. 248–64; Macmillan, *Department of English at the University of North Carolina*, pp. 75–82.

"more earnest."—Robert Fitzgerald, *Enlarging the Change: The Princeton Seminars in Literary Criticism, 1949–1951* (Boston: Northeastern University Press, 1985), p. 11.

155 **"ever known."**—Kenneth Lynn, "F. O. Matthiessen," in *Masters: Portraits of Great Teachers*, ed. Joseph Epstein, (New York: Basic Books, 1981), p. 110.

156 **"*Understanding Fiction.*"**—Young, *John Crowe Ransom*, p. 85.
at Oxford.—Young, p. 72.
"of language."—Young, p. 85.
"values anywhere."—Young, p. 241.

157 **"our fatuities."**—Anthony Hecht, "John Crowe Ransom," in Epstein, *Masters*, p. 181.
"art itself."—Young, p. 267.
"literary quality."—Young, p. 302.
"setting whatever."—Ransom to Tate, quoted by Young, pp. 299–301.
"the way."—Young, pp. 298–300.

158 **"be teachers."**—Young, p. 386.
"made one."—George Lanning, quoted by Young, p. 388.

159 **"Kenneth Burke."**—Fitzgerald, *Enlarging the Change*, p. 121.

160 **"first speculations."**—Fitzgerald, p. 11.
"the room."—Fraser, *Mingled Yarn*, p. 260.
"actually interesting."—Fraser, p. 260.

161 **"of literature."**—Wellek, "American Literary Scholarship," p. 311.

Chapter 10. General Education and the Pedagogy of Criticism: 1930–1950

Page

162 **"curricular reforms."**—Allen, *Romance of Commerce and Culture*, p. 106.

163 **"the ages."**—Allen, p. 102; I am heavily indebted to Allen in the account of general education at Chicago in this chapter.

164 **high school.**—Allen, pp. 83–84.
"of scholarship."—Mortimer J. Adler, quoted by Allen, p. 82.
of Kansas.—Allen, p. 85.
"with them."—Robert Maynard Hutchins, *The Higher Learning in America* (New Haven: Yale University Press, 1936), pp. 85–87.

165 **"and why."**—Hutchins, pp. 117–18.
"gaining insight."—Harry Gideonse, *The Higher Learning in a Democracy* (New York: Holt, Reinhart and Winston, 1937), p. 3.
"earlier period."—Gideonse, "Inaugural Address," *Bulletin of the Association of American Colleges* 25, no. 4 (December 1939): 493–96.

166 **"own times"**—Dewey, "President Hutchins' Proposals to Remake Higher Education," in Hofstadter and Smith, *American Higher Education*, pp. 951–53; first published in 1937.
"5,000 people."—Allen, *Romance of Commerce and Culture*, pp. 99, 104; in *Chicago: The Second City*, A. J. Leibling noted the seeming ubiquity of Great Books groups in the city during the early fifties: "Everybody you meet belongs to a Great Books Discussion Group. . . .

In Chicago intellectual circles, a man who can't do a psychoanalysis between two Martinis ranks with a fellow who can't change a tire" (*Chicago: The Second City* [New York: Alfred A. Knopf, 1952], p. 108).

166 **world government**—Allen, *Romance of Commerce and Culture*, pp. 106ff.

167 **"the janitors."**—Allen, p. 88.

"of values."—James Bryant Conant, *Education in a Divided World: The Function of the Public Schools in Our Unique Society* (Cambridge: Harvard University Press, 1949), pp. 108–9.

"national policy."—Conant, p. 5.

168 **"more curricula."**—Conant, Introduction, in Harvard Committee, *General Education in a Free Society* (Cambridge: Harvard University Press, 1945), p. v.**"that question."**—Harvard Committee, *General Education in a Free Society*, p. 5.

"bookish curriculum"—Harvard Committee, p. 32.

"human being."—Harvard Committee, p. 4.

"of work"—Harvard Committee, p. 14.

"or both."—Harvard Committee, p. 32.

"or Dante"—Harvard Committee, p. 206.

169 **"the course."**—Harvard Committee, pp. 205–7.

"the work."—Harvard Committee, p. 110.

"of information."—Harvard Committee, p. 208.

"educational chances."—Harvard Committee, p. 113.

"of tradition"—Harvard Committee, p. 111.

"human preoccupations."—Harvard Committee, p. 207.

170 **"or whole."**—Harvard Committee, p. 108; these recommendations concern the teaching of literature in the secondary schools, but I find little difference in philosophy between them and the recommendations for the college course.

"literature courses."—Harvard Committee, p. 108.

"school generations."—Harvard Committee, pp. 108–9; again, I conflate secondary school and college recommendations.

171 **"external context."**—Bell, *Reforming of General Education*, p. 213.

chronological order.—See Thomas W. Wilcox, *The Anatomy of College English* (San Francisco: Jossey-Bass, 1973), p. 139.

"with events."—Bell, *Reforming of General Education*, p. 213.

172 **"is lacking."**—Bell, p. 210.

"into contact."—A theory of the "correlated curriculum" was developed in the mid-thirties and tried at a number of high schools and colleges, till evidently abandoned in the early forties. See the NCTE volume *A Correlated Curriculum: A Report of the Committee of the National Council of Teachers of English*, ed. Ruth Mary Weeks (New York: Appleton Century, 1936). This experiment deserves study.

"intellectual discipline."—Trilling, "The Uncertain Future of the Humanistic Educational Ideal," in *Last Decade*, p. 166.

173 **incentives depended.**—See, for example, Wilcox, *Anatomy of College English*, pp. 107–9.
174 **"of view."**—René Wellek and Austin Warren, *Theory of Literature*, 3d ed. (New York: Harcourt Brace Jovanovich, 1956), pp. 21–22.
175 **"invaluable clue."**—I. A. Richards, *Practical Criticism: A Study of Literary Judgment* (New York: Harcourt, Brace, n.d.; first published 1929), p. 41.
as "excuses"—Richards, p. 82 (italics in original).
"of Judgment."—Richards, p. 45.
"for them."—Marilyn M. Cooper, "Context as Vehicle: Implicatures in Writing," in *What Writers Know: The Language, Process and Structure of Written Discourse*, ed. Martin Nystrand (New York: Academic Press, 1982), pp. 107–8.
176 **"golden grove."**—Richards, *Practical Criticism*, p. 83.
"their powers."—Richards, p. 296.
"even reactionary"—Paul Bové, *Intellectuals in Power: A Genealogy of Critical Humanism*, p. 53; the explicit charge of "panopticism" appears on p. 69.
"capitalist society."—Bové, p. 76.
"tolerate difference."—Bové, p. 51.
177 **"American culture."**—Bové, p. 55.
than "oppositional"—Bové, p. 54.
wide appeal.—See above, p. 170.
178 **" 'naive' responses."**—Bell, *Reforming of General Education*, pp. 230–31.
"historical reference."—Irving Howe, *A Margin of Hope: An Intellectual Autobiography* (New York: Harcourt Brace Jovanovich, 1982), p. 179.
"abide it."—Howe, p. 179.

Chapter 11. History versus Criticism: 1940–1960

Page

184 **"a history."**—Wellek, "Literary History," pp. 115–16.
185 **"modern literatures."**—A. O. Lovejoy, *The Great Chain of Being: A Study in the History of an Idea* (Cambridge: Harvard University Press, 1936), pp. 16–17.
"been before."—A. O. Lovejoy, *Essays in the History of Ideas* (Baltimore: Johns Hopkins University Press, 1948), p. 6.
"in dilution."—Lovejoy, *Great Chain of Being*, pp. 16–17.
"of imagination."—Wellek, "American Literary Scholarship," p. 306; "Literary History," p. 109; *Theory of Literature*, 1st ed., p. 111.
of Lovejoy.—R. S. Crane, "Philosophy, Literature, and the History of Ideas," in *Idea of the Humanities*, 1:173–87.
"ideas elsewhere."—Lovejoy, *Essays in the History of Ideas*, p. 4.
186 **"in itself."**—Douglas Bush, "The New Criticism: Some Old-Fashioned Queries," *PMLA* 64, suppl., part 2, (March 1949): 18–21.

186 **Pooh Perplex**—Frederick C. Crews, *The Pooh Perplex: A Freshman Casebook* (New York: E. P. Dutton, 1965), pp. 138–50.

"themselves, inadequate."—Bush, pp. 13–14.

187 **research publication.**—Eliseo Vivas, "Criticism and the Little Mags," *Western Humanities Review* 16, no. 1 (Autumn 1951): 9–11.

188 ***"poetic meaning."***—Cleanth Brooks and Robert Penn Warren, *Understanding Poetry: An Anthology for College Students*, rev. ed. (New York: Henry Holt, 1950), pp. xxi–xxii; emphasis in original.

"historical' meant."—Howe, *Margin of Hope*, p. 177.

"his poetry."—Cleanth Brooks, "The Poem as Organism: Modern Critical Procedure, in *English Institute Annual, 1940* (New York: Columbia University Press, 1941), pp. 35–36.

"of authors."—Wellek, "Literary Scholarship," p. 131.

"and biography."—Wellek, "Literary History," pp. 94–95.

"or brother."—W. K. Wimsatt and Monroe Beardsley, "The Intentional Fallacy," in *The Verbal Icon: Studies in the Meaning of Poetry* (Lexington: University of Kentucky Press, 1954), p. 10.

189 **"in them"**—Cleanth Brooks, "Literary Criticism: Poet, Poem, and Reader," in *Varieties of Literary Experience: Eighteen Essays in World Literature*, ed. Stanley Burnshaw (New York: New York University Press, 1962), p. 105.

"into literature."—Wellek, "Literary History," p. 109.

"something else."—Wellek, p. 130.

"something else."—John Crowe Ransom, "Criticism as Pure Speculation," in *The Intent of the Critic*, ed. Donald Stauffer (Princeton: Princeton University Press, 1941), pp. 101–2.

"language exists."—Wellek, pp. 117–18.

"of ideas"—Wellek, *A History of Modern Criticism: 1750–1950* (New Haven: Yale University Press, 1955), 1:8.

"their audiences."—Martha Woodmansee, "Deconstructing Deconstruction: Toward a History of Modern Criticism," in *Erkennen und Deuten: Essays zur Literatur und Literaturtheorie: Edgar Lohner in Memoriam* (Erich Schmidt, 1983), p. 25.

190 **tried elsewhere.**—See Graff, "Literary Criticism as Social Diagnosis," in *At the Boundaries: Proceedings of the Northeastern University Center for Literary Studies*, ed. Herbert L. Sussman (Boston: Northeastern University Press, 1984), 1:1–16.

"about itself"—Brooks, "Literary Criticism, p. 114.

191 **"to internal."**—Wimsatt and Beardsley, "Intentional Fallacy," p. 14.

192 **"with them."**—Brooks, "Literary Criticism," pp. 106–7.

"twentieth century."—R. S. Crane, "The Critical Monism of Cleanth Brooks," in *Critics and Criticism*, ed. R. S. Crane (Chicago: University of Chicago Press, 1951), pp. 104–5. An earlier version of Crane's essay appeared in *Modern Philology* in 1948.

193 **"a period."**—Jonathan Culler, "Literary Criticism and the University," to appear in *The Organization of Knowledge in American Society,*

1920–1970, to be published by the American Academy of Arts and Sciences. I thank Professor Culler for showing me a typescript of this essay.

Chapter 12. Modern Literature in the University: 1940–1960

Page

195 **"historical commentary."**—Ransom, "Criticism, Inc.," p. 336.

196 **"outmoded style."**—Rewley Belle Inglis, Mary Ries Bowman, John Gehlmann, and Wilbur Schramm, eds., *Adventures in American Literature*, 4th ed. (New York: Harcourt, Brace, 1948), p. iii.

"entire safety?"—Pattee, "Old Professor of English," p. 220.

197 **courses (17.5).**—Northwestern University Archives; these enrollment figures do not account for students enrolling in more than one course, for borderline courses hard to classify as either "modern" or nonmodern, and so on.

"of promotion."—L. S. Wright, letter of August 21, 1943, Northwestern University Archives.

198 **"2,500 years."**—Bush, see above, p. 186.

"apprehending mind."—Vivas, "Criticism and the Little Mags," p. 6.

but be.—See my discussion of this misconception (still sometimes heard even at this late date) in an appendix, "The Poet Nothing Affirmeth," to *Poetic Statement and Critical Dogma*, pp. 180–83.

"Roebuck catalogue."—Brooks, "The New Criticism," *Sewanee Review*, 87, no. 4 (Fall 1979): 593.

199 **"a businessman."**—Bush, "New Criticism," p. 20.

"necessarily untrue."—Harold Rosenberg, "Everyman a Professional," in *The Tradition of the New* (New York: Horizon Press, 1960), pp. 69–70.

200 **"poetic belief"**—Rosemond Tuve, *Elizabethan and Metaphysical Imagery* (Chicago: University of Chicago Press, 1947), p. 47.

"reasonable discourse."—Tuve, p. 19.

"conceptual meaning."—Tuve, p. 415, n. G.

in them.—Rosemond Tuve, *A Reading of George Herbert* (Chicago: University of Chicago Press, 1952), pp. 23–99. See Barbara Leah Harmon's useful account of the controversial history of Herbert criticism in *Costly Monuments: Representations of the Self in George Herbert's Poetry* (Cambridge: Harvard University Press, 1982), pp. 1–38.

"new orders."—Robert B. Heilman, quoted by W. R. Keast, "The New Criticism and *King Lear*," in *Critics and Criticism*, 118; first published in *Modern Philology* (August 1949).

"of calculation"—Robert B. Heilman, *This Great Stage: Image and Structure in 'King Lear'* (Baton Rouge: Louisiana State University Press, 1948), p. 35

"any work."—Keast, "The New Criticism and *King Lear*," pp. 136–37.

In *The Business of Criticism* (Oxford: Clarendon Press, 1959), Helen Gardner argued along similar lines against Brooks's interpretation of the imagery of "the naked babe and the cloak of manliness" in *Macbeth* (pp. 53–75).

201 **"perspectives available."**—J. V. Cunningham, "Ripeness is All," in *Tradition and Poetic Structure* (Denver: Alan Swallow, 1960; first published 1951), p. 136.

"Christian theology."—Cunningham, p. 141.

tripartite soul.—J. V. Cunningham, "Logic and Lyric: Marvell, Dunbar, Nashe," in *Tradition and Poetic Structure*, p. 45.

"inferior sense."—R. B. McKerrow, quoted by Cunningham, p. 57.

have meant.—Wesley Trimpi, "The Practice of Historical Interpretation and Nashe's 'Brightnesse Falls from the Ayre,'" *JEGP* 66 (October 1967): 501–18.

202 **"always meant."**—Catherine Belsey, *Critical Practice* (London: Methuen, 1980), p. 18.

"many ages."—Wellek and Warren, *Theory of Literature*, p. 42.

"is possible."—Wellek and Warren, pp. 177–78; the authors cite Louis Teeter's 1938 article ("Scholarship and the Art of Criticism," *ELH* 5 [1938]: 173–93), which anticipated Cunningham's on the "vegetable love" problem.

"about intention."—Wimsatt and Beardsley, "The Intentional Fallacy," in *Verbal Icon*, p. 281, n. 7.

203 **"literary art."**—Wimsatt and Beardsley, "Intentional Fallacy," p. 3.

"impoverish it."—Wellek and Warren, *Theory of Literature*, p. 42.

"in itself"—Cunningham, "Ripeness Is All," p. 140.

"and concerns."—Wellek, "A Rejoinder to Gerald Graff," *Critical Inquiry* 5, no. 3 (Spring 1979):577; the rejoinder was to my "New Criticism Once More" in the same issue (pp. 569–75), a response to Wellek's "The New Criticism: Pro and Contra," *Critical Inquiry* 4 (Summer 1978): 611–24.

204 **until 1967**—I refer to the four essays, "Critical and Historical Principles of Literary History," later collected in *The Idea of the Humanities*, 2:45–156.

"a mistake."—Bush, "New Criticism," p. 18.

"of poetry."—Donald Stauffer, quoted by Huey S. Guagliardo, "Cleanth Brooks and the Romantics" (Ph.D. diss., Louisiana State University, 1980), pp. 62–63.

205 **"is untrue."**—T. S. Eliot, "Dante," in *Selected Essays*, new ed. (New York: Harcourt, Brace and World, 1950), pp. 230–31; first published in 1929.

"an adage."—Brooks and Warren, *Understanding Poetry*, 1st ed. (1938), pp. 548–49.

"dramatically appropriate."—Cleanth Brooks, *The Well Wrought Urn: Studies in the Structure of Poetry* (New York: Reynal and Hitchcock, 1947), p. 165.

"dramatic context."—Brooks, p. 141.

205 **"and anarchy"**—T. S. Eliot, " 'Ulysses,' Order, and Myth," in *Selected Prose of T. S. Eliot*, ed. Frank Kermode (New York: Harcourt Brace Jovanovich, 1975; first published in 1922), p. 176.
"friends wrote."—Eliot, *To Criticize the Critic and Other Writings* (New York: Farrar, Straus and Giroux, 1965), p. 16.
206 **"sufficiently liberated"**—T. S. Eliot, "Milton," in *On Poetry and Poets*, p. 183
207 **"historical commentary"**—See above, p. 195.

Chapter 13. The Promise of American Literature Studies

Page

209 **"serious literature."**—Edward Wasiolek, "Wanted: A New Contextualism," *Critical Inquiry* 1, no. 3 (March 1975): 623.
"outside it."—Northrop Frye, quoted by Wasiolek, p. 625.
210 ***"into literature."***—Stanley Edgar Hyman, *The Armed Vision: A Study in the Methods of Modern Literary Criticism*, rev. ed. (New York: Vintage Books, 1955; first published 1948), p. 3 (italics in original).
"a heart."—Randall Jarrell, "The Age of Criticism," in *Poetry and the Age* (New York: Vintage Books, 1959), p. 81.
"past them."—Jarrell, p. 85.
211 **"it is?"**—Culler, "Literary Criticism and the University."
"American literature."—Pattee, "Old Professor of English," p. 210.
212 **"of it."**—Pattee, pp. 214–18.
"of America."—Pattee, "A Call for a History of American Literature," in *Tradition and Jazz*, p. 233.
"moral quality."—Van Dyke, *Spirit of America*, pp. 265–66.
213 **"civic note."**— Perry, *American Mind*, p. 82.
"or bloodlessness"—Perry, p. 108.
"American literature."—Perry, pp. 96–97.
"great war."—Pattee, see above, p. 130.
"the globe."—Matthews, see above, p. 71.
"old professor"—Pattee, "Old Professor of English," p. 221.
214 **"blind pursuit"**—Norman Foerster, ed., *The Reinterpretation of American Literature: Some Contributions toward the Understanding of Its Development* (New York: Harcourt, Brace, 1928), p. xiv.
Hugh Holman.—MacMillan, *English at Chapel Hill*, pp. 48–49.
215 **"but itself."**—Harry Hayden Clark, "American Literary History and American Literature," in *Reinterpretation of American Literature*, pp. 170–71.
nonacademic critics.—V. L. Parrington, *Main Currents in American Thought*, 3 vols. (New York: Harcourt, Brace, 1927–30); on Parrington's strengths and weaknesses, see Ruland, *Rediscovery of American Literature*, pp. 186–91.
"on parade!"—Howard Mumford Jones, *The Theory of American Literature* (Ithaca: Cornell University Press, 1965; first published 1948), p. 141.
"the actual."—Lionel Trilling, "Reality in America," in *The Liberal*

Imagination: Essays on Literature and Society (New York: Viking Press, 1950), p. 1; an earlier form of this essay was first published in two parts as "Parrington, Mr. Smith, and Reality," *Partisan Review* no. 1 (January–February 1940), and *Nation* (April 20, 1946); Jonathan Arac truncates Trilling's statement, making it sound more culpably categorical than it was about Parrington's continued dominance; see Arac's "F. O. Matthiessen: Authorizing an American Renaissance, in *The American Renaissance Reconsidered*, ed. Walter Benn Michaels and Donald E. Pease, English Institute Essays, 1982–83 (Baltimore: Johns Hopkins University Press, 1985), p. 110, n. 20.

215 **and Jones**—On Jones's defense of literary-historical orthodoxy against critical attacks, see above, p. 142. Jones much later wrote an entertaining memoir, *An Autobiography* (Madison: University of Wisconsin Press, 1979).

216 **of ideas**—See above, pp. 184–85.

"the bourgeoisie."—Trilling, "Realty in America," pp. 7–11.

"brutally crude"—Yvor Winters, "Post Scripta" to *The Anatomy of Nonsense* (New York: New Directions, 1943); reprinted in *In Defense of Reason* (Denver: Alan Swallow, 1947), p. 559.

217 **theological impulses**—Perry Miller, *The New England Mind: The Seventeenth Century* (Boston: Beacon Press, 1953); Perry Miller, "From Edwards to Emerson," in *Errand into the Wilderness* (Cambridge: Belknap Press, 1956), pp. 184–203; first appeared in *New England Quarterly* 13 (December 1940); other important early essays by Miller include "Thomas Hooker and the Democracy of Connecticut" (1931), "The Marrow of Puritan Divinity" (1935), and "From Edwards to Emerson" (1940), all collected in *Errand into the Wilderness*; see also the prefaces to the two-volume anthology *The Puritans* (1938), edited by Miller and Thomas Johnson.

"to drink."—Winters, *In Defense of Reason*, p. 157.

218 **"man alone"**—Alexis de Tocqueville, *Democracy in America*, trans. Henry Reeve (New York: Random House, 1945), 2:77.

219 **"social class."**—Cushing Strout, "Tocqueville and the Idea of an American Literature," forthcoming in *New Literary History*; see also Strout's essay "Politics and the American Literary Imagination," in *The Veracious Imagination: Essays on American History, Literature, and Biography* (Middletown, Conn.: Wesleyan University Press, 1981), pp. 92–116.

"traditional institutions."—Marx, *The Machine in the Garden: Technology and the Pastoral Ideal in America* (New York: Oxford University Press, 1965), p. 364.

"is necessary."—Irving Howe, *Celebrations and Attacks: Thirty Years of Literary and Cultural Commentary* (New York: Harcourt Brace Jovanovitch, 1979), p. 248.

"nominally part."—F. O. Matthiessen, *American Renaissance: Art and Expression in the Age of Emerson and Whitman* (New York: Oxford

University Press, 1968; first published, 1941), p. 475; on Matthiessen as a culture critic, see Ruland, *Rediscovery of American Literature*, pp. 257, 283; Giles Gunn, *F. O. Matthiessen: The Critical Achievement* (Seattle: University of Washington Press, 1975); Frederick C. Stern, *F. O. Matthiessen: Christian Socialist as Critic* (Chapel Hill: University of North Carolina Press, 1981); Jonathan Arac, "F. O. Matthiessen: Authorizing an American Renaissance"; on Matthiessen as a teacher, see Kenneth Lynn, "F. O. Matthiessen."

220 **"'hopefully obsolescent.'"**—Arac, "F. O. Matthiessen, p. 93.

"historical integer."—Warner Berthoff, "Ambitious Scheme," *Commentary* 44, no. 4 (October 1967): 111.

"or vanishes."—Howard Mumford Jones, Postscript in *Theory of American Literature*, p. 204.

at will.—Ruland, *Rediscovery of American Literature*, pp. 5–6; another telling comment in a different mode was John Seelye's parodic novel *The True Adventures of Huckleberry Finn* (Evanston, Ill.: Northwestern University Press, 1970), an "improved" version of Twain's work that brings it into line with the prescriptions of the critics—or "crickits," as Seelye's Huck calls them—by literally rewriting the book. In deadpan fashion, Seelye creates a Huck consumed with existential *Angst* who, instead of lighting out for the Territory, can only conclude, with obligatory tragic resignation: "But dark as it was and lonesome as it was, I didn't have no wish for daylight to come. In fact, I didn't much care if the goddamn sun never come up again" (p. 339). Seelye's satire was directed at the solemn fault-finding of academic critics in general rather than at the theorists of American literature in particular, but one implication of his satire was that "Americanness" had become reducible to a few formulas.

221 **"American classics."**—Berthoff, "Ambitious Scheme," p. 111.

"founding fathers."—Jones, *Theory of American Literature*, p. 203.

"is jargon."—Jones, p. 205.

"social action."—Berthoff, "Ambitious Scheme," pp. 110–11.

literature canon—See Paul Lauter, ed., *Reconstructing American Literature: Courses, Syllabi, Issues* (Old Westbury, N.Y.: Feminist Press, 1983); see also my discussions of work by Lauter and Jane Tompkins above, pp. 13, 71; for an excellent and comprehensive study of theorizing about American literature, see Russell Reising, *The Unusable Past: Theory and the Study of American Literature* (New York and London: Methuen, 1986).

political conflict.—See, for example, Carolyn Porter, *Seeing and Being: The Plight of the Participant Observer in Emerson, James, Adams and Faulkner* (Middletown, Conn.: Wesleyan University Press, 1981); the essays in Eric J. Sundquist, ed, *American Realism: New Essays* (Baltimore: John Hopkins University Press, 1982); see also two collections edited by Sacvan Bercovitch, *Reconstructing American Literary History*, Harvard English Studies 13 (Cambridge: Harvard University

Press, 1986), and *Ideology and American Literature*, (Cambridge: Cambridge University Press, 1986).

222 **"racial conflict."**—Michael Paul Rogin, *Subversive Genealogy: The Politics and Art of Herman Melville* (New York: Alfred Knopf, 1983), p. 16.

"the canon."—Nina Baym, "Melodramas of Beset Manhood: How Theories of American Fiction Exclude Women Authors," in Elaine Showalter, ed., *Feminist Criticism: Women, Literature and Theory* (New York: Pantheon Books, 1985), pp. 74–75; Judith Fetterley had made a similar argument in *The Resisting Reader: A Feminist Approach to American Fiction* (Bloomington: Indiana University Press, 1977).

"and Thoreau."—Richard Brodhead, *The School of Hawthorne*, forthcoming. I thank Professor Brodhead for showing me his manuscript.

223 **about him**—F. O. Matthiessen, *Theodore Dreiser*, American Men of Letters Series (New York: Sloane, 1951).

his work.—Ellen Moers mentioned that her generation was not encouraged to read Dreiser, in *Two Dreisers* (New York: Viking, 1969), p. vii.

"toward realism."—Leslie Fiedler, quoted by Strout, "Tocqueville and the Idea of an American Literature," forthcoming.

" 'their' totalitarianism."—Donald E. Pease, "*Moby Dick* and the Cold War," in *The American Renaissance Reconsidered*, p. 116. On the "Lefter Than Thou" trend (in Michael Bernstein's phrase) in current criticism, see my essays "The Pseudo-Politics of Interpretation," *Critical Inquiry* 9, no. 3 (March, 1983): 597–610, and "American Criticism, Left and Right," in Bercovitch, *Ideology and American Literature*.

224 **"[American] experience."**—Robert E. Spiller, "Address to the Reader," in *The Literary History of the United States*, ed. Robert E. Spiller, Willard Thorp, Thomas H. Johnson, and Henry Seidel Canby (New York: Macmillan, 1948), p. xix.

"our time." Wellek, "Literary Scholarship," p. 145.

"of knowledge."—Culler, "Literary Criticism and the University."

CHAPTER 14. RAGS TO RICHES TO ROUTINE

Page

226 **"the universities."**—Cleanth Brooks, "Mr. Kazin's America," *Sewanee Review* 51 (1943):59.

"ruling methods."—Wellek, "Literary Scholarship," p. 123; in his later revision of this essay (1963), Wellek changed "apparently outdated" to "obviously outdated."

"mechanical imitation."—Wellek, "The Main Trends of Twentieth-Century Criticism," pp. 359–60.

227 **"extravagant 'symbol-mongering.' "**—Cleanth Brooks, "Literary Criticism: Poet, Poem, and Reader," in *Varieties of Literary Experience*, p. 95.

"bad sense."—Wellek, "American Literary Scholarship," p. 314.

"of literature."—See above, p. 161.

228 **"beyond them."**—See above, p. 143.
"stale game."—F. O. Matthiessen, *The Responsibilities of the Critic: Essays and Reviews*, ed. John Rackliffe (New York: Oxford University Press, 1952), p. 19; title essay first published in 1949.
"his colleagues."—Jarrell, "The Age of Criticism," p. 75. Jarrell could have chosen a more apt example: Quentin Anderson's *The American Henry James* (1957), to which he alluded, was as much a work of "scholarship" as of criticism and, though debatable in its contentions, by no means "absurd." Jarrell's recently published letters show that he worried that the critics associated with the *Kenyon Review* (where his essay first appeared) "may think it an unkind tactless piece more or less directed at them, among others—as it is" (*Randall Jarrell's Letters*, ed. Mary Jarrell [Boston: Houghton Mifflin, 1985], p. 270).
229 **poem "communicates"**—See above, pp. 151–52.
"literary work."—Robert Casillo, *The Genealogy of Demons: Anti-Semitism, Fascism, and the Myths of Ezra Pound*, forthcoming.
of doctrine.—For instance, Gary Saul Morson has shown that the same pattern arose in Slavic studies with respect to Dostoevski's anti-Semitism. See "Dostoevskij's Anti-Semitism and the Critics: A Review Article," *Slavic and East European Journal* 27, no. 3 (Fall 1983): 302–17.
230 **"the meaning."**—Irvin Ehrenpreis, *Literary Meaning and Augustan Values* (Charlottesville: University Press of Virginia, 1974), p. 106.
"complete sentence."—C. F. Main and Peter J. Seng, eds., *Poems* (Belmont, Calif.: Wadsworth, 1961), p. 66; see my earlier comments on this passage in *Poetic Statement and Critical Dogma*, p. xii.
"for that work."—Edgar V. Roberts, *Writing Themes about Literature* (Englewood Cliffs, N.J.: Prentice-Hall, 1982), pp. 89–90.
232 **"well-rounded men."**—Lionel Trilling, "On the Teaching of Modern Literature," in *Beyond Culture: Essays on Literature and Learning* (New York: Viking, 1968), p. 27; essay first published in 1961.
233 **"contains nonsense."**—Hershel Parker, *Flawed Texts and Verbal Icons: Literary Authority in American Fiction* (Evanston, Ill.: Northwestern University Press, 1984), p. 11
"to supply."—Parker, pp. 139–43.
234 **"of English."**—See above, p. 148.
"of art."—R. S. Crane, "Criticism as Inquiry; or, The Perils of the 'High Piori Road,' " in *Idea of the Humanities*, 2:25–27.
historical methods.—"Critical and Historical Principles of Literary History," in *Idea of the Humanities*, 2:45–156.
235 **"of theory."**—Crane, "Criticism as Inquiry," p. 29.
Karl Popper.—See Crane's use of Popper in "On Hypotheses in 'Historical Criticism': Apropos of Certain Contemporary Medievalists," in *Idea of the Humanities*, 2:245–46.
"poetic texts."—Crane, "On Hypotheses in 'Historical Criticism,'" p. 251.

235 **"the surface."**—D. W. Robertson, Jr., "Historical Criticism," in *English Institute Essays, 1950*, ed. Alan S. Downer (New York: Columbia University Press, 1951), p. 14.

236 **"instrumental value."**—Crane, Introduction, in *Critics and Criticism*, p. 13.

"the future?"—Crane, "Criticism as Inquiry," pp. 31–33.

237 **of parody.**—See the parodies by Frederick C. Crews, "A Complete Analysis of Winnie-the-Pooh," in *Pooh Perplex*, pp. 87–99; and W. B. Scott, "The Problem of Tragedy," in *Chicago Letter and Other Parodies*, ed. Gerald Graff and Barbara Heldt (Ann Arbor, Mich.: Ardis Publications, 1978; reprinted as *Parodies, Etcetera and Stuff* [Evanston, Ill.: Northwestern University Press, 1985], pp. 13–16).

read it.—Crane, "On Hypotheses in 'Historical Criticism,'" p. 248.

see print.—See particularly Crane's essay, "Every Man His Own Critic," in *Idea of the Humanities*, 2:193–214.

239 **"of plurisignation."**—Philip Wheelwright, *The Burning Fountain* (Bloomington: Indiana University Press, 1954), pp. 52–75.

"up production."—Richard Levin, *New Readings vs. Old Plays: Recent Trends in the Reinterpretation of English Renaissance Drama* (Chicago: University of Chicago Press, 1979), p. 7.

to endorse.—Crane cites Hirsch's essay, "Objective Interpretation," *PMLA* 75 (1960), reprinted as appendix I in *Validity in Interpretation*, pp. 209–44, as "an admirably reasoned defense of the conception of interpretation I am presupposing here" ("On Hypotheses in 'Historical Criticism,'" p. 247).

240 **was over.**—See Richard Foster, *The New Romantics: A Reappraisal of the New Criticism* (Bloomington: Indiana University Press, 1962).

"of art"—Susan Sontag, *Against Interpretation* (New York: Farrar Straus and Giroux, 1967), p. 14.

to enforce.—Jacques Derrida, "Limited Inc., abc," in *Glyph*, Johns Hopkins Textual Studies no. 2 (Baltimore: Johns Hopkins University Press, 1977), p. 250; Derrida says that "the police is always waiting in the wings" to enforce the linguistic conventions codified by speech-act theorists like John Searle.

241 **"bloody act"**—Josué Harari, Preface, in *Textual Strategies: Perspectives in Post-Structuralist Criticism*, ed. Josué Harari (Ithaca: Cornell University Press, 1979), p. 72.

"coming years."—Paul de Man, "Semiology and Rhetoric," in Harari, *Textual Strategies*, p. 138; on the tautological aspect of de Man's argument, see my *Literature against Itself*, pp. 173 ff.

242 **"referential aberration."**—de Man, p. 129; a considerable literature has already accumulated on the assimilation of deconstruction to the explication industry. Among the best statements are Jonathan Culler, "Beyond Interpretation," in *The Pursuit of Signs: Semiotics, Literature,*

Deconstruction (Ithaca, N.Y.: Cornell University Press), pp. 3–17; Cain, *Crisis in Criticism*, pp. 31–50; Michael Fischer, *Does Deconstruction Make Any Difference? Poststructuralism and the Defense of Poetry in Modern Criticism* (Bloomington: Indiana University Press, 1985), pp. 104 ff.

Chapter 15. Tradition versus Theory

Page

247 **New Criticism**—Geoffrey Hartman, for example, makes this equation throughout *Criticism in the Wilderness: The Study of Literature Today* (New Haven: Yale University Press, 1980).

248 **"all time."**—Foerster et al., Preface, in *Literary Scholarship: Its Aims and Methods*, p. v.

"with life."—Bush, see above, p. 186.

the soul."—Greenlaw, *Province of Literary History*, p. 4.

"old times."—See above, p. 140.

252 **metaphysical standpoint.**—See Walter Benn Michaels and Steven Knapp, "Against Theory," in *Against Theory: Literary Studies and the New Pragmatism*, ed. W. J. T. Mitchell (Chicago: University of Chicago Press, 1985), pp. 11–30; originally published in *Critical Inquiry* (Summer 1982). My conception of theory is close to the ones proposed by Steven Mailloux and Adena Rosmarin in their responses to Michaels and Knapp.

253 **"become greater."**—T. S. Eliot, *The Use of Poetry and the Use of Criticism: Studies in the Relation of Criticism to Poetry in England* (London: Faber and Faber, 1933), p. 22

"of poetry."—Matthew Arnold, "The Study of Poetry," in *Works* (London: Macmillan, 1903), 4:15.

their principles.—F. R. Leavis, *The Common Pursuit* (London: Chatto and Windus, 1952), pp. 211–22; Wellek's critique appeared in *Scrutiny* (March 1937).

255 **"casual passerby."**—Helen Vendler, "Presidential Address 1980," *PMLA* 96, no. 3 (May 1981): 344–48.

256 **"as presupposed."**—Jonathan Culler, "Presupposition and Intertextuality," in *Pursuit of Signs*, p. 114.

"was composed."—Robert Scholes, *Textual Power, p. 21.*

"discourse occurs."—Ross Chambers, *Story and Situation: Narrative Seduction and the Power of Fiction* (Minneapolis: University of Minnesota Press, 1984), p. 3.

"in readers."—E. D. Hirsch, "Cultural Literacy," *American Scholar* 53, no. 2 (Spring 1983): 165.

257 **"upon it."**—Don H. Bialostosky, "Dialogic Narration and Narrative Theory," unpublished paper. As Bakhtin himself puts it, we should "imagine the work as a rejoinder in a given dialogue, whose style is determined by its interrelationship with other rejoinders in the same

dialogue (in the totality of the conversation)." "Discourse in the Novel," in *The Dialogic Imagination*, ed. Michael Holquist (Austin: University of Texas Press, 1981), p. 274.

"and constraints."—Chambers, *Story and Situation*, p. 4.

"as well."—Scholes, *Textual Power*, p. 33.

259 **"ageless 'classics.'"**—Elaine Showalter, "Introduction," in *The New Feminist Criticism*, p. 11.

260 **"in English."**—Gail Godwin, "One Woman Leads to Another," *New York Times Sunday Book Review*, April 28, 1985, pp. 13–14.

"thematic relevance."—Denis Donoghue, "A Criticism of One's Own," *New Republic* 194, no. 10 (March 1986): 31.

"Regency ladies."—Godwin, "One Woman Leads to Another," p. 13.

261 **pairing courses**—Brook Thomas, "The Historical Necessity for—and Difficulties with—a New Historical Approach to Teaching Introductory Literature Courses," unpublished essay.

"those texts"—James R. Kincaid, "The Challenge to Specialization: A Clarion Call or a Nostalgic Wheeze?" Unpublished essay.

Unpublished (1986)

Index

- relationships among faculty + disciplines (differences?)
- Michael Berube - What's Liberal about the Liberal Arts?
- focus on Yale, Harvard, etc. (see introduction)